D1527375

EGYPT UNDER THE KHEDIVES, 1805–1879

EGYPT
UNDER THE KHEDIVES
1805–1879

From Household Government to Modern Bureaucracy

F. ROBERT HUNTER

UNIVERSITY OF PITTSBURGH PRESS

Published by the University of Pittsburgh Press, Pittsburgh, Pa. 15260
Feffer and Simons, Inc., London
Manufactured in the United States of America

Library of Congress Cataloging in Publication Data

Hunter, F. Robert, 1940–
  Egypt under the khedives, 1805–1879.

  Bibliography: p. 267.
  Includes index.
  1. Egypt—History—19th century.   I. Title.
DT100.H8   1984   962'.03   83–47617
ISBN 0–8229–3808–1

For my mother and father, and my wife Joan

▲▲▲
CONTENTS

▲▲▲
TABLES

▲▲▲
ILLUSTRATIONS

PREFACE

This study is based on my doctoral dissertation, which contains information collected during two years of research in Cairo (1968–1970) and two lengthy visits to England, the last in 1975 when I was Junior Associate Member of St. Antony's College, Oxford. The American Research Center in Egypt and the Social Science Research Council provided generous financial assistance for my work in Egypt and England.

I wish to express my special appreciation to L. Carl Brown, Roger Owen, and, above all, to Albert Hourani, the teacher and friend of a generation of young scholars. My thanks also goes to the following persons, who contributed in different ways and at various stages in the long history of this project: Alexander Schölch, Ken Jones, Harold Hanham, Sawsan Abd al-Ghani, Ilse Lichtenstadter, Louis Halim, Don Reid, Noury Al-Khaledy, Barbara Roberson. To those persons whose names have been omitted, I ask your forgiveness.

▲▲▲
TEXTUAL NOTE

In this work, I have followed in a general way the system used by the U.S. Library of Congress for the transliteration of Arabic words. Thus, the "l" of the definite article is always written as "l" whether it is followed by a *sun* letter or not, and the *ta' marbuta* of a word in a construct state is written as "t." I have, however, modified this system wherever I felt it to be cumbersome. The Arabic *ʿayn* and the *hamza*, represented by ʿ and ʾ, respectively, have been deleted when possible (for example, *ulama*). Double consonants are indicated, but all long vowels have been omitted. No distinction is made between the Arabic consonants ز and ظ, which are both transliterated as "z." My goal throughout has been to simplify the spelling of Arabic words and to eliminate diacritical marks in order to avoid confusing readers unfamiliar with Arabic. Well-known geographical place names (such as Cairo) and words with familiar spellings (such as bey) have been retained, but less well known place names and words have been transliterated in accordance with the system I have adopted.

A note on currency: In Egypt, the monetary unit was the piastre. Piastres were coined in silver, copper, and gold, and the 100-piastre gold piece was called the Egyptian guinea or pound. According to the rate of exchange fixed by the Egyptian government, 97½ gold piastres equaled one pound sterling. A "purse" (Arabic, *kis*) consisted of 500 piastres. (McCoan, *Egypt As It Is*, pp. 378–79.)

EGYPT UNDER THE KHEDIVES, 1805–1879

▲ 1 ▲
INTRODUCTION

In Tunisia, Egypt, and Ottoman Turkey during the first three-quarters of the nineteenth century, new power states emerged containing centralized bureaucracies, European-style armies, and directed by elites made up in part of men educated in the West. These states greatly augmented the power of autocratic rulers over their subjects, who became increasingly subordinated to the demands of the central administration. In time, however, tensions arose within these new structures, owing partly to the economic and political influence of Europe. The result was a political crisis of major proportions involving bankruptcy, the rulers' loss of control over key elements of their ruling elites, and the establishment of European fiscal controls. In Tunisia and Egypt, European intervention produced popular rebellions and resistance, and led ultimately to the occupation of these countries by foreign troops. As a result, the power of the rulers was so severely weakened that one can no longer speak of autocratic government. The occupation of Tunisia by France (1881) and of Egypt by Britain (1882) brought an end to a long period of personal absolutism. Yet the state machines that had been built up by these rulers endured, for they formed powerful social and institutional combinations, drawing support from indigenous and foreign groups, and possessing hierarchical structures with a strong technological base. These state machines became the embryos of the bureaucracies of the twentieth century.

Between 1805 and 1879, Egypt passed through a complete cycle from the creation to the disintegration of a highly centralized system of personal rule based upon the domination of one man who was Ottoman viceroy in name only. Personal rule was made possible by a political structure that was both an administrative body and a social class. At the center was a bureaucracy consisting of a hierarchical chain of command and government departments with new regulatory functions. Occupying crucial positions in this hierarchy and presiding over a new conscript army was an elite of mostly Turkish-speaking officials who were directly dependent upon the ruler for favor. This arrangement sustained viceregal autocracy in Egypt for over three-quarters of a century.

This study examines the evolution of the new state system in Egypt after the death of Muhammad Ali in 1849; my purpose is to show how Egypt's viceroys were able to maintain themselves in the face of financial crises and humiliations by Europe, and, more important, to explain the rapid collapse of viceregal autocracy between 1875 and 1879. The decline and fall of viceregal absolutism is viewed as integrally related to changes in Egypt's political/administrative order—in particular, the establishment by key members of the ruling elite of ties outside the viceregal household which weakened their loyalties and attachments to the ruler. European intervention in 1875–1879 precipitated the breakup of a ruling group which had already been penetrated by "outside" influences. The establishment of imperialism in Egypt, then, is seen to have been a more complex and subtle phenomenon than is commonly thought—one with profound cultural as well as economic roots, and a strong indigenous base. Without the support of collaborating officials bent upon "reform," European control could not have been established as it was after 1875.

This study also sheds light upon the new pattern of government in Egypt. Between 1849 and 1879, important structural changes occurred in both the institutional and social bases of viceregal power. The expansion and development of a centralized bureaucracy contrasted sharply with the informal and concessionary administrations of the past. Within the bureaucratic elite, old social and occupational distinctions were breaking down, and the elite was becoming less Turkish and more representative of indigenous elements. These and other changes constituted an important break with medieval practices and signified a movement toward the nation state.

Finally, this study demonstrates the dangers inherent in the rapid development of a country's material infrastructure when that country must depend upon massive outside assistance and when no political adjustments are made to accommodate the new social forces that invariably arise in response to these changes. The decision by Egypt's viceroys to "develop" their country—a policy designed to enable them to become the intermediaries between Egypt and the capitalist economies of Europe—enhanced their power in the short run, but ultimately led to a destabilization of the polity. Egypt's viceroys of the nineteenth century fell victim to the very medicine which they themselves had prescribed.

In undertaking this work, I faced two problems. The first was the virtual absence of information on the Egyptian bureaucracy and the power elite in the 1849–1879 period. There are of course many old studies of the collapse of viceregal power written by contemporary European observers, but these express strong partisan viewpoints and concentrate upon the superstructure (for example, the person of the ruler) to the almost complete exclusion of the political/administrative order upon which the ruler's power was based. Recent studies by Rauf Abbas and Ali Barakat on landownership have shown how the monopolization of the state apparatus led to the buildup of wealth of Egypt's high-ranking officials; and Alexander Schölch's study of the 1879–1882 period has examined the activities of leading members of the power elite after the ruler had been fatally weakened. These works, however, are far from adequate for my purposes, and at any rate did not exist at the time I was beginning my research.

This study would therefore have been impossible without the discovery of hitherto unexploited documents in the Egyptian archives and the use of published collections of documents (such as those of Amin Sami) that have been more or less neglected by writers of Egyptian history. From these materials, I have fashioned the first systematic study of Egypt's administrative elite in the 1849–1879 period and of the bureaucratic apparatus which supported the ruling group.

The discovery of new archival sources led to a second major problem: my inability to establish a complete record of the careers of high officials who served between 1849 and 1879. There are many reasons for this. First, a foreigner dealing with records kept in more than one language and arranged in accordance with more than one system faces many obstacles. For example, the pension dossiers—a principal source—were sometimes very difficult to read, not only because of the script, in which Turkish words were mixed with Arabic, but also because of the use of Muslim, European, and Coptic dating systems interchangeably (such as giving the year according to the Coptic calendar while taking the month from the Muslim year). Because of this and other problems (pages and occasionally entire dossiers were missing), it was frequently impossible to obtain a full account of an official's career. Biographical dictionaries (as, for example, Ali Mubarak's al-Khitat), the writings of European observers, other archival materials, and the documents published by Amin Sami were used to supplement the pension dossiers. Yet owing to the time consumed in reading individual dossiers and my need to consult other archival collections, I was not able to examine the dossiers of every high official who served between 1849 and 1879. In all, I accumulated biographical data on 124 high-ranking officials. Of these biographies, thirty-nine must be regarded as "weak," since they contain only fragmentary information, while many of the other biographies have gaps that could not be filled. Fortunately, I was able to acquire a great deal of archival information on the most influential officials and, of course, the biographical data themselves form only part of the voluminous archival and other materials presented here. My study is not the final word on the political/administrative order in Egypt; however, as the first of its kind, it will chart the course of future research in this area.

▲▲▲▲ PART I ▲▲▲▲

The Emergence of the New Power State,

1805–1848

▲ 2 ▲
THE THEMES OF EGYPT'S
GOVERNMENTAL TRADITION

A political and administrative history of modern Egypt requires some comparative measure by which the reader can distinguish the new and changing elements from what is old and continuous. Thus I concentrate in this chapter upon certain themes of the Egyptian governmental tradition, expressing them as simply as possible. My observations are drawn from that long transitional period between classical and modern times which extends from the rule of the Ayyubids (1169–1250) through the Ottoman conquest of 1517, when Egypt was incorporated into a new imperial system, to the eighteenth century.[1] Despite many dissimilarities between Ottoman Egypt and the preceding periods of Egyptian independence under the Ayyubids and Mamluks (1250–1517), political and administrative life showed a broad continuity.

One recurring phenomenon was the tendency of Egypt's government to pass in cycles from strong central control to much less direction from the center, and back again.[2] Each new ruler's takeover of power in Cairo followed a common pattern. After the pacification of the capital, which lay at the center of a vast agricultural hinterland and permitted easy access up and down the river, military expeditions were sent into the delta and to the provinces of upper Egypt to drive the nomads and other marauders from the cultivable land and to resettle peasants in their villages, where they were offered inducements (such as the elimination of tax arrears) to remain on the land and resume its cultivation. Having begun repair of the regional irrigation canals, a new ruler customarily launched a land survey to ascertain the productivity of the soil and the amount of taxes that each parcel of land could bear. Taxes were then fixed and portions of land or revenues therefrom were allocated to members of the ruling group in return for their performance of administrative or other duties. Although the Ottomans established briefly a direct system of rural administration by appointing salaried tax collectors, the normal situation clearly was one of indirect administration through concessionary privileges. The ruler thus controlled Egypt's rural surplus and through it the land itself.

For strategic reasons and to profit from Egypt's position as middleman in East-West trade, strong governments in Cairo frequently included in their spheres of influence the Hijaz, northern Sudan, and Syria (the Palestinian coast was a traditional invasion route into Egypt). They exercised this influence directly by stationing armies there, or indirectly through local allies or client regimes.

The sine qua non of centralized government was the ruler's control over the administrative machine that levied taxes and enforced their collection.[3] This was achieved through a personally dependent elite who held senior positions in the army and directed the rural administration. These were the ruler's personal retainers, forming his court or household, and were known to their Egyptian subjects as Turks. Egypt's rulers therefore were Turkish-speaking military men whose courts contained large numbers of fellow Turks, many of them imported. The ruler's household was a nucleus around which groups from Egyptian society could be organized, but the key to his maintenance in power continued to be control of a personally dependent elite; this control was more important than even a steady supply of revenue.

Military power and control of the land enabled centralized governments to impose their will upon Egyptian society, but not as bureaucratic states enjoying total power in the manner postulated by Wittfogel.[4] Rather, these governments were personal autocracies, petty despotisms with characteristics that call to mind Weber's model of the patrimonial household.[5] Power was exercised arbitrarily by the ruler whose proprietary right to land and labor was expressed in periodic confiscation and redistribution of wealth and in the reallocation of administrative offices to keep all important posts in the hands of his personal aides. No separation existed between public and private revenues because the ruler *was* the state.

Central control, however, usually did not last long. In theory, the ruling group could be weakened in two ways. Some of its members might develop wider affiliations and interests which conflicted with their loyalties to the ruler and which, if unchecked, could split the elite into rival factions. Developments beyond Egypt's borders or in the provinces might produce a similar effect. A military defeat by an invading force could stimulate local resistance to a regime and produce opposition within the army, or a high Nile flood could destroy Egypt's crops, bringing famine and disease to the rural areas and food shortages, inflation, and riots to the capital. Whatever the cause, the social combination upon which state power was based would be split up, and

Egypt plunged into a round of disorders until power was reconstituted by a new ruling group.

One of these cyclical periods was the roughly two and a half centuries of Ottoman rule from 1517 until the late eighteenth century. Like previous conquerors, the Ottomans reorganized the administration, carried out a cadastral survey, and reclaimed large areas of land for the state; they also imposed upon the country a system of government in which power was exercised by a viceroy (wali). The proper context for most of this period, however, is an empire in decline, one losing its centralized power. By the seventeenth century, the viceroy had lost much influence over Egypt's administration; he no longer controlled the tax system, the land, or even the six Ottoman military corps which had been stationed in Egypt at the time of the conquest, and which had begun to merge with Egyptian society.

During times of weakened central authority, it was customary for powerful men to emerge and play a kind of brokerage politics which Albert Hourani has called the politics of notables.[6] Notable politicians possessed an independent source of power (based on land or other resources) which they used to gain access to the ruling authority and then, through patronage, to move their clients into key administrative positions. Existing only in societies structured along lines of personal dependency, this form of politics led to the buildup of powerful machines that were used to promote and defend local interests.

In the eighteenth century, this role was assumed by military men called mamluks. In the period preceding the Ottoman conquest, *mamluk* (literally meaning owned or enslaved) had designated a white male slave of non-Arab extraction recruited from the Caucasus to serve the elite ruling caste that governed Egypt from 1250 until 1517. After the Ottoman conquest, this ruling class disappeared, but Ottoman military commanders and others continued the recruitment of white male slaves, who were enrolled in their military forces. By the seventeenth century, these mamluks were able to organize themselves into groups whose leaders bore the titles of amir and bey.[7] Possessing coercive powers but no original social base, the mamluks established ties with leading groups in society, especially the *ulama* (Muslim scholars and theologians who had instructed them in the tenets of Islam when they were young). The mamluks patronized the *ulama* by cash donations and other gifts, and in turn the *ulama* used their contacts with the urban guilds and brotherhoods to generate support for them in Cairo.[8] The mamluks used their influence to obtain positions in the Ottoman administration, which enabled them to reward clients and build up even more strength until by the mid-eighteenth century they had replaced the viceroy and the Ottoman military corps as the real power in the land.

Using their own personal retainers as a core, and drawing upon the active support of leading groups in local society, the mamluks built up powerful household organizations. Such households, of course, had been the chief form of politics since the mamluks took over power from the last of the Ayyubid sultans in the thirteenth century, but in the eighteenth century they became vehicles for the creation of a political society. Surrounded by high walls enclosing stables, barracks, food reserves, and other materials, the patron's palace was the physical center of a household. Inside the palace could be found Coptic scribes, Jewish bankers, Egyptian merchants, *ulama*, Turkish soldiers, and other functionaries. These political combinations were used to fight other factions and impose their will upon the Ottoman governor. After 1750, some of these households became powerful enough to compel Ottoman recognition of their autonomy and create short-lived, independent states. The most successful of these was that of Ali Bey al-Kabir (1768–1772), who sent military expeditions against Bedouin raiders in the countryside and conducted military campaigns in the Hijaz, Yemen, and Syria.[9]

Though powerful, these military households were unable to reconstitute central authority in a way that would bring real security to the country. Part of the reason was that although their power had declined considerably, the Ottomans continued to meddle in Egyptian affairs (even reinvading the country in 1786). Part of the trouble, too, lay in the instability of the households themselves, which were continually upset by ambitious clients who had forced their way up the ladder only to break away and form households of their own. The chief problem, however, was the inability of the mamluks to maintain an army that could both overwhelm all internal opposition and take the offensive against the Ottomans. Impressed by European military organization, Egypt's mamluk rulers purchased European weapons, hired European military advisers, and imported foreign mercenaries. But armies built along European lines were very expensive, and when the existing system of taxation proved insufficient, Egypt's rulers were driven to desperate lengths to raise revenues. Households fought one another for control of the rural surplus, and the competition between them plunged Egypt ever more deeply into political disorder.

This competition also led to the breakdown of the so-called *iltizam* system, the means by which the Ottomans had exploited Egypt's rural wealth. Established in the seventeenth century, *iltizams* were revenue-producing lands or tax farms, assigned by the treasury temporarily to private individuals who, in return for making a fixed annual payment, received the right to collect their taxes and direct their administration. To place the breakdown of this system in a wider context, however, we must digress briefly on the administration of the towns and cities. Government in eighteenth-century Egypt was "minimal"—that is, its functions were limited primarily to defense and taxation. Egypt's urban infrastructure, therefore, was maintained not by official action, but by informal arrangements between members of the ruling class and leading groups in society. Private individuals from the ruling elite provided investment capital for the construction and repair of streets, waterworks, sanitation, and other facilities, while prominent merchants, *ulama*, and other communal leaders (who also made investments) managed the infrastructure and helped guarantee order and security. As the eighteenth century wore on, and as increasing numbers of mamluks became incapacitated in the fighting between rival households, the informal arrangements that had maintained urban society began to dissolve. While the *ulama* emerged to maintain a degree of order in Cairo, a far greater problem arose in the provinces where the *iltizam* system was breaking down.

Because of internecine fighting and their need for revenues, mamluks began to lease or transfer portions of their tax farms to the highest bidders. Thus *iltizams* became so fragmented that some of them amounted to no more than a fraction of an acre. According to Abd al-Rahim, the number of *iltizam* holders (*multazims*) rose from 1,714 in 1658–1660 to 4,420 in 1797.[10] *Iltizams* also became hereditary, and many owners converted them into religious endowments (*al-awqaf*), exempt from taxation—a tremendous revenue loss to the government. A new means of exploiting Egypt's rural wealth clearly had to be found, but this could not occur without a stable central authority.

A complicating factor was European intervention. Faced with the need for a steady food supply and a market for their woollen cloth, the French significantly increased their volume of trade with Egypt. By the 1790s, this action and other Western commercial activities had severely weakened the position of some Egyptian artisans and textile manufacturers, and led to the monopoly of Egypt's European trade by European merchants and their allies. In 1798, a French army occupied Egypt, and subsequent efforts by Britain to remove it produced two short-lived British occupations. The French invasion of Egypt was a significant event, for it led to the takeover of the Eastern Mediterranean by the British, who thereby acquired a paramount interest in Egypt as a link in their channel of communications with India.[11] More significantly, by destroying the mamluk armies, the French facilitated the rise of the man who found a new solution to the twin problems of political and economic order in Egypt.

▲ 3 ▲
THE RECONSTITUTION OF GOVERNMENT BY MUHAMMAD ALI

▲▲▲ FIRST MAN OF A NEW AGE OR LAST OF THE MAMLUKS?

Few Middle Eastern rulers in modern times have been subjected to as much debate as Muhammad Ali, who governed Egypt as a virtually independent sovereign from 1805 until 1848. Some writers have regarded him as just another mamluk ruler, while others consider him the founder of modern Egypt.[1] Muhammad Ali was both. If his actions followed closely the pattern established by previous centralizers, and if many of his policies were anticipated by mamluk rulers in the eighteenth century, Muhammad Ali succeeded where they had failed and went beyond them. It was Muhammad Ali who reestablished political order after more than a half-century of disorder, found a solution to the breakdown of the *iltizam* system, and laid the basis for a new kind of state.

Born in the Aegean seaport of Kavalla, Muhammad Ali was a Balkan Turk who had come to Egypt as a junior officer in an Ottoman army fighting against the French. Following their departure, he became a contender for power and was named viceroy by the Ottoman sultan in 1805. In his desperate search for revenues, Muhammad Ali began taxing *iltizam* lands held by mamluks and the *ulama*; and when they protested, he moved quickly against them, breaking the power of the *ulama* by 1809 and eliminating the mamluks as a factor in politics by massacring their leaders in 1811. Since these two groups were the only forces capable of mobilizing public opinion against Muhammad Ali, this action paved the way for the establishment of order. The elimination of the mamluks and the suppression of the *ulama*—the key elements in the political coalitions of the late eighteenth century—are crucial in understanding the period that followed, for their removal facilitated the rise of a new ruling combination and the creation of a centralized administration.

After 1811, raids against government forces ceased, upper Egypt was pacified, peasants began returning to their lands, and a cadastral survey was launched. As this survey proceeded, old taxes were abolished, peasant rights to lands previously held by tax farmers were confirmed, and a uniform tax called *kharaj* was established on all cultivable lands. By 1813, the state—that is, the ruler and his men—had reestablished control over the rural surplus and found a new means for its exploitation. Henceforth, a fixed *kharaj* tax, its amount varying in accordance with the quality of land and the types of crops grown, would be collected directly by government agents.

As with the mamluk rulers of the late eighteenth century, Muhammad Ali's goal was to win Ottoman recognition of his independent rule of Egypt, and he similarly sought to achieve this by creating a military machine modeled after the armies of Europe. Previous efforts had either failed miserably or enjoyed only short-lived success because Egypt's mamluk rulers could not find revenues sufficient to support an army capable of defeating the Ottomans.

Muhammad Ali solved this problem ingeniously by taking over the produce of the land itself. By 1816, all of Egypt's major crops had been brought under control of his government, which supplied the peasants with capital and purchased their crops at prices fixed by Muhammad Ali, who then sold the produce to Europeans for a healthy profit. Government monopolies had of course existed before, but these usually had taken the form of exclusive rights granted to private parties to develop resources in which the government had a special interest, and they had never covered the entire economy. Muhammad Ali's monopolies were therefore a truly revolutionary step that led to organization of Egypt's economy along the lines of a modern European state.

Beginning in 1820, Muhammad Ali succeeded in organizing an army that became known as the *Nizam Jadid* (New Order). Like the armies formed in the late eighteenth century, it relied heavily upon European advisers and technology, but unlike them, it was based upon Egyptian conscripts. This army defeated the Ottomans in two major campaigns and helped Muhammad Ali win recognition of his family's hereditary right to rule Egypt as Ottoman viceroys.

The formation of a large modern army created a need both for more revenues and for institutions to support it. The first requirement was met in 1821 by the introduction and widespread cultivation for export of a long-fiber cotton called Jumel (after the French engineer who invented it). According to Roger Owen, this new crop provided between one-fifth and one-quarter of Muhammad Ali's total revenues in periods of good harvests and high prices, and about one-tenth at other times.[2] The second need was filled by launching massive government development projects, including new social institutions.

MUHAMMAD ALI IN FULL DRESS UNIFORM
From Benis, *Une mission militaire*, vol. 1, plate II.

To produce engineers, physicians, and other technically trained men for the army, Muhammad Ali's government established a new educational system consisting of preparatory and special schools in Cairo and student training programs in Europe.[3] To permit summer irrigation and facilitate the cultivation of Jumel, the government launched the construction of new deep-water canals, a Nile barrage north of Cairo, and other public works projects that would eventually lead to the establishment of a perennial irrigation system. Muhammad Ali's government also created a modern industry replete with iron foundries, tanneries, bleaching establishments, a printing press, and twenty-nine cotton factories in 1837.[4] It established public health facilities, which included clinics in Cairo for the treatment of eye diseases, and began the construction of a modern transportation system. These departures were not insignificant. Previous mamluk rulers had not given a thought to creating new schools, providing health facilities, or conscripting Egyptians into the army. They had simply been too busy searching for new revenue sources and struggling to establish order and security in the countryside. Because Muhammad Ali had solved these problems, he was able to intervene in society and the economy in a new way and so bring an end to minimal government in Egypt.

▲▲▲ BUREAUCRATIC CENTRALISM

One of Muhammad Ali's most important reforms was to establish a centralized bureaucracy which gradually replaced the old concessionary administration. Unlike his monopoly system and the new industries, which were dismantled in the last years of his reign, the centralized structure he created not only survived his death but also grew so rapidly in subsequent years that "bureaucracy" became almost synonymous with the modern state in Egypt.

Muhammad Ali's bureaucracy was an outgrowth of his system of direct taxation and the government's assumption of new social and economic functions. Both called for an organization with clear lines of command capable of providing direction from the center. Yet there was also a powerful political motive for its creation. In the early years, Muhammad Ali struggled to establish his control over Egypt's administrative factions. At first, he made use of Ottoman institutions like the *Ruznama* (the executive department of the old Ottoman treasury) and the rudimentary system of provincial government composed of Turkish governors general called *nazir*s and their subordinates (*kashif*s) at the top, and Egyptian village headmen (*shaykh*s al-balad) at the bottom.[5] He also had to rely upon officials of the Coptic scribal corporation, some of whom kept the government account books in their homes. Whenever possible, Muhammad Ali appointed men from his own household to supervise these officials.[6] As time passed, the account books were called in and stored in the state archive, high officials appointed by the sultan were won over to Muhammad Ali's side, and the Coptic scribes were placed upon regular monthly salaries, as were the leaders of other influential urban groups such as the heads of the residential quarters (shaykhs al-hara).[7] Quite early, Muhammad Ali had reorganized his financial administration and set up the organs of his household government, but it was not until after the military reform and the introduction of long-fiber cotton that a hierarchical bureaucracy fully emerged.

In 1824 Muhammad Ali decided to form a new administrative hierarchy with a line of command that ran from Cairo to the villages.[8] Egypt was divided into twenty-four parts and these were arranged into subdistricts (khutts), districts (qisms), departments (ma'muriyas), and provinces (mudiriyas). Directing these units and replacing the Ottoman kashifs and nazirs were new types of officials sent from Cairo (table 1). This structure was superimposed upon village and other local officials, who remained in the administration. Sometime later, this new provincial organization was brought under the general supervision of the Department of Inspectorate (Diwan Umum al-Taftish), headed by the inspector general (mufattish umum).[9]

Officials in the new hierarchy fulfilled two broad types of functions. In addition to their administrative role, they were assigned strictly political tasks. Thus provincial governors were given general responsibility for all government projects (as well as judicial functions) and were also expected to supervise the officials directly below them in the hierarchy (the ma'murs) to ensure that orders were being implemented and the taxes collected properly. The mudirs and the ma'murs were required to send regular reports to Cairo enumerating all measures undertaken and requesting the viceroy's approval. The ma'murs, in their turn, heard complaints against local officials and dispensed appropriate punishments, advised in agricultural matters, inspected the factories, examined personally the condition of land and crops in their localities, and directed the officials below them. The district chiefs examined village accounts and appointed the khawlis and qa'im maqams, and so on.[10]

In the central administration, power became concentrated in two governmental bodies that were part of an administrative structure made up of departments (diwans) and councils (majlises). Presided over by the viceroy or a close aide, these central bodies supervised and coordinated the day-to-day affairs of government in the capital and also played a role in the provincial administration. The first was the Department of Civil Affairs (*al-Diwan al-Mulki* or *al-Diwan al-Khidiwi*).[11] This large administration had responsibility for Egypt's internal affairs, except for financial matters, which it shared with other administrative bodies. It fixed the salaries of government employees, made decisions on requests from other administrations, issued orders to the provinces, made disbursements, and received accounts from the provinces. It contained offices for the administration of religious endowments for public purposes (*waqf*s), the postal service, the quarantine, passports, the census, and building services. By 1837, it was administering the Mahmudiya canal, the mint, the arsenal at Bulaq, the civil hospitals, the councils of commerce, and the *Ruznama*. The Department of Civil Affairs also served as a court of justice, investigating and trying cases of misdemeanors in Cairo as well as of murder and treason. To assist it, two councils (*majlis*es) of internal affairs were established, one in Cairo, the other in Alexandria. The Cairo council seems to have become quite important, frequently superseding the Department of Civil Affairs itself.

The second major organ of the central administration was the vice-

TABLE 1

THE REFORMED STRUCTURE OF PROVINCIAL ADMINISTRATION
UNDER MUHAMMAD ALI

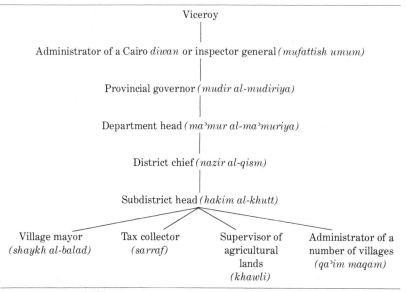

Sources: Rivlin, *Agricultural Policy*, pp. 78–79, 87–99; Clot, *Aperçu*, vol. 2, pp. 184–87; Mengin, *Histoire sommaire*, pp. 235–36; Guémard, *Les réformes*, pp. 256–59.

regal cabinet, known in Arabic as *al-maʿiya al-saniya*, or viceregal entourage. Located at the viceroy's palace, the viceregal cabinet contained officials who met regularly to coordinate and supervise all government affairs—military and civil. The cabinet illustrates the lack of separation between the government administration and the viceregal household (see table 2). Muhammad Ali's household, comprising an estimated 1,500 persons, consisted of his court and harem.[12] Occupying spacious apartments elegantly furnished with beautiful carpets, the court contained buffoons and brusque Turkish officers, magicians and men of state, cooks and military commanders—all pressed into the service of a common master. But Muhammad Ali's court existed not only to satisfy the physical and emotional needs of the ruler; it also provided officials to help run the government; and of these, none were more important than the men of the viceregal cabinet.

The cabinet served as Muhammad Ali's channel of communication with the rest of the administration.[13] It collected information on the work of other administrative bodies, investigated anything in need of clarification, and informed the viceroy. Once Muhammad Ali had made his decisions, it issued orders in his name. The viceregal cabinet also possessed considerable power of its own: it supervised accounts, appointed and dismissed government officials, corresponded with foreign powers, adjudicated administrative disputes, disciplined officials for minor offenses, and formed a high court to try officials accused of crimes. As can be seen, some of its functions overlapped with those of Civil Affairs, but as Deny has made clear, these bodies were separate, and in all matters the cabinet's authority was final.

TABLE 2
IMPORTANT COURT OFFICES UNDER MUHAMMAD ALI

Director in chief, viceregal cabinet *(bashmuʿawin)*
Chief interpreter *(bashmutarjim)*
First lieutenant of the Viceroy *(katkhuda)*
Chief treasurer *(khaznadar)*
Grand master of ceremonies *(tashrifati)*
Keeper of the seal *(muhurdar)*
Sword-bearer *(silahdar)*
Chief physician *(hakim basha)*
Inkstand-bearer
Key-bearer
Pipe-bearer
Chief eunuch

Sources: Guémard, *Les réformes*, pp. 278–79; Mengin, *Histoire de l'Egypte*, vol. 2, pp. 258–59; Yates, *Modern History*, vol. 2, p. 215; Deny, *Sommaire des archives*, p. 95.

As time passed, Muhammad Ali grew dissatisfied with the tendency of his officials to submit every matter, however trivial, to one of the central departments, causing considerable delay. In 1837, prompted by a crisis in his finances, he reorganized his administration to provide greater scope for the functional departments that had begun to emerge (see table 3). All councils (*majlis*es) were abolished, existing departments were reorganized, and new departments were created. The Organic Law issued in that year provided for six departments (exclusive of Civil Affairs): Finance, War, Marine, Industry, Foreign Affairs (including commerce), and Education (which also contained a division of public works).[14]

Although Muhammad Ali's reform marked the beginning of a movement toward bureaucracy, the substitution of direct for indirect administration did not bring an end to office prebends or other concessionary features, nor did the Egyptian bureaucracy develop in a straight, unbroken line. In Muhammad Ali's time and after, administration retained many of its concessionary features, largely because the delegation of privileges contained enormous advantages for the ruler, whose power rested on personal obligation and dependency. In Muhammad Ali's day, offices continued to be bought and sold; customs dues were farmed out; private parties received rights to collect taxes

TABLE 3
PRINCIPAL UNITS OF THE CENTRAL ADMINISTRATION
UNDER MUHAMMAD ALI

Viceregal Cabinet *(Diwan al-Ma'iya al-Saniya)*
Department of Civil Affairs *(al-Diwan al-Mulki)*
Council of Civil Affairs, Cairo *(al-Majlis al-'Ali)*[a]
Department of War *(Diwan al-Jihadiya)*
Council of Military Affairs *(Majlis al-Jihadiya)*
Department of Finances *(Diwan al-Maliya)*
Department of Foreign Affairs and Commerce *(Diwan al-Umur al-Ifranjiya wa al-Tijara al-Misriya)*
Department of Public Education *(Diwan al-Madaris)*
Department of Marine *(Diwan al-Bahr)*
Department of Industry *(Diwan al-Fabriqat)*
High Court of Justice *(Jam'iyat al-Haqqaniya)*[b]
Office of the First Lieutenant of the Viceroy *(Diwan al-Katkhuda)*
Department of Inspectorate *(Diwan Umum al-Taftish)*
Advisory Council *(Majlis al-Shura)*

Source: Deny, *Sommaire des archives.*
[a] In 1830, a second Council of Civil Affairs was formed in Alexandria.
[b] Founded in 1842.

on salt, fruit, wine, and small river craft; and after 1837, Muhammad Ali's personal retainers were given villages to administer as tax farms.[15] Such practices illustrate the complexity of the administrative process and the difficulties of generalizing about it.

Moreover, this new bureaucracy was hardly novel; there were many historical precedents for Muhammad Ali to draw upon. He was surely aware of the centralized system of salaried tax agents (*amins*) through which the Ottomans had governed Egypt for a short time after their conquest. Muhammad Ali's experiment, however, was unusual in being based on European models, and in particular the highly centralized organization realized by Napoleon. His provincial structure, for example, was a carbon copy of the Napoleonic prototype. Recognizing the French influence on the new geographical arrangements, European observers applied French designations to the administrative units: *arrondisement* for *qism*, *canton* for *khutt*, *préfet* for *ma'mur*, and so on.[16] This self-conscious borrowing from Europe was not limited to the bureaucracy. Egypt's conscript army was an adaptation of the French *levée en masse*; the new government-supported educational system was inspired by the Napoleonic example; French law codes were translated and introduced into the army and navy.[17] In short, Muhammad Ali used Western forms to achieve something traditional: the reconstitution of power in his own hands and its imposition upon the rest of society.

▲▲▲ A HOUSEHOLD RULING ELITE

Though Muhammad Ali borrowed European models and even justified his reforms by using such words as "progress" and "civilization," his was household government in the purest sense. After 1805, one man and a house of personal retainers ran the government and became the state. Muhammad Ali had no need of the private militias of the religious brotherhoods to provide security and political support because he possessed a conscript army. He could dispense with the administrative services of the *ulama* and other "intermediaries" because he had a centralized bureaucracy to carry out these tasks. And for technical advice, equipment, and ideas, he relied upon Europe. These formed the elements of a new political order.

Like previous household elites, Egypt's new ruling class consisted almost entirely of Turkish military men imported from abroad.[18] By employing Turks, Muhammad Ali could take advantage of sentiments of ethnic solidarity and obviate the problem of family connections which the introduction of non-Turks into the higher administration would have presented. A common sense of Turkishness was reinforced by ties of locality. A number of Muhammad Ali's Turkish officials, perhaps more than is realized, had come to Egypt from the viceroy's hometown of Kavalla. Unacquainted with the land and people they ruled, Turkish officials were dependent on Muhammad Ali, who tried to keep them there through calculated appeals to their self-interest and by preventing them from establishing ties with Egyptian society. Turkish officials were paid higher salaries than non-Turks holding the same positions; they received money gifts and other favors; they were paid more regularly than other officeholders; and not until late in Muhammad Ali's reign were they allowed to develop landed estates in the countryside.[19]

The men of Egypt's new household elite were of four types (see table 4): first, the blood relatives of Muhammad Ali; second, his in-laws, many of whom were related to him before he became viceroy; third, freed white slaves, or mamluks; fourth, those not related to him in any of the above ways but who had entered his service by private agreements or were clients by virtue of their household affiliation.

Of these, Muhammad Ali's kin were given the highest offices and the most challenging assignments (see table 5). Whenever the viceroy needed someone to lead an important military expedition, govern a recalcitrant province, or perform other difficult tasks, it was usually to one of his relatives that he turned. Since many of Muhammad Ali's sons died in infancy or were cut down early in their careers after promising starts, the principal burden of assistance fell to his son Ibrahim, the heir apparent, and to Abbas, his grandson. Having governed provinces and commanded military units since the age of sixteen, Ibrahim was known as unscrupulous, violent, and fearless.[20] Abbas, on the contrary, was brooding, superstitious, and reserved. Perhaps the fact that he would someday govern Egypt (Abbas was next in line after Ibrahim) best recommended him for leadership tasks. Prince Sa'id, born in 1822, was too young to be given serious responsibilities until the last decade of his father's reign when he received command of the Egyptian navy.[21]

Ibrahim and Abbas were given civil and military assignments inside and outside Egypt. Both had held important military commands (Abbas in Syria), and Ibrahim was commander in chief of the Egyptian army during most of his father's reign. In Egypt, these two men helped Muhammad Ali consolidate and maintain his authority. They presided over the central departments, supervised government officials, went into the provinces on special assignments, and governed in the viceroy's absence. In 1829, Ibrahim was placed in charge of the

TABLE 4
MUHAMMAD ALI'S RULING ELITE

	Birth-place	Civil Position	Household Position	Relation to Viceroy	End of Service
Ibrahim Pasha	Kavalla	Treasurer	Viceroy's first lieutenant[a]	Son	d. 1848
Abbas Pasha	Egypt	Inspector general[b]	Viceroy's first lieutenant[a]	Grandson	d. 1854
Khurshid Pasha	Georgia	Governor of al-Daqahliya	—	Freed slave	—
Ahmad Yagan	Kavalla	War director	—	Nephew	d. 1855?
Ibrahim Yagan	Kavalla	Governor of al-Gharbiya	—	Nephew	d. 1846
Ahmad Manikli	Turkey	War director	—	—	d. 1862
Muhammad Bey	Turkey?	Treasurer	—	Son-in-law	d. 1833
Boghos Bey	Smyrna	Director of foreign affairs	Translator	—	d. 1844
Baqqi Bey	Greece	Director of finance	Viceroy's first lieutenant[a]	—	Exiled by Abbas
Sami Bey	Greece	—	Director in chief,[c] viceregal cabinet	—	Exiled by Abbas
Muharram Bey	Kavalla	Governor of Alexandria	—	Son-in-law	—
Muhammad Sharif	Kavalla	Director of finance	Viceroy's first lieutenant[a]	Nephew	Exiled by Abbas
Yusuf Kamil	Turkey	—	Director in chief,[c] viceregal cabinet	Son-in-law	Exiled by Abbas

Sources: Sami, pt. 2, p. 528n1; Douin, Une mission militaire, p. 78; Douin, L'Egypte de 1828 à 1830, p. 165; "Note sur les pachas d'Egypte," Murray/Palmerston, no. 1, 1 Jan. 1847, in FO 78/107; Hamont, L'Egypte, vol. 2, p. 69; WM, no. 33, 9 L 1262/30 Sept. 1846; Wilkinson, Modern Egypt and Thebes, vol. 1, pp. 199–200; Zaki, A'lam al-jaysh, pt. 1, pp. 50, 59–61.

Note: Dashes indicate information not available.
[a]Katkhuda.
[b]Mufattish umum.
[c]Bashmu'awin.

entire administration. Visiting the treasury two or three times each day, he directed government affairs and initiated reforms for his father. When Muhammad Ali's health began to fail during the last years of his reign, Ibrahim, Abbas, Saʿid, and a few other high officials ran the country for him.[22]

Muhammad Ali's sons and grandson could not bear alone the heavy burden of administration, so a large number of other family members were brought into the government. (Only the most prominent names are listed in table 4.) As can be seen, some were from Kavalla. This was true of the sons of one of Muhammad Ali's sisters, Ibrahim Yagan and Ahmad Yagan, who had followed their uncle to Egypt where they enjoyed distinguished military careers. Another nephew was Muhammad Sharif, who at various times held the offices of first lieutenant of the viceroy (*katkhuda*), governor of lower Egypt, governor of Damascus, director in chief of the viceroy's cabinet (*bashmuʿawin*), and director of finances. Ahmad Tahir, also from Kavalla, received the governorship of upper Egypt and led a military expedition to crush a revolt there.[23] Other high officials married into Muhammad Ali's family, such as Muharram Bey (president of the Council of Civil Affairs in Alexandria and commander of the navy), Yusuf Kamil (director of the Department of Civil Affairs and of the viceregal cabinet), and Muhammad Daftardar Bey, who had been appointed treasurer by the sultan early in Muhammad Ali's reign, and whose marriage to Princess Nazli made him more dependent on the viceroy.[24]

Muhammad Ali also employed a large number of mamluks, most of them originally from Morea or the Caucasus.[25] Clot has suggested that mamluks were even preferred to Turks, but the distinction between the two was not very firm. Mamluks spoke a Turkish dialect, dressed like Turks, and entered into ties of kinship and patronage with them. Muhammad Ali owned the largest number of mamluks, estimated at five hundred. Some of them were assigned to the princes as tutors and playmates, but most were appointed to positions in the civil and military administrations. The officer corps of the army seems to have been composed almost entirely of mamluks from the viceroy's household, and Muhammad Ali's mamluks could also be found as provincial governors and in high offices of the central administration. Muhammad Ali requested his Turkish grandees to contribute some of their own mamluks for service in the military, and the few who had survived the massacre of 1811 were likewise enrolled in the government.

Muhammad Ali also drew upon the talents of administrators who were neither relatives nor freed slaves, and who had entered his service by means of contracts or understandings made directly with him.

TABLE 5
THE MUHAMMAD ALI FAMILY[a]

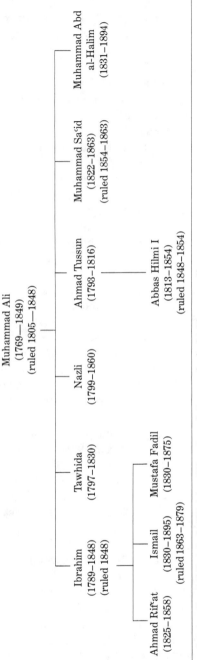

Muhammad Ali
(1769—1849)
(ruled 1805—1848)

Ibrahim
(1789–1848)
(ruled 1848)

Tawhida
(1797–1830)

Nazli
(1799–1860)

Ahmad Tussun
(1793–1816)

Muhammad Saʿid
(1822–1863)
(ruled 1854–1863)

Muhammad Abd
al-Halim
(1831–1894)

Ahmad Rifʿat
(1825–1858)

Ismail
(1830–1895)
(ruled 1863–1879)

Mustafa Fadil
(1830–1875)

Abbas Hilmi I
(1813–1854)
(ruled 1848–1854)

Source: Combe, *Précis de l'histoire d'Egypte*, vol. 3, genealogical table, appendix.
[a]List not inclusive.

One such official was Boghos Bey, who shortly after his arrival in Egypt in 1810 entered into a contract with Muhammad Ali for the management of the customs house in Alexandria.[26] Boghos subsequently became chief translator in the viceroy's household, and for twenty years directed Egypt's commercial and foreign affairs.

Boghos shows that there were exceptions to the rule of a Turkish elite. Although Boghos was born in Smyrna and spoke fluent Turkish, he was an Armenian Christian. Because of his proximity to the viceroy, Boghos became the patron of a handful of Armenian officials, several of whom rose to high positions in the 1840s.[27] Also exceptional were the Coptic officials in the financial administration. Early in his reign, Muhammad Ali had used them to assist in his land survey and to help collect the land tax. Later, he arrested and imprisoned their leaders and confiscated their wealth, yet he could never dispense entirely with their services. After the death of Muallim Ghali, leader of the Coptic scribal corporation, Muhammad Ali relied heavily upon his son, Basilius Bey, who as director of the office of accounting (*mudir al-hisabat*) was frequently at the viceroy's side.[28]

Muhammad Ali's household was the axis and pillar of his government. Court officers received appointments to positions in the civil administration or were assigned governmental tasks as part of their household duties.[29] The viceroy's *katkhuda*, for example, had charge of the Department of Civil Affairs and was governor of Cairo in all but name. These courtiers were also given ad hoc assignments. If Muhammad Ali wished to check into the activities of other officials, or needed something done that required a man of trust, or simply wanted a job accomplished quickly, a personal associate was usually given the task. Baqqi Bey visited government offices, inspected accounts, and dispensed punishments to wrongdoers; Muhammad Sharif went into the provinces to supervise the harvest and make sure that government registers were sent to Cairo on time; Boghos Bey distributed government orders to officials and collected revenues for the viceroy. Ibrahim Pasha carried out darker assignments. Ordered to kill a recalcitrant tax collector if he would not cooperate, Ibrahim allegedly did the job with his own hand. Again on instructions from his father, Ibrahim reportedly murdered Muallim Ghali, the influential head of the Coptic corporation. These assignments were specific and provisional, and the appointee was usually held accountable for any failure. By such means, Muhammad Ali was able not only to maintain his control over state institutions, but also to project his power into society. Once again in Egyptian history, a personally dependent elite helped make one-man rule possible.

BOGHOS BEY (1768–1844)
From Benis, *Une mission militaire*, vol. 2, plate XXIV.

By combining a household elite with a new bureaucracy, Muhammad Ali was able to build up an almost unlimited and virtually independent autocracy which had a far greater impact upon society than that of previous centralizing rulers. Though Muhammad Ali's autocracy came under strain between 1837 and 1848, the highly centralized absolutist government he created remained strong right through the 1870s. The state—that is, the ruler and his men—once again became the major causal force in Egypt's political and social evolution.

In practice, personal rule meant the concentration of all governmental powers in the hands of the ruler, who possessed a standing army, and who could fix prices, impose new taxes, confiscate land, and order arrest and imprisonment without need to show cause. Within the administration, high officials possessed only delegated powers, and had to have the ruler's permission for almost everything.[30] Muhammad Ali could confer titles, increase salaries, bestow generous pensions, and pardon criminals. Conversely, he could deprive an official of his rank, salary, and office; a peasant of his livelihood, produce, and land; and each, if he wished, of his life. If Muhammad Ali was the Great Benefactor (*Wali al-Ni'am*), the Source of all Truth (*Ayn al-Sawab*), he was also the great disposer.[31]

Sanctified by custom, these ruling prerogatives were never fully spelled out in a formal document, although they were occasionally mentioned in laws and decrees. The Organic Law of 1837 affirmed the viceroy's right to pardon a criminal or reduce a prison sentence; an order from Ismail Pasha asserted his privilege of rewarding and punishing at will.[32]

Such actions derived from a proprietary view of government that for centuries had guided the behavior of Egypt's rulers. For Muhammad Ali, as for his predecessors, Egypt was the proverbial milch cow; its people, a needle that clothed others but itself remained naked. Egypt's soldiers were regarded as Muhammad Ali's "property"; officials were "his" employees (*khadamat sa'adatihi*); even the government offices and departments, he said, belonged to him. Officials had no right to remuneration for their services, not even to government pensions, which were considered to be "gifts" from the ruler.[33]

Muhammad Ali endeavored to direct and supervise all state affairs. On a typical day, the viceroy rose about four A.M. and went directly to his office where he received bundles of memoranda, petitions, and dispatches that were read to him and to which he gave his replies. He spent the remainder of the morning receiving officials, giving interviews to Europeans, and making unexpected visits to government

MUHAMMAD ALI (1769–1849)
From Benis, *Une mission militaire*, vol. 1, plate XII.

offices. After lunch, Muhammad Ali returned to his office where he remained until ten or eleven in the evening. He also conducted official business in his palace, which contained special rooms for the work of administration; and in his harem a trained female secretary was available to assist him in affairs of state. Muhammad Ali spent part of the year in Alexandria, supervising the Departments of Civil Affairs, Commerce, and Marine. Twice a year he made inspection tours of the provinces, directing the planting of crops, inspecting irrigation works, examining accounts, receiving petitions, and dispensing summary justice.[34]

The imposition of highly centralized personal control profoundly altered political life in Egypt. Muhammad Ali's destruction of the mamluk households and his creation of a bureaucracy had moved politics off the streets and into the halls of administration. During his reign, the principal kind of politics was that of the court, where influence was held by those closest to the ruler. The chief political actors, then, were the household officials themselves, who used their access to the viceroy to assist friends and family members. A lesser but not unimportant forum for politics was the new bureaucracy, through which officials opposed to Muhammad Ali's policies could try to obstruct them without challenging him directly. The new bureaucracy, however, was not strong enough to supersede the court as the forum for "indoor" politics in Muhammad Ali's time. Not until the 1870s would the political struggle move back into the open.

By 1837, it was clear that Muhammad Ali had carried his centralism too far, for it was beginning to produce a reaction which would lead to the curtailment of his programs. Excessive government demands for revenue and workers had exhausted the land and produced a massive flight of the peasantry into the larger towns and desert, emptying entire villages. In 1837, Egypt was also hard hit by an international monetary crisis that caused bankruptcies among merchant houses upon which the government had relied for credit. In that year, too, Muhammad Ali began planning another war with the Ottomans, and its outbreak in 1839 led to European military intervention that forced the viceroy to accept the London treaty of 1840. In return for recognition of his family's right to rule Egypt as hereditary Ottoman viceroys, Muhammad Ali had to agree to reduce his army to 18,000 men, cede all territories conquered from the sultan (except the Sudan), and accept the Anglo-Turkish Commercial Convention of 1838 which banned all monopolies in the Ottoman empire.[35]

Faced with a serious loss of revenues, Muhammad Ali began granting to himself, his family, and personal aides parcels of land in the provinces. Military commanders and high officeholders received villages in concessions known as *uhda*s. In return for paying the village's tax arrears and guaranteeing future tax liabilities, a concessionaire could work a piece of land tax-free in his *uhda*.[36] His responsibilities included the supervision of cultivation and the provision of working capital. Lands granted by the ruler to himself and his family members were known as *shafliks*, which were formed either from villages in tax arrears or from uncultivated lands not on the cadastral registers. Uncultivated lands were also granted to high officials and others who were not members of the viceregal family; these estates became known as *ab'adiya*s.

This policy of land grants was adopted in order to ensure payment of the land tax and to reduce government expenditures, but it was also a clever way of preserving the viceroy's monopoly system. Until the winter of 1844–1845, Muhammad Ali was able to dictate the crops grown on these estates and to purchase them at his prices.[37] After this, however, European merchants increased substantially their purchases of crops from the peasant cultivators, and by 1848 Muhammad Ali's monopoly system was dead.

Because of the enforced reduction of the Egyptian army, the infrastructure created to support it was significantly weakened after 1837. Egypt's new factory system was almost completely abandoned: in 1849, only two textile factories remained in existence. The government schools also fell upon hard times, receiving little funding after 1841 and experiencing severe cutbacks.[38]

If the 1837–1848 period suggests a decentralization of power, viceregal autocracy was never in any real danger because its bases were not seriously shaken. The new conscript army, now considerably smaller, continued to be a pillar of support for the viceroy. The centralized bureaucracy remained intact in the provinces where it provided a framework for the administration of the *shaflik* and *ab'adiya* estates. Egypt's household elite—the cornerstone of viceregal power—was still totally dependent upon Muhammad Ali, who used it after 1837 to perpetuate his control over land in the countryside. Taxes collected by the holders of *uhda* estates continued to be based on entries in the cadastral registers, and the *uhda* system itself was almost completely dismantled within a few years of Muhammad Ali's death. The central government maintained public works, sent students to study in Europe (a large educational mission went to France in 1844), and collected taxes directly from the land. If some of Muhammad Ali's programs collapsed entirely and all became weakened after 1837, government in Egypt did not revert to the "minimal" government of the eighteenth century.

▲▲▲▲ PART II ▲▲▲▲

Changes in the Political/Administrative Order,

1849–1874

▲4▲
ADMINISTRATIVE DEVELOPMENT UNDER VICEREGAL ABSOLUTISM

▲▲▲ THE KHEDIVATE AND THE WORLD SYSTEM

To Europeans, Egypt's highly centralized system of personal government was known as the khedivate. Derived from an old Persian title meaning lord or master, the word *khedive* is commonly associated with Ismail Pasha (1863–1879), who purchased the right to bear this title from the sultan.[1] Ironically, Ismail's reign saw the collapse of the absolute power that he and his predecessors had wielded for three-quarters of a century. In 1875, Europe began a political intervention that led to Ismail's deposition and exile in 1879. In four short years, viceregal power was dismantled piece by piece until little was left of the edifice of absolutism constructed by Muhammad Ali. After 1879, Egypt's viceroys continued as khedives, but the absolute power symbolized by this title was gone forever.

The decline and fall of viceregal power in Egypt cannot be explained by European intervention alone, but was also related to social and institutional changes in the state system between 1849 and 1874. The rise of a civil bureaucracy, the emergence of "private" viceregal administrations (called *dairas*), and the partial withdrawal of the viceregal cabinet from daily administration reflected a shift in the distribution of administrative power that anticipated the later separation of the viceregal household from government. The 1849–1874 period also saw the appearance of a new body of officials who directed the bureaucracy and the machinery of coercion. Highly diverse in social origins and education, these men who rose to high position under Abbas and Sa'id composed a distinct generation of elite officeholders.

After 1875, men from within this elite began to separate themselves from the viceroy. Some collaborated with the Europeans to compel the ruler to surrender his financial resources and a large measure of his power; others, while not breaking with the ruler, began to join the movement of protest against Europe that was developing in the countryside and the capital. In this way, the ruling combination of men grouped around an autocrat was broken up, and highly centralized power collapsed.

The loss by the ruler of men who originally formed part of a personally dependent elite raises a question about their possession of ties outside the administration. During the middle years of the century, Egypt's high officeholders had rapidly passed from being simply servants of the viceroy to men with interests that coincided, overlapped, and then conflicted with his. This development can be attributed to the profitability of landholding, the protection offered some officials by European consuls, the promotion of wealthy and influential Egyptians to high state positions, and the growth of the bureaucracy. By the 1870s, two new kinds of interests had emerged: a local, rural interest where certain officials possessed social and economic power in the countryside; and a European interest, where officials pushed "reforms," helped advance the policies of particular European states, and facilitated the spread of European civilization generally. These ties signified the presence within the administration of "intermediaries," high officials who were both members of a ruling establishment and representatives of "society."

Despite this change, Egypt's viceroys suffered no diminution of power before 1874. This can be explained by the elite's continued dependence on the ruler for favor. In the 1849–1874 period, the dominant mark of the relationship between the viceroy and his men was cooperation. Egypt's high-ranking officials helped the viceroy maintain control over the instruments of power and he in turn gave them a share of the surplus and other benefits. This cooperation provides a clue as to how Egypt's viceroys could endure more than a decade of fiscal crises and still maintain their power.

Before examining the growth and development of the Egyptian state system after 1849, focusing both upon social relationships and the administrative structure, we must first locate the sources of change within it. What pushed the evolution of the Egyptian state structure in the direction it took? The answer to this is exceedingly complex, since it involves the actions of the viceroys and developments on the other side of the Mediterranean. To begin, the world economic and political orders were altering fundamentally the relationship between Egypt and Europe. This change was expressed, on the one hand, in a shift in the terms of trade by which Egypt became a receiver of manufactured goods and a provider of raw materials to Europe; and, on the other, in the rapid growth of European political influence and a loss of viceregal control over Europeans residing in Egypt. The sources of Egypt's growing dependency were in part exogenous: the rise of merchant capitalism in Europe, the establishment of regular steamship lines in the Mediterranean, and the actions of European governments in support of their nationals in Egypt; but other factors were also important—among them, the determination of Muhammad Ali and his successors to rule Egypt independently of Ottoman control, and their efforts to make themselves and their government the mediators between Egypt and the world economy. However complex the causes, by the 1870s Egypt had been reduced to the status of a client state, its delta provinces forming one vast export sector in the world commercial system.[2]

Within this new international context, there were three important agents of change. The first was the introduction of long-fiber cotton, whose cultivation increased rapidly after Muhammad Ali's death until by the 1870s it had become the dominant crop in Egypt's plantation economy. Cotton production propelled construction of new dock and harbor facilities, the improvement of internal waterways, the building of railways, and the erection of new port cities. Most of these activities came under the direction of the state administration, and this meant that new officials had to be hired, state departments reorganized, and new governorates created. The cotton boom of 1862–1864 was a particularly important stimulus to the development of Egypt's administrative system. Owing to the rapid expansion of agriculture, officials in the regular hierarchy came under such heavy pressures that the viceroy was compelled to permit a devolution of administrative authority and sanction the formation of new agricultural, judicial, and administrative institutions in the provinces.

The second agent of change was the intervention of the European consuls, who represented the interests of the European community. Consular influence was linked to the extension of the Capitulations, privileges granted by the Ottoman sultan in the sixteenth century to Europeans, exempting them from taxation (save for the payment of a low duty on imports) and giving them the right to be tried under their own laws.[3] Muhammad Ali had allowed a modest enlargement of these privileges, but was strong enough to prevent their abuse. After his death, the European consuls compelled his successors to grant further extensions and then used these "rights" to intervene on behalf of fellow nationals. Consuls threatened and blustered, made humiliating demands, and resorted to gunboat diplomacy to obtain a redress of grievances, real or imagined.

Less well known is the influence which the European consuls exercised within the administration through intermediaries who were either viceregal subjects or Europeans employed in the government. European officials served as channels of communication between their consuls and the viceroys. Consuls intervened on behalf of these Europeans, pressing for a reinstatement here, a salary increase there, until Egypt's European employees attained a privileged status unequaled by that of any other group of officials. Europeans employed in the railway administration in 1857, for example, could not be penalized, fined, or even reprimanded without reference to their consuls.[4]

The other kind of intermediary was the viceregal subject who received protection as a consular protégé. European representatives could formally protect some of the viceroy's subjects by employing them as interpreters or consular servants, which gave them all of the privileges enjoyed by Europeans under the Capitulations.[5] But consular protégés could also enjoy informal protection. European consuls extended patronage to high Turkish and Egyptian officials by defending them against rivals, arguing their case before the viceroy, and generally supporting them in their struggles for power and influence. Some of Egypt's leading officeholders received grants of protection and even European citizenship. More than a few high officials owed their success to such patronage, and the viceroys frequently consulted the consuls before making changes in administrations where European influence was strong.

The third important agent of change in later nineteenth-century Egypt was the buildup of an enormous public debt that led eventually to the bankruptcy of the state (see table 6). This was largely the result of the rapid emergence of a European and Levantine fiscal-commercial bourgeoisie.[6] The two most important components of this class were the promoters whose companies undertook the construction of public works, and the merchant-financiers who established banks and had ties with investment houses in Europe. These men not only represented an institutional base for Egyptian trade with Europe, but most important, they also provided a new means of financial support for Egypt's rulers. The viceroys used these Europeans to facilitate the extension of cash crops, and European merchants and bankers became a source of easy credit by providing short-term loans and purchasing government bonds. Egypt first went into debt because money could be borrowed easily, the necessary institutional mechanisms for contracting large debts existed, and lenders profited from making loans to the viceroys. Therefore, the rulers had little incentive to establish a more efficient system of financial administration—though, as we shall later observe, their need for the support of their officials also explains the virtual absence of effective regulation in this area.

The viceroys, of course, also bear considerable responsibility for the bankruptcy of their state. Sa'id's blunder in awarding a concession to the De Lesseps company to build a canal across the Isthmus of Suez marked the beginning of Egypt's plunge into indebtedness.[7] To pay for the 176,000 shares of company stock which he had committed his government to purchase, Saʿid issued government bonds, borrowed from European merchants, withheld salaries from state employees, and was forced to take out Egypt's first public loan in 1862. In return for Fr 53,500,000, Saʿid agreed to pay back Fr 198,000,000.

When Saʿid died in 1863 amid Egypt's cotton boom, his successor Ismail immediately began borrowing from European merchant-bankers to finance agricultural development schemes. After the boom burst in late 1864, these obligations came due at the very time Ismail was saddled with the payment of a huge indemnity (Fr 84,000,000) to the Suez Canal Company for the return of rights to land and labor conceded by Saʿid.[8] Because of this, Ismail could no longer avoid a public loan, and in October 1864, he obtained the first of three loans taken out in only two years. Reverberations were immediately felt in Egypt. Ismail raised the land tax not once but twice, and when this proved insufficient, he raised the increase from six to ten to twenty piastres per *faddan*. Reluctant to impose such a heavy burden upon the peasants by his own authority, he created a new administrative body (the Consultative Chamber of Delegates) composed of leading provincial notables to "approve" his decision. One public loan, however, only led to another. In 1868, Ismail contracted his largest loan yet (at 11.5 percent interest), and by 1870 one-third of Egypt's revenue was being diverted to the service of its debt. Forced into desperate financial straits, Ismail in 1871 issued the *Muqabala* Law, which provided that landholders who paid an amount of six times their annual tax payment in advance would be relieved of half of all future land tax liabilities and receive full ownership rights to their lands. This meas-

TABLE 6
MAJOR LOANS NEGOTIATED DURING ISMAIL'S REIGN

Title or Lender	Date	Amount Realized (£)	Nominal Amount (£)	To Be Repaid[a]
Oppenheim	1864	4,864,063	5,704,200	9,304,000
Daira	1865	2,750,000	3,387,000	—
Railway	1866	2,640,000	3,000,000	—
Mustafa Pasha	1867	1,700,000	2,080,000	—
Oppenheim	1868	7,193,334	11,890,000	28,599,129
Daira	1870	5,000,000	7,142,860	—
Oppenheim	1873	19,973,658	32,000,000	76,970,150
Total		46,621,055	68,497,160	

Source: Hamza, *The Public Debt of Egypt, 1854–1876*, pp. 256–57.
[a]Figures from Stephen Cave, "Memorandum on the Financial Position of Egypt and on Measures for Restoring Its Credit," in FO 78/2539 A. Other figures not available.

ure raised over £8,000,000 in the first two years, but even it could not prevent the inevitable. Ismail was eventually forced to discontinue the payment of interest on the debt. By 1875, his state was bankrupt.

If Egypt was directly affected by forces emanating from the world economic and political orders, the principal cause of change in the administration remained the viceroy himself. The first reason for this, to which we shall return, is that Egypt's administration was part of the viceroy's system of domination, and his intervention was therefore necessary to maintain his control over the ruling elite and the rural surplus. The second reason is related to the decision of Sa'id and Ismail to continue Egypt's development, using the administration as their *point d'appui*. Such a strategy was apparently designed to counteract the serious loss of revenue to European merchants that had followed the breakup of Muhammad Ali's monopolies, and to take advantage of opportunities presented by a market economy.

The first consequence of this decision was a revival of many of Muhammad Ali's schemes, especially under Ismail. To produce trained men for government service, Ismail opened new civil schools in Cairo, established national primary schools in the provinces, founded a teachers' training college, and sent many more young men to study in Europe than had gone under Abbas or Sa'id.[9] Ismail also revitalized Egyptian industry. While only three or four government manufacturies existed in 1856, Ismail created an extensive industrial establishment that included railway workshops, a paper factory, two weaving mills, and seventeen new sugar factories (located on his estates).[10] Ismail also invested heavily in enlarging the irrigation system and building railways. Sa'id had completed Egypt's first railway line from Alexandria to Suez and repaired the delta barrage. Ismail authorized the construction of 112 new canals and expanded the railway network until it embraced 1,200 miles of track. Such investments were not wasted. Government revenues doubled between 1863 and the mid-1870s.[11]

The second consequence of the viceroys' decision to develop Egypt was the buildup of large private landed estates, whose growth was made possible only by their owners' association with the state apparatus. Egypt's rulers, especially Ismail, seized thousands of *faddans* of village and uncultivated lands and reallocated them to themselves, members of their families, state officials, and military officers who received legal rights to them. High state officials and others used their administrative positions to enlarge their properties, while the vice-regal estates benefited from free use of the state railways and corvée labor.[12] By granting such lands and encouraging the production of sugar and cotton for the market, Egypt's rulers hoped to find money with which to continue Egypt's development, pay their creditors, and achieve greater independence from Turkey.

The viceroys also began to rely upon the assistance of new social elements who were brought directly into the governmental system. The promotion of native Egyptians from the provincial notability to high administrative positions was a very important step. It not only brought the rulers into contact with men who possessed an intimate knowledge of the financial resources of the countryside, but also introduced into the government those very family connections which Muhammad Ali had been able to avoid by basing his power on an alien elite. Egypt's rulers also sought the assistance of those educated during Muhammad Ali's reign, and this led to the emergence of a technocratic elite in the higher administration composed of men familiar with European science and somewhat sympathetic to European civilization. In this way, the viceroys themselves helped stimulate changes within their ruling system.

▲▲▲ THE DEVELOPMENT OF THE BUREAUCRACY

In the mid-nineteenth century, the Egyptian bureaucracy underwent a development so rapid as to eclipse the growth that had occurred during the years of Muhammad Ali's reforms. Old Ottoman offices and positions disappeared entirely or were absorbed into an expanding civil administration. New functional departments were created, and new conciliar bodies emerged. The legislative and judicial functions of government became ever more distinct from those of the executive. Salary laws were passed; a pension system was worked out; civil ranks were set up. In short, administration was becoming more specialized in function and bureaucratic in form.

Did Egypt's government have to develop in this way? With the benefit of hindsight, we may consider it logical, almost necessary, that government should become more bureaucratic and specialized once it had acquired new regulatory functions and Muhammad Ali's successors had made the critical decision to continue developing their country. How else but through a centralized bureaucracy could Egypt be developed and personal rule still maintained? Even more important: how far had this process gone by 1874? Is it possible to speak of a rationalized and completely functioning bureaucracy by then?

Egypt at mid-century owed much to the reforms of Muhammad Ali. Since antiquity, the country had fallen into two great natural divisions (see table 7): lower Egypt (*al-bahri*), which included the delta, and upper Egypt (*al-qibli*), which began south of Cairo and extended to the northern Sudan. A subordinate division was sometimes recognized between middle Egypt (the provinces of Bani Suwayf, al-Fayyum, and al-Minya) and the area to the south, known as the Sa'id. As shown in table 1, Muhammad Ali had organized these regions into provinces or *mudiriyas* (usually numbering fourteen after his death); each province was administered by a governor (*mudir*) and was subdivided into departments (*ma'muriyas*, later called *markaze*s) headed by *ma'mur*s, districts (*qism*s) governed by *nazir*s, and subdistricts (*khutt*s) headed by *hakim*s. At the bottom of this hierarchy were the villages, administered by native officials called *shaykhs al-balad* or *umda*s.

Possessing both judicial and executive powers, the governors of the provinces lived in the provincial capitals (*bandar*s) where the garrison troops, consisting of infantry and cavalry as well as Bedouin auxiliaries, were also stationed. Here too were the religious courts and the central police headquarters, whose officials supervised the local police and traveled through the provinces, making reports on suspicious or improper behavior.

Some of Egypt's towns and cities enjoyed special status as governorates (*muhafaza*s), which meant that they were administered independently of the provinces by a *muhafiz* or governor. Amin Sami's list of official positions for the last year of Muhammad Ali's reign reveals four governorates: Damietta, Rosetta, Qusayr and Suez.[13] Above the governorates and provinces stood the inspector-general, one of the most powerful officials in the land. Through the Inspectorate, he and his men coordinated the entire provincial administration and supervised all of its officials, even the provincial governors. Like them, the inspector general combined executive and judicial powers.[14]

TABLE 7
THE PROVINCES OF EGYPT IN 1878

Lower Egypt	al-Buhayra
	al-Gharbiya
	al-Minufiya
	al-Daqahliya
	al-Sharqiya
	al-Qalyubiya
Upper Egypt	al-Jiza
	Bani Suwayf
	al-Fayyum
	al-Minya and Bani Mazar
	Asyut
	Jirja
	Qina
	Isna

Source: Fikri, *Jughrafiyat Misr*, pp. 4–7.

After Muhammad Ali's death, this simple yet reformed structure of administration was modified, first, by the expansion of already existing units, and second, by the creation of new, specialized structures. Perhaps the best example of simple, numerical increase is the governorates. Within twenty years after Muhammad Ali's death, five new governorates had been created, a governor general of the Suez Canal had been appointed, and the sleepy old governorate of Suez had been transformed into a bustling center of commerce and transit traffic. Until 1854, Cairo itself had been administered by a powerful household official, the *katkhuda* or first lieutenant of the viceroy. In November of that year, that position was abolished, and Cairo was given separate administrative status as a governorate, which included jurisdiction over the city police, the arsenals, and some important government administrations.[15] The creation of the Cairo governorate was followed by the establishment of three others: al-Arish (1855), Port Saʿid (1866), and Ismailiya (1870), the last two being created right out of the desert. (Alexandria had become a governorate by 1851.) The work of these governorates was facilitated by the establishment of police departments with boards to hear complaints and receive cases. In Cairo, this new organization made redundant the old Ottoman post of *muhtasib*, whose occupant in Muhammad Ali's day had been the market inspector and one of the city's top-ranking police officers.[16]

The chief reason for the expansion of these governorates was the development of land and water communications. Ismailiya and Port Saʿid, for example, resulted directly from the construction of the Suez Canal, and the early growth of Suez was so intimately linked to the traffic between England and India that it needed a governor who spoke English.[17]

Much less information is available on the development of Egypt's provinces, but it appears that they experienced a quite rapid growth. In 1855, for example, Saʿid Pasha added five district heads (*hakims*) and twelve assistants (*muʿawins*) to the 144 officials employed in the province of al-Daqahliya.[18] Government expenditures for all provinces rose from an estimated 34,423 purses (one purse = five Egyptian pounds) in 1868–1869 to a total of 40,546 purses in 1874–1875.[19] The internal growth of these units derived from the expansion of agriculture, particularly the development of cotton. During the cotton boom, the provinces enlarged considerably. In July 1863, owing to the increased workload in the provinces, new officials were appointed to seven provinces in lower and upper Egypt. In August 1864, the number of officials employed in al-Minufiya was increased from 335 to 362, and in 1866 additional funds were allocated for five provinces in lower Egypt.[20]

Qualitative changes also took place. During the 1860s and 1870s, a new judicial administration emerged in the countryside, and administrative and agricultural councils were formed to supplement those provincial units of government created by Muhammad Ali.

Muhammad Ali had made no substantive changes in the provincial court system. In Cairo, his Department of Civil Affairs shared judicial authority with the viceroy's first lieutenant, and two commercial courts were established (one in Alexandria). After 1842, crimes committed by officials were tried in Cairo by a new but short-lived organization, *Diwan al-Haqqaniya*. In the provinces, executive officials exercised considerable judicial authority, and the *sharia* courts held sway in religious and civil matters.

The growing burden of administration gradually began to compel a separation of judicial from executive functions. During Abbas's reign, courts of first instance (*majlises ibtida³i*) were set up to try criminal and civil cases in the provinces, but these government courts were too few and too weak to be very effective.[21] Egypt's cotton boom, and the rapid, almost frenetic development of the country during the 1860s overwhelmed the officials of the provincial hierarchy and created a need for more highly specialized structures. Within days after his accession, Khedive Ismail began authorizing the formation of new courts of first instance. In January 1863, he opened five provincial courts with 124 members, excluding staff. By 1870, there was such a court in every province of Egypt.[22] Courts of appeal (*majlises isti³naf*) were also set up in lower and upper Egypt to review cases handled by the lower courts.

Because of the heavy weight of criminal and civil cases, these courts were unable to relieve local officials of their judicial functions. To lighten the burden upon the regular administration, new courts were created. In 1871, a village court (*majlis da'awi al-balad*) was established in each of the large villages of Egypt, and a *bandar* court (*majlis da'awi al-bandar*) was formed in every provincial capital to carry out the responsibilities of the village courts there.[23]

These new courts handled minor violations of civil or criminal law. The village courts, which dealt primarily with disputes in which reconciliation was possible, could imprison persons for up to twenty-four hours, impose fines up to 25 piastres, and award damages of not more than 500 piastres.[24] Their decisions were appealed to the *bandar* courts, which had the power to imprison up to five days, impose fines up to 100 piastres, and award damages not in excess of 2,500 piastres. These courts also supervised charitable institutions and the local government schools, whose accounts they checked. Civil and criminal cases of a more serious nature were submitted to the courts of first instance, whose decisions could be reviewed by a court of appeal. By 1871, if not earlier, courts of appeal were sitting in Cairo, Tanta, Alexandria, Jirja, and Bani Suwayf. At the top of this judicial pyramid stood the Council of Justice (*Majlis al-Ahkam al-Misriya*), located in Cairo. In 1872, perhaps because of the growing need to control and coordinate the various elements that now made up the legal order, an executive organ, the Department of Justice, was created. The formation of these courts was the last step in the elaboration of a new judicial administration for Egypt. As the *Egyptian Gazette* stated at the time of their establishment, judicial powers were at last separated from executive functions.[25]

The creation of separate administrative and agricultural councils marked another departure from Muhammad Ali's system of administration. Like the new courts, these councils were designed to lighten the burdens of administration which until then had been borne almost exclusively by officials in the provincial hierarchy. During the cotton boom, this structure had come under considerable strain. Its officials were forced to take more jobs than they could reasonably fulfill, and the work of administration in the provinces had consequently been slowed. In 1869, five agricultural councils (*majlises taftish al-zira'a*) were formed, three for upper Egypt, and two for lower Egypt.[26] Headed by a president and a deputy (who was also an engineer) and composed of local notables, these councils directed local agricultural operations. They ascertained what supplies were necessary, and obtained precise information about the number of local villagers, the condition of the land, and the state of the irrigation works.

The next step in the devolution of provincial authority came in 1871 when an administrative council (*majlis idarat mashyakhat al-balad*) was established in each of the large villages, and an analogous council (*majlis baladi*) was formed in the provincial capitals. The village councils were empowered to supervise local public works projects, direct the procurement of corvée labor in a fair way, and maintain local tombs, mosques, and antiquities. They were also to supervise the collection of taxes, ensure that taxes collected were properly recorded, make disbursements for work done, and register births, deaths, and the arrival of newcomers.[27] These functions had previously been discharged by officials in the regular provincial hierarchy.

Because of this new arrangement, the duties of some provincial officials were redefined. Governors were now given responsibility for implementing the decisions of the agricultural councils, and they became a kind of liaison between the latter and the new local councils. Governors were to make preliminary investigations and submit the results to the appropriate court. They were still held generally responsible for everything occurring in their provinces, and they could recommend that a local council be placed on trial for delay of work.[28] The duties of the inspector general were similarly modified. Petitions alleging violations of the law were to be sent to the proper court without even a preliminary investigation, unless they contained charges against government officials. This was also true of any violations uncovered by the Inspectorate, unless they concerned a provincial governor or his deputy. At the same time, the inspector general was enjoined to watch closely the operations of the councils of agriculture, and to report any delay or irregularity to the Privy Council.[29]

The central government experienced still more growth and change. In the capital, the quickening pace of government activity led to the enlargement of existing institutions, the creation of new ones, and to an ever greater separation between the legislative and the executive. This development was crystalized by the emergence of conciliar bodies and the evolution of distinct executive departments.

Egypt's executive departments were originally known as *diwans umum*, or general administrations, to distinguish them from other *diwans*, which were only offices. Like the provincial governors, directors of departments were called *mudirs*. Under Saʿid, these departments received the appellation of *nizara* (meaning supervision or control), and their directors the title of *nazir*. By the time of Ismail's accession, these new terms had almost completely replaced the old ones, as indicated by Sami's annual lists. The departments, composed of offices called *qalams*, received jurisdiction over smaller units—*maslahas* (administrations), *majlises* (boards), and *diwans* (offices), which were not always attached to executive departments. They were of course a creation of Muhammad Ali. As we have seen, during the later years of his reign there had been six *diwans umum*: Finance, War, Marine, Industry, Education, and Foreign Affairs.

After Muhammad Ali's death, five more departments were created: the Department of Charitable Endowments or *al-Awqaf* (established in 1851, recreated in 1863), Interior (1857), Public Works (1864), Justice (1872), and Agriculture (1875); a railway administration (*maslaha*) also emerged in 1852.[30] Not all enjoyed a continual existence; some were abolished and reformed, and some were merged with other departments. As time passed, these administrations grew larger and were given new responsibilities until they became a permanent feature of government.

As elsewhere in the administration, the 1860s was a time for growth for these new departments. In most, the work load was greatly increased, and this led to their expansion. In 1863, Khedive Ismail authorized adding personnel to the Department of Finance.[31] In June

1864, salaries were increased and seventeen new officials were employed in the Department of Charitable Endowments, whose monthly expenditures rose from 42,805 piastres to 59,880. In the Department of Public Works—the administration most directly involved in building Egypt's material infrastructure—monthly salaries went from 159,082 piastres in 1866 to 366,750 in 1872. The budget of the Department of Education was increased in November 1863, and rose still higher the following March. Such growth, however, was not continual or uniform throughout the administration. In 1872, for example, the Interior Department budget was less than it had been in 1859.[32] Until more data are available on the personnel and expenditures of these administrations, it is impossible to do more than trace the outlines of their development.

Muhammad Ali's executive departments, save perhaps for those of finance and education, had taken few responsibilities. Their directors passed on nearly every problem, great or small, to the central *diwans*, through which Egypt had been administered. As we have seen, Muhammad Ali was displeased that his central *diwans* spent most of their time resolving the minutiae of administration. To remedy this, he passed laws defining further the duties of his departments. He even created new ones, but only after his death did the situation change.[33]

Beginning in 1849, Egypt's administration was reorganized and the departments were forced to assume responsibility for matters which until then had devolved upon the great central *diwans*. About this time, the old Department of *Ruznama*, which had been administered by Muhammad Ali's Department of Civil Affairs, was made a branch of the Finance Department.[34] New functional departments were also set up. Public works, for example, had previously been administered by Civil Affairs, though the work of construction and repair was apparently carried out by a little-known office, *Diwan al-Abniya*.[35] In 1864, Egypt's first real Department of Public Works (*Diwan al-Ashghal*) was created. It was responsible for the building and repair of dams, canals, and dikes, and the construction of buildings in Cairo and Alexandria. It also received administrative jurisdiction over the barrages, the quarantine, the office of engineering, and a short time later, the railway administration. In May 1866, this department was employing 182 officials whose monthly salaries totaled 159,082 piastres.

A far better example of structural development may be found in the Department of the Interior (*Diwan al-Dakhiliya*), established in 1857.[36] When the Department of Civil Affairs was abolished, this department was created to take over some of its functions. In March 1857, the Interior Department received jurisdiction over the Suez Canal project, the Shubra stables, the civil hospital, the printing press, the government primary schools, and the offices of health and engineering. The following September, the Cairo governorate came under its jurisdiction, and in October an office of European affairs was created in it. By April 1859, this department was receiving petitions and complaints from Egyptian subjects and officials in Cairo and the provinces, reviewing the minutes of sessions of the Council of Justice and the commercial councils, and deciding which of the material it received should be sent to the khedive. The Interior Department was made up of three offices: Turkish records, Arabic records, and Arabic petitions. It also contained translators, assistants, guards, and sixty-two officials of the engineering administration, over which it had jurisdiction.

Although this department was abolished in September 1859 and reestablished during Khedive Ismail's reign, its internal organization remained essentially unchanged until 1874. An archival document from 1872 shows that it was still composed of the three offices, and that it possessed the old complement of copyists, watchmen, clerks, and others, though not in the same number. In November 1874, the offices of petitions and Turkish records were fused, and three new offices were created: one for the executive departments, another for the provinces, and one for notes from other administrations.[37]

Despite their structural development, Egypt's executive departments had a very spare and "unmodern" aspect. In appearance at least, they could hardly have been mistaken for ministries.[38] The central room of a department contained a half-dozen straw chairs and a low sofa (*diwan*) with cushions on three sides. On the corner of the *diwan*, crosslegged, sat the minister, transacting business with his clerks. An inkstand, a sponge, several reeds, tobacco pipes, and coffee utensils were its only materials. Adjoining this were smaller rooms, each occupied by an office chief, his clerks, and assistants, all of whom sat on floor mats. Beside them were small boxes, into which the account books and papers were thrown at the end of the day. Inkstands, knives, and scissors were taken home. These features did not begin to change until the 1870s. Edmond About, who visited the government departments in 1868, described a scene not dissimilar from the one given by Hekekyan in 1856. Officials still sat on *diwan*s in sparsely furnished rooms, with a crowd of hawkers and beggars outside. Business, too, was conducted in the same old way—the minister swaying back and forth as he quickly read the paper which had been placed on the floor in front of him, interrupted occasionally by an aide who whispered in his ear; then, having affixed his seal, throwing the paper down on the rug for one of his assistants. However much they may have changed, Egypt's executive departments were not yet ministries.

The other principal unit of the central administration were the conciliar bodies. These were the truly effective organs of government where laws were hammered out and the details of policy formulated. These bodies studied and debated matters submitted to them by the executive departments or by the viceroy, and issued decisions which, once approved, had the force of law. They dealt with every conceivable subject, from taxes to the structure of government. During most of the period under study, there were two conciliar or quasi-legislative bodies: the *Majlis Khususi* (Privy Council), and the *Majlis Ahkam* (Council of Justice). In 1866, a third conciliar body was created, *Majlis Shura al-Nuwwab* (Consultative Chamber of Delegates), which possessed advisory functions and was considerably less important than the other two councils.

The Privy Council, created in January 1847, was Egypt's most important conciliar body.[39] An outgrowth of the administrative reorganization that occurred during the late 1840s, it dealt mostly with problems arising within the administration. It deliberated upon matters sent to it by the Consultative Chamber of Delegates, and handled problems that the Council of Justice could not solve. Save for a short period during Sa'id's reign (it was twice abolished by him), the Privy Council was hierarchically superior to the Council of Justice.

During Ismail's reign, the membership and organization of this body underwent considerable change. In 1847, the Privy Council was made up of five high-ranking officials, most of them belonging to the viceregal family. By 1849, it had acquired a staff of three, and a membership of twelve. In May 1850, there were seven officials on this council, and in September 1854, eight officials sat on a *Majlis Khass*, formed to administer Egypt temporarily in Sa'id's absence.[40] Soon after his accession, Ismail reorganized the Privy Council. He decreed that it meet regularly (between one and three times a week), that it convene in the place where his own cabinet met, and that it be formed of six officials: the directors of the Department of Finance and the Department of War, the head of the viceregal cabinet, the governor of Cairo, the president of the Council of Justice, and Ratib Pasha, a favorite of the khedive.[41] The debates of this council were not always attended by Ismail, but he at least found time to read the notes of its meetings. In 1869, a special committee was established inside the Privy Council to meet daily and consider problems submitted to it. In May 1873, two new offices were created: one for statistics, another for European affairs. By the early 1870s, the commander in chief of the army, the chairman of the committee in the council, the presidents of the Consultative Chamber of Delegates and the Council of Justice, and the directors of Finance, War, and Interior had been established as regular members (in 1871, the director of Foreign Affairs had also joined the Privy Council). It had become customary for a small number of the ruler's personal associates to sit as members, as well as a few advisers from the departments. When the directors of Justice and Public Works were added as members in June 1873, all the heads of Egypt's executive departments were at last members of this council, which numbered seventeen men.[42]

Perhaps this is why some have referred to the Privy Council as a Council of Ministers.[43] This epithet is dangerously misleading, because it implies a greater development than had actually occurred. The members of this council served at the pleasure of the viceroy to whom they were individually responsible and by whom they could be removed at will. They had in common only the fact that they debated and resolved problems together, by majority vote in council, and that as individuals they ranked among the highest officials in the land. While some were appointed to this council because of merit, others had been given their positions as rewards for past services, or as a parking place until another appointment could be found for them.[44] For these reasons and because the *Majlis Khususi* both advised the ruler and legislated for him, this administrative body more nearly resembled a privy council than a cabinet or council of ministers.

Deny has correctly pointed out that the Privy Council functioned as a supreme tribunal.[45] It could try officials, including its own members, but it spent much less time as a court than as a legislative body. Its primary function, as its original statute makes clear, was to regulate the administration by issuing laws. In fact, this council enjoyed a wide range of functions. It defined the procedure of criminal investigation, created new taxes and increased old ones, established a pension system and made specific determinations of the claims of pensioners, and authorized the payment of some salaries and approved increases and decreases in others. This council also established administrative structures. It created a customs administration for Port Saʿid, established a board to supervise finances, and set up commercial and criminal courts. It even issued a statute prescribing the duties of village watchmen (*ghafirs*). The activities of the Privy Council went far beyond the traditional conciliar duty of giving advice. By Ismail's reign, its value to the ruler had become great indeed.

Like the Privy Council, Egypt's Council of Justice spent most of its time resolving problems submitted to it and issuing laws, which had to be approved by the Privy Council or the viceroy himself.[46] Its legislation dealt mostly with legal matters, but it also could function as a high court, and not infrequently served a strictly administrative purpose.

Since this council met daily, its members did not hold other positions in the administration. They were also drawn from the ranks of high officials, but perhaps not so high in rank as the men of the Privy Council. In continuous operation during the reign of Abbas, this council had ten members in 1854. Under Saʿid, the Council of Justice was organized into five offices and three workshops (warshas), one each for upper and lower Egypt, and one for the central administration. Abolished in April 1860, but reestablished in June 1861, this council enjoyed a continuous existence during Ismail's reign.

The Council of Justice concentrated judicial functions which had previously been distributed among several government organs. Until 1842, Egypt had not had an administrative body to deal specifically with judicial affairs.[47] In February of that year, a High Court of Justice was created, but by 1849, this body had been superseded by the Council of Justice. It reviewed and approved the sentences of the local courts, and could set their decisions aside in favor of its own rulings; it also tried cases submitted to it, particularly those involving officials, and could even determine what the punishments for violations should be. Because of its considerable powers, it was Egypt's chief judicial body.

Almost as considerable were its powers of legislation. Like the Privy Council, the Council of Justice deliberated upon administrative problems (though usually of less important nature than those considered by the Privy Council), and could issue laws binding upon the departments of government. Its scope of authority depended upon what the ruler was willing to give it. For a short while during Saʿid's reign, it seems to have been given preference over the Privy Council, though both organs were abolished and reformed more than once during that time. Under Saʿid, this council was empowered to debate financial questions (especially those involving taxes), issue laws for the improvement of agriculture, and establish regulations for the Department of Education. It even issued a law governing land sales to officials.[48] Official documents from the reigns of Saʿid and Ismail leave no doubt about the importance of this body for Egypt's administration.[49]

The third conciliar body to emerge during the mid-nineteenth century was the Consultative Chamber of Delegates (Majlis Shura al-Nuwwab), established in 1866 to advise the ruler in matters of administration. This institution has received more attention than any other administrative body of the time. Scholars and other who have equated constitutional change with representativeness have taken this body as a convenient signpost, if not the starting point, for the development of representative institutions in modern Egypt. It has even been stated, incorrectly, that between 1866 and 1876, the Chamber developed into a parliamentary institution with a significant decision-making role and a willingness to assert itself against the ruler.[50]

As an advisory body with legislative functions, the Consultative Chamber of Delegates (numbering seventy-five members) occupied a unique position. Like the Privy Council and Council of Justice, it passed resolutions on matters covering both general categories and specific instances.[51] Its members were elected for three-year terms on a proportionate basis from the entire country. They were drawn from among Egyptian notables who by law could not be employed in the government at the time of their selection. Many came from families long associated with the administration, and most had been or would become provincial officials (some were given such appointments even before the expiration of their term in the Chamber). Because of the special place of this body within the administration and the importance attached to it by many writers, it bears repeating that this Chamber was never an extragovernmental institution.

The membership of this body reflected the changing social reality of Egypt's administration. Muhammad Ali had first introduced native Egyptians into the bureaucracy and the army. After his death, Egyptians continued to be brought into the administration, and some rose to high positions. By Ismail's reign, Egyptians could be found almost everywhere in the government. In the provinces, for example, the village courts, the courts in the provincial capitals, and the administrative and agricultural councils were staffed by notables whose friends and relatives held positions in the administrative hierarchy. In Cairo, Egyptian notables could be found in the executive departments. A few even sat on the prestigious Council of Justice.[52]

The establishment of a legislative body consisting entirely of Egyptians gave its members an opportunity to acquire experience and knowledge of a kind unavailable to them anywhere else. They learned how to draft and debate proposals, they gradually learned the art of reconciling divergent interests, and they acquired knowledge of administrative detail. Since they also discussed and debated financial matters and were allowed to examine some government records, they became familiar with the methods of record keeping and with some details of Egypt's revenues and expenditures. On one occasion, the Chamber received a list of all *kharaj* and octroi taxes collected by the government over the previous twenty years.[53] This gradually gave some of its members a sophistication that would later prove of inestimable value. The behavior of the Chamber after 1876 cannot be understood without reference to its members' early training in the art of government.

The exact reasons which led Ismail to create the Chamber may never be known. D. M. Wallace suggests that it was intended to check the influence of the high Turkish officials. Jacob Landau, on the other hand, implies that Ismail wished to bring the notables themselves under better control. Abdel-Maksud Hamza asserts, quite credibly, that Ismail regarded its creation as a means of strengthening Egyptian credit and facilitating a loan.[54] Egypt's unhealthy financial condition must certainly have figured prominently in Ismail's decision, but on the basis of the work actually assigned this Chamber, we may suggest two other reasons. The first was to legitimize Ismail's unpopular and oppressive administrative and fiscal policies. Indeed, some of the Chamber's work can be explained only in this way. When Ismail confiscated land near the village of Turuja and reallocated it to some members of his family, he had the Chamber ratify his action. There was no compelling reason for him to do so save the unpopularity of a land policy which was imposing such hardships upon the *fallahin* that there were actually riots on the viceregal estates.[55] The Chamber was asked to establish taxes on uncultivated lands and to specify the conditions on which they should be granted by the ruler, and it also approved new taxes and tax increases.[56] In 1868, it sanctioned a one-sixth increase in land and personal taxes, and approved a head tax on livestock and an octroi tax on vegetables entering towns.[57] The Chamber also became involved in government efforts to extend its control over the population. It authorized a census that was to cover every hamlet, encampment, and village in Egypt, and it further authorized stationing a military engineer and two soldiers in every district.[58] One can only marvel at Ismail's shrewdness in transferring the onus of unpopular policies to a "popular" assembly.

If the Consultative Chamber of Delegates had existed only to legitimize the actions of Ismail, it would merit but a footnote here. Ismail desperately needed money, but he also needed men familiar with conditions in the countryside and capable of assisting him in his development schemes. Ever since Muhammad Ali, the viceroys of Egypt had relied increasingly upon Egyptian notables, and with the rapid development of the country after 1863, their assistance became even more vital. The creation of this Chamber, then, may also be regarded as a response to the administrative realities of the 1860s.

The Chamber passed resolutions covering a wide range of internal projects, from the establishment of new educational institutions to the proper maintenance and construction of irrigation canals.[59] In 1869, a resolution from the Chamber requesting that the Ibrahimiya canal be extended to Suhaj within the year prompted the formation of a committee of high officials who, upon examining the matter, decided that though its extension to Suhaj was impossible that year, the canal could be extended to al-Minya. This Chamber also helped organize and regulate the administration. In 1868, it issued a resolution calling for increased allocations for officials' pensions and salaries and for the work of the departments. It authorized the establishment of courts of appeal and first instance, and was responsible for forming new agricultural councils. The Chamber served as a catalyst in initiating debate within the government that led to the creation of administrative councils and courts in the villages and provincial capitals. During a discussion on the growing difficulties of collecting taxes and resolving cases in the provinces, several members of the Chamber suggested that the principal cause of the problem lay in the heavy and increasing responsibilities given to provincial officials. To provide relief, they suggested that two councils be set up in every village, one for administration, the other for legal matters. The Privy Council discussed and approved this project, and Khedive Ismail authorized it. This Chamber played a more active role in the administration than has generally been realized.

If the Consultative Chamber of Delegates had been in operation more frequently, it might have attained an importance comparable to that of the Privy Council and the Council of Justice. However, it met only for an average of three months when in session, and was convened only six times between 1866 and 1875—not meeting at all during 1872, 1874, and 1875. Yet even when out of session the Chamber was still apparently needed. When an engineering problem arose on the barrages in 1875, Ismail wrote that this should be considered by the Chamber. But since elections for the next session had not yet been completed, he finally decided to form an ad hoc body of notables to examine the problem.[60] Because of its infrequent appearance, the Chamber thus remained subordinate to Egypt's two other conciliar bodies.

▲▲▲ THE LIMITS TO ADMINISTRATIVE RATIONALIZATION

The development of an administrative system must also include laws regulating the machinery of government. This process is often described as "rationalization," a term associated with a number of interconnected developments. The process by which an administration becomes rationalized is generally understood to include such elements as civil ranks, a salary scale, a pension system, a regular scheme of promotion and advancement, an improved organization of accounts and records, penal codes, and rules which define and confine spheres of administrative authority. In other words, rationalization is associated with the development of a "civil" or government service. To what extent was the Egyptian administration becoming rationalized? Of which elements was it composed?

The outlines of a new civil order had first appeared during the reign of Muhammad Ali. After his new military establishment was formed in the 1820s, government officials were given military ranks. Even village headmen wore military uniforms.[61] While a distinction between civil and military spheres could be discerned as early as 1828, the emergence of a government service apparently dates to the creation of separate ranks for officials in the mid-1830s.[62] Government employees not affiliated with the Department of War were requested to apply for these new civil ranks, and Muhammad Ali issued an order prohibiting military officers from holding civil (*mulki, madani*) positions. The number and type of civil ranks available during Muhammad Ali's reign are not known, but by 1855 five civil ranks had been formed.[63] Below the fifth civil rank, there existed only military ranks and titles. By 1863, the highest civil rank, al-*rutba* al-*ula* (first rank), had been subdivided into first and second grades.

The elaboration of a salary scale was a corollary of the new ranking system. Despite disagreement over the criterion for awarding salaries, the principle of salary by rank rather than by position or quality of work became firmly established during Muhammad Ali's reign.[64] There were, of course, exceptions. The salaries of district chiefs (*nazirs* al-*qism*), for example, were fixed by position. In 1860, Sa'id established monthly salaries for civil officials by ranks as follows:

Second rank (first grade)	8000 piastres
Second rank (second grade)	5000 piastres
Third rank	3000 piastres
Fourth rank	2500 piastres
Fifth rank	1500 piastres
Equivalent of captain	750 piastres
Equivalent of lieutenant	500 piastres

In 1863, Ismail fixed the salary of officials holding first rank at 10,000 piastres, and increased the amounts previously set for the positions of district chief and subdistrict chief to 1,750 and 750 piastres, respectively.

In addition to salaries, officials received food allowances (*badal ta-'yin*), fodder (*aliq*) for their horses, and a uniform (*kiswa*). The food allowances could augment one's salary considerably. While director of finances in 1270/1853–1854, Salim Pasha was registered for a monthly food allowance of 3,959 piastres and a salary of 16,111 piastres. During a prior appointment, he had received a salary of 12,083 piastres and drawn 8,685 piastres in food allowances. As time passed, however, the amount of these rations was reduced, and in 1860 they were abolished for all civil and military employees above third rank.[65]

The third component of government service was a pension plan for unemployed or retired officials. Egypt's retirement system was based upon the statute of August 1844; Sa'id Pasha's pension law of December 1854; and the law of January 1871. The statute of 1844, the first pension law for civil servants in the history of modern Egypt, resolved an earlier debate over the basis for awarding pensions by establishing as criterion the period of service. To be eligible, civil officials had to have served thirty years. The amount of their pensions was then determined by the salaries they had drawn. Thus officials whose monthly salaries had been in excess of 1,000 piastres received one-quarter of their salaries as pension, while those who had earned between 1,000 and 250 piastres were given one-third of their original salaries in pension.[66]

The law of 1844 was superseded by the statutes of 1854 and 1871, which became the basis for awarding pensions for the remainder of the century. Retired officials who had entered government service before 1871 came under the provisions of Sa'id's law, which stipulated a minimum period of fifteen years' service and calculated pensions strictly on the basis of time served. Those who had served fifteen years received an amount equal to one-quarter of their salary, no matter what they had earned; those who had served forty years or more were given their full salaries as pension.[67] Retired officials who had entered the government after 1871 came under the tougher provisions of the 1871 law, which harkened back to the code of 1844. A minimum of thirty years' service was reestablished, and pensions were calculated according to the amount of salary received.[68] This pension system was supplemented by a scheme of provisional retirement by which officials dismissed because there was no further need for their services were given one-half of their salaries until a new assignment could be found for them.[69] (This practice may have been an ingenious adaptation of the long-standing British custom of "half-pay" officers in the military.)

To bring more order into the administration, regulate the behavior of its officials, and provide guidance for the courts, other laws and statutes were passed. Until 1855, such legislation was composed primarily of laws and decrees instituted during Muhammad Ali's reign, administrative statutes issued by Abbas in 1849, and the so-called code of Abbas (*Code d'Abbass*), which seems to have been a summary of Muhammad Ali's penal legislation.[70] The chief characteristic of this body of law was its great profusion and its indigenous inspiration. No Ottoman codes were applied in this Ottoman province.

In late 1854 or early 1855, an organic law was issued which became known as the Egyptian *Tanzimat* code. Derived from the Ottoman penal code of 1851, this law provided the legal basis for government during Saʿid's reign.[71] A comprehensive piece of legislation, it contained a penal code for government officials and rules establishing procedures to be followed by the Council of Justice and the government courts. The Egyptian *Tanzimat* code also regulated agricultural operations and defined the relationship between the authorities and the population, at least to the extent of what should not be done. Punishments were prescribed for natives who violated the law. Although its origin was non-Egyptian, this law contained few provisions that were not suitable to Egypt. In fact, it was more nearly Egyptian than Ottoman. At least one of its provisions had been borrowed from a previous Egyptian law, and many of those articles based upon the Ottoman code itself had been changed to suit conditions in Egypt.

Soon after his accession, Ismail requested the Council of Justice to bring together all laws (*qawanin*) and statutes (*lawaʾih*) issued by Muhammad Ali, Abbas, and Saʿid.[72] After his visit to Istanbul, where he acquired a codification of Ottoman laws that included a copy of the penal code of 1858 (based upon French laws), Ismail on July 5, 1863, ordered that the Egyptian *Tanzimat* law be abolished and the new Ottoman penal code be introduced into Egypt. The following September, however, Ismail modified his stand by ordering that those parts of the *Tanzimat* law which were suitable to Egypt be added to the new code. In September 1875, after twelve years of preparation, the new criminal code was finally issued. During the interval, some French penal laws were apparently being applied. In 1865, for example, Ismail ordered that officials guilty of bribery, theft, and embezzlement be punished in accordance with an article in the French law. Translations of French civil and commercial laws were also made and published during the 1860s.

It would seem that real progress had been made toward a more rational administrative order, one based upon laws. But had it? Were salaries regularly paid, as stipulated by law, and on the basis of rank? Were the laws actually made known to government officials? The fact that two different pension laws were being applied concurrently, and that the ruler could whimsically set aside the law, raises doubts.

Rationalization existed mostly on paper. Salaries were not paid with any regularity, nor in the amounts legally specified, nor according to fixed rules. Salary arrears were chronic, particularly during Sa'id's reign when it almost became a rule that salaries would be paid late, if at all.[73] Government salaries were also subject to viceregal interference. In 1858, Sa'id ordered the governor of Qusayr to pay his officials only one month out of four. Several years earlier he had reduced by one-quarter the monthly salaries of officials in Asyut and Jirja who earned more than 500 piastres. In 1875, Ismail ordered that the salaries of tax collectors be docked one month each year.[74] Other officials received more than they should have: in 1876, Qasim Pasha was given twice his designated salary while on assignment, while Ahmad Khayri Pasha was awarded 1,250 piastres a month above the salary of his rank. Salaries were not very stable, as demonstrated by the following amounts received monthly by Hasan al-Shari'i while holding second rank:[75]

1856	5000 piastres
1858	8000 piastres
1863	5000 piastres
1867	4000 piastres
1867	5000 piastres
1871	4000 piastres

Egypt's viceroys could not agree upon salary rules. In 1846, Muhammad Ali ordered that the highest salary be 150,000 piastres a year; Abbas gave his son Ilhami 600,000 piastres annually; Sa'id assigned Prince Ahmad Rif'at 1,000,000 piastres a year and apologized for so small an amount![76] Such high salaries, of course, were given only to a few officials. A much clearer instance of rule changing occurred in 1871 when the basis for awarding salaries was shifted from rank to position.[77] The motive for this seems to have been economic, because salaries designated for certain positions were reduced. Provincial governors, who had not uncommonly received 8,000 piastres a month by virtue of their rank, were to be given 4,000 piastres for that position. This "reform" introduced still more confusion into the administration. Officials began petitioning the Privy Council to restore their salaries to former levels, and when Khedive Ismail himself began to readjust upward the salaries of some high officials, his example was followed elsewhere in the administration, even though it was technically a violation of the law.

Pension laws were treated in the same cavalier manner. During Sa'id's reign, retired officials were assigned pensions without a proper determination of the causes of their dismissal or their periods of service. Retired officials could even be found wandering about the countryside, destitute.[78] The registration of retirees was considerably improved under Ismail. Beginning in 1863, the year of his accession, the number of dossiers made out for retired government officials more than tripled that of the preceding three years. The subsequent fluctuations in the numbers of these dossiers, however, reinforce a suspicion that many retired officials were not properly registered for pensions even during Ismail's reign. Unfettered by their own rules, Egypt's viceroys granted pensions as gifts (*ihsan*) in whatever amounts they desired. This practice, when added to the sheer inefficiency of the administration, helps explain why some pensions were above the legal limit.[79] Not only this, but also payments in cash were frequently replaced by bills of exchange and even parcels of land. The practice of granting uncultivated lands in lieu of pensions, begun about 1856 as result of a crisis in finances, became almost commonplace during Saʿid's reign, but was abolished by Ismail in 1863.[80] By 1867, however, it had been reestablished as official policy.

The wide gulf which separated the rules of administration from reality was apparent everywhere. The Egyptian *Tanzimat* code was evaded by officials and violated at will by the ruler.[81] Some Europeans became convinced that codified legislation did not exist in Egypt, while others believed that it simply was not made known to the officials and the native population. "No pains are taken to render public the laws and decrees passed from time to time," wrote the British consul Borg, "and the population are for the most part entirely ignorant thereof."[82]

Moreover, areas of administration which might be expected to come under formal regulation were left virtually untouched. Thus there were no laws setting time limits for the completion of work, or limiting the number of positions that could be created within a department, or specifying progressive salary increases, or regulating advancement and promotion within or even admission to the administration. A formal pattern of recruitment and advancement simply did not exist.

Neither was there any reform of Egyptian finances, particularly the system of accounts. One feature of Egyptian finances was the weak control of the Department of Finance over revenue and expenditures. Administrative departments, governorates, and even the provinces frequently controlled their own accounts as well as those of the administrations attached to them. When a lesser administration, as for example the Ottoman *Ruznama*, was detached from a department and made independent, it often was given charge of its accounts. Of course, departmental and other accounts were frequently placed in the Department of Finance, but usually not for long.[83] Their fate was left entirely to the ruler's discretion. Many government expenditures, including the salaries of some officials, were not made by the Department of Finance, but came directly from departmental treasuries, which were assigned specific items of revenue. Government expenditures naturally had to be authorized by the ruler, but since receipts usually were not given, departmental budgets were nonexistent, and irregular accounts existed from which officials could spend freely without accountability, it was impossible for anyone to know precisely how much had actually been disbursed. The Department of Finance exercised supervisory authority over Egyptian revenue, but in practice this meant only that it received and examined the accounts (or sometimes just financial statements) submitted by the administrations, usually at the end of each year. Even this practice was not strictly followed; in 1855, some provinces had fallen six years behind in the submission of their registers and papers. Officials from the Finance Department or the viceregal cabinet were frequently empowered to visit and check the accounts of Egypt's administrations.

Given such informal organization, it should be no surprise to learn that the government never produced a budget worthy of the name. Budgets existed, but they were no more than estimates of expenditures and anticipated revenue, the latter based upon lists drawn up by village notables. These lists were revised upwards by the government on the basis of revenue collected from the preceding or a previous year.[84] In gathering taxes, no distinction was made between operations for one year and those for another, no dates were fixed for the actual collection, and no provisions were made for deficits arising from a bad Nile.[85] Nor were budgets even published until European pressure and the need for public loans compelled the ruler to do so. These "official" budgets, issued during the 1860s and 1870s, were not very trustworthy. Items were juxtaposed incongruously. A railway in the Sudan and a canal in Egypt, for example, were listed under one sum.[86] Little faith could therefore be placed in them.

Nor did firm controls exist for the new government structures. In an administration presumably becoming rationalized, one would expect to see a stabilization of jurisdictions and administrative affiliations. Yet while punishments were prescribed for officials who exceeded their authority, their jurisdictions were loose, their departments were continuously being combined and recombined, and their spheres of authority were never definitely fixed.

Egypt's provinces are a case in point. In lower Egypt, the number of provinces oscillated between six (exclusive of al-Jiza) and four. In 1856, al-Sharqiya was abolished (its districts were divided between al-Qalyubiya and al-Daqahliya) and al-Gharbiya was combined with al-Minufiya to form a single province known as Rawdat al-Bahrayn. In 1863, it was broken up into its former divisions, but was reestablished as a single unit in 1866.[87] Two years later, there were once again six provinces in lower Egypt. Sami's annual lists show that the provinces of upper Egypt between 1863 and 1879 were likewise subjected to administrative juggling.

Discontinuity can also be observed in the central administration. It has already been mentioned that the Privy Council and the Council of Justice did not have a continuous existence—both were abolished twice during Sa'id's reign.[88] Egypt's government departments were also abolished and reformed, or otherwise modified by being joined together or by having their administrations stripped away. When Ismail Pasha, director of Interior, died in 1860, his department was abolished and its functions divided between the Departments of Finance and Foreign Affairs.[89] The Department of Interior was not reestablished until Khedive Ismail's reign, and even then it was combined with other departments. Egypt's lesser administrations were affiliated sometimes with one department, sometimes with another, and occasionally were made independent. Between 1864 and 1876, the Railway Administration (which sometimes had charge of all communications facilities and was then known as the Railway and Communications Administration) was placed three times under the jurisdiction of Public Works, once under the Cairo governorate, and was made independent five times.[90]

This crazy-quilt pattern is perhaps best illustrated by the Department of Public Works, created in 1864.[91] Because it was directed by Nubar Pasha, an influential Armenian official, this department initially assumed jurisdiction over Railway. It also was given supervision of the delta barrages, which had until 1864 been controlled by the Department of War. In September 1865, the War Department resumed control over the barrages because of their close relationship with some nearby fortifications and also because work on the barrages had continued to be done by the Department of War when they were technically under Public Works. After the removal of Nubar in 1866, the Railway Administration was separated from Public Works, which was made into an office (*qalam*) of the Interior Department. Public Works was subsequently reconstituted as a department and was combined with Education into a single administration, yet by 1869 it seems to have resumed an independent existence under its own director. In 1870, Public Works was joined to Education and Charitable Endowments; in November 1871, it was converted into an office of engineering and placed under Interior. By 1872, it had been reestablished as a department; in August of that year it was joined again to Education and Charitable Endowments; twelve months later, owing to the transfer of its director to Interior, it was returned to Interior; two months after that, it was joined to the War Department; in 1875, Public Works was reattached to Interior.

By now it should be obvious that only a modest degree of rationalization was actually achieved in the years after 1849. Many areas of administration were not brought under formal regulation, and even those that were do not seem to have been very well regulated in practice. Much of the instability that plagued Egypt's bureaucracy can of course be attributed to the recurrent fiscal crises that shook the entire administration, directly and indirectly. Reducing government salaries and paying officials in depreciated treasury notes, granting uncultivated lands to retired employees in lieu of pensions, placing officeholders on provisional retirement, disbanding some government bureaus—these were clearly economy measures. We should also remember that Egypt's bureaucratic structure had only recently been established and had not yet taken firm root. However, these considerations do not explain such things as the capricious transfer of departmental accounts from one official to another, or the absence of rules governing advancement and promotion, or the existence of illegally high salaries.

It is important to distinguish between the *process* of rationalization—the movement toward more formal regulation—and a rational administration, where the structure is reasonably well adapted to the objectives of the ruler. To assert that administration in Egypt did not become highly rationalized during this period is not to suggest that it was irrational. It was no accident that areas of administration most directly touching the ruler's interest were exempt from regulation, that jurisdiction was shifted from one official to another, and that laws were not followed. For Egypt's bureaucracy was an integral part of the ruler's system of control. It was an object to be manipulated, an instrument to bind men to him, a machine to serve his interests. To have instituted a budget, to have defined the mode of advancement and promotion, to have kept a strict record of every piastre spent: these would have limited the ruler's freedom to maneuver. As long as the viceroy's personal power was paramount, and until something happened to weaken his position, a true bureaucracy in Egypt could not emerge.

How and to what extent was the ruler's control maintained in the years after Muhammad Ali's death? What, for example, did the growth of bureaucracy imply for household government? Let us now consider the changing relationship between the ruler and the political/administrative order after 1849, and examine how the viceroy endeavored to manipulate and control it.

▲▲▲ THE VICEROY AND THE ADMINISTRATIVE APPARATUS

After 1849, despite important institutional and social changes, the viceroy continued to employ the old tactics for maintaining personal rule—using political manipulation and clientage as well as bureaucratic devices to control the distribution of power and, through it, the financial surplus. Government therefore remained dependent upon the ruler, who *was* the state. The subordination of administration to the wants and needs of the ruler can be illustrated by examining the place of the viceregal cabinet in the government, the emergence of "private" viceregal administrations (*dairas*), and the tactics used by the viceroy to control a ruling elite of mostly civil officials.

In Muhammad Ali's time, the viceregal cabinet provided an important link between the household and rest of the administration. Having wide-ranging judicial and executive functions and a membership proportionate to the number of state departments, the viceregal cabinet had managed the business of government. It supervised factories, canals, and bridges; directed civil and military affairs; and contained offices for viceregal properties. Even before the death of Muhammad Ali, however, this household office began losing some of its powers. The management of viceregal properties, for example, was assumed by another administration, the *Daira Saniya*, and in the late 1840s other matters were transferred to the new bureaucratic organs.[92]

The viceregal cabinet seems to have become increasingly preoccupied with protocol and correspondence. Accounts from the 1870s suggest that it had become more concerned with the needs of the ruler than with the daily supervision of government. In 1877, Khedive Ismail is described as being attended by secretaries and chamberlains who stayed at their posts until he retired for the night. Of the ninety-two officials employed in the cabinet in 1878, there were six masters of ceremonies, one chief physician, one keeper of the seal, one treasurer, a number of European and Turkish secretaries, and fifty-nine sergeants at arms and soldiers.[93] Perhaps the best way of illustrating this apparent change is to compare the offices of the cabinet in 1843–1844 with those existing in 1876.[94] Although the actual number of offices seems to have varied little, their titles suggest a radical change in functions:

1843–1844	*1876*
Accounting and Budget	European correspondence
Shaflik properties (estates of the ruler and family)	Protocol
Uhda properties (lands held by persons who had given a tax guarantee)	Translation
Military & Civil Affairs & Petitions	Arabic correspondence & Petitions
Provinces and *Jurnal* (reports on daily operations sent by government offices)	Turkish correspondence
Revenue	[no equivalent]

In appearance at least, the viceregal cabinet had become ever more an organ of personal service.

This household body, however, remained an important mechanism for the viceroy's control of government. Whenever the ruler became impatient with the work of his administration or wished to strengthen his position, he simply conferred temporary authority upon the cabinet. Thus Saʿid decreed that the accounts of the provinces and the state departments be supervised by his cabinet rather than submitted to the Department of Finance.[95] Members of the cabinet continued to receive ad hoc assignments outside the household. Some cabinet officials were empowered to issue orders to the administrations on behalf of the ruler. (His orders to his administrations continued to be sent through the cabinet.) Others were named provincial governors, deputy governors, and heads of state departments. In 1864, Ismail Raghib, the director in chief of the cabinet, was made president of the Privy Council; in 1866, he became president of the Consultative Chamber of Delegates and later director of Finance and Interior. According to British Consul General Colquhoun, the head of the viceregal cabinet was the highest-ranking official in Egypt. If this household body no longer directed the daily business of government, it continued to be a very important instrument for the viceroy.

The 1849–1874 period also witnessed the emergence of large "private" viceregal administrations or *dairas*. As we have seen, in the 1830s the viceroy began to build up landed estates. To recover tax arrears and preserve his control over the rural surplus, Muhammad Ali began seizing land and granting parcels of it to himself and his family.

The ruler's confiscation and reallocation of land was sanctioned by a time-honored belief in his absolute right to the soil and its produce. He could take land for himself, concede parts of it to clients, divide it into estates, grant it as private property and then reclaim it. During Ismail's reign, the lands of peasant cultivators (called *kharajiya* after the tax levied upon them) were confiscated on a very large scale.[96] Entire villages were appropriated. Fifty-four villages along with 56,000 *faddans* were confiscated in a single decree. Lands previously given in lieu of pensions were also resumed by the government, their holders compensated only if buildings had been constructed on them. Ismail felt he had full authority for such arbitrary actions. "In keeping with the right of free disposal [*tasarruf*] which I possess," he wrote to his director of finances, "I have ordered that 320 *faddans* of *waqf* land in the village of Zaira in the province of al-Minufiya be exchanged for lands in al-Sharqiya province, and that the aforementioned Zaira be given to Nubar Pasha." Such action gives meaning to the words of the *qadi* (judge) who told Lady Duff Gordon in 1865 that if Ismail chose to have a man's land, he could take it with or without payment.[97] By the 1870s, the estates of the viceregal family embraced one-fifth of the cultivable land in Egypt.[98]

Large administrations emerged to manage these properties. In 1872, for example, there were *dairas* for the queen mother (102,406 *faddans*); for Ismail's daughter Tawhida (20,033); for Prince Tawfiq (10,200); and for Prince Husayn Kamil (22,999). These viceregal *dairas* were usually formed into a single family administration, the *Daira Saniya*, though the viceroy's own *daira* (*al-Daira al-Khassa*) was sometimes administered separately.[99]

These administrations kept their own accounts, had their own treasuries, and possessed considerable equipment and property. The *daira* of Ilhami Pasha, son of Abbas, owned six steamboats, six palaces, 3,855 animals, an unspecified number of factories and carriages, and a primary school for the owner's male slaves. It paid monthly salaries and pensions of 129,531 piastres to 666 employees and former employees, including translators, accountants, and clerks.[100] The payment of pensions to officials hints at the private character of these administrations. *Dairas* paid their share of the pensions of retired government officials who had once been in their employ.[101]

Khedive Ismail's *daira* grew rapidly during the cotton boom. It acquired a factory at Mahallat al-Kubra, bought the Bulaq printing press, hired new personnel, purchased a house in Cairo, and brought tens of thousands of *faddans* under its administration.[102] By 1870, its landholdings had become so vast that two offices of inspection were created with a total of sixty-eight employees and a monthly payroll of 56,800 piastres; by contrast, only forty-six officials were employed by the government's own Office of Inspectorate in 1866.

At first sight, these new administrations give an impression of an evolving private sector gradually separating itself from the governmental or public arena. To be sure, by providing a means of managing the ruler's money separately from the government's, the *dairas* made possible such a distinction. Following Saʿid's death, Ismail ordered the Department of Finance to ascertain the amount of money that Saʿid's *daira* had drawn from the government treasury and vice versa, and after learning that it had received £E 57,015 from the government as against £E 37,205 sent to it, he ordered that the difference be returned. On another occasion, Ismail directed the Finance Department to send 118,272 piastres to his private treasury to replace the amount that his *daira* had spent on a government matter.[103] But this is not very significant, for the *dairas* and the state apparatus were really inextricably linked. As we have just seen, these administrations had free access to government revenue.[104] Saʿid, for example, ordered that the monies collected in taxes from Bani Suwayf and al-Buhayra provinces be sent to his *daira* rather than the state treasury. Most *daira* officials came from the state bureaucracy and returned to it after serving on the viceregal estates. *Dairas* occasionally received administrative control over government offices and materials. *Dairas* could also employ corvée labor and use the state railway. Thus the viceregal *dairas* should be regarded as extensions of state power rather than a limitation of it.

Egypt's administrative order was not only an institutional structure but also a social body, and here too a shift was occurring. Muhammad Ali's ruling elite had been composed of courtiers, many of them military men and most related in some way to the viceroy. After 1849, as the household offices were superseded in their administrative functions by new bureaucratic departments and councils, Egypt's men of state were no longer centered in the court to the degree that they once had been, and the opportunities for advancement provided by the bureaucracy had begun to produce a pool of men for the viceroy who no longer needed to rely so strictly upon kin, freed slaves, in-laws, and other relations. This was a subtle and gradual process, and the lines between the household and state bureaucracy were never well defined, but the change from courtiers to bureaucrats is clear.

The rise of a new elite of mostly civil officials can be attributed not only to the growth of the bureaucracy but also to such events as the succession fight between Abbas and the sons of Ibrahim, which split the Muhammad Ali family and led to the removal of many members of the former elite; the enforced reduction in the size of the military after 1840 and its gradual subordination to the state bureaucracy; and the coming of age of those young men whom Muhammad Ali had sent to Europe for an education and who after 1849 began assuming positions formerly occupied by Turkish military commanders and officers of the viceregal household.[105]

How were Egypt's viceroys able to maintain their control over these officials? The relationship between the viceroy and his men contained elements both of cooperation, arising from their need for each other, and of conflict over control of the surplus. In the 1849–1874 period, cooperation predominated, in no small part because of the viceroy's skillful use of all the resources and powers at his command. The ruler secured the cooperation of his men (1) through clientage and political manipulation; (2) by encouraging the buildup of landed estates which were virtually exempt from taxation; (3) by giving high officials a large share of the spoils of their offices. Thus participating in the appropriation of the surplus, these men had a reason to support the viceroy and the unequal distribution of power.

A high administrative official had a unique opportunity to exploit fiscal and other resources.[106] Individual officeholders, many of whom held more than one position simultaneously, could benefit from powers delegated to them by the viceroy, which might include control of the treasury from which their employees' salaries were paid. Some officials also drew money from unrecorded accounts set up by the viceroy for their own private use. The directors of Public Works and War, for example, had special accounts supplied by monies taken from the war tax, military exemption payments, and the Nile works. As we have seen, officials were assigned salaries much larger than those set by law, and some received cash, houses, and even female slaves from the ruler. Heads of departments also rode the railway for free.

Owing to the loose administrative structure and the relative absence of formal controls, officials tended to go far beyond what the viceroy would allow.[107] They arbitrarily increased their salaries and those of their friends, withholding pay from other officials; they awarded temporary assignments to family members and others, retaining them on the government payroll long after their work had been completed; they deducted money from departmental income before it was recorded, purchased goods and other items at discounted prices, spent money without authorization, and embezzled funds, sometimes on a very large scale.

Officials in the countryside imported and sold goods at high prices, gave offices to friends or sold them to the highest bidders, confiscated cattle and equipment belonging to peasant laborers, shifted lower officials from one place to another without informing the authorities in Cairo, disposed on their own of the revenue they collected, and extorted money from the peasant population.[108] High officials also levied unauthorized fees more or less regularly. The governor of al-Buhayra province, without permission from Cairo, authorized the collection of fees for guarding cotton brought to public places, and the director of the Cairo Octroi arbitrarily increased the amount of taxes levied on goods brought into the city. The sums of money drained off in this way cannot be accurately estimated; suffice it to say that European observers and others commented frequently on the peculations customarily practised by government officials.[109]

To counteract this drain of the surplus, the viceroy had a variety of means at his disposal. One method was to pass legislation defining illegal behavior and prescribing punishments for it. Laws, statutes, and other enactments issued during this period reflect a great concern with bribery, theft, forging documents, official cover-ups, and embezzlement. In fact, the first efforts to define the rights of the subject population seem to have been intended to check abuses by government officials.[110]

Far more effective were the informal methods of control combining personal supervision with a vigorous assertion of the viceroy's right to reward and punish at will. The ruler subjected his men to fines, loss of salary, reduction in rank, and a host of other punishments. He withdrew accounts from the control of officials and placed them under Finance Department supervision, transferred administrations from one official's jurisdiction to another's, and broke up administrative offices, dividing their functions among several officeholders. The viceroy usually did not allow officials to remain in one position for very long, transferring them regularly. Muhammad Ali stated in an early order that officials who remained too long in their posts would establish contacts with the local population, and that this would lead to ever greater losses for the treasury.[111]

The most frequent and effective way of curbing peculation was dismissal from office. This was done in a particularly humiliating manner: an official's successor would arrive at the office one morning with a viceregal decree of dismissal which frequently contained the words, "Go to your home." The deposed officeholder was then obliged to walk home in full sight of the people—a painfully embarrassing experience.[112] Removal of a high official often entailed the wholesale dismissal of his subordinates. When Bahjat Pasha was removed as head of the engineering inspection office for upper Egypt, its employees were also fired and the office transferred from al-Jiza to another site.[113] Thus a dependent elite was maintained.

Landholding exhibits a similar pattern. After Muhammad Ali's death, Egypt's viceroys continued to be the principal agents for the establishment of large landed estates, which were formed from grants made by them to members of the ruling elite. Because they controlled the administrative machinery, high-ranking officials could extend the area of their estates without the ruler's knowledge. Officeholders made unrecorded land purchases, confiscated the properties of villagers who were indebted to them, and seized peasant land outright. Egypt's rulers counteracted these moves by issuing laws prohibiting officials from purchasing lands in the areas of their employment, except by public auction, and offering rewards to persons who revealed the location of unregistered, reclaimed land. They also attempted to launch surveys of landed property, not only to locate concealed land but also to reclassify land so as to levy taxes on it.[114] Sa'id and Ismail each made a great effort to have land registered, and both carried forward the practice, begun by Muhammad Ali, of granting landholders certain rights to their property. By the 1870s, this had resulted in the establishment of full private property ownership in law.

One such measure was Sa'id's land law of 1858, which gave full ownership rights, including compensation for land requisitioned for public use, to holders of ab'adiyas (uncultivated tax-free land given notables and officials) and shafliks (lands owned by the viceroy and his family).[115] Inasmuch as this enactment was intended to bring about the registration of land so that it could be taxed by the ruler, it is not surprising that many landholders responded to it with little enthusiasm. Some objected to a provision of the 1858 law which granted peasant property holders rights to their kharajiya land, since this would thwart their efforts to seize more peasant property for themselves.[116] This land law, therefore, may be regarded as an attempt by the ruler to increase his control over his men.

Egypt's rulers, however, had to balance their revenue requirements against their need for the support of those who made autocracy possible. Hence they made many concessions, and nowhere is this more evident than in their tax policy. In 1854, Sa'id imposed a very modest tax upon revenue-producing ab'adiya and shaflik lands, hitherto entirely exempt from taxation. Henceforth they were known as ushuriya lands, after the tithe (ushr) levied upon them.[117] Sa'id wished to tax these lands even more, but felt compelled to make compromises; landholders were allowed to participate in the assessment of their taxes, and individual officials were partially exempt from paying land taxes. By the time of Khedive Ismail, even after several tax increases, owners of ushuriya lands were paying an average of only £E 0.303 per faddan as against £E 1.162 levied upon each faddan of kharajiya property. With such fiscal advantages, the elite had every reason to support the status quo.

By making concessions, offering inducements, and employing shrewdly their powers to reward and punish at will, Egypt's rulers succeeded in maintaining a personally dependent elite between 1849 and 1874. Though conflict existed, cooperation prevailed. The relationship between the ruler and his men, and their competition for control of the surplus, provides a key to understanding the bureaucracy and how it worked; it was the critical factor in maintaining the political/administrative order created by Muhammad Ali. Thus we must examine this relationship in more detail.

▲▲▲ ISMAIL AND HIS OFFICIALS: A THEORY OF COOPERATION

Khedive Ismail is remembered by many Egyptians as the second great reformer of the nineteenth century. His reign witnessed a rapid, almost frenetic, growth of commerce, education, agriculture, communications, and urbanization. Moreover, he showed an unaccustomed respect for Egypt's antiquities, took pride in promoting its "olive-skinned" inhabitants to high offices, and was the first viceroy to give the people of his "Egyptian kingdom" (al-Mamlaka al-Misriya) a political education.[118] Ismail shrewdly appreciated the value of propaganda. The establishment of a "free" press subsidized almost entirely by him stands as a monument to his political genius.

Ismail began his reign confronted by problems that would have daunted the ablest and strongest ruler. Egypt's economy was growing faster than its administrative infrastructure. A disastrous Nile flood had washed away the cotton plants just when Egyptian cotton was fetching its highest prices. Government revenue had been mortgaged to pay Egypt's debts. Contractual rights to land and labor were held by European companies. Levantine and European merchants, roaming freely in the countryside, were driving its cultivators into debt and alienating their crops.

Ismail's weakness was revealed most dramatically in an incident that occurred during the first month of his reign. After a French national had been beaten by several Muslim soldiers in Alexandria, Ismail received an ultimatum from the French consul who demanded that the offenders and their commanding officer be brought in chains before him, cashiered, and sent off to a penal colony. If not, the consul threatened to summon marines from a ship stationed in Alexandria harbor. Unsupported by the other members of Egypt's consular body, and unable to resist on his own, Ismail had no choice but to comply.[119]

KHEDIVE ISMAIL (1830–1895)
From Sami, *Taqwim al-Nil*, pt. 3, vol. 1, facing p. 202.

If such challenges were to be met and Ismail's other problems resolved, the young viceroy needed help. But where was he to turn? Previous rulers had been aided by sons, brothers, cousins, and other relations. Abbas had depended to a great extent upon freed male slaves and other personal retainers; Saʿid had relied heavily upon the sons of Ibrahim, who had returned to Egypt after the death of Abbas. Ismail, however, could not take advantage of traditional family support to the same degree. His sons were too young at his accession to be given any public responsibilities, and since 1849 the family had been torn by rivalries growing out of the succession struggle.[120] Ismail's relations with his two most logical supporters, Prince Mustafa Fadil (his brother) and Prince Abd al-Halim (his uncle) were badly strained when he took the throne. When Ismail went to Turkey in 1863 to receive his oath of office, Prince Abd al-Halim became acting viceroy and also served as president of the Privy Council. But this overture (if it was that) failed, and Prince Abd al-Halim resigned as president of the council in October 1864. The two men remained bitter enemies for the rest of their lives.

In the virtual absence of real help from his family, Ismail turned to men from Egypt's new administrative elite who had been rising within the government under Abbas and Saʿid. Some, like the Yagan brothers, whose father had been a nephew of Muhammad Ali, were distantly related to Ismail; a few were protégés from Ismail's household; and one, Ismail Siddiq, was the viceroy's foster brother who had worked in the administration of his private estate. But most of the men called to Ismail's service, while known personally by him, were not part of his household. Rather, they were bureaucrats with considerable experience in civil and military affairs.

To gain and hold the support of these men, Ismail showered favors upon them.[121] In February 1864, he raised the salaries of the directors of War, Foreign Affairs, Finance, and the viceregal cabinet to 25,000 piastres a month (considerably more than the law stipulated). He gave pensions as gifts and awarded favorites higher ranks. He repealed Saʿid's tax increase of 5 percent on tithed (ushuriya) land while retaining the increase on kharajiya property, paid some of his officials' debts, and bought homes for others. Ismail Siddiq, for example, was given money to buy a house in Alexandria, an adjoining garden, and property in Tanta. The viceroy tacitly encouraged rake-offs, and closed his eyes to the widespread sale of offices, particularly in the provinces. He made gifts of harem slaves to his officials, and permitted some officials to marry into his family. Muhammad Ratib, one of his favorites, was not the only high officeholder to have a wife from Ismail's harem. Mansur Yagan, Muharram Pasha, and Mustafa Siddiq married daughters of the khedive. Ismail also gave landed estates and cash as gifts. Such grants were not unprecedented, but the scale on which they were made, especially during the 1860s, may have been. Records kept by Amin Sami reveal gifts of cash totaling £E 78,820 made by Ismail to various high officials during the first three years of his reign; one high official, Nubar Pasha, received £E 15,000 in a single grant.

Ismail also began delegating temporary executive powers to selected high officials. These deputations of authority sometimes included the right to appoint, dismiss, and transfer other officials. While understandable in view of Egypt's burgeoning administration, the delegation of authority to men outside the ruler's own family marked a departure from previous practices. It also provides the best evidence of Ismail's reliance upon a group of officials whose support was indispensable for the maintenance of his absolutism.

Within days of his accession, Ismail gave Husayn Pasha, director of the Cairo police, the right to choose his deputy director, appoint accountants, and supervise all matters connected with this administration.[122] Abd al-Rahman Rushdi, director of the railway administration, and Munis Bey, head of the postal service, were also delegated wide powers. Ahmad Daramalli, director of the Alexandria police, received the right to appoint and dismiss its officials. Nubar Pasha, who influenced many decisions made during Ismail's reign, was appointed director of Public Works and Railway, and was subsequently authorized to act on the viceroy's behalf in raising loans. As director of the railway, Nubar could appoint and dismiss its officials, spend freely from its revenue (which was independent of the Department of Finance), issue promissory notes to raise cash, and import carriages, trains, and equipment. Ismail Siddiq, who as inspector general became the viceroy's intermediary with the provinces, was granted unprecedented powers to transfer and dismiss all provincial employees save the governors. Officials in the provinces were ordered to submit their problems to Ismail Siddiq rather than the khedive, though matters urgently needing resolution could be sent directly to the viceroy by the governors. However, the khedive insisted upon approving all of the decisions of his men, and was in regular communication with them.

These officials assisted Ismail in various ways. A few became advisers to his sons, who were placed at the head of some government departments during the 1870s. (The youthfulness and inexperience of the princes, however, meant that their advisers were the real directors.) Others governed Egypt when Ismail went abroad. Four times between 1865 and 1868, Egypt was administered by high-ranking officials formed into councils headed by Muhammad Sharif Pasha—the first time someone from outside the Muhammad Ali family had run the government in the ruler's absence.[123] These officials also played a vital role in levying and collecting taxes. As members of conciliar bodies, they legislated the taxes, surcharges, and extraordinary levies imposed upon the people of Egypt during Ismail's reign. As individuals, they were frequently given ad hoc assignments to enforce collection of these taxes. Shahin Pasha, a leading military commander and administrator, became notorious for his tax-gathering forays into the countryside (he also put down peasant revolts on Ismail's estates).[124] These officials likewise helped to legitimize Ismail's seizure of land. We have already noted the role played by the Consultative Chamber of Delegates, but the Privy Council, it seems, performed a similar function. In 1864, it received a petition from the inhabitants of a group of villages requesting that they and their lands be taken over by the viceroy. Denouncing this as a cheap tactic, Abd al-Halim Pasha (the president of the council) told its members that if Ismail wanted these lands, he should simply take them over. This petition was nonetheless approved.[125] Ismail ran this council by telling its members what he wanted, and letting them work out the details. Their resolutions (*taqarir*), of course, had the force of law.

These officials became an integral part of Ismail's scheme to reassert his sovereignty over the Europeans. Shortly after his accession, Ismail decided to counteract European commercial activities in Egypt by forming government companies endowed with exclusive rights. His Egyptian Steam Navigation Company was given a monopoly to services in the Red Sea and the Mediterranean, and the Egyptian Commercial and Trading Company received the right to develop upper Egypt and parts of the Sudan. Ismail's officials became directors and stockholders in these newly formed companies, whose governing boards read like a *Who's Who* of high state employees.[126] Government officials also began to obstruct the activities of European merchants in the countryside. In al-Qalyubiya, cultivators were instructed to stop borrowing money on interest from Europeans and to take loans instead from the provincial governors, who lent money on the account of one of the development companies, while Ismail's officials diverted labor from European establishments and caused delays in their supply shipments.[127] These early efforts, though, were short-lived. The disastrous settlement with the Suez Canal Company (July 1864) and the sudden bust of the cotton boom ended Ismail's hopes of reasserting himself. Yet signs of cooperation could still be seen in the protection given to officials who were in debt to Europeans, whose claims were frustrated by the government's seizure of these officials' property, while they continued to live on and cultivate their "sequestrated" lands.[128]

The mutually beneficial relationship between Ismail and his officials gave him a strength that he might not otherwise have enjoyed. Their cooperation helps explain how Ismail was able to sustain his power within the country despite its weakness vis-à-vis Europe. Instead of growing weaker, Ismail thoroughly dominated Egypt's resources and people.

Ismail ruthlessly exploited the country through a tax policy that fell heavily on the poor.[129] Taxes levied upon peasant proprietors of *kharajiya* land, as we have seen, were more than triple those paid by high-ranking officials who held tithed *ushuriya* land. *Kharajiya* taxes were raised in 1864, increased by one-sixth in 1868, and raised again in 1870, this time by ten percent. Legal fees were instituted for the handling of cases by the government; taxes were imposed upon barley, corn, beans, and other foodstuffs; octroi fees were levied upon nearly every manufactured item sold in Egypt. Even prostitutes paid special taxes. These impositions crushed the poor, but they increased revenue to such an extent that government income was estimated at more than three times what had been collected by Muhammad Ali.

Ismail's despotism can be illustrated by various incidents.[130] Lady Duff Gordon wrote of a discussion she had with a wealthy Egyptian landowner whom she met on board a boat bound for the Sudan. Having been summoned to the Citadel by Ismail, allegedly to transact business, he had been summarily arrested, and was being shipped up river to be imprisoned in a penal colony without a trial or even a chance to say goodbye to his family. When Lady Duff Gordon's purse was stolen by pickpockets in Karnac, her friends beseeched her to avoid mentioning the incident to anyone; if the news of it reached Ismail, she was told, the viceroy might take a broom and sweep away the village. The attitude of ordinary Egyptians toward Ismail was expressed by a group of Nubians traveling to Cairo to serve in the Consultative Chamber of Delegates. When Lady Duff Gordon told them that they would at last have a chance to govern the country, they replied that there was no one in Egypt who could say "anything but *hader* (ready), with both hands on the head, and a salaam to the ground even to a Mudir; and thou talkest of speaking before the Effendina [the khedive]! Art thou mad, Effendim?" In Egypt, Lady Duff Gordon wrote, there was no law or justice, but only "the will, or rather the caprice, of one man."

The administration, of course, depended entirely upon Ismail. "From the negotiation of a treaty or a loan, to the approval of a contract for coals or machinery," J. C. McCoan wrote in 1877, "he is cognisant of every detail of public business, and nothing above the importance of mere departmental routine is done without having first passed under his eye."[131] When Ismail left Cairo to visit the provinces, administration came to a virtual standstill. In July 1863, wrote the British consul general, his absence from the capital resulted in the "cession of all business. For nothing, however trivial, is done without his approval." In April 1868, government business was again interrupted by the viceroy's visit to the provinces.[132]

Despite his other preoccupations, Ismail paid great attention to the details, even the minutiae, of administration.[133] He sanctioned the laws and resolutions issued by his conciliar bodies, and he had reports drawn up on the work of his officials. He insisted upon approving the appointment and transfer of even the lowest-ranking officials. Increases in pay and the transfer of salaries from one location to another could not be made without an order from him. Ismail kept a watchful eye on the expenditures of his administrations, sanctioning increases, ordering cutbacks, and freezing the movement of money by decree.

Ismail also made sure that the government departments remained close to him.[134] In 1863, the Privy Council was instructed to hold its sessions at the Citadel in the room where the viceregal cabinet met. When Ismail was at his palace in al-Jiza, the Privy Council went there. In 1865, the War Department was transferred from its location at the Citadel to Ismail's palace at Qasr al-Nil to make room at the Citadel for the viceregal cabinet, whose work was temporarily being carried out by the Interior Department. There were, of course, exceptions. When Ali Mubarak the prominent engineer and administrator, became director of Education, Public Works, and Charitable Endowments, these administrations were transferred to a site near Mubarak's home in new Cairo. With Mubarak's removal from Public Works and Education, however, Charitable Endowments was moved back to the Citadel, and so presumably were the other departments. Egypt's major administrations were situated at the Citadel until the 1870s when they were transferred to locations within a mile of Ismail's new official residence at Abdin Palace.

Throughout his reign, Ismail successfully employed the tactic of circulating his officials, playing a very effective game of musical chairs (see table 8). Within days of his accession, he had begun replacing Saʿid's men with his own, and by March 1863, most of his predecessor's appointments had been revoked.[135] Officials were continuously transferred from one position or assignment to another, or dismissed outright; few remained in one place very long. Ali Mubarak, for example, was given fifteen major appointments in ten years (see chapter 6).

TABLE 8

Government Officials' Average Tenure in High Office, 1848–1879 (in months)

	Abbas's Reign	Sa'id's Reign	Ismail's Reign
Directors of departments	20	16	13
Governors of towns and cities	14	18	11
Governors of provinces	12	18	8

Source: Sami, pt. 3, vols. 1–3, annual lists of appointments.

Amin Sami's annual lists of appointments to high offices reveal that Ismail was more successful than either Abbas or Sa'id in keeping tenures in office brief.

Ismail surrounded his men with regulations that restricted their movements and gave government service a strong involuntary character. Officials had to have permission to travel to other places in Egypt to visit their families, and even then they had to take reduced pay (those who violated this rule were liable for dismissal).[136] Refusal of an appointment, a transfer, or an order for reinduction into the administration was almost unheard of. Save for ill health or old age, officials could not leave the government except under severe penalty. In 1864, Ismail ordered that those who expressed a wish to resign their posts must serve an additional year and were then to be fired.[137]

Ismail also was careful to limit the authority that he delegated.[138] Thus the chief of police in Alexandria was given the right to dismiss soldiers who were poorly trained, negligent, or who had committed misdemeanors, but not those who had been charged with felonies. The aforementioned Abd al-Rahman Rushdi (director of the Railway Administration) was denied the right to appoint and dismiss officials or import equipment, and Munis Bey (head of the postal service) was requested to submit his accounts to the Department of Public Works and defer to it on important matters. Ismail permitted some of his provincial governors to appoint assistants, but he limited their number to four and stipulated that their employment be temporary. Governors in lower Egypt were allowed to dismiss poorly trained clerks and to appoint others in their places on the condition that salaries not be increased. Even when Ismail Siddiq was delegated wide powers, he was told that these privileges were for him alone, as an exceptional case. When things did not go right, Ismail was always ready to assert himself, even against his favorites. In 1871, he admonished Ismail Siddiq for appointing, dismissing, and transferring provincial officials without informing him, and one year later transferred him out of the Department of Finances. Authority was delegated from a position of strength, not weakness.

Few challenged Ismail's personal control. Despite their importance —nay, their indispensability—and despite Ismail's growing weakness vis-à-vis Europe, his officials made no attempt to limit or curb his power. This is not to say that they were unwilling to make their feelings known. Officials could object to viceregal policies and decisions, and occasionally even tried to legislate in their own interests. When Nubar was ordered to join Ismail in Europe, Nubar prevailed by inducing the viceroy to return to Egypt.[139] Ismail's Privy Council also indulged in a limited kind of self-assertion. Its members once told Ismail that his *daira* employees could not be exempted from payment of the general professional (*wirku*) tax. On another occasion, they declared that some newly appointed officials could be dismissed only for a crime, and then only after legal proceedings. They also ruled that village *shaykhs* could not be dismissed until the Privy Council had examined their cases and determined that crimes had indeed been committed.[140] These rulings, designed to prevent arbitrary actions by other officials, upheld principles that were in direct opposition to Ismail's own actions.

The members of the Consultative Chamber of Delegates also were not shy about expressing their opinions. Among the resolutions and proposals of this body were those calling for regular tax collection, the abolition of the head tax on males in the towns, an end to the beating of village *shaykhs*, and the dismissal of provincial governors (*shaykhs* may also have been meant) only for proven crimes.[141]

But beyond this modest kind of self-assertion, officials would not go. They might try to influence the viceroy or express their displeasure with his actions, but once it became clear that Ismail was determined to have his way, they readily complied. In spring 1868, when Ismail wished to gain approval of the Consultative Chamber of Delegates for new taxes, its members were allowed to debate the financial question for the first time. In his opening speech, Ismail explained why some of the proposals passed earlier by the Chamber—specifically, one calling for the fixed and regular collection of taxes—had not been carried out (the Chamber later blamed this failure on Saʿid's misgovernment). When the Chamber was informed that the government was considering the contraction of a new loan, its members requested from the Director of Finances information on Saʿid's debts and a detailed account of the government's current expenditures. These revealed that Egypt's debts were far greater than Chamber members had realized. Further efforts to ascertain the seriousness of the problem met evasive responses from officials called to testify; the government was unwilling to reveal the amount of the floating debt. Once the delegates realized that Ismail did not want a full-fledged investigation into his finances, they dropped their questions and voted the new taxes.[142] Only in March 1873 was the amount of the floating debt finally revealed to the Chamber. At that session, a "budget" was produced; yet despite glaring irregularities in Egypt's finances, no discussion of them was ever broached.[143]

The Consultative Chamber of Delegates, like the rest of Egypt's administrations, was in no position to resist a viceroy who could change its members, determine when and for how long it met, and reject its resolutions. Service in it gave some of its members influence, as witnessed by the large bribes paid for their "election." A seat in the Chamber brought its members to the attention of the ruler, and led to high position elsewhere in the government. Under such circumstances, the delegates could hardly have been expected to rise up in arms against the viceroy.[144]

Administration, then, continued to "belong" to the khedive, and government remained viceregal government (*al-Hukuma al-Saniya*).[145] But this could not have happened without the support of the high-ranking officials who enabled Ismail to control the formal instruments of power or bypass them when necessary, thereby retaining control of his resources. Yet, as we have stated, we are seeking to explain not only how viceregal power was maintained but, more important, why it collapsed after 1874. Cooperation between the ruler and his men in the 1849–1874 period constitutes only part of the story. During these years, fundamental changes were occurring in the nature and composition of Egypt's ruling elite—the most critical element in the political/administrative order. Thus we must also examine the structure of the bureaucratic elite and the sources of its influence.

▲5▲
THE FORMATION OF THE
BUREAUCRATIC ELITE

If Egypt's high officeholders succeeded in helping maintain vice-regal power in the face of mounting budget deficits and political humiliations by Europe, they should not be regarded merely as creatures of the ruler. For they were also developing interests of their own which coincided and conflicted with his. As we shall see, these "outside" interests contributed to the decline of viceregal power after 1874, just as cooperation between the ruler and his men previously accounted for its preservation.

This chapter examines this elite, focusing upon their links with Europe and their ties with the land and people of Egypt. This involves a scrutiny of the sources of their wealth, particularly the acquisition of landed estates that could be translated into social power. And since such power derived in no small measure from their position as bureaucrats, we also need to consider how an official position could be used to advance personal and group ends.

Egypt's high officeholders were known as *al-dhawat*, an Arabic plural which means upper class or aristocracy, and which in this case may best be translated as "persons of high state rank."[1] This term was applied not only to officials serving in the state bureaucracy, the viceregal household, and the agencies administering the viceregal estates (*dairas*), but also to the military commanders and sometimes to members of the viceregal family.[2] The families of Egypt's military officers and high state functionaries likewise seem to have been included under this heading, since a register of tithed *ushuriya* lands held by *al-dhawat* in 1870 contains entries for their wives, freed slaves, sons, and other relatives.[3] It is impossible, however, to ascertain the exact size of this state aristocracy. The 1870 land register has main entries for 437 men and their families, and many others are named in the subheadings. This elite totaled at least several thousand persons.

We can be much more precise about how many made up the civil bureaucracy. According to the annual lists of Amin Sami, 126 individuals were given high positions in the central and provincial administrations by Abbas, 122 by Sa'id, and 216 by Ismail. Many of these, of course, held high posts under more than one viceroy, but the aggregate total still exceeds 300. Some, especially the governors of provinces, were military officers; some were from the viceregal household; but the majority had come up through the state bureaucracy, where they had spent years of service. Since we are concerned with high-ranking officials in the state administration rather than with Egypt's military commanders or the officers of the court per se, we shall henceforth use the term al-dhawat to designate such officials, bearing in mind that it could also be applied to others in the state employ.

Until 1871, government service in Egypt was defined by rank (see table 9).[4] Rank, or occasionally salary alone, signified admission to the bureaucracy. Once a man received a rank and salary, an administrative appointment almost always followed. Salaries were usually given in accordance with rank rather than office. At retirement, pensions were based on the length of salaried employment. This period did not necessarily correspond with the time spent in office because officials could retain part of their salaries while out of office. Senior officials were distinguished from junior state employees (muwazzafun) by rank and by title. After receiving second rank, a government official was considered to be among the dhawat.[5] He was then given the corresponding title of bey (the title of pasha accompanied first rank).[6] Junior state officials held no titles and were known simply by the honorific designation of afandi (in Turkish, efendi), which meant a respected person, though senior officials were also called afandi (for example, Muhammad Sharif Basha afandi).

TABLE 9
EGYPTIAN CIVIL RANKS, 1855

	Equivalent
First rank (pasha)	mirmiran
Second rank, first grade (bey)	mir al-liwa
(al-mutamayyiza)	
Second rank, second grade (bey)	mir alay
Third rank	qa'im maqam
Fourth rank	bikbashi
Fifth rank	saghqul aghasi

Source: Sami, pt. 3, vol. 1, p. 126.
Note: By 1863, the first civil rank had acquired two grades; below fifth rank, all ranks were military (Sami, pt. 3, vol. 2, p. 483).

Egypt's higher officials were a status elite distinguished by privileges stemming from their ranks and not available to their inferiors.[7] They were addressed by honorific titles—*Sahib al-Izza* for beys, and *Sahib al-Sa'ada* for pashas. At official ceremonies, they stood at the head of the line in full dress uniforms to receive greetings and gifts from the khedive. They were given medals encrusted with diamonds and gold, and like others in the high-ranking elite, they could not be interrogated or examined by officials of lesser ranks. Though Egypt's penal laws were explicitly designed to apply equally to all viceregal subjects, *al-dhawat* sometimes received favored treatment. Beatings were commonly meted out as punishment for middle- and lower-level employees, but corporeal punishment was rarely, if ever, prescribed for *al-dhawat*.

To these honors can be added the privilege of high office. Departmental directors and their deputies, provincial governors and deputy governors, town governors and other officials were appointed from the first or second elite ranks. Of the 1,033 appointments to high offices made between 1848 and 1879 (as recorded annually by Amin Sami), 983 went to beys and pashas. Though these titles are associated with high office, they designated, more accurately, those persons of senior ranks from whom the high offices of state were filled. There were times when as many beys and pashas could be found unemployed as were employed. An official position might be won and lost, but rank and title, once acquired, were rarely lost (although rank was not heritable). The ruler could deprive a man of his rank and title, but rarely did so. As long as we keep this distinction in mind, we may describe these men as high officeholders.

The term *al-dhawat* had also designated high-ranking officials in Muhammad Ali's time. His beys and pashas, however, did not dominate the government after his death. The high officials of mid-century were a new and distinct body of men, patricians of rank bridging the gap between Muhammad Ali's imported Ottoman-Mamluk ruling class and the Europeanized, highly technocratic service aristocracy that began to surface during the second decade of the British occupation (the 1890s). There were, then, three generations of high bureaucrats in nineteenth-century Egypt. The first, with a few exceptions (Adham Pasha, for instance), did not survive the succession struggle between Abbas and the sons of Ibrahim.[8] Within several years of Abbas's accession, most of the old ruling class were exiled, pensioned, or dead. They were succeeded by a new generation educated during Muhammad Ali's reign. Although by 1849 most of the second generation of officeholders could be found somewhere in the government, and many rose to high rank and position before Ismail's accession, their careers reached peaks during his reign. After his deposition, many of these men began leaving office. Some continued to hold high positions during the first fifteen years of British rule, but by the 1890s nearly all of them had been pensioned or had died. Their sons, educated differently, took over from them.

It is difficult to classify the second generation of high officeholders. They cannot be categorized by avenues of recruitment and promotion because the boundaries between the civil bureaucracy, the military, the viceregal household, and the *dairas* had not yet been clearly demarcated, and also because offficials did not always move upwards in one channel, but moved laterally from one institution to another. The official who spent an entire career in one sector of the state administration was the exception.

As a body, Egypt's higher officials are extraordinarily difficult to classify. They did not have a common outlook or training. They were pluralistic, men of diverse origins brought together to serve a common master. This does not mean that these men were any less an elite, for they had much more in common than state rank and high administrative positions. As we shall see, a common interest in land and a commitment to reform were important bases of cooperation that helped bridge differences of education and background.

Differences in origin and training, however, do provide a clue as to how high government officials may be classified. But first we must discuss the changes made by Muhammad Ali in the pattern of bureaucratic recruitment. Early in Muhammad Ali's reign, officials were recruited for their presumed loyalty to the ruler or because their personal qualities were needed at the moment. As time passed, two new criteria were added. First, an intimate connection between scientific knowledge and administrative service was established, and men were recruited because they knew a European language or possessed other technical skills acquired in Europe or in Egypt's new European-style schools. Second, the khedive's increasing need for the support of Europeans and of Egypt's rural notables led to the introduction into the administration of men from these two privileged groups.

Muhammad Ali's high officials had for the most part been Turks, but by mid-century changes in recruitment had led to the appearance, at the upper level of administration, of distinct subgroups of *al-dhawat*, new types of men. The high officeholders of mid-century, then, reflected a basic realignment of social forces taking place throughout the state. This new generation still contained a strong Turkish element, but it also included four other types of officials: Egyptian technicians, employed in the central administration, many of whom had received a scientific education in Europe; Egyptian provincial officials drawn from the ranks of village headmen (*shaykhs al-balad*); a number of Europeanized and well-educated Armenians; and Europeans who fulfilled both administrative and technical functions.

Arranged in this way, Egypt's high officials may be regarded as a composite of five groups, distinguished by an ethnic or an educational principle of differentiation. The Turks were the most influential and numerically the largest group of Egypt's polyethnic elite. The majority still came from outside Egypt, particularly Morea (the Peloponnesus of Greece) and the Caucasus. Those from Morea had been brought to Egypt as slaves during Muhammad Ali's reign, but most Turkish officials were freemen who had come to Egypt with their families or tribes, or who had been recruited from abroad by the viceroy or a member of his family.[9]

Unlike the Egyptian technicians and Armenian officials, the Turks were the only group of higher officials who could be found everywhere in the government. They held the majority of high positions in the provincial administration, the viceregal cabinet, and the viceregal *dairas*. They were also given charge of departments in the central administration. Because of their close ties with the ruling family (to which many Turkish officials were related), Turks received assignments of great trust and sensitivity. They were sent on secret missions abroad, particularly to Istanbul where many of them had friends and relatives in high positions. They were called upon whenever the ruler needed strong men who knew how to assert authority. If a province fell too deeply into tax arrears or the peasants became rebellious, the government sent a Turk to collect back taxes or snuff out a revolt.

Turks had a well-developed capacity for command that derived from their belief in an inherent right to rule. Had not Turks governed Egypt for centuries? Was not the present ruling family Turkish? *They* were Egypt's rightful and natural rulers, not the despised natives—those "dogs," those "oxen," fit only for the plough, whose lot was to labor for the benefit of the only "pure element" (*unsur salih*) in the state.[10] As officeholders, Turks relegated to subordinates the minutiae of administration which they believed was beneath their dignity. When Ali Mubarak volunteered to teach reading and writing to soldiers in the field, Adham Pasha, a Turk, expressed surprise, suggesting that Mubarak should have too much pride to undertake such a lowly assignment. "How could I not desire to take the opportunity of educating Egyptians and spreading the benefits of knowledge?" Mubarak wrote in his autobiography.[11] Mubarak, however, was an Egyptian.

Despite a common and in many ways unchanging character, Turkish officials were divided in one important respect. Table 10 indicates that some knew European languages and had received a scientific education, while others had not. This difference reflected the impact of Muhammad Ali's reforms which had created a split among Turkish officials. These reforms had led to the emergence of a new, younger generation of "reformed" Turks educated in Europe or in Egypt who assumed the trappings of European civilization in dress and manner. By the mid-nineteenth century, they had become high-ranking officials. Side by side with them were other Turkish officials who remained rather old-fashioned in their habits and spoke out strongly against European influence. They were, however, relics of a bygone age, less and less able to cope with the new conditions. Yet exposure to the Western world was not necessarily associated with a formal, scientific education, and opposition to Europe was not confined to a certain category of Turks. Muhammad Sharif, for example, had been educated in France, professed sympathy for European constitutional ideas, and even married the daughter of a French officer (who had converted to Islam); yet he was violently opposed to the extension of European influence in Egypt, and disliked Europeans and their ideas.[12]

If Turks holding high office was nothing new, the sight of Egyptian beys and pashas certainly was. By the mid-nineteenth century, perhaps for the first time since the pharoahs, significant numbers of native Egyptians could be found in high posts in the provinces and in Cairo. Turks drew no distinctions among Egyptians: they were all common peasants (*fallahin*). Yet the new cadres of Egyptian officials were not peasants by the standards of native society. Quite the contrary, they represented some of Egypt's most prominent native elites. A few came from merchant families in Cairo, some from the religious aristocracy (*ulama*), but most were drawn from families of provincial *ayan*, loosely translated as "notables."[13]

Notables were local or communal leaders.[14] The term had a secular connotation; there were, for example, Coptic ecclesiastics and Coptic notables, respected men of wealth and influence, but the term applied almost exclusively to leaders of the countryside. Notables consisted of village headmen (*shaykhs al-balad*), their families, and a large number of *shaykhs al-hissa* who administered a designated part (*hissa*) of a village and who frequently performed minor religious functions. These village leaders were a privileged, crafty, and proud lot; many traced their ancestry to Arab tribes that had settled in Egypt following the Muslim conquest.

Egypt's provincial notability provided most of the young Egyptians who under Muhammad Ali had been taken into the government for an education or for service in the provinces. Most of those enrolled in the viceroy's new schools were trained as teachers, engineers, physicians, and translators. Some were sent to Europe to complete their educa-

TABLE 10
Turkish Officials in High Government Positions, 1849–1879

	Muhammad Zaki Pasha	Ali Dhu al-Fiqar Pasha	Ismail Raghib Pasha	Muhammad Hafiz Pasha
Origin or birthplace	—	Greece	Greece	Bosnia (born in Egypt)
Education	Egypt, state school (administration)	—	Egypt, state school	Egypt, state school (accounting)
Languages (other than Turkish)	French, Arabic	Greek, French, Arabic	Greek	English, Arabic
First post, civil service	In Council of Education, 1835/36–	President, Council of Justice,[a] 1857–	Translator, Office of the *Jurnal*,[b] 1834–	Clerk, 1835/36
First post, military service	In artillery regiment, 1837/38–	In Egyptian fleet, 1834–	—	None
First post, viceregal service[c]	Translator, viceregal cabinet, 1850/51–	Deputy director, Sa'id's *daira*, 1844–	Transferred to viceregal cabinet, 1836–	In Ibrahim's *daira;* director, Ismail's *daira*, 1863–
Highest post, viceregal cabinet	Master of ceremonies, Ismail's reign	Chief of protocol, 1891–	Head of cabinet, 1863–	—
Highest post, the *Khassa/ Daira Saniya*	Director, the *Daira Saniya,* 1880–	None	—	Director, the *Daira Saniya,* 1862/63; director, the *Khassa,* 1868
First high post, central administration[d]	Director of railroads, 1872–	President, Council of Justice, 1857–	Director of finance, 1859–	Director of finance, 1864–
First high post, provincial administration[e]	Governor of Alexandria, 1871–	Governor of Alexandria 1866–	Inspector, lower Egypt, 1863–	—
Last post	Director of finance and public works, 1888–	Chief of protocol, 1891–	President, Council of Ministers, 1882	Director, the *Daira Saniya*
Date of retirement (or death)	1894	1892	1884	1886

Source: Compiled by the author from archival sources and various published works.
Note: Dashes indicate information not available.
[a]*Majlis al-Ahkam.*
[b]The Office of the *Jurnal* issued daily reports from the administration to household officials.
[c]Includes service in the *Khassa, Daira Saniya,* or *Ma'iya Saniya.*

TABLE 10 (Continued)

	Ahmad Tal'at Pasha	Abd al-Qadir Hilmi Pasha	Muhammad Sharif Pasha	Hasan Rasim Pasha
Origin or birthplace	Greece	—	Istanbul	—
Education	—	Egypt, Austria (military science and medicine)	Egypt, France (St. Cyr)	—
Languages (other than Turkish)	English	—	French	—
First post, civil service	In Department of Education, 1841–	Surveyor, 1858	Director of foreign affairs, 1858	Employed at Bulaq arsenal, early 1830s
First post, military service	—	In Battalion of Engineers, 1884–	Colonel in infantry, 1854 (Sa'id's reign)	—
First post, viceregal service[c]	In viceregal cabinet, 1838–	Officer in the Daira Saniya, Sa'id's reign	Colonel in viceregal entourage (?),[f] Sa'id's reign	Deputy director the Daira Saniya, 1857–
Highest post, viceregal cabinet	Keeper of the seal, 1851–	Chief of protocol, 1887–	—	—
Highest post, the Khassa/ Daira Saniya	—	—	—	Director, the Khassa, 1863; director, the Daira Saniya, 1865–
First high post, central administration[d]	—	Chief of police, Cairo, 1874–	Director of foreign affairs, 1858–	President, Council of Justice, 1873–
First high post, provincial administration[e]	—	Governor of Port Sa'id, 1876	—	Governor of Damietta, 1860–
Last post	Chief of secretariat, viceregal cabinet, 1880s	Director of war and marine, 1884–	President, Council of Ministers, 1882–	—
Date of retirement (or death)	1884	1887	(1887)	1882

[d]Includes the posts of department director, president of the Privy Council, the Council of Justice, the Consultative Chamber of Delegates, and chief of police of Cairo or Alexandria.

[e]Includes provincial governors, governors of towns or cities, the inspector general and his deputies, and the heads of provincial councils or departments.

[f]The Ma'iya Saniya.

tion, and upon return received rank, salary, and a government position in Cairo. In 1833, Muhammad Ali authorized the appointment of village headmen to positions in the provincial administration. Confined at first to the lower posts of district chief (*nazir al-qism*) and subdistrict leader (*hakim al-khutt*), these parvenus percolated slowly upward until by the late 1830s they could be found at every level of provincial administration save that of governor.[15]

Muhammad Ali's experiment was reversed during the 1840s when Turks recaptured many (though not all) of the positions previously lost. The 1850s, however, marked a turning point. For the first time, Egyptians began replacing Turks at the highest levels. In 1850, two French-educated Egyptian engineers, Hammad Abd al-Ati and Ali Mubarak, were awarded second rank and appointed head of the office of engineering and director of the government schools, respectively. For four years, Mubarak presided over Egypt's educational system and carried out many reforms. In 1856, Egyptian notables were again appointed to the provincial posts of district and subdistrict chief.[16] Soon, Egyptians were appointed provincial governors. By the 1870s, Egyptian governors were common.

In the central administration, however, Turks continued to direct most government departments, although the Departments of Education and Public Works were sometimes headed by Egyptians. In 1868, the Turks lost control of the Finance Department to an Egyptian, Ismail Siddiq, who was also inspector general. Ismail Siddiq was the first non-Turk to hold these two powerful offices. But, such exceptions aside, Egyptian high officeholders remained a distinct minority in the central administration. Only eight Egyptians received what may be called "ministerial" appointments between 1849 and 1879.[17]

Egyptian and Turkish officials did not get along. The latter resented the intrusion of "peasants" into "their" administration, while Egyptians thought Turks dull-witted and spoke of them disparagingly as latecomers to Islam.[18] This antagonism can be traced to the reign of Muhammad Ali, whose own Turkish officials had found it difficult to accept his reforms.[19] Some refused to enter the new schools of medicine, agriculture, and engineering; others neglected the irrigation works, slept on the job, and let the new cotton plants rot in the ground. When Muhammad Ali appointed Egyptians to posts in the provinces, his Turkish officials refused to work with them. "I hear that some of you," Muhammad Ali told them, "have begun spreading rumors that the nazirs of qisms are [only] Arabs while 'we are Turks'; . . . you have asked how is it possible for Turks to be placed under the administration of Egyptians? Do you not know that many other Egyptians have had government office and done well?" Since Muhammad

Ali's time, tension had existed between these two groups, to end only after the total Egyptianization of the administration. If the Egyptian high officeholders were different from the Turks in their attitudes and origins, they varied among themselves as to education and, to a lesser extent, function. Egyptian high officials fall into two categories: the technicians, with scientific skills obtained through a formal European education; and the notables, village *shaykhs* with limited education, but who were recruited because of their knowledge of the countryside. (See table 11.)

TABLE 11
EGYPTIAN TECHNICIANS IN HIGH GOVERNMENT POSITIONS, 1849–1879

	Mustafa Bahjat Pasha[a]	Abdallah Fikri Pasha	Mahmud al-Falaki
Origin or birthplace	Village of Miniyat Abi Ali (al-Sharqiya)	From *ulama* family (mother from Morea)	Village of al-Hissa
Education	Egypt, Preparatory School, Engineering School; Paris, 1826–	Egypt, al-Azhar	Egypt, Naval School, Cairo Polytechnique; Paris, 1850– (math, astronomy)
Languages (other than Arabic)	French, Turkish	Turkish	French
First post, civil service	Headmaster, Preparatory School, 1836?	Turkish office of *Diwan al-Katkhuda*, 1851–	Teacher and translator, Cairo Polytechnique, 1840–
First post, viceregal service	Chief engineer, viceroy's *shaflik*, early 1840s	Attached to Sa'id's entourage	—
Date of becoming bey or pasha	Bey, 1845; pasha, 1858	Bey, 1865/66; pasha, 1879	Bey, 1859; pasha, 1881
First post, Abbas's service	Engineering inspector, 1850/51–	In *Diwan al-Katkhuda*, 1851–	Sent by Abbas to study in France
First post, Sa'id's service	Surveyed Sa'id's lands	Attached to Sa'id's entourage	Surveyed and mapped lower Egypt, 1859–
First post, Ismail's service	Engineering inspector 1863–	Accompanied Ismail to Turkey	—
First high post, central administration	Director, Public Works and Education, 1870	Director, Education, 1882	Director, Public Works, 1882
Last post	—	—	Director, Education, 1884
Date of death (or retirement)	1872	—	1885

Egyptian technicians could boast of a scientific education in one of Egypt's new schools or abroad. All knew at least one foreign language, usually French. As a group, they had a highly "civil" character. Only one official in table 11—Ali Mubarak—had served in the military. These Egyptians were usually employed in the central administration; if they went into the countryside, they did so as representatives of the

TABLE 11 (Continued)

	Ismail al-Falaki Pasha	Ali Pasha Ibrahim	Salih Majdi Bey
Origin or birthplace	—	Village of al-Fazara	From merchant family
Education	Egypt, Cairo Polytechnique; Paris, 1850– (astronomy)	Egypt, Preparatory School, Artillery School; Paris, 1844– (engineering)	Egypt, School of Languages (translation), Cairo Polytechnique; Paris (engineering)
Languages (other than Arabic)	French	French	French, Turkish
First post, civil service	Assistant, Shubra observatory, 1845–	—	Deputy director, office in Translation Office, 1836/37
First post, viceregal service	—	Attached to Abbas's entourage, 1849–	—
Date of becoming bey or pasha	Bey, 1864	Bey, Abbas's reign; pasha, 1879	Bey, 1871/72
First post, Abbas's service	—	Various assignments, including tutoring Abbas's son Ilhami	In School of Engineering
First post, Sa'id's service	—	Assistant in War Department	Translator, 1854–
First post, Ismail's service	Director, Cairo Polytechnique and Observatory, 1866–	Translator for khedive; director, Preparatory School, Cairo	Translator in Translation Office, 1863–
First high post, central administration	—	Director, Education, 1879–	—
Last post	Director, Engineering School, Cairo	Director, Justice Department, 1882–	Judge in mixed courts
Date of death (or retirement)	1901	1899	1881

central government or as part of the viceroy's traveling entourage. Egyptian technicians were most numerous in the Departments of Education and Public Works. As a whole, they were not highly skilled. Engineers, for example, were generally poorly trained, and some were

TABLE 11 (Continued)

	Rifaʻa Tahtawi	Hammad Abd al-Ati Pasha	Ali Mubarak Pasha
Origin or birthplace	From *ulama* family	Village of Dayr al-Janadala	Village of Birinbal al-Jadida
Education	Egypt, al-Azhar; Paris, 1826– (translation)	Egypt, Preparatory School, Cairo Polytechnique; Paris, 1844– (engineering)	Egypt Preparatory School, Cairo Polytechnique; Paris, 1844– (engineering)
Languages (other than Arabic)	French	French, Turkish, English, German	French
First post, civil service	Translator, School of Medicine, 1832? 1833?	Director, Office of Engineering, 1850–	Teacher, Artillery School, 1849–
First post, viceregal service	—	—	Attached to Abbas's entourage, 1850
Date of becoming bey or pasha	Bey, 1845/46	Bey, 1853	Bey, 1850; pasha, 1868
First post, Abbas's service	Headmaster, School of Khartum, 1850 (in exile)	Inspector in provinces and other assignments	—
First post, Saʻid's service	Deputy director, Military College, 1855–	Dismissed by Saʻid, then reattached to entourage	Officer in Crimea, 1854–
First post, Ismaiľs service	Director, Translation Office, 1863–	Teacher, Cairo Polytechnique, 1863–	Director, Preparatory School
First high post, central administration	—	—	Director, Public Works and Education, 1868–
Last post	Director, Translation Office	Judge in mixed courts	Director, Education, 1888
Date of death (or retirement)	1873	(pensioned 1901)	1893

Source: Compiled by the author from archival sources and various published works.
Note: Dashes indicate information not available.
ᵃAlthough Bahjat Pasha had a Turkish father, he was related through his Egyptian mother to a family of provincial notables. He spoke fluent Arabic and was closely associated with Egyptian engineers throughout his career, which followed a pattern similar to theirs.

downright incompetent. The most skilled among them had spent years in Europe, but these formed a minority.

These high Egyptian officials had a technocratic mentality; they tended to regard the solution of problems as a matter of finding the right technique. Answers lay in organization and in method, a typically bureaucratic approach. Egypt's hydraulic economy would be mastered by the proper irrigation techniques, just as the Egyptian people could be "improved" by the right kind of education. There was a certain conceit about these men, whose esprit de corps derived from a feeling of indispensability and a conviction of their own superiority.

The notables offer a contrasting stereotype (see table 12). As youths, they had memorized the Quran and learned the rudiments of reading and writing in a village school. They were not formally educated, and few knew a European language. They spent most of their government careers in the countryside, where they served in the provincial administrative hierarchy, sat in the provincial courts, and worked as agricultural managers on the estates of the viceregal family. Later in their careers, some entered the central administration or served in the Consultative Chamber of Delegates.

A fourth group were the Armenians, unmatched in breadth of learning and sophistication (see table 13). Educated in the sciences and humanities, and well acquainted with both Europe and the Middle East, these Europeanized officials were shrewd and urbane men of the world. Most of them had spent years of study in Europe, often at the very best schools. They knew the principal European languages as well as Ottoman Turkish. Few, however, knew the language of their adopted country. The only Armenian official I have found who knew Arabic was Joseph Hekekyan (Yusuf Hikakyan).[20] In addition to their multilingualism, Armenian officials were connected with influential persons in Europe and Ottoman Turkey.[21] Nubar Pasha, for example, had married into a prominent banking family in Istanbul. A former slave of Hekekyan served in the household of the heir apparent to the sultan. Artin Bey reportedly had contacts with Lord Palmerston and other leading European statesmen.

Armenian officials frequently held positions in the Departments of Foreign Affairs and Education, where their strong background in commerce (some, such as Artin Bey, came from highly successful merchant families) and their knowledge of many languages were put to good use. The positions of chief translator (bashmutarjim) in the viceregal cabinet and director of foreign affairs frequently went to Armenians.

Joseph Hekekyan and Nubar Pasha have left vivid records of their government experiences.[22] Hekekyan's papers show the deep imprint that a European education had made upon him. Hekekyan was a champion of civilization with a capital "C." He eagerly embraced the doctrines of free trade and liberalism, and believed firmly in the superiority of European ways. An internationalist at heart, Hekekyan imagined a single world order in which everyone could benefit from expanded trade and modern communications.[23] His sympathies lay not with the Egyptians, nor with Egypt's Turks, whom he considered a "retrograde" element. "Nobody," he wrote in 1845, "thinks or is persuaded that methods different from those used by themselves or their forefathers will succeed or be profitable. Hence it is that [Turks] are slow, negligent, dilatory, careless, apathetic, unheeding, and stupid." Hekekyan poked fun at the superstitions of Turkish officials, ridiculing their contempt and "hatred" of Christians, and delighting in stories of their "unprogressive" attitudes. He wrote in his diary of two Turkish officials who requested a change in the badges of rank in order to distinguish Muslims from Christians. These men said that occasionally they were "deceived into the humiliating error of saluting Christians and of showing them the politeness and attentions which a Muslim should confer only on Muslims." To Hekekyan, and no doubt to many of his Armenian colleagues, the Turks of his time were unreformable barbarians. "Your day is past," he wrote in 1846, "and your children, differently educated, will occupy shortly your places with better sentiments."

Another strongly prejudiced group of high officeholders were the Europeans (see table 14). European officials, of course, were not new to Egypt. Muhammad Ali had employed many of them as experts to implement his reform schemes, and by mid-century, the European technical presence had become firmly rooted. Europeans seemed to be everywhere in government, particularly in the Department of Public Works and the communications administration. This was largely due to the rapid development of a transportation system. In 1852, construction began on Egypt's first railway, built by George Stephenson to link Cairo with Alexandria. This line was completed during the reign of Sa'id, and was extended to the Red Sea. By the late 1870s, as we have seen, Egypt was crisscrossed by 1,200 miles of rail. New opportunities were created for Europeans, who found employment as stationmasters, engine drivers, mechanics, and supply clerks.

Muhammad Ali had avoided giving Europeans high administrative positions for fear of offending the religious feelings of his Muslim subjects. Turks had been placed over the European experts employed by him. By mid-century, this had begun to change. For the first time, Europeans were appointed as directors and deputy directors of major government departments. The first European to be placed at the head

TABLE 12
Egyptian Notables in High Government Positions, 1849–1879

	Sulayman Abaza Pasha	Ali Badrawi Bey	Muhammad Sultan Pasha	Hasan al-Shari'i Pasha	Muhammad Shawaribi Pasha	Ahmad Bey Mustafa
Origin or first local post	From family of shaykhs, al-Sharqiya	Shaykh of subunit of village[a] of Samannud, al-Gharbiya	Village shaykh[b] of Zawiyat al-Amwat, al-Minya	Village shaykh[b] of Samallut, al-Minya	From family of Arab shaykhs, al-Qalyubiya	Village shaykh[b] of al-Malij, al-Minufiya
First post, civil service	District chief[c] in al-Qalyubiya, 1840	Subdistrict chief,[d] district chief,[c] departmental governor,[e] Muhammad Ali's reign	District chief[c] of Qulusna, in al-Minya, 1857	District chief[c] of Qulusna, al-Minya, 1856–	Member, Consultative Chamber of Delegates, 1866–	District chief,[c] Sa'id's reign
Date of becoming bey or pasha	Pasha, 1875	Given rank and title of bey by Sa'id	Pasha, 1869	Bey, 1856	Bey, 1871–72	—
First appointment as deputy governor of province[f]	—	—	Deputy governor, Bani Suwayf, 1859–	—	Deputy governor, al-Qalyubiya, 1869/70	Deputy governor, al-Qalyubiya, early in Ismail's reign
Appointments as provincial governor	Governor of al-Gharbiya, 1869–; governor, al-Qalyubiya, 1871–; governor, al-Sharqiya, 1871–	Governor of Fuwwa (which was his land concession, or uhda)	Governor of Bani Suwayf, 1860–; governor of Asyut, 1863–; governor, al-Gharbiya, 1864–	Governor of al-Daqahliya, 1858; governor of al-Jiza, 1858–; governor of Bani Suwayf and al-Fayyum, 1867–	Governor of al-Minufiya, 1871/72–; governor of al-Qalyubiya, 1875–	Governor of al-Minufiya, 1869–

	First post, central administration	Work done for viceregal family	Last high post	Date of death (or retirement)
	In Department of Finance, 1879–	Employed in viceroy's private estates,[g] 1863/64; inspector, the Daira Saniya, al-Sharqiya, 1864–	Director, Education Department, 1882	1896 (pensioned 1886)
	Supervisor of factories in Cairo, Abbas's reign	Director of viceroy's private estates,[g] Muhammad Ali's reign; developed viceroy's private estates, Abbas's reign	—	1867
	—	Inspector of viceroy's properties, upper Egypt, 1865; director of viceroy's private estates,[g] al-Minya and al-Fayyum, 1872?	President, Legislative Council, 1883	1884
	Member, Cairo Court of Appeals	—	Director, Department of Charitable Endowments[h]	—
	—	—	—	1913

Source: Compiled by the author from archival sources and various published works.
Note: Dashes indicate information not available.
[a] Shaykh al-hissa.
[b] Shaykh al-balad.
[c] Nazir al-qism.
[d] Hakim al-khutt.
[e] Ma'mur.
[f] Wakil al-mudiriya.
[g] Shaflik.
[h] al-Awqaf.

TABLE 13
ARMENIAN TECHNICIANS IN HIGH GOVERNMENT POSITIONS, 1849–1879

	Khusraw Sikyas Bey (Khusrow Bey)	Istafan Rasmi Bey (Stephen Bey)	Dikran Pasha (Tigrane D'Abro)	Artin Shukri Bey	Yusuf Hikakyan (Joseph Hekekyan)	Boghos Nubar Pasha
Birthplace	Istanbul	Sibastiya	Cairo	Istanbul	Istanbul	Smyrna
Education	Paris, 1826 (diplomacy)	Paris, 1826 (diplomacy)	Italy	Istanbul; Cairo; Paris, 1826 (administration)	England, 1817– (engineering)	Switzerland, France
Languages (other than native Armenian)	French, Turkish	French, Turkish,	English, French, Turkish, Italian	Turkish, Italian, French	French, Turkish, English, Italian, German	French, German, Italian, Turkish
First and second posts, civil service	—	Translator, War Department, 1832/33–; Council of Education, 1836	In Department of Railroads, 1864–; secretary and head of Office of Foreign Affairs, 1877–	Translator, Department of War, 1834–; director, School of Administration at Citadel, 1835–	Teacher and supervisor of cotton mills, 1831; director, School of Engineering, 1835	Chargé d'affaires, Vienna, 1853–; director, Railroads and Communications, 1858–
Appointments as deputy director or director of government department	—	Deputy director, Foreign Affairs, 1846/47–; 1850–	Deputy director, Foreign Affairs, 1879–; director, Foreign Affairs, 1891–	Director, Foreign Affairs/Commerce, 1844–; president, Tribunal of Commerce, 1854–	Director, Council of Health, 1849–	Director, Railroads and Communications, 1858–; director, Public Works and Railroads, 1864–

Highest post, civil service	—	Director, Foreign Affairs, 1854–	Director, Foreign Affairs, 1893–	—	—	President, Council of Ministers (three times)
First and second posts, viceregal service	In viceregal cabinet, 1834–; second secretary to Muhammad Ali, 1839–	—	—	First secretary and interpreter for Muhammad Ali, 1839–	—	Interpreter in viceregal cabinet, 1840s; secretary and chief interpreter for Ibrahim
Highest post, viceregal service	First secretary and interpreter for Muhammad Ali, 1844–	—	—	First secretary and interpreter for Muhammad Ali, 1839–	—	Chief interpreter
Other important assignments	First secretary and interpreter for Abbas, 1850–	In entourage of Artin Bey, 1841/42	At outset of career was secretary to Nubar	Member, Council of Education, 1835–	Member, Council of Education, 1836–	Director, Foreign Affairs, 1866–
Last post	—	—	Secretary, Foreign Affairs, 1894–	Member, Governing Council, 1857–	—	President, Council of Ministers, 1894
Date of death	1873	1859	1904	1859	1874?	1899

Source: Compiled by the author from archival sources and various published works.
Note: Dashes indicate information not available.

TABLE 14
EUROPEAN OFFICIALS IN HIGH GOVERNMENT POSITIONS, 1849–1879

Nationality		Position	Date Appointed	Date Entered Service
Betts Bey	British	Deputy director of railroads	1859	—
DeMartino Bey	Italian	Director, Office of European Affairs, viceregal cabinet	1879	1872
Goudard Bey	French	Chief of viceregal secretariat	Ismail's reign	1859
Green Bey	British	Director of railroads and communications	1855–1856	—
Koenig Bey	French	First secretary of viceregal cabinet	Saʿid's reign	—
Linant Bey (Linant de Bellefonds)	French	Director of public works	1869	—
Lubbert Bey	French	Deputy director of foreign affairs	1857	—
Rousseau Bey	French	Deputy director of public works	—	1870
Tonino Bey	Italian	Assistant grand master of ceremonies, viceregal cabinet	1877	1842

Source: Compiled by the author from published works and archival sources, especially "Etat nominatif des fonctionnaires européens au service du gouvernement égyptien," in FO 78/3436.
Note: Dashes indicate information not available.

of a department was an Englishman named Lee Green (Green Bey). Previously agent of the Egyptian communications administration, he was appointed director of Railway and Communications by Saʿid.

Europeans also occupied high positions in the viceregal household. Most European officeholders in the viceregal cabinet were members of its secretarial staff, but a few possessed real influence. A French orientalist named Koenig had originally come to Egypt to improve his Arabic. Employed by Muhammad Ali to translate French laws, Koenig became tutor to his son Saʿid.[24] Teacher and pupil developed a close bond of friendship and trust, and when Saʿid became viceroy, Koenig Bey became first secretary in the viceregal cabinet. Reportedly the only European trusted by Saʿid, Koenig ranked among the most influential officials. Another European favorite in Saʿid's court, Paolino (Draneht) Bey, received high position outside the household. In 1861, he was named director of Railway and Communications.[25]

The rise of Europeans to high government position introduced yet another source of tension into the bureaucratic elite. European sentiments of national and racial superiority ran up against similar feelings

among Turkish, Egyptian, and Armenian officials, and made cooperation among them very difficult. Europeans seemed most hostile toward
the Turks, whereas they commonly regarded Egyptians as intelligent
but docile and too imitative.[26] Green Bey's engine drivers (all Europeans) would leave him, he said, if he hired natives. British engineers
did not want to see Egyptians promoted, and the majority shunned the
few Englishmen among them who thought differently. Such views
were bound to lead to dissension, especially between European and
Turkish officials. Abdallah Pasha, a Turkish director of finances under
Sa'id, came into conflict with Linant Bey (a Frenchman), and Turkish
intrigues against Green Bey were unceasing.[27]

These five categories of officials composing Egypt's bureaucratic
elite are not absolute or all-encompassing. Not every high-ranking
official can be so easily classified. Ismail Siddiq, the previously mentioned Egyptian director of finances, did not possess a European education and spoke only Arabic, yet he hardly qualifies as a "notable." Of
obscure family origin, his mother had been wet nurse to Prince Ismail,
and he had grown up as the future viceroy's foster brother. There
were also a few Coptic officials of high rank, but too few of them to
constitute a group. Coptic officials could hardly be found at the upper
levels of administration.[28]

At this point one may ask, why did not the sharp differences between elite subgroups lead to rivalries so fierce as to threaten the stability of the state? This did not occur, first because Egypt's political/
administrative order was not a purely competitive system in which
everyone was scrambling against everyone else for a finite set of rewards. It was possible for all groups and individuals to gain in wealth,
and there was room at the top for everyone. Second, certain forces
brought members of the elite closer together and pushed them toward
cooperation. Important common material interests were being forged
among elite subgroups, who shared much more than high rank and
administrative position. This is illustrated by the new elite's life style
and investment patterns, and particularly their acquisition of property
in the countryside.

▲▲▲ A COMMON MATERIAL CULTURE AND INTEREST IN LAND

Personal wealth became an increasingly important objective of
Egypt's high officeholders. Wealth was identified with land and also
with cash, whose place in the economy was growing daily. The emergence of cotton as a commercial crop, the increased money available, and the political reality of a centralized, absolutist state in which
no official could hope to gain supreme political power made private

wealth a more highly regarded prize of office than ever before. A means of ostentation as much as a medium of exchange, wealth became a very important raison d'être of officeholding. Officials strove to accumulate as much capital as they could, by any means possible, on the assumption that the appearance of wealth brought status and that its substance would somehow bring them influence.

Thus land and cash were the two expectations of high office. By mid-century, it was taken for granted that every high-ranking official would have at least one landed estate. Although high officeholders did buy property, most of their landholdings were gifts of the viceroy, following a precedent established by Muhammad Ali. Not only did senior officials expect to accumulate cash, but also they were expected to spend it according to their positions. They felt obliged to live in a certain way, to buy the "right kind" of home and furnish it appropriately. So much had always been true, but the pattern of investment at mid-century marked a departure from that practised by Muhammad Ali's higher officials. By the late 1860s, officials bought fewer slaves and more steam engines, smoked oriental pipes less and European cigars more, and preferred to ride in expensive carriages rather than on horseback. In other words, they were beginning to mix oriental and European habits of consumption.

This new cultural mode was quite different from Egypt's traditional mamluk household culture (see table 15). The typical eighteenth-century elite household had been centered on a palace containing many rooms and passageways, including a place for the harem and a reception room. The household included the owner's family and numerous slaves, male and female, white and black—concubines, eunuchs, and domestic guards. Outside were barracks for the master's troops and a large stable of horses. Bristling with weaponry, these households were like armed fortresses, reflecting the high stakes involved in the struggle for power between rival beys. Muhammad Ali destroyed the power of these military households, but he did not destroy the tradition they represented. Like the mamluks of the eighteenth century, Muhammad Ali's senior officials owned spacious palaces and possessed retinues of armed followers. In the marketplaces of Cairo and Istanbul, slaves were purchased in large numbers. In 1825, an estimated 1,610 mamluks resided in the palaces of about twenty-nine higher officials. Upon reaching maturity, these mamluks were freed and given horses and other forms of wealth. Some remained in their masters' service, others were given ranks and salaries in the civil administration or entered the military service.[29]

By mid-century, this mamluk household culture was being replaced by a more refined but expensive mode of living. A new type of house-

TABLE 15

THE MAMLUK HOUSEHOLDS OF EGYPT'S GRANDEES, 1825

	No. of Mamluks Owned
Muhammad Ali	500
Ibrahim Pasha	300
Abbas Pasha	150
Viceroy's first lieutenant[a]	60
Director, War Department	80
Tussun Bey	30
Sharif Pasha	40
Muhammad Daftardar	150
Muharram Bey	100
About twenty other officials dismissed by Muhammad Ali	200
Total	1,610

Source: Douin, Une mission militaire, p. 78.
[a]Katkhuda.

hold was emerging, reflecting new tastes engendered by contact with Europe. Perhaps the most discernible change was the popularity of a new type of residence, representing European and Turkish influences, known as the Constantinopolitan. Though introduced in the 1830s, it was not accepted until after Muhammad Ali's death.[30] It was characterized by a flat roof (the Istanbul version had slanted roofs) and numerous high, narrow windows covered by grillwork and panes of glass. This new style implicitly rejected some features of the old mamluk and Arab culture. The traditional arched windows, for example, were replaced by rectangular ones, and wooden latticework (mashrabiya) was forbidden to be used as decoration for the new buildings. These new mansions were enclosed within high walls, and the entrance gates were designed to prevent outsiders from having a direct view into the interior. By 1856, the Constantinopolitan was the most popular style of building among the well-to-do in Cairo.

It was customary for high-ranking officials to buy and furnish homes of this type, though some preferred to live in palaces, like the viceregal family. The cost of building or buying such a home plunged more than one official into debt. Because of the expense, viceroys frequently made cash gifts to chosen officials to help them defray the costs of their homes.[31] Tal'at Pasha received 1,500 purses or £E 7,500 for a new house, and Ahmad Rashid was given £E 12,250 for a home by Khedive Ismail. Expenses never ceased. Hekekyan had to spend £E 1,750 just to maintain his home. These new residences were located in both old and new sections of Cairo, in Bab al-Luq and Darb al-Jamamiz as well as al-Sayida Zaynab and Azbakiya. Some officials owned buildings on the island of al-Rawda and along the Shariᶜ al-Muski. In the 1870s, these residences were filled, sometimes to overflowing, with expensive European bric-a-brac. Large mirrors, paintings, fine china, toilet accessories, gold- and silver-plated utensils and other baubles were uncrated and placed on display as soon as they arrived from Europe.

The new life style was most obvious in the appearance and public behavior of Egypt's officials and their families.[32] The men wore frock coats rather than robes, fezes rather than turbans; they sported mustaches and smoked cigars and cigarettes. By the 1870s, they and their harem women could be seen riding in European carriages. A visitor to Cairo could stand in front of his hotel and see the harem ladies pass by, "dressed in the latest Parisian modes—all except the face, which half-hidden, half-revealed, [was] covered with a gossamer veil." The same observer, Edwin de Leon (former American consul general in Egypt) wrote in 1877, "European costume is now the rage in the hareems, and Lyons silks of brightest colors, and French boots with impracticable heels, have succeeded the flowing draperies and shuffling slippers and baggy breeches of the Eastern fair ones."

Of course, many old practices persisted. If there were no longer military barracks or armed retainers, there were still slaves. Despite protests from European consuls, and despite viceregal decrees abolishing the practice, it remained fashionable for high-ranking officials to keep female slaves as concubines. Officials did not, however, have more than one wife at a time, though many were married two or three times. The number of concubines and attendants was usually not large, generally no more than five. Turkish officials owned the largest number; Hasan Rasim, for instance, had five Circassian slave girls, one of whom bore him two sons.[33] It was customary for officials to manumit and marry concubines who had given them children, and some arranged marriages between their female slaves and their sons. Since families were not very large, male slaves were rare. The Abyssinian slave of Sultan Pasha, and the mamluk owned by Muhammad Thaqib were exceptions.[34] Aside from the household of Ismail Siddiq, which seems to have rivaled the great mamluk establishments (*bayts*) of the eighteenth century, bureaucratic households of mid-century were not comparable even to those of Muhammad Ali's time.

Intermarriage between Egyptians and Turks also occurred. Some high Egyptian officials (such as Ali Mubarak) took Turkish wives, and many Egyptian officeholders purchased Turkish women (who were famous for their beauty) as concubines. Rifaᶜa Tahtawi, for example, owned a Circassian concubine, and Hasan al-Shariᶜi had a Turkish slave girl who gave him three children.[35] Indeed, a few high officials of the second generation were themselves of mixed Turkish-Egyptian parentage, but our sources do not yet permit knowledge of the true extent of this assimilation.[36]

Although the mixed life style of Egypt's high officials at mid-century marked them as a transitional generation, theirs was the first generation of officials to display a real interest in developing landed property. By the 1860s, for the first time in the century, landholding had become a privilege of high office. During roughly the first three decades of Muhammad Ali's reign, there was no association between office and landholding. In fact, the viceroy took pride in having prevented his high officials from becoming landowners.[37] Yet by mid-century nearly every high-ranking official in Egypt owned at least one landed estate and was keenly interested in developing it.

This important and rapid development followed Muhammad Ali's decision to begin granting landed estates, which made the viceroy the mechanism for transferring property, and the conversion of landed estates into an economic asset. These were in turn connected with the expanding production of cotton, Egypt's growing entanglement with Europe, and the viceregal family's desire to be free of Ottoman control.

As we have seen, owing to the great expense of wars with the Ottomans in Syria and a loss of tax revenue within Egypt, Muhammad Ali began assigning villages as tax farms (*uhdas*) to many of his followers. He also granted lands (*shafliks*) to himself and his family members, and gave leading officials and military commanders estates called *ab'adiya*s, from land which had been surveyed but was uncultivated and therefore not on the cadaster. The latter were granted tax-free, with the proviso that they be brought under cultivation. Muhammad Ali once told the governor of al-Daqahliya that his policy was to give an *ab'adiya* estate to every provincial governor on condition that it not be cultivated while he was in office.[38] (The viceroy feared that officials would use their positions to extend their estates at the expense of the peasant proprietors.) It is not known, however, how general this practice became, but it can be reasonably assumed that most highly placed state employees received such tax-free estates.

Even though land was now being granted under Muhammad Ali, it was not regarded favorably by most recipients.[39] Excluding the viceroy's family, who got the best estates, officials considered land to be an obligation rather than a privilege, and accepted estates under compulsion; no one could refuse the gift of an *uhda* or *ab'adiya*. Severe restrictions controlled the sale of cotton and grain, and holders of *uhda*s had to sell their produce to Muhammad Ali at his price. Bring-

ing an *ab'adiya* estate under cultivation required an enormous investment of capital and time. Animals had to be purchased, waterwheels
constructed, and dams erected—all to fructify a piece of land that had
not been touched by the plough for decades. For most officeholders,
Muhammad Ali's land grants were a punishment, not a privilege.

The next stage came during the years between Muhammad Ali's
death and the accession of Khedive Ismail. This period represented an
advance over the previous one in two important respects. It marked
the origins of the estates held by the second generation of high
officeholders, and it produced the first signs that land could be an
economic advantage.

We must distinguish between the landholdings of Muhammad Ali's
higher officials and those of the succeeding generation. Most of the
land granted by Muhammad Ali went to his own *dhawat*, an ephemeral
ruling elite that did not survive the succession struggle between Abbas
and the sons of Ibrahim. Following Muhammad Ali's death, most of his
men left Egypt, never to return. Of course, Muhammad Ali's land
grants contributed to the formation of estates that flourished under his
successors. As Ali Barakat has shown, some of the relatives of Muhammad Ali's elite managed to remain in Egypt and to hold onto and
even extend their lands; some even attained high state position. Yet
most high officials of the second generation did not come from the
families of Egypt's former ruling *dhawat*, who in any case lost vast
amounts of property when Abbas confiscated their *uhdas*.[40] Muhammad Ali's contribution to the development of estates owned by Egypt's
second generation of high officials, therefore, may be less than is commonly supposed. The *Dhawat* Land Register of tithed *ushuriya* lands,
whose entries go back to the 1830s, reveals that out of eighteen prominent high-ranking officials and their families, thirteen received their
first piece of land during the reign of Abbas or Sa'id, whereas only one
entry shows land obtained during Muhammad Ali's reign. From this, it
may be deduced that the landed estates of this elite were first acquired
between 1849 and 1863 (see table 16).

This period also produced the first signs that landholding could be an
economic advantage. Egypt's growing tie with the European market
and the end of Muhammad Ali's restrictive monopolies had stimulated
the Egyptian economy during the first half of the 1850s. Perhaps because free sales were now possible, cotton production increased significantly between 1850 and 1852.[41] Yet this was nothing compared to
the boom in wheat sales between 1854 and 1856. Propelled by rising
cereal prices because of the need to victual Turkish, British, and
French troops fighting in the Crimea, Egyptian wheat sales rose dramatically and enriched many landholders. Yet, as Owen has pointed

TABLE 16
Lands of Officials in High Government Positions, 1849–1879

Landowner	Date of First Acquisition	Under What Ruler	No. of Faddans Acquired Under Abbas and Sa'id
Ismail Raghib	3 Mar. 1841	Muhammad Ali	1,104
Muhammad Thabit	26 Aug. 1849	Abbas	1,332
Amin Pasha	30 Sept. 1849	Abbas	2,189
Abd al-Latif	1 Dec. 1849	Abbas	1,050
Ahmad Rashid	8 June 1850	Abbas	750
Ali Mubarak	30 Dec. 1850	Abbas	300
Nubar Pasha[a]	13 Aug. 1852	Abbas	1,300
Mustafa Riyad	16 Jan. 1853	Abbas	290
Ali Dhu al-Fiqar	11 Nov. 1853	Abbas	1,650
Muhammad Hafiz	27 Dec. 1856	Sa'id	—
Abd al-Qadir Hilmi	21 June 1857	Sa'id	300
Ismail Abu Ja'bal	17 Jan. 1861	Sa'id	426
Muhammad Sultan	29 Mar. 1862	Sa'id	437
Ahmad Sadiq	11 July 1862	Sa'id	200
Arif Fahmi	27 Jan. 1863	Ismail	
Ismail Siddiq	15 June 1863	Ismail	
Shahin Pasha	15 June 1863	Ismail	
Muhammad Sharif	26 June 1863	Ismail	

Source: Egyptian National Archives, Daftar zimam atyan ushuriya: Dhawat, no. 1343.
Note: Dash indicates information not available.
[a] In 1846, Nubar received a grant of 494 faddans of uncultivated tax-free (ab'adiya) land according to Barakat, Tatawwur, p. 175.

out, only a small portion of the profits made during this time was invested in agriculture. A highly developed land market did not yet exist, and landholders preferred to invest their cash in government bonds.[42] The Crimean War boom, however, was important. It showed that land could be an asset rather than a liability.

As already noted, Abbas and Sa'id converted precedent into practice by continuing Muhammad Ali's policy of granting land as favors.[43] Sa'id, however, went beyond this by authorizing the sale of state lands to persons who promised to improve them.[44] He also offered the holders of big estates an opportunity to exchange their unproductive ab'adiyas for cultivated lands, and began giving untilled ab'adiya lands to retired state employees in lieu of pensions. According to Barakat, 70,414 faddans were granted by Sa'id to state retirees during the last three years of his reign. By 1863, at least 2,532 persons had received land in this way.

While landholding was being regarded more favorably when Ismail became khedive, the cotton boom galvanized agricultural activity within Egypt. No effort was spared to bring as much land as possible under cultivation. To spur development, Khedive Ismail began making grants of land on a much larger scale than before. Amin Sami's records reveal the magnitude of this change. Between January 1863 and December 1865, Sami records a total of 77,620 *faddans* granted to government officials and military officers, while the viceroy bestowed 132,941 *faddans* upon himself and family members.[45]

Most of the land received by Egypt's high officials was *ab'adiya*.[46] Abandoned properties were also granted, as were "survey surpluses," unregistered and unsurveyed lands (*ziyadat al-masaha*). Once the khedive had decided to give an estate to someone, he would send an order to a provincial governor or to his inspector general, who was requested to locate and delimit a specified amount of land and to send a statement to the Department of Finance, which would issue the title deed (*taqsit*) to the new owner. During Ismail's reign, 876,863 *faddans* of land of all types were granted in this way.[47]

If a large estate were to be built up, the 1860s was the time to do it. The brisk land sales and exchanges of this time reflected not only higher land values but also the increased amount of capital in circulation during the boom years. The fate of Abbas Pasha's large private estate of 13,370 *faddans* at Mahallat al-Kubra is illustrative. Between the summer of 1862 and the winter of 1867, as recorded in the *Dhawat* Land Register, thirty-three individuals, many of them beys and pashas, purchased 11,196 *faddans* of this prize property. Perhaps the best indication of the growth of estates after 1863 is the proportion of land acquired by high-ranking officials after that date. Table 17 shows that almost three-quarters of the land held by twenty *dhawat* officials had been acquired after Ismail's accession in January 1863.

The development of large estates as a concomitant of holding high office provided a basis for cooperation among officials of differing ethnic and cultural backgrounds. As property holders, they supported policies designed to protect the position of those who owned land and cooperated generally in promoting the buildup of their estates. Before examining this matter further, however, we need to make three general observations. First, great variability existed in the landed possessions of *dhawat* officials. Some owned fifty or a hundred *faddans*, others several thousands. At the same time, landholding seems to have followed ethnic lines. There was a large disparity between the amounts of land held by Turkish officials and Egyptian notables, on the one hand, and the Egyptian technicians, Armenian and European officials on the other. Estates of high Turkish officials customarily ran to several thousand *faddans*, and notable officials also held very large estates, although their property was as often inherited as granted by

TABLE 17

INCREASE IN LANDHOLDING AFTER ISMAIL'S ACCESSION

Landowner	No. of Faddans Acquired Between 1863 and 1870	Total Faddans Held in 1870
Abd al-Latif	791	1,841
Ismail Abu Ja'bal	1,808	2,491
Shahin Pasha	2,006	2,006
Muhammad Thabit	594	1,600
Ahmad Tal'at	975	2,128
Ismail Raghib	2,911	7,061
Ismail Siddiq	4,024	4,024
Ahmad Rashid	2,027	2,779
Abd al-Qadir Hilmi	1,275	1,574
Muhammad Sultan	1,582	1,905
Nubar Pasha	1,343	2,193
Umar Lutfi	723	723
Arif Fahmi	6,561	6,561
Abdallah Pasha	1,353	1,980
Ahmad al-Daramalli	2,186	2,186
Mustafa Riyad	878	1,119
Ali Dhu al-Fiqar	999	3,689
Amin Pasha	2,850	4,519
Muhammad Sharif	2,507	2,507
Ahmad Sadiq	662	862
Total	38,055	53,748

Source: Egyptian National Archives, Daftar zimam atyan ushuriya: Dhawat, no. 1343.

the ruler. Lands held by officials from other *dhawat* groups were much less impressive. According to the register recording tithed *ushuriya* lands, Rifaʿa Tahtawi, Ali Mubarak, and Abdallah Fikri—all Egyptian technicians—are credited with lands totaling 2,020 *faddans*, while Ahmad Rashid, Ismail Raghib and Ali Dhu al-Fiqar, three leading Turkish officials, possessed a combined 13,478 *faddans*. This disparity is reinforced by figures from Amin Sami on landed estates granted by Ismail during the first three years of his reign. Turkish officials consistently received large grants. Muhammad Sharif was given 1,197 *faddans*, Ali Dhu al-Fiqar 1,000, Ismail Raghib 3,000, and Ahmad Tal'at 1,000. Ali Mubarak and Mahmud al-Falaki, on the other hand, received a paltry 300 and 200 *faddans*, respectively. No other Egyptian technicians mentioned in table 13 are recorded by Sami as having received land during this period.

High-ranking European officials also do not seem to have acquired much land. Of the land grants recorded by Sami, very few went to

European *dhawat*. (Draneht Bey, who received 1,485 *faddans*, was an exception.) The register of *ushuriya* lands contains the names of only a few European officials, whose landholdings may have been even less substantial than those of the Egyptian technicians. Armenian officials, with the exception of Nubar and a few others, did not fare much better. By contrast, Egyptian notables possessed considerable landed properties. In 1870, Muhammad Sultan held 1,905 *faddans*, Muhammad Minshawi, 1,030, and Rifaʿa Tahtawi 1,546, while Ali Badrawi owned 4,000 *faddans* at the time of his death in 1867.[48]

Turkish officials were the most favored group of landholders because of their proximity to the viceroy, but Turks were also advantaged, as were Egyptian notable officials, because the leading positions in the provincial administration were filled almost exclusively from these two elite subgroups. Egyptian technocrats, Armenians, and European officials did not become governors or deputy governors of provinces, but remained closely bound to the central administration.

Our second observation is that not all high officials reaped profits from their lands. Many were in debt. This sprang from a variety of causes: the difficulty and expense (before the 1860s) of bringing land under cultivation, mismanagement of property, the instability of tenure for those in high positions, and the expense of adopting the prevailing life style, which caused some officials to live far beyond their means. Within a single career could be found great extremes of wealth and poverty, and indebtedness was more common than is usually realized.[49] Muhammad Thaqib Pasha, Muhammad Khulusi Bey, and Ali Mubarak all fell into debt at some point in their careers; Mustafa Bahjat, an engineer, died a poor man after having owned a textile factory, a house in Bulaq, a small estate in al-Jiza, and land in the provinces.

Third, we need to bear in mind that a basis of mutual cooperation also existed between officials and the ruler in view of their monopolization of the best lands and their joint ability to build up their estates. The viceroy, his family, and state employees held by far the greater part of all land designated as *ushuriya* which by 1877 had reached 1,282,000 *faddans*.[50] They also held considerable amounts of *kharajiya* property, the other category into which land had been divided for tax purposes, which altogether amounted to 3,461,000 *faddans*. (Most of this *kharajiya* land, however, was held by peasant farmers.) Though some evidence exists that Ismail seized the lands of many officials shortly after his accession, the estates of Egypt's high officeholders seem to have been less liable to confiscation during his reign than in previous periods.[51] This was not because of private ownership rights, which in any case existed merely on paper, but more likely because the ruler desired to see the country developed as rapidly as possible in hopes of broadening its tax base and augmenting his revenue. However, confiscation remained a potential threat.

Owing to the cotton economy, Egypt's high officeholders found it in their interest to cooperate in acquiring and developing their properties.[52] Officials favored each other in public auctions of government lands, which were purchased at considerably less than their real value. They formed "conspiracies of silence" to conceal their acquisition of lands confiscated from peasant holders for nonpayment of taxes or debt or because they had been left vacant. They undervalued the tax assessments on their lands, had portions declared tax-exempt, and worked together to reclassify their *kharajiya* land as *ushuriya*, thereby lowering their taxes. While the amount of *kharajiya* land varied little between 1863 and 1877, the area of *ushuriya* land doubled, amounting to about a quarter of the total cultivated area.[53] Officials purchased steam pumps and other equipment at reduced prices, and joined together to "persuade" the peasants of a village or district to work for low wages in return for delayed loan repayments or reduced interest charges. Officials also made sure that their lands were watered before those of the *fallahin*, and they conspired to avoid registering reclaimed land. To gain additional protection, they alienated portions of their land as *al-awqaf*—endowments made for pious or public purposes—which removed lands from taxation and helped prevent their seizure. According to Barakat, by January 1874, 87,941 *faddans* of *ushuriya* land had been endowed in this manner.[54]

There can be little doubt that the buildup of landed estates among Egypt's officials helped to break down regional and ethnic divisions between Turks and Egyptians in the provinces, and between the countryside and the urban areas. Turkish landholding officials employed in the provinces needed the cooperation of local notables, and vice versa. High officeholders in the central administration required the assistance of provincial officials, since as absentee landowners they could not supervise their estates themselves. Provincial officials in turn needed contacts in Cairo in order to gain access to the political center (that is, the ruler) and to push for projects favorable to the development of their estates. The purchase by rural notables of second residences in Cairo was both cause and manifestation of an increasing interaction between center and periphery.

Yet the real question is: how far had this process gone? Can we speak of the transformation of *dhawat* officials into a new landed class? This, of course, presumes both self-consciousness and a common level of wealth, both of which were lacking in the period covered by this study. If every official held at least one landed estate, differences in the size, value, and fate of their holdings remained great indeed, and their self-perception as an economic elite was vitiated by strong ethnic feelings which were to a degree reinforced by the allocation and division of land. Cooperation among officials did not lead to the organization of large combinations to advance and defend their landed interests because they had neither the capacity nor a compelling reason to do so. All were subject to the power and caprice of the ruler, who was at the same time their chief patron and protector. If common possession of land was not the most distinguishing factor in their formation, however, one can argue that the rapid accumulation of landed estates by Turkish and Egyptian notable officials made it possible for the members of these two groups to begin perceiving themselves as part of an agrarian bourgeoisie.

▲▲▲ LINKAGE POLITICS

Egypt's officials employed the bureaucratic apparatus to help extend and develop their landed estates, but they also used their positions to advance and protect interests of a more political nature. At the highest levels of administration, three kinds of interests were represented. Officials worked to realize certain personal and family goals, and they also possessed two new outside associations: a European interest and a local or rural interest. Before examining these, however, we must first understand the arrangements by which officials were able to achieve their objectives.

In Egypt, administration was not entirely synonymous with bureaucracy. There was also a strong informal component which derived not from prescribed rules but from ties of personal obligation and dependency. Officials entered into alliances and formed networks based on personal ties known as *al-intisab*, usually translated as "personal connections." Rooted in a value system in which loyalties were given to local units (family, tribe, village), *al-intisab* had broad implications. Within the government, knowing the "right" person was crucial for promotion, a prolonged tenure, protection from enemies, and a return to office after being dismissed. According to the law, state employees dismissed for certain crimes could reenter government service by the intercession of high-ranking officials who vouched for their integrity. Occasionally, a person was promoted without patronage, but this was so rare as to elicit comment when it happened.[55] At the same time, *al-intisab* could serve as a basis by which officials banded together in pursuit of a common goal. Temporary coalitions called *shillas*, or alliances of equals, were formed among higher officials to block the promotion of rivals or to realize some other objective. In 1861, forty-two high officials signed a petition requesting that Saʿid delay his proposed trip to the Hijaz. Unfortunately, Saʿid reacted by dismissing all the petitioners, including most of his departmental directors![56]

The other (and more common) type of bureaucratic alliance was the faction, composed of a patron and a number of clients, usually family, friends, acquaintances and co-workers. Kinfolk were the cement of a faction, since they could be trusted to act in the family interest and could help enlarge the patron's following by acquiring clients of their own. Marriage was commonly used to place others under obligation or to ensure the loyalty of clients. One of the largest factions was that of the Yagan family, linked by marriage to Egypt's viceroys.[57] Khedive Ismail's son Prince Husayn Kamil was married to the daughter of the late Ahmad Yagan, and Ismail's daughter Tawfida was the wife of Mansur Yagan. The Yagans drew many high officials into their faction through patronage and other ties. Muhammad Asim Pasha and Ahmad Pasha al-Daramalli both married Circassian slaves from this family. In 1863, eight members of the Yagan family were among Egypt's highest-ranking civil and military officials.

The family core of the faction and its usefulness to a patron can be illustrated by Egypt's Armenian officials, many of whom were relatives of Nubar Pasha or Artin Bey.[58] (Artin, incidentally, was not a full member of the second generation of elite bureaucrats. His career, and also those of Khusrow Bey and Hekekyan Bey, reached a peak during the 1840s, though all three continued to enjoy high rank and influence after Muhammad Ali's death.) Khusrow and Hekekyan were Artin's brother and brother-in-law, respectively. Arakil Bey, a high-ranking civil official, was Nubar's brother. In 1853, the two were posted to Europe as commercial agents of the khedive—Arakil in Berlin, Nubar in Vienna. Arakil subsequently became chief translator (1856), then governor of Khartum and Kordofan. In 1868, Arakil's son, along with Iram Bey, Nubar's brother-in-law, could be found in the viceregal cabinet, where Iram was appointments secretary for the khedive. In Istanbul, Abraham Bey, one of Khedive Ismail's agents, and Kevork Bey, Ismail's banker, were also related to Nubar.

Influential Armenian officials like Artin took great care to associate family members or fellow Armenians with them in their rise to power. When Artin became first secretary in the viceregal cabinet, his brother Khusrow was made a secretary. After Artin was appointed director of Foreign Affairs (1844), Khusrow became first secretary in the viceregal cabinet and Artin's assistant in Foreign Affairs. In Artin's absence, Khusrow even directed that department (1850).[59] The rise of Stephen Bey was similar. In the early 1830s, Stephen was attached to Artin's entourage. He worked alongside Artin in the School of Administration, served with him as co-translator in the War Department (1834), sat with him (and Hekekyan) in the Council of Education (1835/1836) and remained with him when Artin became first secretary and chief interpreter. Stephen served as deputy director of Foreign Affairs (1846/1847) at the time Artin was director. After Artin's dismissal, Stephen became deputy director, then director of Foreign Affairs.[60] Similar patterns can be discerned in the relationships between Artin and Hekekyan, and between Nubar and Tigrane.

In this way, Armenians acquired a dominant influence in certain areas of administration. For thirty-six years during the period 1824–1894, the Department of Foreign Affairs was headed by officials from Nubar Pasha's family. Including the tenures of two other Armenian directors of foreign affairs, Artin and Stephen, this department was controlled by Armenians for forty-five years.[61]

One purpose served by the bureaucratic faction was self-protection. Hekekyan Bey steadfastly maintained that during a crisis in his career, only the presence of his two brothers-in-law in high office prevented Muhammad Ali from having him strangled or knifed to death. At the time, the viceroy was greatly dependent upon Hekekyan's relatives (Artin and Khusrow), and they would have left office had anything happened to him.[62] The most common objective of the bureaucratic faction, however, was control of revenue. The behavior of Artin Bey as director of foreign affairs and commerce illustrates this point.[63] In 1849, Artin (who already held the Department of Foreign Affairs) procured by intrigue the downfall of the director of Egyptian commerce and induced Abbas to join that department to his own. One of his relatives was then made government broker, and another was set up as a banker in Alexandria. This made it possible for Artin to monopolize a large share of the country's commerce. He sold cotton, wheat, and other products whenever and however he pleased, and enjoyed "as comfortable a family compact of monopoly as could be imagined." By selling government produce in secret rather than by public auction, Artin was able to accumulate a tidy sum and eventually became so powerful that some officials lived in fear of him. When he finally fled Egypt (Artin was also mixed up in the succession feud), he took with him a fortune estimated by French newspapers at Fr 2,500,000.

As we have said, family and individual interests were not the only ones advanced by these arrangements. Within the higher administration, officials could be found with ties to Europe and to rural Egyptian society, and who therefore represented something beyond the family or private group. Muhammad Ali had been rather successful in preventing his senior officials from developing interests that might conflict with his own, and thus tolerated their private rivalries and petty intrigues. Following his death, however, the realignment of social forces within the higher administration led to the appearance of outside interests among the very group upon whom viceregal control rested.

A link with Europe could take several forms. A high-ranking official could receive support from a European consul, favor a certain kind of reform, support the policies of a particular European state, or simply feel sympathetic toward European civilization. Links between these officials and Europe existed on two levels: (1) the ideological plane of attitudes and beliefs, and (2) the material level of self-interest and mutual benefit, which involves the ties between *dhawat* officials and the European consuls.

As for the first, the appearance of men possessing attitudes favorable to European civilization was directly related to Muhammad Ali's introduction of Western technology into Egypt, and the establishment of a new educational system which included sending students on study missions abroad. Between 1809 and 1849, 349 young men were sent to Europe, most to France and Britain, and almost 11,000 youths passed through the new schools in Egypt.[64] Scientific study was of course accompanied by learning European languages, and this ineluctably led to a familiarity with European culture and ideas. Students formed friendships with their foreign instructors, who lost little time acquainting them with the writings of Locke, Montesquieu, and Rousseau. Antoine Clot, director of Muhammad Ali's medical school, worked sedulously to inculcate ideas of nationalism in his Egyptian students.[65] In time, this broad exposure produced a profound cognitive change, a new weltanschauung in which the European experience was regarded as normative and which led to a new perception of the land and people of Egypt. Those who went to Europe for an education returned home impatient with the system and eager to inform their elders of the "proper" way to conduct their business and other affairs.[66] The assimilation of European culture sometimes went to extreme lengths. Young Armenians arriving in Egypt after years of study in Paris are described by Hekekyan as "complete Parisians," with "long [finger] nails and large heads of hair." Some had even forgotten their mother tongue and had to converse with their parents through an interpreter!

During Muhammad Ali's reign, a cadre of "new men"—physicians, engineers, geographers, metallurgists, printers—began to emerge. Employed by Muhammad Ali in various jobs, from translating French law codes to managing medical dispensaries in the countryside, these young men worked their way through the ranks of the bureaucracy until by the 1860s many had become part of Egypt's administrative elite. Although they appear in our tables and elsewhere as "technicians," they became the cutting edge of a new society.

Egypt's technician officials were all broadly committed to "reform," which in the most general sense meant the introduction of European knowledge or know-how. Most understood the relationship between Europe's technological advances and certain new attitudes and values. Progress therefore came to be associated with a determination to break with past customs and chart new paths. These officials, however, differed greatly as to what reforms should be implemented, or how rapidly and to what extent. Ali Mubarak was wholly committed to the elixir of a scientific education, not only to produce "forward-looking" leaders, but also to change the values of his society. On the other hand, Muhammad Sharif was perfectly willing to argue the case for a modern system of communications, but for some future generation, not his.

These men built up support for their ideas by promoting or favoring others who thought as they did, and in this way formed a bridge across ethnic divisions that enabled those with similar goals to cooperate with each other, at least in a general way. However, ethnic and religious differences, not to speak of personal rivalries (for example, between Nubar Pasha and Muhammad Sharif) made prolonged cooperation difficult. There was no common agreement on a specific program of reform.

One aspect of this cognitive change was the development among some Egyptian technicians (such as Ali Mubarak, Rifaʿa Tahtawi) of a new concept of Egypt. Because of their exposure to European ideas, they began to explore their country's pharaonic origins and developed a notion of Egypt as a living reality with continuous links to its pre-Islamic past. In their writings, they began referring to Egypt by the Arabic word *al-watan*, which had customarily meant "birthplace" in the sense not only of house or plot of ground but also of homeland.[67] *al-Watan* was used in this latter sense to convey a meaning of Egyptianness, the assertion of the indigenous element against outsiders, and had even found encouragement in the statements of Muhammad Ali (who had once declared Egyptians to be the equals of Turks), of Saʿid (who suggested that Egyptians, not Turks, should rule their country) and of Ismail.[68] This use of *al-watan* as *patrie* or "fatherland" was later to form the core of a new national identity.

Finally, some of these men (as, for example, Muhammad Sharif, Nubar Pasha) developed a sympathy with the idea of constitutionalism, and a few began to see in the application of European concepts an opportunity to limit the autocracy of the khedive. We can find an inkling of this sentiment in statements made by Artin and Hekekyan to

Nassau Senior in the mid-1850s.[69] "What we want in Egypt," Heke-kyan told him, "is good government. What we have is . . . mere sub-jection." Both men were sharply critical of viceregal autocracy and spoke of the need to limit the khedive's power and impose upon him a civil list (an appropriation of money for the ruler and his household) and the other checks that had reduced monarchical power in Europe. Artin expressed the hope that someday the European consuls would compel the khedive to accept limits on his power, and Hekekyan con-fessed that the best thing which could happen to Egypt would be a French or British occupation. How many other technician-reformers were thinking similar thoughts?

It is impossible to separate ideas from their material basis. Behind every professed commitment to reform lay a private ambition of one sort or another which, to be realized, needed assistance. Of course, the viceroy could give this support, but by mid-century the European con-suls had emerged as a new source of patronage. For this reason, we must examine the growing ties between the representatives of Europe and certain reform-minded officials.

As we have seen, the European consuls were the new politicians of Egypt. Their support of their own nationals and the pressures that they could bring to bear upon the ruler are well known. The consuls forced Abbas to reverse his decision to expel Greeks from Egypt; they prevented Sa'id from establishing mixed tribunals, and caused him to change his mind about conscripting Copts for military service.[70] In the days following the assassination of Abbas, consular intervention pre-vented a fight between two factions of the viceregal family and ensured the accession of Sa'id.[71] Little wonder that these "wolves," as Sa'id once called them, were feared and hated by Egypt's viceroys.

Of course, these consular representatives were not the only influen-tial Europeans with whom elite officials had contacts; these ties were established in the context of a new urban society that contained Euro-pean merchants and financiers, *shaykh*s of the Azhar, journalists, Muslim merchants, religious reformers, and others. Particularly im-portant meeting grounds were the Freemason lodges that had been founded by Europeans of various nationalities. At first patronized ex-clusively by Europeans, Levantines, and a few *dhawat* reformers, these societies by the mid-1870s had become centers for the exchange of ideas among many segments of society.[72] Here, members of the Consultative Chamber of Delegates, high Turkish officeholders and others met to discuss the problems of Egypt. In these lodges, elite officials formed relationships with the leaders of local society and with prominent Europeans, and, above all, consolidated ties of patronage and protection with the foreign consuls.

As Egypt's new politicians, the European consuls worked hard to protect the interests of their allies within the administration. Highly placed Europeans in the viceroy's court regularly sent information to them.[73] European officials subjected to fines, reductions in salary, and dismissal from their posts sought consular help in obtaining redress of their grievances, and were frequently successful.[74] Because of consular support, European officials acquired a privileged status not available to any other group of state employees. When Sa'id decided to withhold payment of government salaries for three months, European officials were explicitly excluded from his order. After an English engineer was flogged by his Egyptian superior for disobeying a command, the latter was dismissed while the Englishman received one year's salary in compensation as well as a paid leave of absence. In 1857, British engine drivers went on strike to obtain a settlement of their claim to salary arrears, an action which non-European employees could not possibly have taken. As director of communications under Sa'id, Lee Green hired additional personnel, fixed their salaries, and renewed contracts without informing the viceroy. But this should not have been very surprising, since many Englishmen were employed in the Egyptian communications administration, and British influence was correspondingly great. As Hekekyan had once observed, Egyptian communications was one of the first steps in the subjugation of the country.

The most important consular allies, though, were officials from within the elite itself, some of whom possessed long-standing ties with Europe. They relied upon consular assistance in their fights for power and influence, and used their positions to advance the policies of European states. Artin Bey, who had been appointed by Muhammad Ali as his representative in negotiations with Britain on a transit agreement, reportedly induced the viceroy to make concessions favorable to Britain, while Nubar Pasha is said to have helped convince Abbas to authorize the construction of the Cairo-Alexandria railway, a project favorable to British interests.[75] Some officials became stereotyped by the consuls as "friendly" or "hostile." Adham Bey, for example, was regarded by the British as a "trustworthy" supporter; Abd al-Rahman Bey was a "Christian at heart," because of the presumed influence of his European wife; Artin Bey (who joined the French side after having helped Britain obtain the transit agreement of 1844) was a "cunning" Armenian grafted onto French stock.[76] The French, on the other hand, never trusted Nubar, because they were convinced that he was a British agent.

The word "agent," however, is highly misleading, since these officials were totally dependent upon viceregal power and were merely taking advantage of a situation in which consular intervention could in certain instances result in an appointment or promotion or, conversely, block an official's advancement. Objections by British Consul General Bruce to Artin's appointment as president of the mixed tribunal of Alexandria caused Sa'id to withdraw the nomination; Stephen Bey was dismissed as director of foreign affairs because of consular pressure.[77] As noted earlier, British consular influence was especially strong in Egyptian communications. Backed by Consul General Barnett, Hekekyan was given control of the transit administration by Muhammad Ali.[78] Nubar's appointment by Sa'id to direct the Department of Communications and Railway received the full support of the British consul. In 1864, a "friend" of Britain (Abd al-Rahman Pasha) was named director of the railway administration. In their contests for power and influence officials had to tread warily, ever mindful of where real power lay. Hekekyan and Nubar both were removed from their posts for having favored British interests.

The ultimate form of consular support was to make an official a protégé or to grant him outright European citizenship. Rumors abounded as to which men held this highly coveted status. Was Nubar a Prussian protégé? Did Muhammad Sharif have French protection? According to the British consul general, Artin Bey possessed naturalization papers enabling him to claim protection as a French subject. On this matter, it is often difficult to separate fact from fiction; however, this form of protection did exist, and high-ranking officials could and did request it.[79]

The emergence of officials favorably disposed toward Europe was a momentous development; but the full impact of this change was not to be felt until after European intervention had weakened the position of the viceroy. It must also be noted that only a small number of officials sought and received consular patronage and that their lives and careers were influenced far more by viceregal power and caprice than by consular influence. Nonetheless, the seeds of collaboration were being sown, and Europe was establishing a base of support at the highest level of the Egyptian state administration.

The second outside interest to emerge among state bureaucrats had equally disturbing political implications. Some high-ranking officials had strong ties with the people of the villages, districts, and provinces. Such an interest, as we have seen, had not existed among high office-holders in Muhammad Ali's time. By the 1860s, however, a new kind of "family" influence had appeared, represented by high-ranking Egyptian provincial officials whose social loyalties and personal allegiances were more local than viceregal.

Power and influence in the countryside were based not only upon owning a landed estate but also to a great degree on who you were, where you served, and how you managed your estate. Most officials in the central administration either rented their lands to persons who subleased them to small cultivators or, more commonly, transferred the administration of their properties to other officials, supervising their work from time to time or merely inspecting the yearly accounts.[80] Egyptian technicians like Ali Mubarak possessed the advantage of having families in the provinces who could manage their estates, but since their holdings were not large, and they were too busy to spend much time in the provinces, Egyptian technicians were unable to translate landholding into social power.

The officials most capable of developing a power base were those who worked in the provinces, and it is here that Egyptian officeholders held an advantage over all other groups. To be sure, Turkish provincial officials owned large amounts of land, had relatively easy access to their estates, and could develop connections with merchants and other leading groups, but as Turks, they were resented by the native population and, lacking a social base, could have no real power. Such was not true of Egypt's notable officials, whose families were the leaders of rural society. Power centers developed around these native officials, who by means of long service in the high administration had acquired great wealth and influence in their home areas. Some became veritable magnates, with influence extending far beyond their own villages and districts. Muhammad Sultan Pasha, born in the district of Samallut in al-Minya province, and owner of thousands of *faddans*, was known as the "king" of upper Egypt. So great was his influence that in 1882, at the height of the Urabi Revolt, one word from him was sufficient to create unrest in upper Egypt against the Urabists, even though Sultan himself was miles away in Alexandria.[81]

These men established a powerful hold over the land and people of a region by manipulating high office so as to strengthen and broaden preexisting local influence deriving from their positions as the *ayan* or leaders of the countryside. For years their families had monopolized the powerful office of *shaykh al-balad*.[82] Muhammad Sultan, for example, hailed from a family well established in the district of Qulusna (later Samallut) where Sultan was *shaykh al-balad* before entering the provincial administration. The Shawaribi family, descendants of the Bedouins, had for centuries lived in Qalyub, where they held local offices. The Abazas, among the wealthiest of *ayan* families, were *shaykhs al-balad* of Arab descent in the province of al-Sharqiya. The Shari'is were a family of village *shaykhs* in al-Minya who claimed descent from the Hawara Bedouin tribe. *Shaykhs al-balad* discharged a variety of functions and enjoyed certain privileges. By the time of

Khedive Ismail's reign, they were not only responsible for the supervision of *ghafir*s (night watchmen) and the recruitment of labor for public works and the military, but also were serving as tax collectors, land classifiers, and tax assessors.[83] They were the linchpins of the rural security and tax system.

It was from the *shaykhly* families that Egypt's viceroys had made appointments to the provincial administration. Once a former *shaykh al-balad* entered the provincial hierarchy, he used the advantages of office to strengthen his local connections. Interestingly, however varied his high positions, throughout his career a notable usually remained close to his home base, which became the center of his growing power and influence.

Three factors made this possible. Notables' earliest assignments were almost always to places in their native provinces. Many began their rise in the provincial hierarchy as *nazir*s and *hakim*s of districts in which their own villages were located. If a notable became governor, it was quite often of a province located near his own, and it was not unusual to be appointed governor or to assume some other high position in one's own province (see table 12).[84] Occasionally, a high-ranking native official received his own village as an *uhda*.[85] Rare indeed was the notable sent to govern a province in a part of Egypt far from his home.

Short tenures, frequent dismissals, and early recalls subjected many notables to periods of unemployment. They often spent these intervals in their home districts where they tended their estates or even resumed their former position of *shaykh al-balad* while awaiting recall to high office.[86]

Of course, high-ranking Egyptian notable officials were sometimes posted to Cairo (scores of them came from the provinces to serve in the Consultative Chamber of Delegates, though technically this was not regarded as government employment). The responsibilities of provincial officials required frequent visits to Cairo, where they took care to establish or renew strategic contacts with high officials in the central administration. Though many notables acquired property in Cairo, few moved there permanently, and their stays in the city were usually brief. During their absence from "home," their interests were cared for by family members, some of whom held positions at the lower level of the provincial hierarchy (for example, as district chiefs).[87]

It was only natural that notable officials' home areas became centers for building up large landed estates. Native provincial officials held an advantage over everyone else, save the ruler himself, because land was acquired not only legitimately, through gifts from the ruler or by purchase, but also through coercion. As one Mr. Harris correctly

pointed out in a report on the provinces in 1856, because of their intimate acquaintance with the possessions and resources of everyone in
their districts, notables who became provincial administrators tended
to get the best lands.[88] Village *shaykhs* may have become wealthy
owing to their growing importance, but the wealthiest "locals" of all
were those in the provincial hierarchy.

The concentration of estates in officials' home provinces is easy to
document. Of the 1,902 *faddans* entered in the *Dhawat* Land Register for Sultan Pasha, 1,019 *faddans* were located in al-Minya. Sultan
Pasha's entire endowment (*waqfiya*) of 4,400 *faddans* was also located
in al-Minya, including 965 *faddans* in a village named after him.[89] Similarly, Ali Badrawi is registered in the *Dhawat* Land Register as holding 519 *faddans*, of which 371 were in his home province of al-Gharbiya.
Mubarak credits him with owning 4,000 *faddans* at the time of his
death, much of it in Samannud, his native village.[90]

These large estates had a sociopolitical significance not yet fully appreciated by students of modern Egyptian history. Estates were not
just a resource base from which notable patrons rewarded clients or
promoted friends. They also enabled them to create and maintain
spheres of personal influence in a district or even a province. These
massive estates employed large full-time staffs which included field
inspectors, veterinarians, engineers, stable managers, night watchmen, and menials. In 1885, for example, 493 persons staffed four estates belonging to Muhammad Sultan Pasha. Estates also contained
one or more hamlets (*izbas*) where numerous field hands lived: 2,608
persons lived in five hamlets on two estates of Shari'i Pasha.[91] The
typical estate might also contain a mosque and a primary school (*maktab*). During the Muslim holy days, its kitchen was opened to feed the
poor and needy from the neighboring countryside. Local persons also
found temporary employment on the estate as surveyors or extra
hands during the annual Nile flood. Merchants and artisans relied
upon the estate as a market for their goods. In short, people from far
and near were drawn into a dependence upon the facilities and services of a large estate. In founding mosques, *madrasas*, and *maktabs*,
and endowing buildings in neighboring villages, landowners helped
support the communal infrastructure of an entire district.[92] In this
way, a "public" obliged to a patron was built up within a province.

The potent combination of high office and a command over land and
people in the countryside made it possible for some notables to play a
double role as representatives of an exploitative government, and as
spokesmen for local interests. High-ranking Egyptian officials un-
abashedly used their offices for their own enrichment, placed allies in
key administrative posts, and rapidly built up family factions. In 1871,

a British subject named Thompson brought to the British consul general's attention a claim that he had made against the departmental head (ma'mur) of Mit Ghamr, who had closed down his steam mill. This local official belonged to a faction headed by his father, Hilal Bey, the former governor of al-Daqahliya and a man of considerable wealth and influence in lower Egypt. One of his other sons was governor of al-Mansura province. Hilal himself was governor of Tanta, and also had friends high in the central administration, one of whom was Nubar Pasha. Hilal had rejected a compromise proposal offered by Nubar, and Thompson feared with good reason that Hilal's allies would protect Hilal's son by refusing to act on the Englishman's claim. The claim was eventually dropped when his consul general refused to support it.[93]

Provincial magnates did not always act from motives of pure self-interest. Being part of their local communities, they could and did act on behalf of the "people." They could protect fallahin from usurious moneylenders by advancing them money from their own pockets, block the implementation of an order harmful to the community, plead the local case for a tax reduction, or in other ways represent the people of a village or district in their dealings with the authorities.[94] If they took more than they gave, they were at least not unremitting tyrants.

The dynamics of the process by which Egypt's notables played this double role must be clearly understood, for this leads to an important point about politics in Egypt. As holders of the highest state ranks with all of the benefits thereof, men like Muhammad Sultan, Sulayman Abaza, Muhammad Shawaribi and their families were an integral part of Egypt's political/administrative elite. Yet they were also leaders of a village notability, estimated at 20,000 families in the mid-1850s, which was coming under tremendous pressure from the officials of the central administration.[95] Village shaykhs were regularly beaten and imprisoned for collecting too little in taxes, and the peasants were subjected to even greater oppression.[96] As supporters of the viceroy and agents of his government, dhawat notables had a strong interest in defending the status quo and preserving the unequal distribution of power, because they were among its chief beneficiaries. But they also represented an elite, Egypt's rural shaykhs, whose interests did not coincide with those of the khedive and the government in Cairo. This dichotomous position gave high-ranking Egyptian provincial officials a heightened importance, but it also presented them with a challenge since they could continue to represent society only by maintaining "access," that is, keeping their government positions.

The need for access and the continued strength of the center (that is, the ruler) explains the absence of any politics other than local. Power in the provinces could not be projected into a national politics without the invitation or tacit consent of the ruler, who was too strong and too jealous of any other power centers to allow Egypt's *dhawat* notables much influence. These new intermediaries, therefore, were unable to achieve the autonomy or the power necessary to become political brokers in the classic sense. Between 1849 and 1874, their interests remained more or less confined to their localities.

This chapter has argued that ethnic and cultural factors were primary in the formation of Egypt's bureaucratic elite. We have demonstrated that landholding and an interest in reform provided a bridge across ethnic divisions without, however, leading to the transformation of the elite as a whole. More important, we have shown how the rise of Egyptian notables and reformers within the administration led to the appearance of outside interests at the highest levels of government; yet the divergence of interest between the ruler and his men did not erupt into a major conflict. Politics continued to be dominated by cliques and factions, and the primary objective of high officeholders was the acquisition of wealth. The 1849–1874 period may therefore be regarded as a time of preparation, when cooperation with the viceroy made sense, but when Egypt's growing economic and political dependence upon Europe was leading inexorably to an explosion that would break the bonds of cooperation.

Before turning our attention to the next period (1875–1879), we must first consider the lives and careers of a handful of important officials who played a key role both in the maintenance of viceregal power before 1874 and in its subsequent breakup and who illustrate the variety of interests represented in Egypt's higher administration.

▲ 6 ▲
EGYPT'S OFFICIALS AND
THEIR INTERESTS

In contemporary accounts of our period, Ali Mubarak, Muhammad Sultan, Ismail Siddiq, Muhammad Sharif, Mustafa Riyad, and Nubar Pasha were virtual household names. The careers of these men illustrate the variety of background, education, and influence among Egypt's high officials, and also their common interests, particularly in land and reform. Ali Mubarak, the father of education in modern Egypt, typifies the Egyptian reformer and nationalist who remained relatively poor throughout his life. The career of Muhammad Sultan, on the other hand, illustrates the process by which native officials, through contacts with the capital and influence in the provinces, became veritable magnates. The life of Ismail Siddiq demonstrates the value of a close personal relationship with the ruler. Muhammad Sharif, the self-proclaimed father of constitutionalism in Egypt, exemplifies the superficially Westernized Turkish loyalist. Mustafa Riyad, three times president of the Council of Ministers, was a conservative Muslim who willingly collaborated with Europe. The career of Nubar Pasha, Egypt's statesman par excellence, shows how far the European "connection" could carry an official. As we shall see later, each of these six men in different ways was destined to play a key role in developments after 1874.

▲▲▲ ALI MUBARAK

In a career that lasted more than thirty-five years and spanned the reigns of four viceroys, Ali Mubarak (1823/24–1893) is regarded by Egyptians today as one of the most prominent Egyptian figures of modern times. (See table 11.) Mubarak was an administrator of the first order, one of the best Egyptian engineers of the nineteenth century. He was also representative of a new type of official: the Egyptian-born technician with a scientific education. Mubarak held a unique distinction among members of this elite, being the first Egyptian Muslim to be appointed director of a government department in modern times. Yet this distinction was not without disadvantages. Perhaps because he was the first native Egyptian to attain "ministerial" rank in an administration dominated by Turks, Mubarak's career reveals an instability remarkable even for mid-nineteenth-century Egypt. There were far more abrupt twists and turns in his official life than in the careers of the five other officials to be examined here. Of course, they shared with Mubarak a common pattern of promotion and demotion, even of dismissal, but none of them experienced the rapid rises and sharp plunges characteristic of Murbarak's checkered career. Deeply imprinted upon his psyche, such vicissitudes cannot have failed to influence his behavior profoundly.

Another major question raised by Mubarak's official life is political in nature. Ali Mubarak is remembered for his participation in the ministry of 1878–1879 which, as we shall see in the next chapter, dispossessed Khedive Ismail of his power and administered Egypt on behalf of European interests. For decades, Mubarak had been a loyal servant of the viceroys, whose reforms he had enthusiastically supported and helped implement. Why should he have been willing to join a ministry bent upon destroying viceregal power and dismantling the political system in which he had been raised? The answers to these questions can be found by examining his early life, his experiences in government, and his attitudes toward Egypt, Europe, and reform.

Described in his later years as a tall, thin, darkskinned old man with grizzled hair, patent leather boots, and independent if outmoded ideas, the aged Mubarak must have felt the quiet satisfaction of having surpassed the wildest expectations of his youth.[1] At a time when he himself thought that only Turks could be rulers, he had dreamed boldly of a government career, but even then could hardly have anticipated the heights to which he would soar.[2] Of course, he was fortunate to be living in a time when more opportunities were becoming available to Egyptians; but then, too, Mubarak possessed remarkable qualities: a shrewd and resourceful intellect, a capacity for hard work, a stubborn pride and determination, and a willingness to make great sacrifices and take risks—important ingredients in his future success.

Born in the village of Birinbal al-Jadida (al-Daqahliya province), Ali Mubarak came from the *shaykhly* nobility of the countryside.[3] Known as the "family of *shaykhs*," the Mubaraks had for generations held positions as prayer leader (*imam*), preacher (*khatib*), and judge (*qadi*), and performed nonreligious duties as well. They regarded themselves as superior to the *fallahin* by virtue of such privileges as a tax-free grant of land and the respect they enjoyed. So great was

ALI MUBARAK PASHA (1823/24–1893)
From Sami, *Taqwim al-Nil*, pt. 3, vol. 2, facing p. 920.

their pride that when, during Muhammad Ali's reign, government officials under pressure to obtain taxes began treating them like common
fallahin, beating and imprisoning them, this family, unaccustomed to
such insults and destitute, fled their ancestral home. Not until Ali
Mubarak's father found a village which treated him with proper respect did he settle down. Pride in a noble pedigree remained an important part of Mubarak's character throughout his life.

According to his autobiography, Mubarak was no more than eight
years old when he began to aspire to a life of wealth, power, and status
unobtainable in the village. He first wanted to be a scribe (*katib*) because scribes wore fine clothes, enjoyed great respect, and were close
to the government officials. But after serving *katib*s who only cursed,
beat, cheated, and imprisoned him, he abandoned this ambition when
he learned of the preparatory school at Qasr al-Ayni, from which officials were chosen. Because he believed the post of scribe too lowly,
exposed, and dangerous, he resolved to enter government service
where presumably he would find more security.

Determined to enter this new school at any price, Mubarak found
out its location and, on the pretext of visiting his family, took a leave
from his employer and struck out in its direction. When he happened
upon a group of students from a nearby government primary school
(*maktab*) who praised his handwriting and said that one could enter
the school at Qasr al-Ayni without a patron by excelling in a government *maktab*, he immediately enrolled himself in their school. But by a
ruse his father and the school director had him removed and returned
to his home where he was locked in his room for ten days and had to
promise to renounce his ambition. Yet no sooner had his family relaxed
their vigilance than Mubarak was gone again. Having sneaked back
into the school without the director's knowledge, the young Ali resolved not to leave by night or day. The time finally came when he was
chosen by the director of *maktab al-khanka* (the school of princes) to
enter the preparatory school. When his father pleaded against this,
the school director gave Mubarak his choice, and he bravely chose a
government education in Cairo over the wishes of his family to stay in
the village.

After a few initial disappointments at Qasr al-Ayni, Mubarak began
receiving excellent grades and soon was selected to enter a technical
training school in Cairo, the Polytechnique or School of Engineering,
where he rose to the top of his class. About that time (1844), the viceroy decided to send a large student mission to Paris, one which included his sons, Husayn and Abd al-Halim, and two of his grandsons,
Ahmad and Ismail, the future khedive. Mubarak was invited to par-

ticipate. Despite the importunings of his French friend Sulayman Pasha to remain at the Polytechnique where he had an assured rank and salary, he decided to go because he realized that to travel to Europe with the relatives of Muhammad Ali would bring him honor, high rank, and knowledge.[4] In the most important decision of his young life, Mubarak was right. Those who went on this mission were destined for fame as future leaders: of the eighty members of the group whose biographies are recorded by Umar Tussun, fifty-four became beys and pashas.[5] Friendships and personal contacts were made that lasted a lifetime, and Mubarak was exposed to a new, powerful, and dynamic civilization which he came to admire.

Once in Paris, Mubarak had obstacles to overcome. Coming from the Cairo Polytechnique, he had not been trained in the military sciences (education at the Paris school was military in character); nor had he learned French, the language of instruction. Consequently, he and others were at first unsuccessful in their work; when their request for special language training was refused, they boycotted classes. Locked up for their trouble, they were ordered to obey the authorities or return to Egypt. Mubarak surmounted his problem with characteristic ingenuity. He purchased a number of French books covering a wide range of subjects and, while others slept, taught himself French. His grades quickly improved. After two years, he and his two lifelong Egyptian friends, Ali Ibrahim and Hammad Abd al-Ati (also graduates of the Cairo Polytechnique) stood at the head of their class.

The reports sent to Cairo by Mubarak's French instructors are enlightening. Mubarak was regarded as proud and stubborn, a discipline problem, someone needing careful supervision and sometimes severe punishment. But his intelligence, industry, and "logical" mind earned their admiration and won him excellent grades.[6] At the examination given after two years, Mubarak received a very high grade and won congratulations from Ibrahim Pasha and a group of French notables who examined him. After this, he and his two Egyptian colleagues were transferred to the Metz school for artillery officers and military engineers. There, sitting in classes with Frenchmen, the Egyptians surpassed many of them. In a class of 1,205 students, Mubarak ranked 697.[7] He then went into the field with the French army and served one year before being recalled to Egypt in 1849 by Abbas.

Within a year after his return, Ali Mubarak had risen from the lowly position of instructor at the artillery school (where he had been assigned shortly after his return) to director of the government schools with the title of bey. This was not only a rapid advance; it was remarkable that this promotion was granted to an Egyptian. How this happened testifies to the importance of personal connections and, more specifically, to Mubarak's adaptability and skills. (Table 18 lists the major positions held by Mubarak during his career.)

To gain the ruler's attention almost always required the mediation of a relative or friend. According to Mubarak, it was Prince Ahmad who intervened on his behalf with the ruler.[8] Mubarak was summoned by Abbas, interviewed, promoted to fifth rank, appointed to the viceroy's entourage, and taken (along with Ali Ibrahim and Hammad) into the provinces to examine engineers suspected of incompetence. Mubarak's reaction to this summons is revealing about the attitudes held by officials toward the ruling family. The good news came as he was sipping coffee in Alexandria with the two Frenchmen, Galice Bey and Sulayman Pasha. Abbas was peremptory: he ordered Mubarak to join him at once on his steamboat. Fearing the dangers that others had encountered in their dealings with the viceregal family, and with his own family members waiting for him in a boat nearby, Mubarak hesitated. Only after Sulayman Pasha had promised to look after his family did he agree to join Abbas. Imagine how much more fearful he must have been when Abbas warned him that if he acted dishonestly in his service he would be dismissed, stripped of his wealth, and forced to dress as a common *fallah*!

After successfully discharging his assignment in the provinces, Mubarak was able to make himself useful to a viceroy interested in reducing administrative expenditures. After Mubarak had discovered a means of facilitating boat passage through the barrages at far less expense than the plan submitted by Mougel Bey (the viceroy's chief engineer), Abbas began consulting him on many matters.[9] Abbas commissioned Mubarak and his two Egyptian colleagues (Ali Ibrahim and Hammad) to draft a plan for the schools which would be less expensive than that of Lambert Bey (a French official). When the three failed to agree upon a program, Mubarak drew up one of his own with a price tag of £E 5,000, considerably less than £E 100,000 attached to Lambert's scheme. Delighted and relieved, Abbas eagerly embraced Mubarak's program, submitting it to the Privy Council where it was adopted after an eight-day debate. Following its adoption, Abbas asked Mubarak to recommend someone to implement it, and the young man indirectly suggested himself as best qualified. In May 1850, Mubarak was made director of the government's primary schools, the Cairo Polytechnique, and the preparatory school. He had become director of education in fact if not in name.

But Mubarak did not keep what he had gained. Shortly after the accession of Sa'id in July 1854, Mubarak was stripped of his functions and thrown out of government service, like many other officials closely

TABLE 18
MAJOR POSITIONS HELD BY ALI MUBARAK PASHA

Under Abbas and Sa'id
Teacher, Cairo Artillery School (1849)
Member of traveling entourage of Abbas (1850)
Director of government primary and preparatory schools and Cairo
Polytechnique (May 1950)
Officer in the Crimea (1854)
Assistant, Office of Legal Affairs, Department of War
Deputy director, Council of Commerce
Engineering inspector in upper Egypt
Director of teaching staff for officers in training

Under Ismail
Director of the school of al-*Mubtadiyan*
Supervisor of the barrages (1863)
Head, Office of Engineering (Dec. 1864)
Director of the barrages (July 1866)
Deputy director, Department of Education (Sept. 1867, removed Sept. 1870)
Director, Departments of Education and Public Works (Apr. 1868)
Director, Department of Communications and Railway (Oct. 1868)
Director, Department of Charitable Endowments (Jan. 1869)
Director, Department of Public Works (Aug. 1869, removed Sept. 1870)
Director, Department of Railway (Aug. 1869, removed Sept. 1870)
Director, Department of Education (Jan. 1870)
Director, Departments of Education and Charitable Endowments (May 1871)
Director, Department of Public Works (June 1871, removed Aug. 1872)
Director, Departments of Education and Charitable Endowments (May 1872,
removed Aug. 1872)
Adviser, Department of Charitable Endowments (1872)
Deputy director, Department of Public Works (July or August 1873)
Member, Privy Council (Oct. 1873, dismissed Mar. 1874)
Head, Office of Engineering (Mar. 1875)
Adviser, Department of Public Works (Oct. 1875)
Director, Department of Education (Aug. 1878)

After Ismail
Director, Department of Public Works (Sept. 1879, Aug. 1882)
Director, Department of Education (June 1888)
Pensioned (1891)

Sources: Mubarak, *al-Khitat*, vol. 9, pp. 43–61; Heyworth-Dunne, *History of Education*, p. 347; Sami, pt. 3, vol. 2, pp. 779, 871, 1015; *al-Abhath*, box 52, dossier "Mawdu'
al-Ta'lim," *Wakil Diwan al-Madaris/Bashmu'awin* 21 D 1279/10 May 1863, and box 53,
dossier "Mawdu' al-Ta'lim," *al-Madaris*/Shafiq Bey, 14 B 1266/26 May 1850; *Mas,
Awamir, Ma'iya Saniya-Arabi*, reg. 1911/80/2, Viceroy/*al-Ashghal*, 28 B 1281/27 Dec.
1864; reg. 1935/137/123, Viceroy/*al-Dakhiliya*, 1 M 1288/23 Mar. 1871; reg. 1935/163/142,
Viceroy/*al-Dakhiliya*, 22 S 1288/13 May 1871; reg. 1936/21/40, Viceroy/Bahjat Pasha, 11
RT 1288/30 June 1871; reg. 1939/160/135, Viceroy/*al-Majlis al-Khususi*, 14 R 1289/22 May
1872; *Mas, Awamir, Ma'iya Saniya-Turki*, reg. 557/110/93 Viceroy/*al-Jihadiya* 20 S
1283/4 July 1866; reg. 573/21/1, Viceroy/*al-Madaris*, 13 J 1284/12 Sept. 1867; *WMC*, box
19, "al-Masalih," no. 239, 26 JA 1285/14 Oct. 1868; no. 267, 12 L 1285/26 Jan. 1869; box 21,
"Muwazzafun," no. 317, 27 RT 1286/6 Aug. 1869; no. 320, 18 J 1286/26 Aug. 1869; no. 528,
15 SH 1290/7 Oct. 1873; *WM*, no. 432, 2 N 1288/15 Nov. 1871; Darwish, *al-Wizarat
al-Misriya*, pt. 1.

associated with Abbas. Without protection and heavily in debt, Mubarak descended into the deepest and longest slump of his career.[10] Soon after his dismissal, he was inducted into the army and sent to the Crimea. With a portion of his salary being set aside to pay his debts, Mubarak made ends meet by finding odd jobs. First assigned to Istanbul, Mubarak was then appointed liaison officer in the Crimea and later became a transport officer in Anatolia. Returning to Egypt after an absence of two and a half years, Mubarak was again dismissed from the service. With barely enough money to survive and sharing a rented house with his half-brother, wealth, high rank and position gone, Mubarak slipped into melancholy and despair. He was no better off than when he had returned from Europe seven years before. Why, he asked himself, had he ever decided to become a government official? Miserable, Mubarak resolved to leave Cairo forever and return to his village to till the soil. But just as he was about to leave, Mubarak was ordered to report for reinduction into military service. Thus compelled, Mubarak was given a succession of low-ranking positions and assignments, none of which lasted very long. He worked in the office of legal affairs in the War Department, drew up plans for military lighthouses, and served as deputy director of the Council of Commerce for two months before being removed because of the intrigues of his Armenian predecessor, who maligned him to Sa'id.[11] At some point, though, Sa'id assigned Mubarak a salary as a member of his entourage and loaned him 100,000 piastres. Still, Mubarak continued to receive lowly assignments and remained in a financial straitjacket. In 1861, he was asked to repay his debt (28,000 piastres were outstanding), but replied that he did not have any cash.[12] Upon learning of this, Sa'id assigned him to examine a damaged bridge and ordered that half of his monthly salary be deducted for the repayment of the loan. This assignment, too, was short-lived, and Mubarak was again dismissed from service. But thanks to the assistance of a friend (Ismail Pasha al-Fariq, a Turkish officer) he was able to buy government property auctioned at bargain prices and to enter (along with some other dismissed engineers) the contract building business.[13]

With Ismail's accession in January 1863, Ali Mubarak's career assumed a somewhat different rhythm. In contrast to his meteoric rise in 1850, Mubarak moved slowly upward in Ismail's administration for over half a decade until he received an appointment as director of education and public works in April 1868. Thus began a four-year period of appointments which brought him to the height of his career, but which was marred by humiliating dismissals arising (at least in part) from a dispute with Ismail Siddiq. In 1872, Mubarak's "golden years" came to an end when he lost the directorship of Public Works and Education to Prince Husayn Kamil.

Khedive Ismail had known Mubarak when the two were fellow students in Paris, but it is doubtful that Mubarak's reemergence can be attributed to this association. By 1863, Mubarak was well known as a skilled engineer, a dedicated educator, and a good administrator who appreciated the value of economy. Indeed, Mubarak was made head of Public Works in 1869 for the explicit purpose of cutting expenditures in that department.[14] Mubarak's skills happily coincided with those required by a ruler bent on reform.

These years gave full scope to the wide range of Mubarak's extraordinary talents. His assignments, described with great enthusiasm in his autobiography, were diverse and demanding, yet always he seems to have risen to the challenge.[15] His tasks ranged from supervision of the Nile barrages, to inspection of the government schools, to participation on a commission investigating lands belonging to the Suez Canal Company, to the discharge of a special mission to Paris. Spending forty days in the French capital, Mubarak visited the schools, studied the latest publications on education, and inspected the city's sewer system for his master, who was planning to build a new Cairo à la Haussmann.

In order to direct Ismail's program of educational reform and superintend the construction of new Cairo, Mubarak was appointed director of public works and education on April 15, 1868. The following October, he was made director of railway and communications. For the greater part of the next four years, Mubarak was concurrently in charge of Education, Public Works, and Charitable Endowments—the first native Muslim in modern times to have enjoyed such a concentration of power.

Ascertaining the course of Mubarak's career during these hectic years is made difficult by omissions and apparent errors in his autobiographical account. Materials from the archives and from Amin Sami, however, help to sort out the complex and shifting pattern of appointments and dismissals that marked his official life during this time. All accounts agree upon the date of his first "ministerial" appointment, but differ as to the duration. Mubarak writes that he did not lose these posts until the end of 1871, but the archives and Sami reveal that he was temporarily removed from Public Works and Education in January 1869, and from the Railway Department the following July (Public Works and Railway were returned to him in 1869, and Education in January, 1870).[16] Nor does Mubarak mention his removal from Public Works, Education, and Railway in September, 1870 (he was reappointed to Education and Public Works the following May and June). But he does write of a dismissal that occurred in November or December 1871, for which there is no corroborative evidence. According to Mubarak, this resulted from a dispute with Ismail Siddiq, who wanted to bring the railway revenues under his administration. Mubarak asserts that he was willing to agree to this transfer, but insisted that Ismail Siddiq also assume responsibility for railway expenditures. This caused the latter to intrigue against Mubarak and resulted in his dismissal.[17] Mubarak remained in his home for two months and was then placed in charge of the government primary schools. In May 1872, he was made head of Education and Charitable Endowments (Mubarak writes that he was also given Public Works), but held these posts only until August when these three administrations were transferred to Prince Husayn Kamil, who retained Mubarak as his adviser. After this, Mubarak continued to serve in various capacities, but not at a "ministerial" level. He suffered another galling dismissal in March 1874, when Siddiq persuaded the viceroy that a book Mubarak was writing contained criticism of his government.[18] Apparently, the years that marked the height of Mubarak's career were not so golden as his own account has made them out to be.

The reason for Mubarak's dismissals and plunges into debt can be found in his lack of protection—that is, the absence of a social or economic base strong enough to sustain him in and out of office. Mubarak had no large estates to retire to when out of favor, and few influential friends to intervene on his behalf. Unhappily, he also had one powerful enemy—Ismail Siddiq. If this were not enough, Mubarak's unabashed effort to acquire protection became a principal source of his indebtedness. Such extreme vulnerability made him all the more eager to hold office, for this was his only resource.

At first sight, it may seem strange that a native from Egypt's *shaykh*ly elite had no significant base of support in the countryside. Although he owned a small estate in his village, Mubarak had only tenuous links with his family in Birinbal al-Jadida. According to his autobiography, the mid-1830s was the last occasion that he spent any length of time with them. When he retired from government service, Mubarak had been away from his village for thirty years.[19] This may be attributed mostly to the nature of his work, but also to rules that restricted freedom of movement of officials. By contrast with those *shaykh*s in the provincial administration who built up strong rural ties, Mubarak was a central administration official who spent much of his time in Cairo and on specific, short-term assignments in the provinces. As he explained it, the demands of his work were simply too great for him to return to his village. Furthermore, Egypt's administrative system was designed to create a dependence upon the ruler and to weaken all other ties. From the moment Mubarak entered the government school system, it became hard for him to move about freely. Leaves of absence were very difficult to obtain and involved partial losses of salary. In 1849, Mubarak managed to visit his family without official approval, circumventing the law when some friends gave him an assignment not far from his village. At that time, he had not seen his mother in fourteen years.

During Abbas's reign, Mubarak attempted to acquire influence and protection by marrying an orphaned Turkish woman who possessed money and land, and whose guardians had connections with the viceregal household.[20] (This was a second marriage; his first wife, the daughter of his former drawing teacher, had died.) The prospect of sharing his wife's fortune and having contacts with highly placed Turks apparently overrode the consideration that his new wife was a simple-minded and childish woman who could not even manage her own affairs.

Unfortunately, Mubarak's marriage did not meet with approval from his wife's guardians, Raghib *afandi* and his wife. Fearing that Mubarak coveted his wife's wealth (they wanted to have it for themselves), these two made an intrigue at the court, won over the queen mother and Hasan al-Munastarli (who was, under Abbas, the most powerful official in Egypt), carried off their ward, and stirred up the palace guards against Mubarak, who began to fear for his life. After the queen mother learned of their deception, however, Mubarak's wife was returned to him. But matters did not stop there. When Mubarak was out of Cairo, her guardians legally dispossessed her of her wealth. Only after Mubarak had submitted a petition to Abbas, followed it through tortuous legal and administrative channels, and withstood intrigues from high-ranking Turks (Mubarak feared that Hasan al-Munastarli would have him banished to the Sudan) was his wife's property returned to her. When these intrigues continued into Sa'id's reign, Mubarak annulled the marriage. He was awarded 25,000 piastres in cash as well as 600 purses, which he had spent in building a house for her, and he left his wife with the house and its furnishings, including the slaves he owned. Toward the end of Sa'id's reign, Mubarak remarried once again, purchased a house in Darb al-Jamamiz (a district in the Ismailiya quarter) and began building onto it. The heavy expenditures incurred as a result of his third marriage, he writes, helped lead him into debt again.[21]

For Mubarak, high office was both bane and boon: bane, because as officeholder he felt compelled to undertake unwise expenditures in order to live at a level commensurate with his position; boon, because high office was the avenue to influence and wealth.[22] Mubarak's influence was expressed chiefly in his patronage of native technicians. During Abbas's reign, he enrolled Egyptians in the schools and helped send them on missions to Europe.[23] Under Ismail, he brought Egyptian friends and colleagues into his departments where they worked to promote reforms. Mubarak's requests for appointments and promotions were usually approved by Ismail, though on one occasion the viceroy refused a request that Ismail al-Falaki be appointed director of both the observatory at Shubra and the Cairo Polytechnique, arguing that the concentration of these two posts in one person would hamper their administration (Ismail al-Falaki received the observatory).[24] Another of Mubarak's favorites was Salih Majdi Bey, a graduate of the School of Languages and the Cairo Polytechnique.[25] Under Ismail, the two wrote articles for the journal of education, *Rawdat al-Madaris*, and collaborated in publishing books for the government schools. Mubarak presumably instigated Salih's promotion to an office in the Education Department, and after that to the position of deputy director of education, directly under Mubarak. When Mubarak left his post in 1870, so did Salih.

There can be little doubt that Mubarak benefited materially from his positions. Described by Bell as a man not disdainful of the emoluments of high office though not personally corrupt, and by Ninet (though a dubious source) as intelligent but greedy, Mubarak did not resist the opportunities for profit available to him.[26] As director of public works, Mubarak probably drew funds from the director's private account containing monies for Nile works and illicitly deducted a portion of his department's expenses. The best opportunities for self-enrichment lay in control of departmental revenue, especially those of the railway, where money could also be made from bribes, fees, and kickbacks for awarding contracts and concessions. Graft in this administration was estimated to have drained off one-fifth of its revenue.[27] Yet, as we have seen, Mubarak did not long remain in control of railway revenue (or even of the railway administration). If his hands were not entirely clean, he certainly was not one of those officials described by Stephen Cave (with considerable exaggeration) as serving a short while and leaving office with a fortune.[28]

One important means to wealth were gifts of cash and land made by the ruler. Mubarak was not entirely deprived of these benefits—in 1870 he received £3,000 as a reward for having increased the railway revenue—but he did not receive these gifts in anything like the number or amount given to many other high officials.[29] As early as 1850, according to the *Dhawat* Land Register, Mubarak had been granted an uncultivated estate of 300 *faddan*s located in two villages close to his home in al-Daqahliya province. Like most lands granted at this time, Mubarak's estate turned out to be a liability. So much money was invested in bringing it under cultivation that it became a cause of his indebtedness.[30] During the 1860s, when many high officials were receiving land grants and building up large and profitable estates, Mubarak seems to have been almost overlooked. Sami reveals one grant of 300 *faddans* made to Mubarak in April 1864.[31] The *Dhawat* Land Register, which does not record the grant noted by Sami, shows only two acquisitions for Mubarak in the 1860s: 64 *faddans* in al-Qalyubiya (21 February 1865), and 9 *faddans* in al-Jiza (25 April 1865). His total holdings (including the grant from Abbas) were a mere 363 *faddans*. As we shall see, this is a pittance compared with the lands held by men like Ismail Siddiq or Muhammad Sharif, but then Mubarak was not one of the most important government officials and he was also an Egyptian. At any rate, with respect to landholdings, Mubarak remained almor⁴ where he had begun in 1850.

The relative lack of socioeconomic strength kept Mubarak insecure and dependent upon the khedive. Although Mubarak needed to hold office because it provided his only real means of existence, it does not necessarily follow that he felt a personal allegiance or responsibility to the khedive. Mubarak was obliged to behave as a loyalist so long as there was no alternative to a strong ruler, but if a political crisis arose that threatened the position of the viceroy, nothing guaranteed that he would stand by his master.

Ali Mubarak was an Egyptian and proud of it. He was not one of those imported from abroad to serve in the viceroy's household. Dependent as he was upon the khedive, Mubarak was fully aware of the differences between the "olive-skinned" Egyptians and the "white and ruddy-faced" Turks.[32] He was a type of official new to Egypt, one with skills and ideas more appropriate to the modern world than to the country's mamluk past. Mubarak was motivated not only by a professional concern, but also by a firm attachment to the people and land of Egypt, with a strong desire to improve their lot. This commitment transcended any loyalty to a ruler or a ruling family.

No one who has read his description of the horrible treatment of *fallahin* taken for the corvée can doubt the depth of Mubarak's feeling and sympathy.[33] His own career provides ample evidence of willing sacrifices that exceeded the requirements of a purely professional commitment. As director of government schools under Abbas, Mubarak showed a concern for his students' welfare unusual for the time. In daily visits he paid attention to nearly every aspect of their work, teaching them how to read and write, even to dress, and making sure their diet was adequate. He also helped reduce the incidence of beatings and other rough treatment customarily meted out to students in the schools.[34] "I looked upon both teachers and students as a father does," he wrote, "and I still believe this to be the duty of every shepherd toward his flock, so that the purpose of education may be achieved." During Sa'id's reign, he willingly undertook an assignment to teach the "three R's" to Egyptian soldiers in the field, visiting them in their tents and sometimes writing the letters on the ground or pavement with charcoal. As his enthusiastic account of his work under Ismail attests, he was willing to go to great lengths to facilitate the education of his compatriots.

This commitment found its justification in a higher purpose, which Mubarak defined as love of country (*hubb al-watan*). Influenced by his European teachers and by his knowledge of the European state system, and perhaps also by the speeches of Egypt's viceroys, including Muhammad Ali, who had once exhorted his officials to love and work for their *watan*,[35] Mubarak used this word to convey the notion of *patrie* or nation in a territorial sense. Whether he fully realized it or not, he was helping to promote a new concept of Egyptian nationhood. As he wrote in the preface to his didactic novel, published in 1882, *Alam al-Din*:

One of the strongest things we feel indebted to and on whose part we, being steeped in its sacred rights, make demands is the great *watan*, in which we are born, on whose ground and under whose skies we live, whose air forever refreshes us, whose water we drink, whose plants and animals nourish us, and which benefits us in all the rest of its components. For at every moment it is enlarging us, benefiting us, giving things to us, and enriching us, just as it has done with our fathers, grandfathers, and ancestors and will likewise do with respect to our sons and grandsons who follow us. We are thus obliged to give it full due as it deserves.[36]

It was love of country, said Mubarak, that motivated his actions and explained his many successes:

I do acknowledge the benefits that my beloved *watan* has conferred upon me; for I was born in its shade, rocked in its cradle, raised in its bosom and care until I became one of its prominent sons and well-known men. I have enjoyed, to great or lesser degree, many of its riches and fruits, and I still enjoy its nice things and it still refreshes me. Even though I have already expended a great share of effort and spent my life in its service, I have not fulfilled one-tenth of the rightful demands it makes of me, and which are incumbent upon me;

. . . because of this, in all the work I have done and all the changes I have been involved in, I have felt an obligation to serve my *watan* with everything I could obtain and with all my power that could be mustered [to do] what I think would more or less benefit it, such as striving to increase the number of *makatib* and *madaris*, bringing to the public learning and culture, publishing helpful books either by composing them myself or by urging others fit for it to do so.³⁷

Every Egyptian, Mubarak told his readers, was obligated to serve his *watan* to the utmost of his ability and in the capacity best suited for him. The best way of serving it and of perceiving its "rightful demands," Mubarak averred, was to acquire a good education, but the *watan* could be served in many other ways too.

If one is an official in a high position among men or [if one] has been entrusted with a job in his village, he must faithfully perform his task and be honest in his work. If he is a merchant, he must act in good faith in his commercial dealings, and if he has an occupation like agriculture or industry he must sacrifice himself for the love of his *watan* by excelling in his trade, even though he be a lowly street sweeper or shoemaker.³⁸

The kind of *watan* Mubarak wanted to see was quite different from the one in which he lived. Egypt, he regretfully acknowledged, had lost the glory that it had attained under the pharaohs and regained for a short while after the Muslim conquest (like other reformers, Mubarak looked to a national past which antedated Islam). He agreed with Europeans who called Egyptians cowards, cheats, liars, and flatterers. But he said this was not their fault; this was the sad result of centuries of domination by foreigners, whose evil actions produced a condition that had altered Egyptian character.³⁹ Just as harmful were superstitions and false beliefs, a point which Mubarak strongly emphasized, for these reflected an insular and tradition-bound society.⁴⁰

What then was the remedy? Egypt could take its place among the world's civilized nations by applying to its needs European science and technology. Because of Mubarak's diverse and prolonged exposure to European culture, he admired the power, wealth, and scientific achievements of the Europeans, whose acquisitive drive he clearly apprehended. An industrious spirit, he believed, had led them to greatness. This spirit was manifestly lacking in Egypt, and Mubarak exhorted his people to acquire the drive and scientific skill that enabled the Europeans to penetrate mountains and dig great canals.⁴¹

Mubarak's cause was no less than the transformation of his country.

Speaking in moral terms, he held that Egyptians had somehow to be taught the necessity of subordinating their private interests to a common good, a belief that underlies Mubarak's persistent efforts (through his writings) to instill the idea of loyalty to an Egyptian *watan*. Regarding Egypt's material condition, three steps had to be taken. Egypt's industry and trade had to be developed to the maximum to bring the country wealth and make it productive. Education had to be rapidly advanced, to change people's attitudes and habits and to teach them the know-how that would make them self-sufficient. Finally, agriculture must be developed to its full potential, with the construction and proper maintenance of a sound irrigation system. Here were the ingredients of Egypt's national development and progress. Here, too, was a standard by which the rulers could be judged. Ali Mubarak may not have been rich or well connected, but this made him no less a patriot.

▲▲▲ MUHAMMAD SULTAN

If Ali Mubarak may be considered representative of Egyptian technicians in the central administration, Muhammad Sultan Pasha (1825–1884) typifies the Egyptian *shaykh* who rose to a new level of power by serving in the provincial administration (see table 12).[42] A natural leader, gifted politician, and widely-acclaimed as "king" of upper Egypt, Sultan had received little formal education and never did learn a European language (for much of his life, he could not even read and write his native Arabic).[43] Yet he enjoyed great wealth, was respected for his influence among the people, and is best known as president of the Consultative Chamber of Delegates during the abortive Urabi rebellion. Perhaps better than any other official of his type, Muhammad Sultan exemplifies how a particular kind of power could be built up and employed. This power derived from combining local wealth and status with service in the provincial administration, a combination that expanded a preexisting base of influence and enabled many provincial notables to play a double role as the government's representatives to the people and vice versa. Association with the new provincial administration, then, was the crucial ingredient. It was as bureaucrats that Egyptian notables became wealthy and powerful. This is how Muhammad Sultan, in 1857 a semiliterate village mayor, could become the pivot of authority in upper Egypt, a man with great influence over the *shaykhs* there, one so powerful that the viceroy felt obliged to transfer his chief engineer out of al-Minya province after he had fallen afoul of Sultan.[44]

Shrewd, intelligent, and eloquent, Muhammad Sultan was known for his frankness, native pride, and overweening ambition.[45] But his greatest initial asset was a position of wealth and status. Though well established in al-Minya, Muhammad Sultan's family was not among its most distinguished residents. Of his father, identified in an archival document as Sultan Agha, little is known. In time, Muhammad Sultan assumed leadership of his family and became *shaykh al-balad* of his village (Zawiyat al-Amwat), where he was able to build up considerable influence and wealth.

The circumstances of his first administrative appointment indicate the extent of his wealth and the importance of his personal connections. As recounted by Fahmi, one of Sultan's friends, Hasan al-Shariʿi (also from a leading family in al-Minya), had done so well as chief of the district of Qulusna (in al-Minya) that Saʿid made him member of a court of appeals.[46] Asked by the viceroy to recommend a successor, Hasan suggested Sultan. When called to Saʿid's palace for a meeting, the young man was asked if he were willing to entertain the viceroy and his entourage in his home (Saʿid wanted proof of Sultan's wealth and high standing in his province). Sultan readily agreed and received Saʿid in his village with great hospitality and display. The guests and their host sat in huge tents erected for the occasion and ate in the Arab manner. Before departing, Saʿid said that he wished to pay another visit to Sultan after his return from the Sudan, but wanted to be received in more impressive surroundings. Having accepted this great honor, Sultan went immediately to Cairo where his friend, Shaykh Ali al-Laythi (one of the *ulama*), introduced him to a good architect who drew up plans for the construction of a great house in which the viceroy and his entourage could be entertained. With Sultan supplying the capital and the labor, the architect produced in a short time a palace with a lovely garden of ten *faddans*. Expensive furnishings were procured, and when the viceroy returned to al-Minya he was so impressed that he at once appointed Sultan to the vacant post of district leader of Qulusna.

Thus began the career of Muhammad Sultan, who was now a bureaucrat as well as a notable and who, because of his association with the government, was able to strengthen a preexisting base of wealth and influence and extend it throughout upper Egypt. Three aspects of Sultan's career are worth noting (see table 19). First, nearly all of his service was spent in the provinces of upper Egypt, including al-Minya, which seems to have been usual for officials of his type. As we have seen, notables appointed to provincial positions below that of governor were frequently assigned to their home provinces or to nearby areas.[47] Second, for fifteen years Sultan enjoyed continuous service, progressively advancing in the administrative hierarchy. Finally, his periods in office were much longer than the average. Between 1857 and 1872, he received but seven appointments. He was governor of Bani Suwayf for three years and four months, considerably above the average, and held his highest and most responsible position (deputy director of the Inspectorate) for over six years. The opportunities afforded by such long tenures in places close to his home base are obvious. It should not be surprising that Sultan is described as a man accustomed to getting his own way.[48]

Sultan's action while district leader (*nazir al-qism*) provides an instructive example of how someone with local influence and position in the administration could block governmental orders in order to benefit both the local population and himself.[49] Finding the lands of many *fallahin* in his district mortgaged to usurers, particularly a Greek identified as Bassili, Muhammad Sultan organized a boycott against these claims. After receiving an order from the governor (who had an alliance with Bassili) requesting his assistance in enforcing payment, Sultan secretly assembled *shaykhs al-balad* and other notables, informed them of the order, and forbade them, upon threat of punishment, to pay anything to Bassili. Order after order was sent from the capital of the province, but to no avail; Sultan's opposition had made them unenforceable. Bassili finally appealed to Sultan, who consented to help him recover his capital provided that he renounce the interest and accept a payment schedule favorable to the debtors. Bassili had

TABLE 19

MAJOR POSITIONS HELD BY MUHAMMAD SULTAN PASHA

District Chief, Qulusna (1857?)
Deputy governor, Bani Suwayf (Jan. 1859)
Governor, Bani Suwayf (Mar. 1860)
Governor, Asyut (July 1863)
Governor, al-Gharbiya (July 1864)
Inspector of viceregal properties in upper Egypt (Dec. 1865)
Deputy director, Inspectorate of upper Egypt (July 1866)
President, Court of Appeals in Khartum (Sept. 1872)[a]
Inspector of viceregal properties in al-Minya (date of first appointment
   not known; dismissed Oct. 1875; reappointed May 1876)
Member, Consultative Chamber of Delegates (1876)[b]
President, Consultative Chamber of Delegates (1881)[b]
President, Legislative Council (1883)

Sources: MM, no. 11369, *Warathat Muhammad Sultan Basha;* Sami, pt. 3, vol. 1, pp. 310, 345; pt. 3, vol. 2, pp. 498, 552, 631, 649–50, 1013; pt. 3, vol. 3, pp. 1276, 1337; al-Rafiʿi, *Asr Ismail*, vol. 2, p. 151; *al-Thawra*, pp. 199, 594.
[a]*Majlis al-Khartum.*
[b]*Majlis Shura al-Nuwwab.*

little recourse but to agree. (As we have seen, the rise of such inter-mediaries within the administration was one mechanism by which the wishes of the government could be frustrated.)

Between March 1860 and December 1865, Sultan performed a wide range of administrative tasks as governor of Bani Suwayf (where he had previously been deputy governor), Asyut, and al-Gharbiya provinces.[50] Admonished by the viceroy to be clever, treat the population fairly, and deal justly with their cases, Sultan must have been very busy during these years when the cotton boom and the viceroy's own frantic efforts to expand and develop his estates were changing the face of rural Egypt. As governor, Sultan selected and detached from the province land which the khedive wished to grant to his favorites or take for himself. When violence erupted in Asyut in 1863, as it had elsewhere in reaction to the great demands being placed upon the peasantry, Sultan was ordered to disarm the villagers and was also authorized to dismiss any *shaykh* who failed to comply with the order. Perhaps as a reward for his successful services in upper Egypt, Muhammad Sultan, who had earlier been praised by Ismail as honest and capable, was made governor of al-Gharbiya province and his salary increased from 5,000 to 8,000 piastres a month.

Sultan's influence became greater still in 1865 when he was appointed inspector of viceregal properties in upper Egypt, for this position gave him not only a wider sphere of jurisdiction, but also great authority over many government officials.[51] More opportunity came his way in 1866 when he was named deputy director of the Inspectorate for upper Egypt, serving directly under Ismail Siddiq, one of the most powerful and feared officials in the country. As we have seen, the Department of Inspectorate was the highest administrative authority in the provinces; its director named virtually every provincial official. Combining the functions of an intelligence service with high executive functions, the Inspectorate communicated viceregal orders to the provinces, saw to their implementation, and discharged a host of formidable responsibilities that included overseeing public works projects, examining complaints, and supervising tax collection. This department also had powers of appointment and dismissal.[52]

It was during these years that Sultan acquired the landed wealth and achieved the personal influence which made it possible for him to become known as the "king" of upper Egypt (see table 20). As the *Dhawat* Land Register reveals, no acquisitions are recorded for him during the time he was district chief or deputy governor of Bani Suwayf. Only after he became governor did he begin to acquire land, and over half of his aggregate holdings were obtained when he was deputy director of the Inspectorate. Not surprisingly, Sultan's land-holdings were concentrated in upper Egypt, most in his home province of al-Minya.

It can be reasonably assumed that many of his acquisitions never found their way into the *Dhawat* Land Register, and, of course, land was also acquired after 1870. Sultan's aggregate landholdings were estimated in the early 1880s at 13,000 *faddans*, of which 10,000 were in al-Minya; the endowment deed (*waqfiya*) of his charitable bequest (*waqf*) shows 4,400 *faddans*, all located in al-Minya; and the 1885 census lists Sultan as the employer of 493 persons on four estates in that province.[53] He also held urban real estate in the provinces and in Cairo. It is stated in his *waqf* endowment deed that he owned many buildings in al-Minya and in the capital, where he held a palace in Bab al-Luq district and a piece of land in Bulaq which contained a mosque, a *salamlik* (parlor) and three shops. As with the entries for his holdings in the land register, this information may only hint at the true extent of his urban possessions.

Sultan was also consolidating personal ties and building up good will in al-Minya and elsewhere. According to Fahmi's biographical account, Muhammad Sultan was well known for his generosity to the common people. He made regular donations to the Azhar (where he counted friends among the *ulama*) and to the mosques of Mecca and Medina.

TABLE 20

LANDHOLDINGS OF MUHAMMAD SULTAN PASHA

No. of Faddans	Date Acquired	Location
300	29 Mar. 1862	
137	16 Oct. 1862	
300	23 Aug. 1863	al-Minya and Bani Mazar
172	4 Aug. 1864	
22	18 Nov. 1866	
3	6 July 1868	
500	14 June 1869	Bani Suwayf and al-Fayuum
500	25 July 1869	
85	25 July 1869	al-Minya and Bani Mazar
2,019 (subtotal)		
−117 (ceded)[a]		
1,902 (total shown in register)		

Source: Egyptian National Archives, *Daftar zimam atyan ushuriya: Dhawat*, no. 1343.

[a]Properties sold or transferred to other persons.

He secretly gave money to great families who had fallen upon hard times. He distributed alms and provided food and drink to the people of his village, which became a kind of rooming house for the poor.[54] Fahmi's laudatory account of Sultan's generosity is partially supported by the provisions of his *waqf* endowment. While the greater portion of his bequest went to family and friends (allies were rewarded in this way), Sultan did provide for the upkeep of three mosques and a school (*madrasa*) where orphans and children of the poor could come to receive an education.[55] (He also set aside funds for a religious teacher to instruct the public in the *sharia*, or religious law.) These actions were an indirect source of political capital, for they placed Sultan in a position to champion popular grievances or protest injustices in the name of the people.

In addition to his large family and many friends in al-Minya, Sultan had friends inside the administration. Mustafa Riyad, Ahmad Khayri Pasha (Ismail's keeper of the seal), and the queen mother (who once made Sultan a present of precious stones) are said to have been his friends.[56] Sultan also knew Nubar and Muhammad Sharif, two of Egypt's most prominent officials who reportedly esteemed his talents highly.

Sultan was also consulted by the khedive. Huda Sha'rawi reports a story that reveals something of Sultan's self-assertiveness: Khedive Ismail, while on an inspection tour of al-Minya, had decided to change a number of provincial officials (some of whom must have been friends of Sultan). Ismail visited Sultan, then deputy director of the Inspectorate, and asked for an opinion about the men he was considering as replacements. "Would Abu Hammadi be a good *mudir* for al-Minya?" the viceroy queried. "He is a good *mudir* of Suhaj because he is from there," Sultan replied; "But what is the matter with the *mudir* of al-Minya? Is he not doing well?" The next day, Ismail continued to press the matter. "Would not Ayyub Bey Jamal al-Din be a good *mudir* of al-Minya?" he asked Sultan. "He is a good *mudir* of Asyut," replied Sultan, who finally became so exasperated that he rudely told Ismail that his first concern should be to improve the condition of al-Minya rather than to spend time changing its *mudir*s. A few days later, when he and Ismail were on a train bound for Cairo, Sultan finally went too far. Ismail had just asked his opinion of the *muqabala* tax. "My lord," Sultan replied, "you have twice asked me about this and that, and I have replied; and now you ask me about the *muqabala*. If you would just concern yourself with improving the condition of the population, then that would be good and more useful." This was too much for Ismail. He instantly ordered Sultan off the moving train, but the punishment was not carried out.

This dispute is alleged by Sultan's daughter to have caused his dismissal as deputy director of the Inspectorate in August 1872—the first setback of his career. Following this, Sultan was ordered to go to the Sudan and assume the position of president of the Court of Appeals in Khartum, an appointment tantamount to exile, but which was soon rescinded. According to Fahmi, Sultan was banished because he told Ismail that the *muqabala* tax was a burden for the country.[57] There is, however, another possible reason for Sultan's removal that may also resolve other questions raised by this episode. Why did Ismail change his mind and rescind the order so soon? And was it not strange that Sultan had been allowed to hold the position of deputy director of the Inspectorate so long before being removed?

The answers can be found in the relationship between Sultan and Ismail Siddiq Pasha, his patron and protector. It is not known when their paths first crossed, but they may have met each other in the mid-1860s when Sultan was helping manage the viceregal properties. It is probably no coincidence that Sultan's appointment as deputy director of the Inspectorate occurred at the very time (July 1866) that Ismail Siddiq was named inspector general.[58] More interesting still, Sultan's removal in 1872 coincided with the temporary demotion of his protector from his position as director of finances to membership on the Privy Council. In fact, the two removals were made in the same order.[59] Moreover, Sultan's pardon was issued only after Ismail Siddiq had been returned to favor. Fahmi has acknowledged that Ismail Siddiq's intervention was responsible for Sultan's pardon, but Huda Sha'rawi mentions other voices raised in protest against his banishment.[60] Nubar, Sharif, and Riyad told Khedive Ismail that the country needed Sultan. The queen mother was asked to discuss the matter with her son, who is said to have granted her every request. Ismail Siddiq and others also interceded with Prince Tawfiq, at whose request the viceregal pardon was finally issued—a classic example of how personal contacts with access to the ruler could change a viceregal decision. Yet one must not lose sight of the overriding significance of the relationship between Ismail Siddiq and Muhammad Sultan, for this certainly was a decisive factor in the latter's success, as for many other notables in the provincial administration. Without the protection of this powerful man, Sultan might never have become "king" of upper Egypt.

▲▲▲ ISMAIL SIDDIQ

The name of Ismail Siddiq Pasha (1821?–1876) figures prominently in nearly all accounts of Khedive Ismail's reign.[61] Of slight, stooped frame, with a great "hooked" nose, Ismail Siddiq is described as resembling a bird of prey.[62] Ismail Siddiq was more commonly known as the *mufattish* because of his long terms as inspector general (*mufattish umum*) and as director of Egyptian finances. From these two powerful and lucrative posts, he amassed a fortune and built up a network of personal ties that enabled him to reach into the lives of many officials. As we have just seen, his support enhanced the career of Muhammad Sultan, but his opposition almost destroyed that of Ali Mubarak.

Ismail Siddiq seems to defy classification. Because his initial success stemmed from the accident that his mother was wet nurse to Ismail and the two boys grew up as brothers, he does not fit any of the elite typologies outlined in the preceding chapter.[63] Holder of the highest administrative positions, he was not a Turk, as were most other officials of comparable positions, but rather an Egyptian. Yet unlike other Egyptian officials, he did not come from the rural nobility, being the son of a humble *fallah*. His service began neither in the provincial administration, like Sultan Pasha's, nor in the central administration, like Mubarak's. Ismail Siddiq possessed no formal education, is said to have known only Arabic, and had no early exposure to European ways, yet he became one of Egypt's most wealthy and powerful officials.[64] He was the only high official of his day not to have suffered the disgrace of dismissal from the government, and he enjoyed an extraordinary degree of freedom in office. The mere mention of his name inspired fear and envy among the Egyptians. Known as the "little khedive," Ismail Siddiq was one of the most remarkable officials of his age.[65]

The precise date of Ismail Siddiq's entry into the administration is not known, but like most other high officials who served under Khedive Ismail, his rise within the government occurred before Ismail's accession. In 1853, Ismail Siddiq was employed by the *Daira Saniya*, the agency administering the viceregal family's estates, as an inspector of Burdin district (al-Sharqiya province).[66] In 1858, he was transferred to al-Santa district in al-Gharbiya province, still as an inspector. In 1858, Ismail Siddiq was elevated to second rank (with the title of bey) and promoted to inspector general of the *Daira Saniya*—a position he held until Ismail's accession.

Ismail Siddiq's climb to high position did not occur overnight (see table 21).[67] To be sure, he received a big promotion from the new viceroy. In February 1863, his salary was increased to 8,000 piastres and less than a month later it was raised to 10,000 when he was given first rank and made director general (*mudir umum*) of the viceregal properties. Yet Ismail Siddiq did not have a seat on the regency council formed to govern Egypt during Ismail's trip abroad in April 1866, and the gifts of land he received from the khedive in 1863 and 1864 were not comparable to those granted the highest-ranking officials (for example, Ismail Raghib, Muhammad Sharif). His rise was more gradual. In May 1865, he was made inspector of lower Egypt and in June, he received authority over the governorates of Damietta and Rosetta. One year later, he was named to the important post of inspector general, a position which established his fortune and fame, and in June 1867, Ismail Siddiq took his place on a regency council formed in the viceroy's absence. When he received control of the Department of Finances in April 1868, Ismail Siddiq had at last achieved a concentration of power that placed him among the most influential officials in the land.

What use did Ismail Siddiq make of the power at his disposal? In Egypt as in other parts of the Ottoman empire, talent was worth little unless one had access to the ruler. In this respect, the inspector (*mufattish*) had a rare advantage, as we have noted, in being Khedive Ismail's foster brother. This explains Ismail's Siddiq's early service in the family *dairas* and his subsequent entry into the government administration. This personal bond was further strengthened by his marriage to a freed slave of Ibrahim Pasha, Ismail's father and former viceroy of Egypt; then, during Ismail's reign, by the marriage of Ismail Siddiq's son to the adopted daughter of the khedive.[68]

But Ismail Siddiq was also a man of talent. European observers did not like him, but readily acknowledged his intelligence and skills.

TABLE 21
MAJOR POSITIONS HELD BY ISMAIL SIDDIQ PASHA

Inspector of Burdin (Sept. 1853)
Inspector of al-Santa (Sept. 1858)
Inspector general, *Daira Saniya* (Dec. 1858)
Director general of viceregal properties (Mar. 1863)
Inspector of lower Egypt (May 1865)
Inspector general of Egypt (July 1866; transferred out of Inspectorate, Oct. 1868; Inspectorate abolished, Oct. 1870)
Director, Department of Finance, in addition to being inspector general (Apr. 1868, Aug, 1869)
Member, Privy Council (Aug. 1872)
Director, *Daira Saniya* (Aug. 1872)
Director, Department of the Interior (Aug. 1872)
Director, Department of Finance (Aug. 1873)

Sources: WMC, box 21, "Muwazzafun," no. 319, 15 J 1286/23 Aug. 1869; *Mas, Awamir, Maʿiya Saniya-Turki*, reg. 573/138/27, Viceroy/*al-Maliya*, 9 B 1285/26 Oct. 1868; Sami, pt. 3, vol. 2, pp. 774, 874, 1011, 1012, 1015; pt. 3, vol. 3, pp. 1042, 1449–51.

Edwin de Leon thought him poorly informed and uncomprehending of any but the most selfish interests, yet credited him with native shrewdness; J. C. McCoan found him clever and energetic, and C. Rivers Wilson saw in him a natural intelligence.[69] Ismail Siddiq's chief advantage was a flexible intellect capable of adapting quickly to any new situation, and an uncanny ability for discovering ways of realizing his master's wishes, which he carried out efficiently and ruthlessly.

This intelligence and resourcefulness can be seen in the events following his appointment as director of finance, which was made in the hope that he could assist the khedive in loan negotiations then under way.[70] Ismail Raghib, his predecessor, had been out of his depth in matters of high finance and in April was made the scapegoat for the failure of a loan signed the preceding February. At the time he became director of finance, Ismail Siddiq was a neophyte in international financial dealings, but he brought with him loyal followers who were skilled in such matters and soon learned the intricacies of high finance on the job. In fact, he learned his lessons so well that he acquired a reputation as a skillful fencer with his government's creditors.

After the failure of the contract signed by Raghib, new offers were entertained. On April 21, agreement was reached between Khedive Ismail and two bankers, Cernuschi and Pastré. Only the formal signing remained to bring into effect the new loan. Cernuschi drew up a contract and Ismail Siddiq promised that it would be signed and returned the next day. But the following morning, he announced that a flaw had been found in the draft and the entire project fell through. One source has attributed responsibility for this "scandal" to the *mufattish* himself and his alleged great influence over the khedive, but another source acknowledges that the Europeans were not without blame.[71] According to Muhammad Sabry, Ismail Siddiq and his master had legitimate fears that the guarantee of the customs revenue stipulated in the contract might lead to French interference in Egyptian finances.

Whatever the reason, a frantic search ensued to find new expedients for raising money. The *mufattish* raised old taxes, imposed new ones, and even proposed floating an internal loan, but these expedients fell short and the government finally had to contract a loan with the banking house of Oppenheim. Yet the skill he demonstrated during months of complicated maneuvering and tortuous negotiations proved his capacity to handle sophisticated financial matters. The *mufattish* thus became his viceroy's chief financial aide, providing ideas on ways of raising money, traveling abroad on the viceroy's behalf, drawing up phony budgets for Egypt's creditors, and becoming adept at sleight of hand in his financial dealings. Without him, Khedive Ismail acknowledged in a revealing letter, it would have been difficult to manage Egypt's finances, because Ismail Siddiq was the only one who really understood them.[72]

Ismail Siddiq was also the only one who truly understood the provincial administration. Through the Inspectorate, he supervised the work of Egypt's provincial officials and watched over the activities of the various councils and courts, but it was by his possession of delegated powers that he acquired real influence in the countryside. In December 1865, while inspector of lower Egypt, he was granted special permission to transfer and dismiss all provincial officials under his jurisdiction except the governors themselves.[73] After Ismail Siddiq was appointed inspector general, provincial officials were ordered to submit all matters connected with the provinces to him instead of to the viceroy, as formerly. After examining these problems, the *mufattish* would then submit them to the ruler.[74] Ismail Siddiq thus became the link with the provinces through whom the khedive communicated his decisions about appointments and dismissals, provincial reorganization, and the allocation of funds. Petitions from the viceroy's subjects were transmitted by Ismail Siddiq to the khedive, who on one occasion received a petition that had been drawn up a year before it reached him.[75]

Ismail Siddiq was not only an intermediary between Khedive Ismail and the provinces; he was also an innovator of schemes whose purpose was to satisfy his master's insatiable appetite for money. Being an Egyptian himself, the *mufattish* knew the natives' tricks for evading payment of taxes, and his long service in the provinces had enabled him to estimate shrewdly the true extent of the country's fiscal resources and to apprise himself of the landholdings and other wealth of prominent local families. His name thus became associated with nearly every new fiscal device introduced by the khedive. It was he who induced Egyptian notables to make "voluntary" contributions to the viceroy's new educational establishments, who squeezed from them funds used to repurchase land which Sa'id Pasha had granted the Suez Canal company, who invented the *muqabala* tax, and so on.[76] Ismail Siddiq knew how to bring in the money, and the viceroy closed his eyes to the methods by which it was done.

It would be a mistake, however, to equate Siddiq's extraordinary freedom of movement with the absence of viceregal supervision or immunity from reproach. The viceroy paid great attention to Ismail Siddiq's work, and always seemed to be exhorting or admonishing him to do this or that. When Ismail Siddiq went too far, he could expect a sharp rebuke, or worse. In July 1871, the viceroy prohibited him from appointing, dismissing, or even transferring low-ranking provincial officials; he was henceforth to refer all such matters to the viceroy and act only after receiving permission from the Privy Council.[77] And as we have seen, in 1872 the *mufattish* was temporarily demoted.

Such examples notwithstanding, Ismail Siddiq used his high positions and delegated authority to build up power unique among high officeholders. His influence pervaded the entire administration: he intervened in the affairs of the other government departments, and became the archrival of Nubar, another official with real influence (Ismail Siddiq's hand was seen behind Nubar's dismissal in 1874 after Nubar had opposed his financial schemes).[78] In the provinces, he became the patron of local officials and notables; his support was indispensable for gaining and keeping a provincial post. Ismail Siddiq intervened with the ruler on behalf of his clients, some of whom were bound to him through marriage or other ties.[79] When elections to the Consultative Chamber of Delegates were held, his support of local candidates was important for their success.[80] So great did his influence become that one of his appointees refused to obey a note from the viceroy ordering his dismissal and had to be removed from his post by force.[81]

Ismail Siddiq used his opportunities to accumulate wealth on a scale exceeded only by that of the khedive himself.[82] His extravagance was the talk of Cairo. People spoke of his palaces containing hundreds of rooms furnished with overstuffed French sofas, satin curtains, and silver washbasins. His clothes and jewelry, his servants and slaves, and his lavish palaces were envied even by the women of the viceroy's harem. A visitor wrote of seeing a portrait of the *mufattish* with one of his wives: he, seated, dressed in an expensive European suit, and bareheaded (it was customary for officials to wear the fez); she, dutifully standing at his side, wearing a fashionable dress of blue velvet and a tiara of diamonds. In some respects, Ismail Siddiq's establishment resembled the great Mamluk households of preceding centuries. His household was formed of three palaces (located in the new Ismailiya quarter) into which were crowded enough servants to populate a small village. De Leon speaks of his thirty-six "wives," each with six white slaves and retinue of blacks, and his harem which contained 300 women and 250 male servants (the *mufattish* is said to have owned more than 700 slaves). The palaces housing this crowd of dependents were furnished in the French style. Dinner guests used forks and spoons of silver and gold. Ismail Siddiq's household jewelry was valued at £650,000—not a prohibitive sum for a man worth between two and three million pounds.

Ismail Siddiq had accumulated his wealth in various ways. Special unrecorded accounts were set up for him. Much money was made in fees and commissions from European contractors and bankers. Large amounts of cash were given by the khedive.[83] But embezzlement and extortion seem to have been the chief avenues to wealth. Ismail Siddiq is said to have boasted openly of having extorted several million pounds more than whatever appeared in the budgets he produced. Large bribes were obtained from clients in the provinces: one person reportedly paid him £3,000 for a gubernatorial appointment. He is even said to have fixed bribes by position. The going rate for governors was between £E 2,000 and £E 3,000; for deputy governors, £E 1,000 and £E 1,500; for district chiefs, £E 500 and £E 750. Little wonder that Egyptians who held these positions came from the wealthiest families in the provinces.

Though much of the cash acquired by the *mufattish* was invested in stocks and bonds (valued at more than a half million pounds), the bulk of his wealth took the form of urban property and landed estates in the provinces (see table 22).[84] Ismail Siddiq owned numerous houses and palaces (the khedive gave him at least six houses alone), many of which were located outside Cairo—in Alexandria, along the Mahmudiya canal, and in Tanta where he had at least five houses and sixteen shops.[85] In the rich delta provinces lay his vast landed estates. Unfortunately, it is impossible to ascertain the true extent of his landholdings, for many acquisitions did not find their way into the record books. The *Dhawat* Land Register shows him with a total of only 4,024 *faddans* of *ushuriya* land in 1870, but evidence from other sources suggests this to be a gross understatement of his actual *ushuriya* holdings.[86] For example, until 1868, the *mufattish* owned 1,180 *faddans* of *ushuriya* property in Bani Suwayf, and in 1870 he acquired 174 *faddans* of *ushuriya* land in al-Sharqiya—figures that do not appear in the register. By the time of his death in 1876, he is credited with owning 30,000 *faddans* of *ushuriya* property. Ismail Siddiq's largest single acquisition of land on record was 36,000 *faddans*, purchased in 1865.[87] If the precise extent of his landholdings cannot be known, there can be no doubt that they were located in the most fertile regions of the country. Almost all of his estates seem to have been in the delta, and many sat alongside major irrigation canals. There were 1,192 *faddans* bordering the Ibrahimiya canal, and, according to Mubarak, the *mufattish* had six steam pumps along the Mahmudiya canal.[88] Ismail Siddiq apparently spent a small fortune on steam pumps, and was extravagant in other ways as well. In the village of al-Jaradat (in al-Buhayra) where he owned 1,206 *faddans*, the *mufattish* had a home for his estate manager, an office for his employees, a mosque supported by his revenues, and a farmhouse.[89]

Ismail Siddiq's unique position can now be fully appreciated. He was an Egyptian, yet his career was quite different from those of Muham-

TABLE 22
LANDHOLDINGS OF ISMAIL SIDDIQ PASHA

No. of Faddans	Date Acquired	Location
434	15 June 1863	
160	8 Sept. 1863	
68	26 Oct. 1863	al-Sharqiya
662	21 Feb. 1864	
283	21 Feb. 1864	
321	17 Apr. 1866–6 Mar. 1867	al-Rawda
493	10 Aug. 1866	
490	2 Aug. 1866	
26	3 Jan. 1867	al-Daqahilya
119	17 Jan. 1867	
1,829	—	
123	—	
150	—	al-Buhayra
175	24 Apr. 1868–12 Apr. 1869	—
1,052	22 Dec. 1868	al-Buhayra
204	14 Apr. 1869	al-Sharqiya
142	15 May 1869	—
4	5 Sept. 1869	al-Sharqiya
450	20 Feb. 1870	
700	10 Mar. 1870	al-Gharbiya
50	15 Apr. 1870	
7,935	(subtotal)	
−3,911	(ceded)[a]	
4,024	(total shown in register)	

Source: Egyptian National Archives, Daftar zimam aytan ushuriya: Dhawat, no. 1343.

Note: Dashes indicate information not available.

[a]Properties sold or transferred to other persons.

mad Sultan or Ali Mubarak. His wealth surpassed that of any other official, even the high-ranking Turks. Ismail Siddiq did not represent any group of officials. If he had an interest outside his own, it lay not in the countryside, or in Europe, and certainly not in "reform." Ismail Siddiq's interest was in preserving that system by which Egypt's viceroys had been able to establish nearly absolute control over the rest of society. The *mufattish* was very much his master's loyal servant.

▲▲▲ MUHAMMAD SHARIF

Muhammad Sharif Pasha (1826–1887) was another loyal ally of the viceroy. Though resembling a European in dress and to some extent in manner, Muhammad Sharif was a Turk, a representative of the old school in attitude and outlook. In a career spanning thirty-three years, Sharif Pasha served variously as director of the Departments of Justice, Foreign Affairs, Interior, Public Works, and Education, and on four occasions governed Egypt as acting viceroy. (See table 10.) During the last years of Ismail's reign, he was the unquestioned leader of the Turkish party in Egypt, and by the time he was pensioned in 1884, he had been four times president of the Council of Ministers. Muhammad Sharif was not only the leading Turkish official of Ismail's reign, but also one of the most prominent administrators of the nineteenth century.

According to a statement made by Sharif at the time of his retirement from government service, he was born on November 26, 1826 in Istanbul.[90] He met the viceroy as a young boy while traveling with his father, appointed judge (*qadi*) of Mecca by the sultan during Muhammad Ali's reign.[91] Muhammad Ali is said to have taken a fancy to the young man and persuaded the judge to place Sharif under his care, promising to treat him as though he were his own son. As a ward of the viceroy, Muhammad Sharif was enrolled in the primary school for the princes (*maktab al-khanka*) where he developed a friendship with the viceroy's grandsons, the sons of Ibrahim. This relationship was enhanced when Sharif was chosen to accompany them on the study mission to Paris in 1844. After staying for a short while at the Paris school, Sharif was transferred to St. Cyr, the famous French military academy, where he spent two years and was appointed to the rank of captain in a French regiment. After five years in France, Sharif returned to Egypt in 1849, after both Muhammad Ali and his son Ibrahim had died.

Presumably because of his association with the family of Ibrahim, Sharif was not promoted by Ibrahim's rival Abbas, who was now khedive. He did become a friend of Sulayman Pasha, the chief of staff, and served in his entourage at the rank of captain.[92] According to al-Ayyubi, Sharif was employed by Prince Abd al-Halim in 1853 as a clerk in his *daira*, a lowly position but one not without potential advantage because of Sharif's proximity to Abd al-Halim's side of the viceregal family. However, his association with the very group that was challenging Abbas may have placed him in immediate danger, for about this time Sharif left Egypt for Istanbul, ostensibly to settle his father's estate. He appears to have remained outside Egypt until 1854; when Abbas was murdered, Ibrahim's sons returned to Egypt, and Muhammad Sa'id, a brother of Ibrahim, became viceroy. Remembering Sharif from his school days, Sa'id promoted him to the rank of colonel and assigned him to an infantry regiment.[93] After serving less than a year in the army, Sharif was briefly unemployed and then was appointed to a position in the ruler's household. After a second period of unemployment, Sharif received a command in another infantry regiment. But high administrative position was not far away. In January 1858, Sharif was given direction of the Department of Foreign Affairs, the first of many distinguished appointments in the civil administration.

Why was Sharif given so many important posts? (See table 23.) First, he got along very well with Europeans, perhaps because he looked and acted the part of a European. He was nicknamed *al-Fransawi* (the Frenchman); his bright and convivial manner, his expert French, his professed admiration for constitutional government, and his marriage to the daughter of Sulayman Pasha, a prominent French officer (and converted Muslim) in the Egyptian army—all made him a favorite of the French in particular and Europeans in general, including the British, many of whom were his friends. It was really difficult not to like a man who enjoyed good cigars, played billiards, loved the hunt, and entertained a mistress—in short, who was an agreeable man of the world.[94] To his British friends, Sharif was a perfect gentleman. Khedive Ismail is reported to have said that he could find no better ambassador to Britain than Sharif, because he loved to hunt and would thus be loved by the English. Without doubt, Sharif knew how to please Europeans.

Second, Sharif possessed certain qualities that made him an ideal choice as minister for the absolutist ruler. Unlike some of his colleagues, Sharif was not overly ambitious, nor given to intrigue. He was in fact one of Egypt's few truly honest officials. No price, it is said, could buy Sharif, and his reputation was never clouded by charges of illegal or improper conduct.[95] He was also unquestioningly loyal to the ruler. This made him a good choice as Sa'id's director of foreign affairs; for Sa'id, wanting to control matters himself, desired men who would not assert themselves in any way. Consequently, Sharif's first high administrative post was of little importance.

Sharif Pasha was a true representative of his "race." D. M. Wallace found it difficult to think of someone so European in speech and appearance as a Turk, but he and others labored under few illusions about Sharif's real character.[96] Europeans regarded Turks as habitually indolent, and Sharif fitted the stereotype perfectly. He loved the easy life; hard work bored him, and he was accustomed to entrusting the details of administration to others. According to a statement in his pension dossier, it was this very want of energy and perseverance that caused him to be dismissed briefly from the army during Sa'id's reign. Bell described Sharif as extraordinarily apathetic and indifferent to

TABLE 23
MAJOR POSITIONS HELD BY MUHAMMAD SHARIF PASHA

Adjutant in staff of Sulayman Pasha (1849)
Clerk in *daira* of Prince Abd al-Halim
Colonel in Egyptian army (Sa'id's reign)
Colonel in Sa'id's entourage
Commander in Egyptian army
Director, Department of Foreign Affairs (Jan. 1858)
President, Council of Justice[a] (June 1861)
Director, Department of Education (July 1863)
Director, Department of Foreign Affairs (Aug. 1863)
Director, Department of Interior (June 1865)
Acting viceroy (June 1865, Apr. 1866)
Director, Departments of Public Works and Interior (Nov. 1866)
Acting viceroy (June 1867)
President, Council of Justice[a] (Sept. 1867)
Director, Department of Interior (Apr. 1868)
Acting viceroy (May 1868)
Director, Department of Justice (Sept. 1872)
Director, Departments of Justice and Commerce (Nov. 1874)
Director, Department of Interior (Sept. 1875)
Director, Department of Justice (June 1876)
President, Council of Ministers (Apr. 1879, July 1879,
  Sept. 1881, Aug. 1882)

Sources: Sami, pt. 3, vol. 1, pp. 234, 351; pt. 3, vol. 2, pp. 494, 608, 610, 641, 643, 695, 711, 783, 985; pt. 3, vol. 3, pp. 1127, 1202, 1291, 1547; *MM*, no. 9598, *Mudad istikhdam Muhammad Sharif Basha;* al-Ayyubi, *Tarikh*, vol. 2, p. 168.
  [a]*Majlis al-Ahkam.*

almost everything. Sharif's affability masked a proud disdain for those who were not Turks. He disliked the Armenian Christians in the administration, and regarded the Egyptians with a mixture of arrogance, contempt, and paternalism. They were like children and good for little else but tilling the soil for their Turkish masters; he was indifferent to their lot. For him as for the rest of Egypt's Turkish rulers, the Egyptians were no more than a conquered race.

Although Sharif could deal with Europeans and had acquired the trappings of European civilization (including an undeserved reputation as a reformer), he was almost fanatically opposed to the extension of European influence in any form and at heart did not like Europeans. Sharif's professed commitment to reform, his interest in constitutionalism, and so on, lacked substance. These might be good for other countries, or even for a future Egypt, but not for the Egypt he knew. Existing abuses must be tolerated. Sharif even objected to improvements in the sanitation system on the grounds that they had not existed in the time of the Prophet, and despite his apparent fran-

MUHAMMAD SHARIF PASHA (1826–1887)
From Sami, *Taqwim al-Nil*, pt. 3, vol. 2, facing p. 504.

cophilia, he objected more strenuously than any other high official to the construction of the Suez Canal.[97] Such were harmful innovations, rooted in a foreign culture, and unsanctioned by the Quran.

Thus Sharif's unquestioning loyalty, honesty, lack of ambition, and ability to deal with Europeans formed a successful combination for high office under Egypt's viceroys. According to Bell, Sharif became the perfect foil for Khedive Ismail, who used him to float ideas that were presented to the consuls as the thoughts of Sharif (hence one source of Sharif's reputation as a reformer).[98] Because he was trustworthy and an ideal cover for the viceroy's projects, Muhammad Sharif began receiving important assignments and rose rapidly to prominence. Within months of Ismail's accession, he was promoted to the rank of general and made president of the Council of Justice (*Majlis al-Ahkam*) and director of education. He was also named to a seat on the board of directors of the Egyptian Steam Navigation Company.[99]

These appointments made it difficult for Sharif to take it easy. As president of the Council of Justice, Sharif was asked to supervise the collection of all laws issued by the Egyptian government since Muhammad Ali's time; to help formulate statutes governing the operation of new councils set up in Damietta, Isna, and in the Cairo Police Department (*Dabtiyat Misr*); and to ensure that all criminal cases tried in the government courts conformed to the new law code that Ismail had promulgated.[100]

But Sharif's tenure in the Council of Justice was short-lived. In August 1863, he was transferred to the post of director of Foreign Affairs (where he must have felt more comfortable) and in 1865 he was given the additional task of directing the Interior Department. Much of his time was spent satisfying the demands of European nationals and their governments. A delicate situation arose in March 1868, when a fourteen-gun frigate from Italy arrived in Alexandria harbor bearing a "request" from the king of Italy for the expeditious settlement of all Italian claims. Such gunboat diplomacy placed Sharif in a difficult position, but he handled matters so skillfully that by the end of April all but one case had been settled and the gunboat had been recalled. During this time, Sharif also presided over the completion of a railway line between Zaqaziq and Suez, which earned him the thanks of the British representative.[101] Sharif may not have enjoyed such hard work, but he had no time to be lazy.

During the 1860s, Sharif also served for short periods as director of Public Works and, once again, as president of the Council of Justice and Interior, but his most prestigious appointment was as regent. Four times during this period Ismail left Egypt in the hands of his loyal "vassal," who nominally directed state affairs in concert with a council of department heads. The 1870s brought a slight easing of his responsibilities. Until September 1872, Sharif was in charge of Interior. Then, in sequence, he was given Justice (with Commerce), Interior, and Justice again, though he did not hold these positions concurrently, as had sometimes been true during the hectic years of the 1860s.

As with other high officials, Muhammad Sharif's rise in the government was accompanied by the buildup of a landed estate (see table 24). The *Dhawat* Land Register shows Sharif owning 2,507 *faddans* of *ushuriya* property by 1870, and Sami's lists reveal 2,197 *faddans* acquired during the 1860s. Judging from these sources, Sharif's estates seem to have been located almost entirely in the delta provinces, though other archival materials reveal holdings in Bani Suwayf, Bani Mazar, al-Jiza, and at least 540 *faddans* in Jirja.[102] Most of this land was apparently granted by Ismail, who favored him in other ways too. Ismail overrode an engineer's objection that a steam pump which Sharif had installed on a canal in al-Sharqiya province (where he owned land) would deprive the surrounding lands of water, and in 1863 the viceroy agreed to remove a tax which had been levied as a surcharge on Sharif's *ushuriya* lands. In 1879, Sharif possessed 3,097 *faddans* of *ushuriya* property, and in 1885 his estates were supporting thirteen hamlets with a population of 4,216 persons.[103] If his land and

TABLE 24

LANDHOLDINGS OF MUHAMMAD SHARIF PASHA

No. of Faddans	Date Acquired	Location
1,000	26 June 1863	al-Rawda
300	25 Sept. 1866	al-Gharbiya
321	4 Sept. 1867	al-Rawda
61	18 June 1868	al-Jiza
546	27 June 1868	—
118	21 Sept. 1868	al-Gharbiya
278	21 Sept. 1868	al-Minufiya
44	22 Dec. 1868	al-Gharbiya
2,570 (total shown in register)		
2,668 (corrected total)[a]		

Source: Egyptian National Archives, *Daftar zimam atyan ushuriya: Dhawat*, no. 1343.

Note: Dash indicates information not available.

[a]According to author's count.

other property were not comparable to those of Ismail Siddiq, they far exceeded the holdings of many other officials.

Sharif's landed wealth, his affability, and his disdain for those not of his "race" made him the favorite of the Turkish grandees who frequented his palace in the Ismailiya quarter.[104] Yet despite his prestige it would be an error to conclude that Sharif was a person of real influence or independence. He enjoyed only a limited patronage—the kind available to every high official—and never received delegated powers comparable to those enjoyed by a man like Ismail Siddiq. Even as acting viceroy, he allowed other officials to run the country's administration.[105] Sharif possessed strong convictions, but he was simply not a self-assertive leader. Lacking ideas of his own, he was completely dominated by the viceroy. Until the last days of Khedive Ismail's reign, Muhammad Sharif was not really the master of his house.

▲▲▲ MUSTAFA RIYAD

Described by some as a devoted public servant and by others as a vain and willful autocrat, Mustafa Riyad Pasha (1834–1911) compiled a record of government service remarkable for its diversity.[106] In a career that encompassed roughly half a century, Mustafa Riyad served as provincial governor, high officer in the viceregal household, and was director of the Departments of Education, Foreign Affairs, Agriculture, Justice, and Interior. After Ismail's deposition in June 1879, this short, stooped, and unsmiling man was three times president of the Council of Ministers. Riyad had neither the breadth of vision nor the tact to be regarded as a statesman, but he did win the respect of his contemporaries for his honesty, industry, and general competence.[107] Riyad was a master of administrative detail, an expert agronomist, and a dedicated educational reformer.

Riyad's youth and early career are shrouded in mystery. His contemporary biographers (Zaki, Zakhura) say nothing about his origins but merely state that his first important appointment was governor of al-Jiza, which Zakhura has mistakenly dated to 1873, but which actually was made twenty years earlier. This same uncertainty was displayed by Riyad's European contemporaries. McCoan knew little about Riyad's early life and, like his biographers, believed that his career had begun under Ismail.[108] Curiously, Riyad himself contributed to this mystery by avoiding mention of his early life. Apparently, he preferred to tolerate rumors and innuendo rather than reveal the details of a past that might have proved embarrassing to a high official in a Turkish-dominated administration.

Riyad may have been Jewish. Though the truth cannot be known, some Europeans and others believed that Riyad was a Jew from Smyrna, a member of a family of usurers and gold weighers called al-Wazzan, and that his real name was Jacob.[109] Riyad's origins, however, are a source of dispute, since other Europeans thought Riyad was Turkish. He spoke Turkish as his first language, and according to Milner was a Turk of Turks—conservative of temperament, a fervent Muslim (he carried his prayer beads wherever he went), a "pure Oriental."[110] Riyad was married to the daughter of Husayn Pasha Tapuzada, a Balkan Turk who came to Egypt with Muhammad Ali. Within the Tapuzada family, however, rumors persisted about Riyad's "Jewish" background, and the children were told never to refer to it.[111] Only in personal appearance—he resembled a Levantine Jew— did Riyad betray a hint of a non-Turkish background. The fact that some of his contemporaries, including Sharif, believed him to be Jewish detracted from the prestige he might otherwise have enjoyed.[112]

There was another reason for Riyad to hide his background. Rumors existed that early in his career he had held positions unbecoming a member of the ruling elite.[113] Riyad's pension dossier reveals that he began his career as an entry clerk and copyist of Arabic documents in an office of the Department of Finance.[114] After a brief period of unemployment, Riyad received an appointment as clerk of Arabic documents (katib Arabi) in the Department of Civil Affairs, but was soon transferred to the office of the lieutenant of the viceroy where he copied and entered documents in the Arabic registers. In 1848 or 1849, Riyad entered the military service (at the rank of lieutenant) as a clerk, then served as a musician in the army. After one year, he was promoted to major, while continuing as a musician. Thus his work during the early years of his career hardly recommended him to his high-ranking Turkish colleagues who regarded Arabic as a contemptible language and believed clerical work beneath the dignity of a member of the ruling class. If these Turkish officials had themselves been too proud to become engineers and physicians, one can imagine their regard for a former musician!

Riyad's career soon turned upward (see table 25). His previous work for Hasan al-Munastarli, the lieutenant of the viceroy, had apparently caused his name to be brought to the attention of the khedive, because in 1850 or 1851 Riyad received an appointment as aide-de-camp (yawur) to Abbas Pasha. This brought him into the court and led to the first big break of his career. In 1852, Riyad was named keeper of the seal in the viceregal cabinet, an important position that carried both prestige and influence. This appointment was accompanied by a promotion to the rank of colonel, which meant that Riyad was now a bey and a member

TABLE 25
MAJOR POSITIONS HELD BY MUSTAFA RIYAD PASHA

Under Abbas and Sa'id
Copyist, Department of Finance (1846/47)[a]
Copyist, Department of Civil Affairs (1848/49)
Copyist, Office of the Lieutenant of the Viceroy[b] (1848/49)
Copyist, *al-Madrasa al-Harbiya al-Mafruza*[c] (1848/49)
Musician in the army (1849/50)
Aide-de-camp in the viceregal entourage (1850/51)
Keeper of the seal (Nov. 1852)
Governor, al-Jiza (Nov. 1853)
Administrative chief, al-Fayyum (1856)
Governor, Qina (Dec. 1856)
Deputy director, Railway Administration (1856/57)
Administrative chief, Rawdat al-Bahrayn (1857/58)
Deputy governor, Rawdat al-Bahrayn (1860/61)
Appointment in the viceregal entourage (1861/62)

Under Ismail
Keeper of the seal (Jan. 1863)
Member, Council of Justice[d] (July 1864)
Director of the viceroy's private office for administration
  of his estates[e] (Oct. 1864)
Chief treasurer in the viceregal entourage (Oct. 1868)
Adviser to the president, Privy Council (Dec. 1872)
Director, Department of Education (Aug. 1873)
Adviser to the director, Department of the Interior (Mar. 1874)
Director, Department of Foreign Affairs (May 1874)
Director, Department of Agriculture (June 1875)
Director, Department of Justice (Sept. 1875)
Director, Department of Education (June 1876)
Director, Department of Justice (June 1877)
Director, Department of Commerce and Agriculture
  (Oct. 1877; June 1878)

After Ismail
President, Council of Ministers (Sept. 1879)
Director, Department of the Interior (Aug. 1882)
President, Council of Ministers (June 1888; Jan. 1893)

Sources: MM, no. 27656, *Mudad istikhdam Mustafa Riyad Basha;* al-Ayyubi, *Tarikh,*
vol. 2, pp. 197–202; Sami, pt. 3, vol. 1, pp. 55, 61, 181; pt. 3, vol. 2, pp. 448, 562, 572, 791,
1028; pt. 3, vol. 3, pp. 1042, 1081, 1159, 1232, 1271, 1355, 1494, 1513; Darwish, *al-Wizarat,*
pt. 1.
  [a]*Katib Arabi;* al-Ayyubi (*Tarikh*, vol. 2, p. 197) records that this appointment was made
on 18 Jan. 1848. Dates used for early appointments are cited in Riyad's pension dossier.
  [b]*Diwan al-Katkhuda.*
  [c]A primary, preparatory, and military/technical training school under Abbas.
  [d]*Majlis al-Ahkam.*
  [e]*al-Khassa.*

of that privileged elite of *Dhawat* officials. He could now begin to forget his past.

In November 1853, Riyad was named governor of al-Jiza province where he remained until October 1856. It is noteworthy that Sa'id allowed Riyad to continue as governor for two years when most of Abbas's high officials were dismissed within several months of Sa'id's accession, and especially since slanderers had charged that Riyad was one of Abbas's lovers.[115] Such rumors notwithstanding, Sa'id appointed Riyad to be administrative chief (*Ma'mur al-idara*) of al-Fayyum and in December 1856, named him governor of Qina. Somewhat later, Riyad was transferred to Cairo as deputy director of the railway administration, but he was soon returned to the province of Rawdat al-Bahrayn. At this point, Riyad's career encountered a setback. During one of Sa'id's inspection tours, negligence was uncovered in the administration of Riyad's province, and in December 1860, Riyad, the governor, and another high official were summarily dismissed (although they may not have been the guilty parties.)[116] Sa'id's anger, typically, was short-lived. Riyad was soon returned to the service with an appointment to the viceregal cabinet and a promotion in rank.

Like most other high officials of his day, Riyad had already attained prominence by the time of the accession of Ismail, who promoted him to first rank and appointed him to the post of keeper of the seal, which Riyad had held under Abbas.[117] Riyad was also made a member of the Council of Justice, and in October 1864, became director of Ismail's private administration, the *Khassa*. Riyad continued in this position for only a month, but held on to the important court position of keeper of the seal for a longer period.[118]

During the 1860s, Riyad, like most other important officeholders, was busy accumulating and developing a landed estate (see table 26). As usual, this was made possible by gifts of cash and land granted by Ismail during the boom years. Between 1853 and 1862, Riyad acquired but 290 *faddans* of *ushuriya* land. Between June 1863 and May 1864, however, he accumulated 1,778 *faddans*, of which 850 are known to have been granted him by the viceroy. Additionally, Riyad received £E 6,000 in cash gratuities from Ismail, and a grant of £ 2,000 to help him pay for a house.[119] Yet Riyad did not appear to be a wealthy man. He dressed quite modestly, and lived inconspicuously in an old part of Cairo. Riyad's unadorned and unfashionable home contrasted sharply with the splendid palaces of Sharif and Nubar. Bell regarded him as impecunious, which he attributed to Riyad's unwillingness to benefit personally from high office.[120]

TABLE 26
LANDHOLDINGS OF MUSTAFA RIYAD PASHA

	No. of Faddans	Date Acquired	Location
From *Dhawat*	57	16 Jan. 1853	al-Jiza
Land Register	233	8 Aug. 1862	al-Jiza
	100	15 July 1863	al-Minya
	478	14 Aug. 1863	al-Gharbiya
	350	12 May 1864	al-Daqahliya
	1,218 (subtotal)		
	− 573 (ceded)[a]		
	1,119 (total shown in register)		
	645 (adjusted total)[b]		
From other	500	4 June 1863	—
records	350	15 Feb. 1864	—
	850 (total)		

Sources: Egyptian National Archives, *Daftar zimam atyan ushuriya: Dhawat*, no. 1343; Sami, pt. 3, vol. 2, pp. 490, 539.
Note: Dashes indicate information not available.
[a]Properties sold or transferred to other persons during the 1860s.
[b]According to the author's count.

In February 1868, Riyad was suddenly dismissed from his post as keeper of the seal and expelled from the viceroy's service. The precise reason for this is unknown, but Ahmad Zaki (a contemporary of Riyad who also served in the viceregal household) has written that Ismail became very angry with Riyad, and that the antagonism between the two men was well known.[121] Perhaps the reason can be found in Riyad's own temperament, which ill suited him to serve such a demanding and tyrannical master. Riyad was by nature very independent, and had a strong stubborn streak; he was also exceedingly vain. Riyad, writes Bell, had no theories, only convictions, and these were presented as absolute truths. Riyad was not content with personal honesty; but waged a private campaign against venality in the government. His criticisms so aroused Ismail's ire that he reprimanded Riyad, who responded by giving the khedive the same lecture on the evils of venality that he had delivered to his subordinates.[122] Unaccustomed to such back talk, Ismail reportedly could not find a single instance of corruption in Riyad's past that could be used to silence him. It is surprising that such temerity did not cause Riyad more falls from grace. But Ismail was a shrewd judge of talent; perhaps he controlled his anger because of Riyad's indispensability.

Riyad was simply too valuable to be kept out of office for long. Eight months after his dismissal, he was reappointed to the viceregal cabinet as Khedive Ismail's *khaznadar* (chief treasurer), a position of great trust since its holder was responsible for receiving and disbursing large amounts of money. Riyad thus had an opportunity to learn the intricacies of viceregal finances as well as to follow the development of Ismail's family estates, for as chief treasurer he was delegated to receive the notes and papers sent to the khedive by the officials of the *Daira Saniya* and the *Daira Khassa*.[123] Riyad thus became the intermediary between Ismail and his private administrations. It has been suggested that Riyad was chosen for this job because he knew Arabic as well as Turkish, and could therefore translate readily the many documents brought to him, but his fiscal integrity must also have been an important consideration. Despite this appointment, Ismail may still have harbored ill feelings toward Riyad, for his salary in this new position was cut by 4,000 piastres a month.[124]

Following his appointment as chief treasurer, Riyad's stock within the administration soared.[125] He was named adviser to Prince Tawfiq (president of the Privy Council). He was given a large increase in salary from 7,500 to 12,500 piastres. And in August 1873, Riyad was made director of education and charitable endowments, the first of many "ministerial" appointments given to him during the 1870s. This first appointment (Riyad was also adviser to the director of the Interior Department and president of the guardianship court for orphans) was perhaps his most important, not by virtue of the influence he acquired, but because at this time he gained a reputation as a reformer which remained with him the rest of his life.

The use of the word "renaissance" by Abd al-Karim to describe Riyad's achievements as director of education is much too generous. Riyad's tenure lasted less than a year; many of his projects were discontinued after he left office and others were implemented only years later. Yet Riyad's work as director of education was not without importance: he carried forward the reorganization begun by Ali Mubarak, whose major contribution was to provide a physical base for a new educational program.[126] Employing teachers, assigning salaries, establishing new schools—these had been the kinds of rudimentary tasks faced by Ali Mubarak, and Riyad built on that foundation. New study programs were organized. Age limits were fixed for students at the elementary, preparatory, and advanced levels. Course requirements were established for passing from one level to another. Plans were laid for a teacher's training school. Parents from high or middle income levels were required to pay for their children's education. This last reform died shortly after Riyad left the department, and the plan for a teacher's training school was not realized for years, but many other reform projects were implemented during Riyad's tenure.

Claiming that he could not find a capable cadre of reform-minded administrators to assist him, Riyad spent most of his time in the field examining students and placing them in the appropriate schools (personal supervision of this kind was indispensable for the success of any new policy or program). Yet Riyad did not have enough time to achieve more than a modest success, and at any rate he was no more than an agent of the ruler for a program whose chief result was ever greater bureaucratic control over education.

When Riyad left the Department of Education in May 1874, he had consolidated his already well-deserved reputation as a reformer. As noted earlier, Riyad was a bold critic of corruption in government, and an opponent of injustice.[127] Above all, he was committed to the improvement and spread of education in Egypt, the depth of his commitment reflected in endowing the revenue from 1,806 *faddans* of land in lower Egypt to support the khedivial library (*al-Kutubkhana al-Khidiwiya*).[128] As specified in his endowment, revenue from these lands was to be used to pay the salaries of the clerks and other personnel, to buy new books and repair old ones, to purchase equipment, and to defray government taxes on the land and buildings. No other official whose endowments were available for this study could boast of a comparable commitment.

Riyad's interest in reform, however, should not be interpreted to mean that he was imbued with new attitudes and beliefs of European origin, or that he supported the wholesale importation of European technology into Egypt. (However, Riyad brought to Egypt the founders of the important journal *al-Muqtataf*, through which many new scientific ideas came to the Middle East.) Riyad's interest in reform appears to have stemmed from sympathy for the ignorance and poverty of the population, and perhaps this is why some observers describe him as a patriot.[129] Riyad also seems to have possessed a strong concept of duty. He was susceptible to requests to serve in the government when they were couched in appeals to his sense of responsibility.[130] Yet Riyad was not a democrat or patriot in the modern sense; his attitude toward the natives was like that of an oriental father toward his sons. The Egyptians, he said, were like children who needed strict supervision and protection from mistreatment. Milner compared Riyad's paternal attitude to that of a feudal baron of the better sort toward his serfs.[131] Riyad was not cruel or unjust, but he believed strongly in exercising a heavy hand. He was certainly no constitutionalist.

Riyad regarded European technology and science as useful within limits, and was apparently impressed by European budgetary methods, but he did not believe that Egypt's revitalization must depend upon an outside stimulus. Recall that Riyad was a staunch Muslim, a vigorous defender of the religious law and tradition. The Muslims had been great once, he said, and they could be great again.[132] Islam, he believed, contained a vitality of its own. Riyad was also aware of the unfair advantage that Europeans had acquired in Egypt. Europeans should be brought under Egyptian laws, he argued, and forced to give up the privileged position that had made them a state within a state.[133] Riyad at least had a more realistic view of the European impact upon Egypt than did other so-called reformers who failed or did not want to see its negative consequences.

▲▲▲ BOGHOS NUBAR

One such reformer was Boghos Nubar (1825–1899), a leading statesman of Armenian origin who did more to advance the cause of Europe than any other official. Bold and outspoken in his opinions, and never really trusted by any of the rulers he served, Nubar nonetheless held the unique distinction of serving as translator in the viceregal cabinet under four viceroys. Under Ismail, he served as foreign minister and was the chief agent in most of the financial and political negotiations of the time. At home in all the major capitals of Europe, Nubar Pasha acquired a reputation as a great reformer, and his stature rivaled that of Ismail Siddiq.

Nubar's life and career contained many elements of paradox. Professing to be a man of high principles, Nubar did not hesitate to fill his pockets if given the opportunity. An ardent champion of the "suffering" *fallahin*, he neither knew Arabic nor possessed roots in native society. The chief negotiator of most of Egypt's loans, he refused to accept any responsibility for their disastrous results. A leading advocate of an independent Egypt, Nubar did more than any other official to make the country dependent upon Europe.

These inconsistencies explain why writers are divided in their judgments of the man.[134] To Alexandre Holynski, Nubar was a great patriot, a civilizer among barbarians, a fighter for the oppressed, the Cobden of Egypt. Dicey and Bertrand are only slightly less restrained in their praise of this "great reformer." To the contrary, McCoan and Wallace portray him as ambitious, eager for high position, and devious, the man who did more than anyone else to undermine viceregal power.

NUBAR PASHA (1825–1899)
From Sami, *Taqwim al-Nil*, pt. 3, vol. 2, facing p. 594.

Because Nubar played such a central and important role in the major issues of his time, we may inquire into the ingredients of his success. How was it possible for such a man to have enjoyed influence and high position under four viceroys for more than thirty years? (See table 27.)

The first element of Nubar's success was his family connections, particularly the patronage of his uncle and influential in-laws in high positions in Istanbul who rendered important services for Khedive Ismail. Born in Smyrna, Nubar was educated at a school in Sorèze in France and then at a Protestant school in Switzerland.[135] After completing his studies, he was summoned to Egypt by his uncle, Boghos Bey Yusufiyan, who for many years had been chief translator for Muhammad Ali. Nubar was immediately brought into the household as an assistant to Boghos, who admonished his nephew to learn Turkish since that would be the basis of his future success. It is not known precisely when Nubar began his work in Egypt. A British archival document records that in 1833 Nubar was acting as interpreter to Muhammad Ali in his uncle's absence. According to Bertrand, Nubar was presented to Muhammad Ali in 1842. In his pension dossier Nubar records that he entered government service in 1844. Whatever the case may be, Nubar worked alongside Boghos for a while, and after his uncle died in 1844, was employed in the office of Khusrow Bey, who had succeeded Boghos as chief interpreter for Muhammad Ali. Without the early patronage of Boghos, Nubar would not have been in a position of direct contact with the ruler or members of his family.

Nubar was soon assigned to the entourage of Muhammad Ali's son,

TABLE 27

MAJOR POSITIONS HELD BY NUBAR PASHA

Translator in office of Khusrow Bey (1843/44)
Translator for Ibrahim Pasha (by Oct. 1847)
Chief translator for Abbas Pasha (Dec. 1850)
Chargé d'affaires in Vienna (July 1853)
Secretary for Sa'id Pasha (1854?)
Director, Department of Communications and Railway (Jan. 1858)
Chief translator for Ismail Pasha (Jan. 1863)
Director, Department of Public Works (Dec. 1864)
Director, Department of Foreign Affairs (Jan. 1866, June 1875)
Director, Department of Commerce (Sept. 1875)
President, Council of Ministers (Aug. 1878, Jan. 1884, Apr. 1894)

Sources: MM, no. 8321, *Mudad istikhdam Nubar Basha; WM*, no. 87, 9 D 1263/19 Oct. 1847; Stephen Bey/Gilbert, 29 Dec. 1850, in FO 141/16, pt. 3; Sami, pt. 3, vol. 1, pp. 58, 234; pt. 3, vol. 2, pp. 444, 582, 608; pt. 3, vol. 3, pp. 1202, 1232, 1518; Darwish, *al-Wizarat*, pt. 1.

Ibrahim Pasha, whom he served as translator and unofficial adviser.[136] About this time, Nubar made an important marriage to the daughter of a prominent Armenian notable from Istanbul, Kevork Bey Iramiyan. This family subsequently became a source of high connections for Nubar, who used his patronage to procure government positions in Egypt for some of its members while they in turn rendered important services in Istanbul for him and Khedive Ismail. Nubar's brother-in-law, Abraham Bey, an intimate of Sultan Abd al-Aziz, subsequently became Ismail's representative in Istanbul, and Kevork Bey became his chief treasurer (sarraf pasha) there. Kevork financed Ismail's visits to Istanbul, remunerated members of the viceroy's family who lived there, and paid the viceroy's agents. Nubar's wife was herself extremely well educated. She became an adviser to her husband and was a tactful and charming hostess—the perfect wife of a statesman.

A second ingredient of Nubar's success was his ability to deal with Europeans. Following Ibrahim's death in 1848, Abbas appointed Nubar chief translator, an extraordinary act for a ruler so hostile to Ibrahim and those associated with him.[137] Abbas had requested diplomatic support from Great Britain in his conflict with the Ottomans, and in return had offered to build a railway to facilitate Britain's overland traffic with India.[138] Unaccustomed to dealing with Europeans, the viceroy needed agents in the upcoming negotiations. In April 1851, four months after his appointment as chief translator, Nubar departed Egypt by steamer for Britain with complete authority to negotiate contracts for the rails, carriages, and other equipment and supplies needed for the construction of the railway.[139] This was only the first of numerous occasions on which Egypt's viceroys called upon Nubar for assistance in their dealings with Europeans. During the reigns of Sa'id and Ismail, Nubar was a principal agent in negotiating their private and public loans. He also led the discussions for the revision of the concession of the Suez Canal Company, and he conducted the tortuous negotiations that resulted in the establishment of the mixed courts (of this, more later).

What made Nubar such an ideal agent? In the first place, he was in many ways more European than oriental. His dress (save for the fez) was entirely Western in style. As a young man, he had spent many years in Europe, and he was fluent in all of the major European languages (he reportedly spoke eleven).[140] He was also well read, especially in European literature, and could discuss knowledgeably a wide range of subjects. He could grasp quickly the point of an argument, and his broad liberal ideas appealed readily to educated Europeans. Second, many Europeans found him irresistibly charming. His grace, logical discourse, and smooth manner made him very persuasive. "I used often to half believe him," wrote Cromer, "when I knew full well he was trying to dupe me."[141] King Louis Philippe was so impressed by Nubar when he accompanied Ibrahim on an official trip to France that he presented the young man with a medal of honor. But above all, Nubar had an adaptable and clever mind; he is described as subtle and devious, a juggler, a man of finesse bordering on duplicity who could cover words with a veil of ambiguity and who always left an opening for a retreat. Perhaps more than any other quality, this suited Nubar for the task of diplomat and ambassador extraordinaire.

Nubar served as chief translator to Abbas until 1853 when, in a curious incident never fully explained, Nubar asked and received permission to leave the government (an action almost unheard of), and then was apparently persuaded by Abbas to become his chargé d'affaires in Vienna (Nubar's brother, Arakil, was named chargé d'affaires in Berlin).[142] Following Abbas's death, Sa'id Pasha closed these agencies, but he too had need of Nubar's talents. Nubar organized the transit traffic between Cairo and Suez, was named secretary in the viceregal cabinet, and in January 1858, was appointed director of Communications and Railway; fifteen months later, however, Nubar's career came to a temporary halt when he was removed from Communications and Railway in disgrace.[143]

The official reason for this dismissal was a delay in the arrival of two guns ordered by the viceroy, but the real reason, as revealed in a British Foreign Office dispatch, was that Nubar had come to rely too heavily upon the support of the British consul general.[144] In announcing the dismissal, Sa'id told Nubar that since he was depending upon others for support, he could go and live with them. Nubar's removal evoked a strong protest from the British representative, who acknowledged that no director of communications could hold his post for long without British protection, but he denied that his government exercised indirect influence over Egypt's officials.

This incident reveals another partial explanation for Nubar's rise and success in government service. From time to time, Nubar received support from the consular representatives of Great Britain and (to a much lesser extent) Germany. The precise nature and extent of Nubar's ties with the British remain a mystery, but it is doubtful that he was actually in the pay of the British government, as the French Foreign Office chose to believe.[145] It is true, however, that on various occasions Nubar acted to favor British interests. He allegedly helped persuade Abbas to build the Alexandria-Cairo railway, and his opposition to the Suez Canal project dovetailed with British objections.[146]

If British consular backing led to his dismissal in 1859, it could on other occasions facilitate his career. Nubar reportedly was maintained in office under Abbas by the support of British Consul General Murray, who is said to have had considerable influence upon the viceroy.[147] In the mid-1860s, Nubar was supported by the British consul general in his successful efforts to have his chief rival, Ismail Raghib, removed as director of the viceregal cabinet. (Raghib was himself aided by the French.)[148] During the 1870s, Nubar may also have had the backing of the German consul general. Support for this view can be found in the protest made by German Consul General Jasmund against Nubar's dismissal as director of foreign affairs in 1874, and his insistence that Nubar be reinstated.[149] Until new information can establish these connections in a more precise way, they remain a subject of rumor and speculation. Yet Nubar's British connection is worthy of attention because of the strong alliance that developed between him and British interests in the years after 1874.

Nubar's chief sources of support, of course, were the viceroys, and none more than Khedive Ismail. During the first year of Ismail's reign, Nubar spent much of his time outside Egypt. He visited Istanbul to present Ismail's views on the revision of the Suez Canal concession, and he also visited Paris to conduct negotiations with the French.[150] After his return to Cairo, buoyed by the confidence that Ismail had reposed in him, Nubar began an intrigue against Ismail Raghib, who as director of the viceregal cabinet and president of the Privy Council was the highest-ranking official in the country. Ismail Raghib, as we have seen, eventually fell out of favor, and by 1865 Nubar had become, in the words of British Consul General Colquhoun, the "first man in Egypt."[151] (Ismail Siddiq, it may be recalled, was just beginning his rise.)

Vain and ambitious, Nubar presumably accomplished this feat by sheer personal effort, since he did not have a large group of followers in the country. He certainly could not have relied upon the support of most other high-ranking officials, who were Turks (Muhammad Sharif was Nubar's bitter rival). In fact, Nubar could count as his friends only a handful of men, mostly Armenian officials related to him; among them were Nubar's brother-in-law, Iram Bey (appointments secretary to the viceroy), Arakil Bey, and Tigrane (Dikran), a nephew.[152] The measure of Nubar's triumph over Ismail Raghib is reflected in his appointment in 1864 as director of public works and railway with powers so extensive as to make him nearly autonomous.[153] Nubar was permitted to spend the revenue of this administration for whatever purposes he liked, issue promissory notes to obtain ready cash, control the department's accounts, and hire and fire officials (including Europeans). He wasted little time in exercising his powers of patronage: Tigrane was given an appointment in the railway administration, and Ali

Mubarak was made director of the office of engineering. By July 1865, Colquhoun could write that Nubar was the mastermind of Egypt's administration—quite an accomplishment for a man who had such a narrow base of support within the country and whose boldness and direct expressions of opinion were not customarily seen in the relations between viceroys and officials.

At this time Nubar was also accumulating land and cash on a scale that within a few years had made him one of the wealthiest officials in the country (see table 28).[154] Nubar seems to have cared little about how his wealth was acquired. Whenever he began to wax indignant about corruption in government, Ismail could quickly end the discussion by referring to one of Nubar's own "dirty" transactions.[155] Nubar was not very trustworthy. In 1875, the negotiations between Egypt and Britain for the sale of Ismail's Suez Canal shares were taken out of Nubar's hands because he was regarded as too shifty and treacherous; as de Kusel observed, Nubar had more cleverness than character.[156] Nubar benefited greatly from the commissions and rake-offs on the loans he negotiated, and his visits to Istanbul must have augmented considerably his wealth. Yet even without this, he would still have been a wealthy man. Nubar's wife possessed considerable wealth of her own, Khedive Ismail generously gave him grants of land, cash, and even an oil concession, and it is assumed that Nubar benefited greatly from speculative dealings on the stock market.[157] The gala balls and lavish dinner parties given regularly by Nubar and his wife reflected no mere pretense of wealth.

Nubar is well known for his role in helping obtain loans for Egypt's viceroys, in conducting the negotiations with Ottoman Turkey that led to the issuance of imperial decrees (firmans) consolidating Egypt's autonomy, and in the establishment of the mixed courts, regarded by many as his crowning achievement. On the basis of this, and as an organizer of Egypt's transportation system, he acquired a reputation as a reformer, which he himself was proud to acknowledge. (If permitted, Nubar would gladly have taken credit for every good thing that happened to Egypt.)[158] Nubar's unshakable conviction was that Egypt's assimilation of the fruits of European civilization would revitalize its government and its society. He was particularly attracted to the idea of the rule of law, universally held principles of right and wrong being infinitely superior to the dictates of kings and emperors; Nubar did not believe in the sacred character of kingship and showed little deference to the viceroys he served. However, this did not make him a democrat. He supported a reform of the judicial system that would check the harshest abuses of personal rule, but did not favor its replacement by parliamentary government. This, he believed, was not suited to the character of Egypt and its people. He also favored the rapid development of the country's material infrastructure (especially communications) by importing European technology and employing European specialists. Thus European civilization was necessary and beneficial to Egypt. Yet his view of reform was more "Nubarian" than European. He had no objections to using Europeans as a lever to pry concessions from the ruler, but he was opposed to direct European intervention. He supported the employment of Europeans, but not the

TABLE 28
LANDHOLDINGS OF NUBAR PASHA

	No. of Faddans		Date Acquired	Location
From *Dhawat*	500		12 Aug. 1852	al-Minufiya
Land Register	800		5 Mar. 1861	al-Minya
	506		14 July 1863	al-Minufiya
	2		24 Nov. 1865	al-Qalyubiya
	328		22 Dec. 1868	al-Minufiya
	300		23 July 1869	} al-Daqahliya
	207		19 Aug. 1869	
	2,643	(subtotal)		
	− 499	(ceded)[a]		
	2,193	(total shown in register)		
	2,144	(adjusted total)[b]		
From other records	494		Muhammad Ali's reign	—
	1,000		Abbas's reign	—
	800		Sa'id's reign	—
	320		6 July 1863	—
	275		23 Jan. 1871	—
	14		19 Apr. 1871	—
	157		22 Dec. 1875	—
	3,060	(subtotal)		
	−1,000	(ceded)[a]		
	2,060	(total)		

Sources: Egyptian National Archives, *Daftar zimam atyan ushuriya: Dhawat*, no. 1343; Sami, pt. 3, vol. 2, pp. 500, 914; *Mas, Awamir, Ma'iya Saniya-Arabi*, reg. 8/32/70, Viceroy/*al-Maliya*, 20 D 1292/22 Dec. 1875; reg. 1935/103/136, Viceroy/*al-Maliya*, 3 D 1287/25 Jan. 1871; *al-Abhath*, box 106, dossier "Nubar Basha," Viceroy/*al-Maliya*, 26 JA 1281/26 Nov. 1864; Barakat, *Tatawwur*, p. 175.

Note: Dashes indicate information not available.

[a] Properties sold or transferred to other persons.

[b] According to the author's count.

abdication of power to them. In short, Nubar had a vision of a reformed Egypt that would still be Egyptian.

There is no reason to doubt the sincerity of Nubar's professed devotion to his adopted country. He had a wide knowledge of Egyptian history and could expiate with great enthusiasm on the glories of Egypt's pharaonic past. He sympathized with the lot of the peasants, deplored the corvée system, and during the last decade of his life worked hard to abolish it. He disliked the harsh and arbitrary tax system which fell heavily upon the poor. The welfare of the Egyptian people was the professed touchstone of his policies.

It is ironic that Nubar's actions helped strangle the country he purported to love, but such was the result of his success in negotiating loans that led to a huge debt and resulted ultimately in foreign intervention. In 1862, Nubar went to Europe to negotiate Egypt's first major public loan, issued by the house of Oppenheim, who was supported by British interests (at this time, rumors circulated that Nubar received kickbacks in return for showing preference to certain contractors).[159] When Ismail came to power, he was immediately pressured by Oppenheim to accept a new public loan, a policy also favored by Nubar.[160] In 1864, Ismail's resistance collapsed, and he took out the first major loan of his reign, which opened the floodgates to further borrowing. By the summer of 1865, Ismail, again in desperate need of money, wanted to borrow two million pounds sterling on the security of the railroads and another three million on his own private property.[161] Negotiations thus were opened between Nubar and Oppenheim, and an agreement was reached in October for a loan (called the "railway loan") on very harsh terms. The following December, a loan on Ismail's *daira* properties was concluded. But Ismail had begun to lose confidence in Nubar, who apparently had been duped by Oppenheim into accepting terms for the railway loan that were much less favorable than they had appeared to be (the real cost was 14 percent instead of the 9 percent which Nubar believed he had agreed upon).[162] Ismail had Nubar inform Oppenheim that he refused to accept the railway loan, but in January 1866, a new agreement was reached on somewhat better terms than the last. By this time, however, rumors were rife of a secret deal made between Nubar and Oppenheim, of favoritism shown by Nubar in awarding concessions and contracts, and of speculation in treasury bonds by Nubar and Ismail's banker, Edward Dervieu. Because of this scandal, Nubar was removed from Public Works and Railway and was transferred to the Department of Foreign Affairs as its new director, a move planned several months earlier, though Nubar had hoped to retain Public Works.[163]

Nubar's place as Ismail's agent in the negotiation of loans was eventually taken over by Ismail Siddiq, who became director of finance in 1868. Nubar continued to be involved in the viceroy's financial affairs—in 1866 he was asked to direct the purchase of the estates of Mustafa Fadil (Ismail's brother)—but as Egypt's director of foreign affairs, he was increasingly abroad, engaged in political negotiations on Egyptian autonomy and the reform of Egypt's judicial system.

Nubar was directly involved in Ismail's successful efforts to widen the scope of Egypt's autonomy vis-à-vis the Ottomans. Shortly after Ismail's accession, he and Nubar began suggesting to influential Europeans the possibility of establishing in Egypt the principle of direct hereditary succession (in the Ottoman domains, succession passed to the eldest male representative).[164] This would give Egypt a dynasty modeled on European lines and emphasize further Egypt's special status within the Ottoman empire. In the negotiations that led to the *firman* of 1866, which granted this privilege to Egypt, Nubar served as Ismail's advocate and agent in Europe where he sedulously worked to persuade France and Britain not to oppose Ismail's efforts to establish hereditary rule.[165] Soon after this *firman* was issued, Ismail made further demands of the Porte, and Nubar was again enlisted to serve his master, but this time in a much more important role. In March 1867, Nubar left Paris for Istanbul to oversee the negotiations himself.[166] Backed by the financial resources of Ismail's government, Nubar told the Ottoman ministers that if they did not grant to Ismail the privileges he wanted, Egypt would quickly withdraw its troops from Crete (Egypt had previously assisted the Ottomans in quashing a revolt there), leaving the Sultan's government to face the disorder alone. Possessing wide discretionary powers that included the right to terminate the negotiations, in June 1867 Nubar finally wrung from the Ottomans an agreement that gave Ismail most of what he had sought. Thanks to Nubar's skillful work, the viceroy was given the right to conclude conventions with foreign powers on matters concerning the customs, transit, the post, and the European police force. He also formally received the title of khedive, and his right to regulate Egypt's internal administration was confirmed.

In 1867, Nubar embarked upon a new campaign that was to occupy him for most of the next eight years. For some time, Nubar and Ismail had been endeavoring to find a way to protect the government from claims brought by Europeans before the consular courts, and from the expense of submitting to the consuls all claims or charges against European criminals and defaulting debtors. By virtue of the Capitulations and subsequent abuses of privilege, the consuls had assumed full jurisdiction in all civil and criminal matters involving their nationals. In civil cases, an Egyptian with a claim against a foreigner had to bring it before the appropriate consular court. The Egyptian government was not the only party inconvenienced, for a European making a claim against a European of a different nationality had to bring the suit before the latter's consulate. As McCoan has observed, the entire system was a denial of justice and a complete scandal.[167]

In 1867, Nubar presented a report to Ismail that marked the beginning of a long fight to create the mixed courts, a new legal system that would replace these consular jurisdictions. Nubar proposed that new courts be established with jurisdiction over civil and commercial cases between foreigners and natives, and full criminal jurisdiction over cases involving foreigners.[168] These courts were to be divided evenly between Europeans and Egyptians, and to apply a code based upon European laws. Appealing to Europe, Nubar emphasized that these courts would constitute an independent judiciary, entirely free from government interference, and that this was to be guaranteed by the presence of European judges. Through a rule of law, he said, European enterprise and capital would be greatly facilitated in Egypt while the rights enjoyed by Europeans under the Capitulations would continue to be protected.

For the next eight years, Nubar fought hard to gain big-power approval of his proposals.[169] Nubar visited Bismarck in Berlin, Menabrea (the Italian premier) in Florence, and conducted a press campaign in England where he singlehandedly put together a lobby in favor of his program. He convened an international commission and showed himself willing to modify important parts of his original proposal in order to save the project (thus Nubar agreed that a majority of judges would be European). Delayed by the Franco-Prussian War, by the objections of the Ottomans who feared that the creation of a new legal system in Egypt was merely another step in its movement toward de facto independence, and by the stubborn opposition of the French foreign ministry, the mixed courts were finally inaugurated by Ismail in June 1875, after having been approved by all of the major European powers except France (although French support was soon forthcoming). Unfortunately, Nubar was not able to establish a criminal jurisdiction for these tribunals that would bring Egyptians under their sway and therefore protect the *fallahin* from viceregal despotism (which seems to have been one of his aims), but the original objective of superseding the consular jurisdictions was attained. The new mixed courts had full jurisdiction in all civil disputes between foreigners of different nationalities and also between foreigners and Egyptians, including the Egyptian government. The moment chosen for their establishment was auspicious, for in 1875 Europe was about to begin an intervention in Egypt's affairs that would lead to the deposition of the khedive. As we shall see, these courts soon became a weapon which was used to weaken viceregal power. In a different way, perhaps, Nubar's wish was realized after all.

Having met the individuals who helped maintain viceregal autocracy before 1874, we can now turn to the 1875–1879 period and observe how European intervention broke the bonds of cooperation between the viceroy and his men.

▲▲▲▲ PART III ▲▲▲▲
The Decentralization of Power,
1875–1879

▲ 7 ▲
THE DISMANTLING OF KHEDIVIAL ABSOLUTISM

▲▲▲ EXTIRPATING THE FISCAL ROOTS OF VICEREGAL POWER

Throughout Egyptian history, centralized regimes had based their power upon the nucleus of a personally dependent elite whose members controlled the state apparatus. This had ensured Cairo's domination over the hinterland and, through it, control of the agricultural surplus. Though the ruling groups and power combinations they represented differed from one period to another, the crucial factor and principal element of success was the elite's direct dependence on the ruler. Centralized regimes broke up when members of the elite developed associations that conflicted with their loyalties and obligations to the ruler. But a catalyst was also needed to produce a reversal of centralization. A military defeat, the sudden death of a ruler, a natural disaster, a powerful outside force: these could precipitate the unraveling of centralized power and bring about a period of political and economic disorder.

In 1875, the catalyst for the breakup of Egypt's ruling combination was the European powers themselves, who began to intervene in Egyptian affairs after it had become clear that Ismail's government could no longer meet its payments on the debt. In less than three years, the Europeans had stripped Ismail of the principal sources of state revenue, and by fall 1878 they were beginning to threaten his political control directly. At this juncture, key individuals from within the power elite left Ismail's side and joined the Europeans to form a ministry headed by Nubar, which dispossessed Ismail of his landed estates and displaced him from the center of power. Collaboration thus ensured European control without an occupation. However, the breakup of the combination on which Egypt's government had previously rested released social forces hostile to Europe; and Ismail, taking advantage of popular resistance, was able to mount a comeback. He was supported by the Turkish and Egyptian notable elite, who feared for the security of their landed estates and who hoped, by allying with Ismail, to guarantee their own safety and to assert themselves. Ismail's return to power forced the Europeans to adopt a tactic that they had long threatened but had always resisted: to bring pressure upon the central government in Istanbul, and in June 1879, Ismail was deposed as viceroy of Egypt.

The deposition of Ismail signified not only the passing of another ruler, but also the end of an age. Though Egypt would continue to be governed by rulers called khedives, never again would their power be so absolute or despotic as it had been in the 1805–1879 period.

The rapidity with which Ismail lost his power in the years after 1875 can be explained by reference to circumstances that had been building up in the preceding period and which by the mid-1870s had reached a critical point; only a spark was needed to ignite a political explosion. This is perhaps most evident in the increasing difficulties faced by the Egyptian government in meeting its debt payments; but the European penetration of Egypt's administrative system and the development of ties between *dhawat* officials, Europeans, and others were equally crucial causes. The decline and fall of viceregal absolutism between 1875 and 1879 follows logically from and in a sense completes the previous period.

The end of Ismail's power, however, did not result in the dismantling or destruction of the political/administrative order that had supported it. We have seen how a new kind of power state, with a hierarchical bureaucracy at the center, came into existence in Muhammad Ali's time, and was built up by his successors. After 1875, new groups struggled with old groups for control of the administrative apparatus, and used it to impose their will upon the country.

Our task here is to examine the process by which European intervention deprived the ruler of control over his resources, to explain the defection of some of Egypt's leading officials and elucidate the consequences, to analyze the role of Turkish and Egyptian notable *dhawat* in helping bring about Ismail's return to power; and, finally, to detail the events that led to his deposition.

The immediate cause of European intervention was the Egyptian government's failure to make interest payments on the debt. Until 1868, its chief financial problem had been the floating debt imposed upon the country by the Suez Canal concession, the arbitration of Napoleon III, and the claims of European speculators, which had led to the uncontrolled issue of short-term paper. With the loan of 1868, however, long-term indebtedness became a very serious problem. Desperate attempts to reverse this process came to no avail. Ismail and his advisers had hoped that the Law of *al-Muqabala* (by which landholders who paid an amount equal to six times their annual tax were relieved of one-half of all future land tax liabilities) would bring in enough revenue to extinguish the debt, but this measure only succeeded in benefiting the wealthiest landholders and raised less than half the expected amount.[1] The goal of unifying and converting the treasury bonds and loans simply could not be achieved. Ismail made one last attempt in 1873 when he raised a foreign loan of £32,000,000 and committed his government to pay almost £77,000,000 in return. With this, Egypt's doom was sealed.

Egypt's creditors became nervous. They began to clamor for their money. They made sure that Egypt's financial difficulties were fully discussed in the press and in the legislatures of Europe. They brought pressure to bear upon their governments. With Egypt verging upon bankruptcy, Britain and France, each eager to establish a predominant influence over Egyptian finances, began their intervention.

In 1875 Great Britain sent Stephen Cave, its paymaster general, to Cairo to conduct an inquiry into Egyptian finances and to submit a report. Upon learning of Cave's objective, a startled Ismail remonstrated that an official investigation into his finances by an employee of a foreign government had not been his intention when he requested Britain to send two men for employment in his Department of Finance. Cave's mission, he said, would only serve as a pretext for intervention by other powers and lead to an abridgment of his administrative privileges. To these objections, the British consul general blandly replied that his government had merely believed the Cave mission to be the best way of responding to Ismail's request, and that it had no intention of interfering in his affairs.[2]

Ismail, however, was right. Soon after the Cave mission was announced, the French government sent a former French consul general in Egypt named Outrey to Cairo. Outrey accused Britain, in Ismail's presence, of wanting a protectorate over Egypt, and threw his weight behind a plan offered by a group of French capitalists to establish a national bank under international control, with commissioners appointed by France, Italy, and England to consolidate the floating debt and pay the coupons.[3] On February 19, 1876, Britain's consul general informed the Foreign Office that the Egyptian government had agreed.[4] Britain strongly opposed the plan, contending that the proposed bank would have no real control over finances. The British government dispatched Sir Rivers Wilson, comptroller of the British national debt, with proposals to counter the French scheme, instructing its consul general to give Wilson full "unofficial" support.[5] To counteract British moves, the French government sent a representative named de Villet, who by mid-March, as a result of strong French pressure, had been appointed adviser to the Finance Department.[6] On

March 14, Stanton, Britain's consul general, wrote to his government that Ismail was at last firmly in the clutches of the French.[7]

The arrival of the Cave report at the Foreign Office on March 13, 1876, the very moment when French interests were triumphing in Cairo, set in motion a series of dramatic events which ruined Ismail's credit. The Cave report, a lengthy and embarrassing statement of the causes and current status of Egypt's financial position, had been drawn up with the understanding that it would remain confidential.[8] Yet within ten days of its arrival, Disraeli made a public statement that fell like a bombshell in Egyptian financial circles. Disraeli said to the House of Commons that he did not object to the publication of Cave's report, but suggested that the khedive did.[9] Nothing, not even the publication of the report itself, could have been better calculated to ruin Ismail's credit. Within hours, Egyptian securities plunged in value, panic set in, and the money markets were closed to Ismail. Those French financiers who had invested heavily in Egyptian stocks in expectation of the consolidation of the floating debt and the formation of a national bank were seriously threatened, but far more important, Egypt's default on the April payment of the coupon was almost a certainty. After a last-minute attempt by the French government to rescue his credit failed, an embittered Ismail announced on April 8 a three-month suspension of the payment of the debt, an action which caused panic among stockholders and brought forth cries for his abdication.

What were the reasons for this European intervention, and how can the differences between Britain and France on the financial question be explained? When one considers the record of European interference in Egypt and especially the financial history of the Suez Canal—the engine of Egypt's ruin—and when one understands that the governments of Britain and France, from the very beginning, consistently supported the claims of their own merchants and financiers, there can be no doubt about the economic motivations behind this new involvement. European intervention was designed to support those very creditors who had mercilessly exploited Egypt. In this, however, Britain and France were competitors rather than allies, in large part because each had quite different interests in the terms of settlement. Of the seven major loans made by Khedive Ismail, five were issued entirely or in part by British-supported interests. The loan of 1867, for example, was issued in sterling by the Ottoman Imperial Bank, the General Bond being deposited in the Bank of England.[10] The loans of 1864, 1866, 1868, and 1873 were made by Oppenheim, who was supported by British interests. The French, on the other hand, held a considerable portion of Egypt's floating debt. The fact that English financiers held the greater part of Egypt's long-term debt while the French held a large share of the bonds and other short-term paper issued by the Egyptian government meant that each power would seek to shape a final settlement that favored its own creditors. It should also be noted that the British government itself had a big financial stake in Egypt. In 1875, Disraeli had purchased (at almost a quarter of the original cost) 176,000 shares of Suez Canal stock from Ismail.[11] Britain, of course, had a long-standing interest in the security of Egyptian communications, especially the railroads, for its own purposes. The French, too, highly valued the Suez Canal and the overland route across Egypt, but Britain's investment was considerably greater than that of France.

In the short term at least, Britain was the loser. Soon after Ismail's suspension of payments, the French-inspired National Bank scheme was revived in a new form. By a viceregal decree of May 2, a Commission of Public Debt (*Caisse de la dette publique*) was formed to receive and disburse the revenue assigned to the payment of the coupons.[12] Although without formal administrative power, and not yet capable of exerting international control (this commission was created unilaterally by Ismail to pacify the powers), the *Caisse de la dette*, whose members were to represent the bondholders and be designated by the governments of France, Italy, Austria, and Great Britain, would show itself to be more aggressive than Ismail had expected. Several days after its formation, a second viceregal decree (May 7) was issued embodying French proposals for settling the debt. Egypt's debt, both long-term and floating, was consolidated into one unified debt of £91,000,000 at 7 percent interest.[13] Welcomed in France, this settlement was poorly received in Britain, whose government adamantly refused to appoint a debt commissioner.

The next important step in the advancement of European financial interests came on November 18, 1876, when a viceregal decree sanctioned a revised settlement of the Egyptian debt (known as the Goschen-Joubert settlement) that provided for joint Anglo-French control over vital areas of Egypt's administration.

This new arrangement grew out of British opposition to the May settlement, which had aroused protests in London from the Council of Foreign Bondholders and from the stock exchange committee.[14] These two groups received promises of "unofficial" assistance from their government, and they and the British government entered into separate discussions with their French counterparts in hopes of inducing them to accept a revision of the debt settlement and the establishment of some kind of control over Egyptian finances. Since without British support not even the May settlement could succeed, the French banking houses finally agreed to accept a reduction (from 25 percent to 10 percent) in the bonus given to holders of Egyptian bonds and to cooperate with the British bondholders in pressing for joint Anglo-French political control over Egypt's financial administration. On the basis of this understanding, a revised scheme for the debt was outlined, and in July 1876 the British bondholders delegated G. J. Goschen to proceed to Cairo on a joint mission with a M. Joubert, representing the French bondholders, to renegotiate the May settlement. This was the G. J. Goschen of Fruhling and Goschen, the prominent London banking firm which, as allies of Oppenheim, had been agents and subcontractors for several Egyptian loans. A former cabinet minister and former president of the Council of Foreign Bondholders, Goschen had been primarily a politician since 1865 and had been building up a reputation as an impartial financial expert. One of Britain's few truly first-rate financiers in the technical sense, Goschen came to Egypt fully confident of success.

But first Ismail had to be induced to accept Goschen and his French colleague Joubert. Ismail, who wanted declaration of bankruptcy, could not be expected to look with favor upon a mission whose purpose was to tighten the screws still more.[15] Consular pressure, therefore, was needed. Baron des Michels, who had been sent as the French consul general to work closely with his former colleague, British Consul General Vivian, in establishing joint European control, was instructed to urge Ismail to accept Goschen and Joubert and also to warn him that he might be deposed if he repudiated his obligations. Ismail must have found it painful to smile when told by Vivian that Goschen only wanted to be fair to both sides, his own and the khedive's. Yet, because Britain and France were now acting in concert, resistance was hopeless, and Ismail reluctantly consented to receive the mission.

Resistance, however, came from another quarter. Former Inspector General Ismail Siddiq vehemently denounced the idea of control as tantamount to handing Egypt's administration over to foreigners, and he attacked the proposed rate of repayment as ruinous to the country.[16] Since May, the *mufattish* had vigorously obstructed the work of the Debt Commission to obtain control of revenue which, in theory, it had the right to receive. When the money received by the *Caisse* during July and August from four Egyptian provinces came to only 14 percent of the estimated revenue, Ismail Siddiq claimed that these estimates were based upon inexact information.[17] When the discrepancy for September and October turned out to be even greater (11 percent of the estimated revenue was actually received), being based upon a new set of estimates which the *mufattish* asserted to be more accurate, the Debt Commission quickly concluded that funds were being diverted to his office. Ismail Siddiq refused to turn over to the *Caisse* the money he had received from the sale of wheat paid in taxes in al-Gharbiya province, and while always promising large sums, he never produced them.

Thus Goschen resolved to bring down the one man, next to the viceroy, who could defeat his mission. Goschen refused to pay even a courtesy visit to the Finance Department, and when his investigation began uncovering false accounts and evidence of speculation by Ismail Siddiq, Goschen used it to discredit him, hoping that he would be replaced by Sir Rivers Wilson.[18] In an interview with the viceroy, Vivian pressed him unofficially to dismiss his chief minister, but was told cryptically that the time was not right. Ultimately, direct action became necessary, and a pretext was found in the *mufattish*'s obstruction of the efforts of the *Caisse* to obtain revenue appropriated to the payment of the debt. On November 4, the Commission of the Public Debt, tacitly supported by the consuls, brought a formal charge of misappropriation of funds against Ismail Siddiq before the mixed courts.[19]

As we have seen, the mixed courts (opened on February 1, 1876) had superseded the consular jurisdictions in civil disputes between Europeans and Egyptians. They thus possessed an independent authority quite unlike that of any other legal body in Egypt. Dominated by European judges who were paid by the Egyptian government but nominated by the European powers for irrevocable five-year terms, these courts had the unusual power to hear cases against the Egyptian government, which was bound by a curious provision of the statute to execute the courts' judgments, even against itself.[20] At the time of Goschen's mission, private creditors had been obtaining judgments against Ismail in these courts, and when the government delayed their implementation, the court of appeals in Alexandria had ordered their enforcement. The decision by the Debt Commission to have recourse to these courts provided a precedent that was later seized upon by the European powers to justify threats to use these courts against the head of state.

The action of the Debt Commission and the unified stand taken by Goschen, Joubert, and the consuls of France and Britain, broke Ismail's support of his favorite minister. On November 10, in stunning succession Ismail Siddiq was arrested for fostering agitation in the provinces, tried and found guilty by the Privy Council, murdered in secret, and his body sent up the Nile in a sealed boat allegedly carrying him to exile in the Sudan.[21] Within twenty-four hours, the khedive notified Goschen and Joubert of his acceptance of their plan in its entirety, and one week later, on November 18, 1876, he issued the decree authorizing the new arrangements.

The truth about Ismail Siddiq's arrest, trial, and murder cannot be fully known because the available information is based almost entirely upon rumor, innuendo, and biased speculation.[22] Certainly the *mufattish* had many enemies, and some may have regarded Goschen as a rallying point around which they could work for his destruction. Rumors suggested that the viceroy and his chief minister had planned to stir up agitation in the provinces, and that Ismail Siddiq was made the scapegoat for the "sins" of his master. Reports also circulated that Ismail Siddiq had tried to blackmail the khedive, that he was plotting against him. Without doubt, Ismail Siddiq was a man who knew too much, someone therefore to be feared, a man for whom a public trial could lead to embarrassing exposures of the khedive's own wrongdoings. This is probably the reason for the extraordinary violence of his removal. The need to silence or punish those who could implicate the viceroy or who might be plotting against him also accounts for the violence with which some of the followers of Ismail Siddiq met their end.

The new settlement accepted by Ismail contained provisions of a financial and political nature. To provide for the payment of interest at a rate which was more favorable to British stockholders than the May settlement, the *daira* debts were joined to the floating debt, forming a separate arrangement (a compromise by the French); the loans of 1864, 1865, and 1867 were removed from the unified debt; and a preference stock of £17,000,000 was created to encourage investment. The consolidated debt was thereby reduced to £59,000,000 and was set at 7 percent.[23]

This settlement also provided for a limited kind of political control as a guarantee to European creditors that the khedive would no longer tamper with revenue allocated to pay the debt. This was achieved, first, by appointing two European controllers general, one to receive and remit to the Debt Commission the revenue pledged to the payment of the loans, the other to supervise the accounts of the government departments; second, by creating a board composed of two Englishmen, one Frenchman, and two Egyptians to manage the railroads and the port of Alexandria. Europeans were now in control of vital areas of Egyptian administration, and Egypt was saddled with debt payments amounting to about 66 percent of its estimated annual revenue.[24]

The last event in the establishment of European control over the viceroy's fiscal and economic resources was the formation on April 4, 1878, of a commission of inquiry into Egyptian finances. This development marked the beginning of a still deeper European involvement, and also reflected the failure of the Goschen-Joubert settlement. In spite of the removal of Ismail Siddiq, the administrations under Europe's charge did not yield the anticipated revenue. Egypt's railroads, expected to produce £900,000 a year, gave up only £30,000 a month; the customs administration ran up a huge deficit; and the three most productive delta provinces were £500,000 in the red.[25] Harsh methods were applied to raise revenue. To pay the coupon due on January 15, the controllers collected taxes in some parts of Egypt six months in advance. The July coupon was paid by an advance collection of nine and even twelve months. By fall 1877, the khedive was telling Vivian that the payment of the next coupon would consume most of the taxes for 1878. These tactics were strictly short-term. By autumn, Egypt's controllers, faced with huge deficits, had to admit that the December coupon could not be paid, a decision which revealed clearly the wreck of the Goschen-Joubert scheme.[26]

The reasons for this failure have been much debated. Some Europeans believed that Europe was asking more than Egypt could produce; others attributed the failure to faulty information given to Goschen, and to the allegedly illegal diversion of funds by Ismail.[27] There can be no doubt that Ismail resisted this settlement with all his might and thus contributed to its failure. He ordered officials to send the revenue they collected to him rather than to the European controllers, and sent trusted agents into the countryside to procure money for him. To improve Egypt's credit, he had deliberately exaggerated the size of the revenue upon which Goschen and Cave had based their estimates. He also sought to place himself in the most favorable light by proving he had spent large amounts of money on useful works. It is of course true that it was extremely difficult for anyone to know how much revenue Egypt was capable of producing. Yet Vivian and Baring were right: Ismail bore a considerable share of responsibility for the difficulties of these years and the failure of the Goschen settlement.

But so did the Europeans, who demanded economy from the khedive and his officials, yet refused to apply this standard to themselves. The controllers general, members of the Debt Commission, and officials of the Railway Board received huge salaries.[28] Because appointments were frequently made with a view to conciliating one European power or another, more European officials were employed than were needed. The appointment of five men for the relatively easy task of administering the railroads, Vivian wrote, was an "unnecessary extravagance." Their high salaries (£12,000 to £13,000 annually) placed a heavy burden on the railway budget.[29] The English directors of the railway and customs administrations filled the offices below them with young men imported from England, whose disproportionately high salaries were a principal cause of the huge deficits that accumulated in these administrations. "All nepotism or selection by favor without regard to qualifications or character," Vivian wrote, "must be avoided in a country like this."[30] Amid mounting deficits, the European consuls continued to support their nationals' indemnity claims (estimated by Vivian to be worth over £2,000,000).[31] Vivian used the threat of the mixed courts to pressure Ismail to settle the claims of British subjects.

Whatever the reason for the growing deficit, the fact remains that Goschen's estimate of revenue (slightly over £10,500,000) was much too high. Twenty years later, the most Egypt could produce was about £11,000,000 annually.[32] When this was combined with such adventitious developments as a bad Nile in 1877 and the Russo-Turkish war, for which Egypt had to provide a contingent of soldiers, the result was disaster. In 1877, Egypt yielded a revenue of only £9,543,000, of which £7,473,909 went to the bondholders. This left the government, after paying the tribute, with £1,070,000 for the expenses of administration.[33]

By fall, it was clear to Egypt's European creditors that additional sources of income would have to be found. Some began to cast covetous eyes upon two sources not yet brought under their control: the rich viceregal properties, estimated at about one million *faddans*, and the revenue that under the previous arrangement had been left to the khedive for the expenses of his household and administration. The Europeans gradually became convinced of the need for still another investigation into Egyptian finances to uncover new sources of wealth.[34] In an interview with Ismail, Vivian proposed that a commission of inquiry be appointed to look into expenditures as well as revenue, and he hinted that if new revenue sources were not found, Ismail might have to surrender his private estates. Was Europe, through this new inquiry, planning to indict Ismail for Egypt's ills and seize his lands? Ismail thought so, and he fought hard against European pressures to sanction a new inquiry. To compel access to expenditures, the controllers brought a suit before the mixed courts which required Ismail's son Hasan, director of finance, to account for all the monies he had received and spent. Vivian's intervention, and joint pressure from Germany, Austria, France, and Italy forced the viceroy's capitulation. On April 4, an exhausted Ismail issued a decree authorizing the establishment of a Commission of Inquiry with full powers of investigation, including the power to subpoena Egyptian officials. It was to consist of Ferdinand de Lesseps as president (although de Lesseps left Cairo shortly thereafter and never participated in the work of the commission), Sir Rivers Wilson (who became its real head) and Mustafa Riyad as vice-presidents, and the four debt commissioners.

The Commission at once set about to establish the fact, hardly surprising to anyone, that Egypt's administration had been entirely dependent upon Ismail, and that he was therefore personally responsible for Egypt's financial woes. Inquiries also began to be made about the size and location of Ismail's landed properties.[35] The commissioners soon realized, however, that the appropriation of viceregal properties was inseparable from the question of the viceroy's political control, for so long as Ismail retained his prerogatives, he could resist attack. European intervention now began to take a new turn. Khedivial power would have to be limited; a new political arrangement would have to be found; but how was this to be done? Ismail, who had fought so hard and resourcefully against the loss of his fiscal resources, and whose authority over the administration and the army was still great, could be expected to fight back with all his strength. In spring and summer 1878, Egypt's European creditors and their supporters were not prepared to see Ismail deposed altogether, nor did they have any military force at their immediate disposal. Yet it was clear that for the type of political operation now being envisaged, help from some quarter was desperately needed.

▲▲▲ THE POLITICS OF COLLABORATION

After 1875, Ismail was deprived in one way or another of the services of nearly all of his most competent and knowledgeable officials, men who had been with him since his accession and who were associated with the major achievements of his reign. The first step in the dissolution of his elite was the death of Ismail Siddiq, whose removal cost the viceroy the only man in Egypt with an intimate knowledge of the country's finances and provincial affairs. Moreover, because Ismail Siddiq had built up an intricate network of personal alliances, Ismail was forced to break up his large faction, which included many high-ranking officials. These clients were dismissed from their positions—Mustafa Bey, the son of the *mufattish*, was removed from his post in the viceregal cabinet and forced to divorce his wife, an adopted daughter of the viceroy—and about one hundred of them were arrested and sent to the Sudan.[36] Some of Ismail Siddiq's most prominent allies met strange and violent deaths. Thus European intervention not only deprived the viceroy of a foster brother and chief adviser in internal affairs, but also threatened the stability of his administration.

While the fate of Ismail Siddiq illustrates the pressure that Europeans could bring to bear upon Egyptian officials who obstructed or opposed them, the European presence also gave positive encouragement to those who had never been reconciled to Ismail's despotism and who saw in European influence an opportunity to assert themselves through association with the new power center. Perhaps most critical to the breakup of Egypt's ruling elite was the formation of the Commission of Inquiry, which made it clear that Europe was preparing to move beyond financial control and attack the superstructure of power itself. At this time, members of the official elite began active collaboration with Europe. These men were few in number but their defections were critical, for they were among Egypt's leading *dhawat* and included the only man capable of giving real assistance to Ismail in his fight against Europe. Their cooperation with European control left Ismail little choice but to acquiesce (at least temporarily) in a political operation that severely limited his power, deprived him of his landed estates, and displaced him from the center of administration.

It is important to remember that these collaborating officials were all reformers. They were intimately connected with Ismail's reform schemes, and were therefore committed to changes European in origin. Private ambition was also vitally important; some, perhaps, thought that they could "use" Europe to achieve their own personal goals. Of course, the sheer fact of European power must also have influenced their decisions, for Europe seemed so obviously like the "future," the winning side.

Mustafa Riyad was the first of these officials to break with Ismail. This defection, which came after Ismail had appointed Riyad to the Commission of Inquiry as "his" man, gave the Europeans an ally with intimate knowledge of the Egyptian bureaucracy, and deprived Ismail of a truly capable administrator. Riyad's appointment came after a dispute regarding Ismail's right to select members of the commission. It was finally resolved by a compromise in which Ismail was permitted to select one man of his choice (France had opposed even this concession on the grounds that such an appointee would merely represent the viceregal interest).[37] Ismail chose Riyad—known for his independent judgment—perhaps because he believed that Riyad's paternal concern for Egypt's welfare and his strong sense of duty would keep him loyal to him, and also because he knew that the Europeans would accept him. Vivian had praised Riyad as "one of [Ismail's] most able and energetic Ministers, a man with the courage of his opinions and whose character for honesty and integrity is unimpeachable."[38]

The first hint of where Riyad's true sympathies lay came late in March 1878 during a fight in which Ismail opposed Great Britain's insistence that Rivers Wilson be appointed first vice-president. During this dispute, which ended in Ismail's capitulation, Riyad did not resign in support of his nominal master, but instead, in Vivian's words, "loyally consented" to remain on the commission as second vice-president.[39] Riyad soon developed into such an active collaborator that by mid-May Vivian expressed concern for his safety: Riyad was doing his job with such "thorough loyalty" to the commission's objectives that his position had become dangerous. "We are bound, I think, to see him harmless," he wrote. Riyad later received promises of protection which shielded him from Ismail's wrath.[40]

It is impossible to know with certainty the motives for Riyad's collaboration. As we noted in chapter 6, his reputation for personal honesty was unchallenged. Though possessing a landed estate in the provinces, Riyad continued to live modestly in an old quarter of Cairo, disdaining all display of wealth. If Riyad had not previously sought high position for self-enrichment, it is unlikely that he would do so in 1878. But if he were not bent upon financial gain, could Riyad have sought power for its own sake?—a motive which cannot be disregarded in a system where short tenures in office were commonplace. Yet Riyad's career prior to 1878 reveals no evidence that he was losing favor through demotion or even temporary unemployment. On the contrary, he was considered a rising star in Ismail's administration.

Perhaps an explanation lies in Riyad's personality and career.[41] Riyad firmly believed in clean government (witness his admonition to dishonest officials and his remarkable reproach to Ismail himself on the evils of peculation). He also believed in a just government. He disliked the corvée and detested arbitrary and heavy taxation. Though a firm supporter of authoritarian government, Riyad did not take kindly to despotism or tyranny, and therefore may have chafed under the heavy hand of Ismail whom he later blamed for much of Egypt's ruin. Riyad was also a staunch Muslim who believed that the Muslim world contained within it the means of reform. While Riyad opposed such reforms as the abolition of slavery on religious grounds, he at the same time wanted to see Egypt regenerated. His record reveals a strong commitment to a modern system of education, which he seems to have regarded as a major tool for Egypt's renewal. Yet he did not advocate the indiscriminate importation of the products of European civilization. Riyad was not blind to European exploitation of Egypt's weakness, and particularly disliked the French and the Syrian Christian officials who entered Egypt's administration after 1876.

Perhaps Riyad regarded cooperation with the Europeans as an opportunity to curb the power of a tyrannical ruler and introduce long-needed changes into the country. He may also have hoped by collaborating to help place Egypt on a sound fiscal footing as a prelude to a thoroughgoing reform of the country by Muslims. After all, European intervention could not last forever, and in 1878 Europe's goal was fiscal reform and collecting monies owed to European creditors. No one could envision a long-term occupation of the country by foreign troops. Riyad told Wilfrid Blunt that his cooperation stemmed from a desire to help Egypt recover from its financial problems and to release the country from European control.[42] Perhaps in his own confident but short-sighted way, Riyad thought that the European presence might somehow be exploited for Egypt's benefit.

This interpretation is borne out by Riyad's ties with two prominent clients: the Muslim reformer and political firebrand, Jamal al-Din al-Afghani, who arrived in Egypt in 1871 and was expelled in 1879; and Ali Mubarak, whom the reader has already met. Reportedly, Jamal al-Din settled in Egypt because of the encouragement of Riyad, who had met him in Istanbul.[43] Riyad used his influence to obtain a government stipend for him and permitted his client to teach at the Azhar, admonishing him to adhere closely to the teachings of the Quran and the canonical law. At some point, however, al-Afghani left the Azhar, but continued teaching in a house in the Jewish quarter of Cairo where he built up a small following.[44]

In 1876 or 1877, al-Afghani joined the Eastern Star Lodge, one of several Masonic groups organized originally by Europeans.[45] Having become a Mason, al-Afghani quickly rose to become master of the Eastern Star Lodge, which had a reported membership of around 300 persons that included Jamal al-Din's earlier followers, some government officials, and perhaps even Prince Tawfiq, who was on poor terms with his father.[46] By 1877, al-Afghani was quietly spreading subversive political ideas among this small following.

Al-Afghani's increased activity coincided with rising agitation in Egypt's cities and towns.[47] This public excitement was the result of the weakening of the khedive's position, the advance collection of taxes being carried out by the European controllers, and the threat which the Russo-Turkish war seemed to pose to the Ottomans, to whom many Egyptians looked for protection against European encroachment. Ugly incidents broke out between Muslims and Europeans. Prayers against Europeans were recited in the mosques, and European travelers to upper Egypt risked personal injury.

Amid this agitation, there arose a movement of ideas and criticism which was primarily the work of religious leaders, teachers in the government schools, and Syrian Christians. It was expressed in a vehicle of protest new to Egypt: political journalism, which according to Muhammad Sabry began about 1877, and which may rightly be called opposition journalism since most of its efforts were spent protesting against European interference and, to a lesser extent, criticizing indirectly the arbitrariness of viceregal power.[48]

Egypt's new press, however, was not independent. Few newspapers could have been founded or maintained without the support of patrons whose views they reflected.[49] Ironically, the original sponsor of the press in Egypt was Ismail himself, who invited journalists to Egypt and subsidized their publications in hopes of gaining help in his battle against Egypt's creditors. In 1878, a sum of £10,869 was entered in the budget of the Department of Foreign Affairs for subscriptions to journals. Prince Abd al-Halim, Ismail's uncle who had been active in Egyptian Masonry and was intriguing against Ismail from outside Egypt, was another influential patron. Abd al-Halim's influence was at least in part behind the publication of the journal *Abu Nazzara*, edited by Yaqʿub Sanuʿ, an ardent champion of Abd al-Halim's claims to supplant Ismail as viceroy, although Sanuʿ himself had earlier been supported by Ismail.

The principal force behind the upsurge of journalistic activity, though, was Jamal al-Din al-Afghani, who emerged in 1877 as a man with considerable influence of his own.[50] Through Riyad, al-Afghani was able to obtain government licenses for his friends to publish their newspapers. It was with Riyad's help, for example, that Adib Is-haq, a Syrian Christian writer, was able to publish his journal, *Misr*. Such newspapers were used by al-Afghani to express his ideas in articles by himself or by his many friends. Al-Afghani's articles, like his speeches, had three purposes: to arouse Egyptians against European encroachment; to bring about a reform of Islam by stressing its past virtues and its capacity, through reason and scientific education, to adapt to modern conditions; and to denounce the evils of arbitrary rule by criticizing Eastern despots (and by implication Ismail) for exploiting their subjects instead of protecting them and obeying the laws. Such tyranny, al-Afghani said, was a basic cause of the backwardness of the Islamic world.

Although we cannot know precisely the relationship between al-Afghani and Riyad during 1877 and 1878, Riyad could not have objected to these criticisms, for Riyad himself believed in the regeneration of Islam and was not averse to using modern science as a means of attaining that objective. Any criticism of Khedive Ismail, however indirect, could only have benefited Riyad who, like al-Afghani, condemned tyranny and believed enlightened despotism to be eminently superior to the arbitrary despotisms then existing in the East. Unlike his client, however, Riyad did not appreciate the virtues of republican or constitutional government.[51]

Riyad's second important ally was Ali Mubarak, the prominent Egyptian engineer and administrator. Mubarak is said to have been a protégé of Riyad, but in a very different sense from al-Afghani.[52] Since the early 1870s, Riyad and Mubarak had a close working relationship which derived from a common commitment to the improvement of education. By the time Riyad became director of education in 1873, Mubarak had already won a reputation for his work of reform, which Riyad carried forward. Mubarak advised Riyad and served alongside him in the Privy Council.[53] In October 1873, Mubarak, accompanied by Riyad (the director of education), took part in an examination of students at a government school even though he had no official connection with Riyad's department.[54]

There may also have been a compatibility of temperament between these two men. Mubarak, like Riyad, had a strong sense of duty and a corollary desire to improve the lot of his fellow Egyptians. Though attracted to some aspects of European civilization, Mubarak did not believe that indiscriminately importing its products would automatically revitalize Egypt, which he believed to have a distinctive character that invalidated solutions workable in other lands. He, too, was convinced that Egypt would have to reform itself, and that this could be accomplished primarily through a system of scientific education geared to meet Egypt's peculiar needs. Like Riyad, Mubarak had links with the intellectual movement. He and his friends wrote nonpolitical articles in the new scientific journals, and one of his friends, Salih Majdi Bey, later became a vocal critic of Ismail's despotism. One of Salih's poems attacked Ismail for using the wealth of Egypt to enrich himself and his friends.[55]

As the 1870s wore on, Mubarak seems to have become disenchanted with the progress of reform. This, at least, is the impression gained from his book, *Nukhbat al-Fikr fi tadbir Nil Misr*, written in the early 1870s, which contained criticism sufficient to justify Mubarak's removal from office in 1874. According to Mubarak, Egypt suffered a rapid decline in the years following Muhammad Ali, who is lavishly praised for having stimulated the development of agriculture, trade, and industry, and for having built a new irrigation system.[56] Mubarak had no praise, however, for Muhammad Ali's successors, whose governments are criticized for failing to maintain Egypt's irrigation system and for allowing local industries to decline. Khedive Ismail is never criticized by name, only indirectly through references to the "bad" government of his day. Mubarak presents tables purporting to show a decrease in land under cultivation and in the value of crops (save cotton); he is critical of the way in which the Ibrahimiya canal deprived much of upper Egypt of water (thereby criticizing Ismail, for whose benefit it was constructed); and he bemoans the neglect of the Nile barrages, which fell into disrepair during the 1860s.[57] Mubarak paints a gloomy picture of a country rapidly going to seed.

To what can we attribute Mubarak's apparent disenchantment? Although after 1872 Mubarak did not hold a departmental directorship and suffered two brief but humiliating dismissals from office, he nevertheless continued in high position just short of the "ministerial" level by acting as adviser to the princes who had been given nominal charge of the Department of Public Works (according to McCoan, this department was actually directed by its adviser); in 1876, Mubarak's salary was fixed at 12,500 piastres a month—no small sum, if it were actually paid to him.[58] It is difficult, therefore, to attribute Mubarak's presumed unhappiness to a loss of position; but he could have become estranged from Ismail for much the same reasons as Riyad. Could not his disenchantment have made him a friend of any government that promised reform, no matter what its origin? As we shall see, Mubarak would soon join Riyad in collaborating with Europe, but only after the viceroy's power had been further weakened.

Riyad was the first of Ismail's own ruling elite to betray him, but his loss was far less important than the second defection. As we know, there were only two officials whose advice was nearly indispensable to the viceroy. By the summer of 1878, one of them—Ismail Siddiq—was dead. The other—Nubar—was in Europe preparing a triumphant return to Egypt where he would denounce Ismail and join forces with the Europeans. For Nubar, this marked the beginning of a period in which he hoped to dominate the politics of Egypt. He was not able to attain this objective, but for a short period Nubar enjoyed exceptional influence and perhaps more than any other man was directly responsible for the downfall of his former master. After Ismail's deposition, Khedive Tawfiq, out of fear of the man whom he blamed for his father's fall, forbade Nubar to return to Egypt.[59]

Nubar is described by some writers as a patriot motivated by an overriding concern for the welfare of Egypt and its people. To all who would listen, Nubar denounced the corvée as an evil system, condemned the methods of tax collection as harsh and unjust, and railed against the confiscation of land by Ismail, whose arbitrary power he identified as the chief cause of Egypt's suffering. According to Edward Dicey, the English publicist employed by Nubar, Nubar stood for an independent Egypt and a limitation of viceregal autocracy by establishing a system of justice and by employing Europeans.[60] These two checks would limit the arbitrary power of the ruler without destroying autocratic government, which Nubar believed was the form best suited to Egypt's stage of development. Thus Nubar's apologist could readily justify his action in having a clause inserted in the statute of the mixed courts which gave European plaintiffs the right to bring claims against the government, and which obliged it to enforce the decisions of these courts.[61]

The extent to which Nubar was a humanitarian reformer at heart cannot be ascertained, but clearly Nubar wanted others to believe that he was. There was another element of his personality that even his apologists cannot deny: Nubar craved power. Those who knew him wrote of his "unlimited ambition," his deviousness, his restlessness, his eagerness to seize any opportunity for a return to office.[62] Only slightly less important was his desire for wealth; he displayed his riches, acquired in part by underhanded dealings, with ostentatious delight. Could such behavior be reconciled with a professed desire for good government? Could a man who had never counted the costs of the loans, *firmans*, and other deals he arranged for Ismail have had the true interests of Egypt at heart? Europe may have thought Nubar a statesman, but in the eyes of many Egyptians, this man (who did not even speak Arabic) was no friend of Egypt.[63]

Nubar seems to have cared more about the removal of a khedive than he did for the government upon which leadership power rested. Muhammad Abduh believed that he had long wanted to see Ismail overthrown. Nubar is said to have described the mixed courts as a mine planted under the authority of the khedive. Some of his intimates even suspected that he had ideas of supplanting Ismail himself, though this is doubtful.[64] In this connection, it is worth remembering that while Nubar's fortune was located in Egypt, his base of social support was not; aside from Ismail, Nubar was supported mainly by the consular corps. If Nubar's insatiable desire for high position and influence was to be realized after 1876, it would likely have to be in an alliance with the Europeans.

In 1875, Nubar began moving closer to the European side. Dicey has explained this as reflecting a change in Nubar's thoughts about the Egyptian question.[65] Having become convinced of the inevitability of European intervention (which he had previously opposed), Nubar came to believe that the best solution was to compel Ismail to surrender his lands and to accept the appointment of a European to administer Egypt's finances, an arrangement to be guaranteed by one or more European powers, preferably Great Britain, which Nubar knew had the greatest stake in Egypt. Such a solution would at least preserve Egypt's administrative independence, albeit under European tutelage.

Soon after the arrival of the Cave mission, Nubar began to conduct intrigues designed to discredit Ismail and involve the big powers more deeply in Egyptian affairs. Though Ismail had forbidden his officials to provide any assistance to Cave, Nubar broke ranks with the khedive by meeting with Cave and painting a very black picture of Ismail's financial situation. He told Cave that the corvée, the advance collection of taxes, and Ismail's large military expenditures were harming the country. He criticized Ismail for growing sugar on his estates when imported sugar could be sold in the market for less, and urged that an Englishman be sent to Egypt to direct the country's finances. Upon hearing of these charges, Ismail became furious and in an interview with Cave denounced all of Nubar's suggestions, especially the idea that Egypt needed a European director for the Department of Finances.[66] But Nubar did not stop there. Acting without Ismail's knowledge, he issued a formal request to the Italian government to send to Egypt a man of high rank to assist him in drawing up a commercial treaty with Italy. Nubar was believed to be responsible for the Outrey mission, and he was also thought to be behind the Russian and German governments' offers of assistance to Ismail against the alleged interference of Britain in Egyptian affairs.[67]

Nubar, it may be assumed, hoped to benefit personally in some way from his intrigues, though precisely how may not have been clear even to him. The kind of reward Nubar may have been expecting may be suggested by a British consular dispatch which states that Nubar had enlisted the support of the Russian General Ignatief to obtain from the Ottoman government his appointment as governor of Erzerum, a Christian province reportedly to be placed on a semi-independent footing. After the grand vizir had turned down Ignatief's request, Nubar's overture was disclosed by the Russian consul general in Cairo.[68] Under these circumstances, Nubar hardly could have expected to remain in power for long. On January 2, 1876, Nubar lost the position of director of commerce. Three days later, he resigned as director of foreign affairs and left Egypt to carry on his intrigues from abroad.[69]

Once in Europe, Nubar campaigned actively to win acceptance for his view that the true cause of Egypt's financial difficulties was neither excessive expenditures nor usurious interest rates but rather the buildup of large, private viceregal estates.[70] This, he argued, was where the bulk of the money raised from taxes and loans had gone. His argument not only held Ismail directly and personally responsible and could therefore be used to justify bondholders' claims against these properties, but also suggested the need to curtail sharply the viceroy's powers. Ismail must be compelled to surrender the lands held by him and his family, and his grip upon the reins of administration must be loosened and permanently weakened by the appointment of a European director of finances. This was a program for a revolution, one that could be carried out by a policy which Nubar euphemistically called "compulsion by persuasion."

Aware that British support was vital to any further European intervention in Egyptian affairs, Nubar spent most of his time in London meeting with persons of influence inside and outside government and publicizing his case through journalists employed by him. In December 1877, Edward Dicey, relying upon information supplied by Nubar, published a widely read article in *The Nineteenth Century* which made a great impact upon English opinion. Nubar's efforts to promote a revolution through foreign intervention seemed at last to be making headway.

During Nubar's stay in Europe, the Commission of Inquiry began its work in Egypt. The line eventually adopted by this body—that Egypt's problems stemmed from "despotic misgovernment" and that Ismail must therefore relinquish all of his property and a share of his power—bore striking resemblance to the course advocated by Nubar, a correspondence of views that elicited much comment and speculation. Edward Dicey himself asserted a causal relationship between Nubar's program and that of the commission. Nubar's wife viewed the commission as Nubar's child, and even Khedive Ismail grumbled that it was merely carrying out Nubar's ideas, a criticism that Wilson admitted was true.[71]

The similarity between Nubar's views and the course adopted by the commission may be explained in part by Nubar's impact on influential Europeans (especially the English), but also by the long-standing alliance between Nubar and the commission's leader, Sir Rivers Wilson.[72] In the spring of 1876, Wilson had become acquainted with Nubar's program for the "salvation" of Egypt. On the eve of his departure for Egypt to inaugurate the inquiry, Wilson met Nubar in Paris; once in Egypt, he remained in contact with him by mail and through Nubar's wife. When Wilson was offered the post of director of finances by the khedive (later withdrawn), he told his wife that he could probably write of this confidentially to Nubar, who had originated the idea and was actively promoting it in Europe. Wilson desired Nubar's return to Egypt and was convinced that if recalled he would be a friend and ally of the commission.

The resignation of Muhammad Sharif, precipitated by Wilson himself, opened the way for Nubar's return.[73] After the death of Ismail Siddiq and the defection of Riyad, Muhammad Sharif (named director of foreign affairs and director of the Department of Justice after Nubar's flight to Europe) emerged as Ismail's "chief minister" and Egypt's most prominent officeholder.[74] Sharif's foolish boast that he would never appear before the commission brought him to the attention of Wilson, who eagerly seized the opportunity to call him to testify. Sharif adamantly refused to be examined by Europeans heading an investigation to which he was opposed; however, as a gesture of conciliation, he offered to answer questions in writing, a response entirely unacceptable to Wilson, who was fully prepared to use all of his power to compel Sharif's appearance. On June 4, Sharif resigned rather than submit to the commission. Riyad was appointed in his place because Ismail knew that Riyad would not be called upon to give testimony before his own colleagues. Wilson has interpreted this fight as a "matter of principle" in which his commission's authority was at stake. Since he was in the habit of initiating fights with Ismail and his officials, this incident may have been merely another in a series of clashes by which Wilson hoped to strengthen the commission's position. On the other hand, one cannot discount an ulterior motive, especially as this resulted in the elimination from office of Nubar's chief rival. On June 8, Vivian wrote of Sharif's resignation and observed prophetically that Ismail might now be compelled to turn to Nubar.

Nine days after Sharif's resignation, Wilson wrote to his wife of his suspicion that Tigrane Bey was carrying a secret message from Ismail to Nubar in Paris, and by June 29, Ismail's overtures to Nubar had become acknowledged fact. Hoping desperately that Nubar could save his land and his power, Ismail told him that if he could clear himself from the suspicions of intrigue against the viceroy in 1876, he could return to Egypt and have any government post he wished.[75] Nubar replied that he would return only if he received three guarantees: first, that before a government was formed, a reform program be agreed upon; second, that his friend Wilson be appointed director of the Finance Department; third, that Nubar himself not be expelled from Egypt again.[76] While negotiating with Ismail, Nubar visited Bismarck in Kissingen and British officials in London where he was given an oral and general expression of support from the British government. On July 23, Nubar received a direct and urgent request for help from Ismail. "He [Ismail] thinks no doubt that Nubar will help and save him," wrote Wilson in Cairo, "so he will, very likely, but not in the way the Khedive hopes."[77] By August 15, 1878, Nubar had arrived in Cairo, and the die was cast.

At their first meeting, Ismail complained to Nubar about European interference and the commission's intention of seizing his lands.[78] But, knowing that Ismail could no longer order him about or dismiss him at will, Nubar disappointed his host. He told Ismail that he had no choice but to submit to the wishes of the commission, and presented him with a three-point program of his own: a system of justice should be established to safeguard the Egyptian people from arbitrary rule; Ismail must surrender some of his powers to a council of ministers which would formulate and implement administrative policies; Ismail and his family must cede all of their property in return for a civil list. These were Nubar's conditions; this was his program for solving Egypt's problems.

Nubar thus showed himself willing to accept the commission's ideas in their entirety. Of course, this came as no surprise to the British government, to which Nubar was already pledged to work for the surrender of the viceregal properties, nor to Rivers Wilson, who had been in communication with Nubar and who expressed pleasure at his arrival at the very time the commission was to issue its report.[79] The commission, he wrote, would need all the influence it could muster to induce Ismail to accept its findings. Almost identical with Nubar's program, the commission's report insisted upon the surrender of all viceregal properties, the issuance of a civil list for the khedive and his family, and the enforcement of the principle of "ministerial responsibility." By this phrase Nubar referred to the establishment of a new type of ministry composed of an Egyptian element but also containing one or perhaps two Europeans (an Englishman and a Frenchman), a ministry which enjoyed the sanction of the European powers, or at least of Britain, and which was presided over by Nubar rather than Ismail. Thus constructed, this new ministry would be able to maintain the principles of the settlement, impose its will upon the khedive, and realize Nubar's objectives of administrative autonomy and Egyptian prosperity.[80]

But first Ismail had to be compelled to accept this solution. The lines of battle between Ismail and the commission were drawn, and in the ensuing struggle, Nubar's influence and arguments proved decisive.[81] Without his assistance, as Wilson himself acknowledged, the commission would not have succeeded so completely. The commission brought pressure to bear on Ismail not only through Nubar himself, but also by virtue of Nubar's private efforts and initiatives. On August 18, Wilson wrote that Nubar was fighting hard to compel Ismail to yield. Nubar and Riyad, he wrote, had been sent by Ismail to negotiate the amount of the civil list with the European members of the commission, but they refused to discuss the matter. On August 22, Wilson joyfully announced the "total" capitulation of the viceroy, who had agreed to surrender his family's entire estate, not just a portion, as the British and French consular agents had earlier told their governments to expect. This was a big victory, "more than anyone had dared to hope," Wilson trumpeted. Ismail also agreed to sanction the formation of a responsible ministry along the lines proposed by Nubar and the commission. The struggle was over.

Until the papers of Nubar and Wilson are thoroughly examined, the arguments, concessions, and other devices used by Nubar to obtain "total victory" over Ismail cannot be fully known. We do know, however, that in return for Ismail's willingness to cede his entire estate, Nubar permitted him and his family to retain small portions of land (mostly gardens) around their palaces and gave him written assurance of payment for his cattle and implements, worth about £300,000, which by local custom did not accompany the purchase of land. Even so, it took Nubar more than two months to wring from Ismail the title deeds for his lands.[82] Ismail may also have been reconciled to the surrender of his estates by the idea of a mixed ministry; Dicey attributed this idea to Nubar, who may have told the khedive that a mixed ministry would obviate the need for direct European control.[83] Ismail also could not have failed to realize that such a change would buy him valuable time. Yet Ismail did not capitulate until after both Nubar and Wilson had made it clear that if their solution were not accepted, they would leave Egypt on August 27, thereby turning the whole problem directly over to the powers of Europe. On the twenty-third, Ismail issued his formal acceptance of the commission's decisions; on the twenty-eighth, he decreed the formation of a responsible ministry to be headed by Nubar, the man of the hour.[84]

▲▲▲ THE FAILURE OF NUBAR'S UNFINISHED REVOLUTION

The events of late August 1878 bore clear signs of an administrative revolution in which executive power was separated from viceregal authority. Ismail's loss of his lands and his acceptance of a civil list forced a distinction between the ruler's revenues and those of the government. The establishment of a Council of Ministers (*Majlis al-Nuzzar*) to replace the Privy Council meant that Ismail could no longer direct the daily affairs of government or manipulate freely its politics. At Nubar's insistence, he was excluded from attending the sessions of *Majlis al-Nuzzar*, whose members were responsible for formulating policy, and whose resolutions were conveyed by Nubar to Ismail for his signature.[85] As directors of Egypt's government departments, the individual members of this council received the right to appoint and dismiss officials and to authorize departmental expenditures. The viceregal cabinet, once the directing agency of the administration, was brought under the jurisdiction of the Department of Finance. By this formula, the makers of Egypt's "bloodless revolution" hoped to bring the viceregal household under their control.

But could this really be a revolution when Ismail's authority as head of the government had been left intact? Ismail's signature was required before any decision of the Council of Ministers could become law. Only he could convoke and prorogue the sessions of the Consultative Chamber of Delegates. Even those who sat in the new Council of Ministers were Ismail's men in the sense that he had appointed them and could in theory replace them. Instead of removing Ismail from the administration, Nubar and his colleagues had created two distinct powers: the viceroy and the Council of Ministers.[86] Not only this; taking advantage of the difficulties into which Nubar's ministry eventually fell, Ismail used his authority to dismiss from office the very man who had been the moving force of this revolution. On February 19, 1879, less than six months after Nubar's stunning triumph, Ismail unceremoniously removed him from power.

Yet the gains made by Nubar and his colleagues were not completely lost with the breakup of his ministry. Ismail never regained control of his property, nor was he able to revive all of his previously undisputed power. Because of Nubar's revolution, Ismail was forced into desperate actions that ultimately led to his deposition. Regarded from this standpoint, the almost six-month period of "ministerial rule" forms an important chapter in the story of the dismantling of khedivial absolutism.

Why was this experiment in ministerial government so short-lived? The problems facing the new ministry, to be sure, were overwhelming. Can its failure be attributed to the intractability of the financial problem, or to Nubar's personal shortcomings, or to the retention of Ismail as viceroy? Why should this experiment fail after six months, when Nubar and Wilson were both thinking of a duration of between two and three years?[87] The Council of Ministers, weak and divided from the very outset, was simply unable to achieve the measure of strength and unity necessary to give the experiment the fair trial that its framers wanted. This situation naturally created an opportunity for intervention by Ismail. To understand the weaknesses of this new government, we must examine systematically the relationship between the Council of Ministers and three forces: the European powers, the Turkish *dhawat*, and the Egyptian notables.

Nubar expected the European powers to help secure and maintain the independence of his ministry. First, he wanted consular support against the khedive in the form of threats and warnings, which he hoped would prevent Ismail from intriguing against him.[88] Such warnings had in fact been issued to Ismail by the French and British consuls who told him to cooperate with the new order and promised to hold him responsible for its failure. Ismail was threatened with his own deposition and even the end of his dynasty. Second, Nubar intended to include an Englishman and a Frenchman in his ministry in hopes of guaranteeing the independence of his government and enabling it to impose its collective will upon the khedive. Ismail would think twice, Nubar told Vivian, before incurring the wrath of Britain and France by dismissing men who had been appointed with the blessings of these two powers. Finally, Nubar expected Europe to allow him a free hand in forming the ministry. It was important, he believed, for the Egyptian people to regard the new government as Nubar's creation rather than the product of the European powers. While willing to grant Europe the right to intervene, Nubar wanted a period of time free from European interference. Only an independent ministry with native representation, he argued, could succeed in restoring law and order in the country.

Nubar immediately set about forming his ministry. In addition to his own appointment as president of the Council of Ministers, Nubar took charge of the Departments of Foreign Affairs and Justice. He then secured the appointment of Mustafa Riyad to the Department of Interior, which had control over internal security as well as the provincial administration.[89] Ali Mubarak, a friend of both Nubar and Riyad, was given the Department of Education. Nubar also announced his choice of Rivers Wilson as minister of finance and formally asked the British government to grant Wilson a leave of absence so that he could take this important post. The other principal ministry, the Department of Public Works, was left temporarily without a head.

The European powers, however, did not leave Nubar alone. Shortly after these appointments had been made, France, Italy, and finally Britain began a series of interventions that eventually destroyed Nubar's freedom of action and made a mockery of the "independence" of his ministry. European interference thus became one of the principal causes of the weakness of Nubar's government.

France was the first to intervene. Eager to retain influence over Egypt's administration and suspicious of Nubar, whose return to Egypt it had opposed, the French government demanded that a Frenchman be given a post in the ministry.[90] French Consul General Raindre suggested that this position be the directorship of Public Works, Commerce, and Agriculture. Nubar angrily replied that he had intended to offer a department to a Frenchman, but one chosen by him rather than by the French. This interference, he complained bitterly, was nothing more than a blatant attempt to impose a European ministry upon him, and would open the door to intervention by other European governments. In a gesture of conciliation, Nubar offered the Department of Public Works to M. Cauvet, but this was opposed by the French government, which tried to force Nubar to appoint Baron de Malaret, the former controller general of expenditures.

In the meantime, just as Nubar had feared, another European power intervened. On September 16, Britain's consul general reported that the Italian government had made a demand for representation in Nubar's ministry.[91] Italy's Consul General De Martino admitted that it would have been better had Nubar been allowed the freedom to choose his ministers, but since this was not happening, he said, Italy was justified in pressing a claim of its own. A few days after receiving the Italian demand, Nubar abolished the Department of Commerce and Agriculture, but his position was clearly growing weaker. If he were forced to accept the principle of foreign interference, he told Britain's consul general, he would prefer to have a minister imposed upon him so that the amount of European influence could be clearly seen and defined.[92]

By late September, the fight between Nubar and the French had begun to focus upon the distribution of power within the ministry. The French government insisted that its candidate for the Public Works Department be given control over all roads, canals, irrigation facilities, railroads, and ports (including that of Alexandria) as well as commerce and agriculture.[93] Nubar replied that he could concede neither the railroads, which he claimed by custom fell under Finance Department authority, nor the ports, whose revenue rightly went to the director of finance. Nubar was willing to withdraw the name of Cauvet and to nominate de Blignières if France would abandon its claim to a seat in his ministry, but France responded that it would grant de Blignières a leave of absence only if his powers as director of public works were "complete."

The French demand for control over administrations in which Britain had an interest aroused concern in London. Great Britain could hardly object to the French claim for representation in Nubar's ministry, but looked askance at the idea of a Frenchman controlling both the railroads and the port of Alexandria, which in the Goschen-Joubert settlement had been placed under a board in which British interests were predominant. Moreover, the ceding of the railroads to a Frenchman could be regarded as a violation of a promise made by Nubar to Wilson that railroads and the customs authority would come under the direct orders of the director of finance. Wilson wasted little time informing Nubar by telegram that the port of Alexandria and the railroads belonged to the Department of Finance.[94]

Since early September, Nubar had been imploring the British government to make haste in granting Wilson an official leave of absence, but the most he could obtain was an unofficial statement of approval of Wilson's nomination. This delay greatly vexed Nubar, who had begun to believe that an agreement might be made between Britain and France without consulting him.[95]

Nubar's growing weakness (his ministry could not be formed until he had reached an understanding with the European powers) created the first of many opportunities for Ismail, who seized the occasion to declare his refusal to surrender the title deeds to 425,729 *faddans* of land which he himself had pledged in August. Since this land had already been offered as security for a new loan, Ismail's action set back the negotiations then in progress with the Paris banking house of Rothschild.[96] Nubar feared that Ismail's unexpected move would force his capitulation to French demands or, worse still, lead to the direct intervention of the European powers. With great urgency, he again implored the British government to accept Wilson's appointment officially so that he could overcome his difficulties with the khedive and succeed in raising the loan which the government so desperately needed.

The delay in obtaining a new loan weakened Nubar's government. This loan, recommended by the Commission of Inquiry, was indispensable for the new regime's success. After Ismail's capitulation in August, Wilson was sent to Europe where he opened negotiations with Rothschild for a loan of £ 8,000,000, pledging as security the viceregal properties. But as difficulties arose between Nubar and the French, negotiations with Rothschild bogged down and the financial position of Nubar's government, which was encountering great difficulties in collecting revenue, became grave. Ismail, however, was not the only party to impede these negotiations. In late September, it was learned that the French government had induced Rothschild not to issue his loan until a settlement had been reached on the prerogatives of the director of public works.[97] This was perhaps the greatest blow yet dealt to Nubar, whose government had to have at least part of the loan very soon, else it would be irreparably weakened.

These difficulties prompted a decisive step. Nubar authorized Wilson to reach a solution with France on the Public Works Department, and in case of emergency, to conclude an agreement. Thus the center of gravity in the talks was shifted to Europe where the negotiations were taken over by the French government and by the British, who supported the French claim in order to render their own influence less obvious.[98] Nubar labored under no illusions; he was fully aware that his decision would cost the Egyptian government its independence. If the Italians wanted a ministry, Nubar sarcastically told De Martino (the Italian consul general), they should go to Paris or London because that was where Egyptian affairs were being decided; he had little choice but to submit to the will of the powers. On October 16, three weeks after Wilson had been authorized to conclude an arrangement with the French, Nubar, who had naively dreamed of Egyptian independence guaranteed by Europe, was asked to approve an agreement reached between Britain and France for the restructuring of Egypt's administration.[99]

This settlement had two parts. The first resolved the dispute over the distribution of power within the ministry. The port of Alexandria was placed under the jurisdiction of the director of finance, while Egypt's other ports and harbors were placed under the French director of public works, de Blignières, who was also conceded jurisdiction over the railroads. No provision was made for an Italian minister, although Baravelli, the Italian debt commissioner, was subsequently appointed auditor general.[100] It was stipulated that should either of the two European ministers be dismissed without the consent of their governments, the system of dual control established by Goschen and Joubert would automatically be reestablished.[101] This settlement gave the two European ministers a position of advantage over Nubar, who had earlier suggested that the railroads, port of Alexandria, and Suez Canal harbors be placed under his administration as president of the Council of Ministers.[102] In addition to the port of Alexandria, Wilson received control over the customs, the public debt, and the financial administration of the provinces. Every government official involved in the collection of revenue came under his direct order. De Blignières received control over the canals, bridges, telegraphs, and the barrages.[103] These two ministers were favored even in the amount of pay they received. Their annual salaries of £E 6,000 were considerably higher than the £E 3,000 allocated to Nubar and his non-European colleagues.[104]

Nubar also lost on the second part of the settlement, the administration of the viceregal properties earmarked to guarantee the Rothschild loan. As we have seen, France had demanded that these lands be placed with the Ministry of Public Works. Wilson had proposed that they be managed by a special administration consisting of an Englishman, a Frenchman, and an Egyptian, but Nubar had objected to Wilson's proposal on the grounds that three men from such different backgrounds could not work in harmony. Nubar preferred that these properties be placed under the Public Works Department.[105] The final decision, reached in Paris by Britain and France, was to set up a special administration composed of one Egyptian, one Englishman, and one Frenchman. The English and French representatives were to be designated by their respective governments, whose consent was needed before they could be removed from their posts. As a concession to Nubar, the Egyptian government was allowed to make the actual appointments of the French and British members of this administration, after first obtaining the approval of Wilson and de Blignières. As a result, the viceregal title deeds were handed over and a loan was granted, but not before Britain and France had established a further measure of control over the Egyptian administration.

The unwillingness of the European powers to support Nubar's efforts to create a strong, unified, and credible ministry was the first source of its weakness. The second was the opposition of the Turkish *dhawat*. Vivian attributed the downfall of Nubar's government (in February 1879) in part to the failure of his ministry to find support from important segments of society.[106] Since the Turks were the dominant element in the higher administration, we need to know, therefore, if an effort was made to represent the Turks in the ministry, and, more important, what lay behind Turkish hostility.

The unquestioned leader of the Turkish party was Muhammad Sharif, who after his resignation had retired to his palace. Because of Sharif's great influence, Nubar or those close to him began to consider seriously the idea of bringing him into the government. As early as July 15, Vivian wrote that the offer of the directorship of the Department of Interior to Sharif was being contemplated, and that Sharif's presence would make a strong ministry.[107] From this point, the sources either diverge or are mute. According to Bell and al-Rafiʻi, Sharif was offered the position of director of war and declined it, but Schölch writes that Nubar did not want his old rival in the ministry under any circumstances. Yet the question of Sharif's participation must have remained open, for on December 14, Vivian again suggested that Sharif be conciliated by the offer of a departmental post, though he doubted that Sharif probably could be induced to serve under Nubar.[108]

Perhaps to placate Sharif, Nubar gave the post of director of war to Sharif's son-in-law, Muhammad Ratib Pasha.[109] Leader of the ill-fated Abyssinian expedition of 1876, Muhammad Ratib was a Circassian Turk (a freed slave of Muhammad Ali) with close ties to the viceregal family, being married to a Circassian woman from Ismail's household, and having long enjoyed the viceroy's favor. But Ratib possessed little influence of his own. An incompetent, bungling administrator, he was the leader of no party, and as director of war was treated as a cipher by Nubar and his colleagues. His presence neither strengthened the ministry nor conciliated Sharif, who remained adamantly opposed to Nubar.

Muhammad Sharif complained that Nubar was an "outsider," that Riyad and Ali Mubarak were loathed by the people, and that the two foreign ministers were representatives of Europe rather than Egypt; but these criticisms were simply a justification for opposing a ministry whose policies threatened the Turks' economic and political privileges in Egypt. Their principal economic grievance, and on which the Turks found common ground with the provincial notables, was related to Wilson's proposal to increase the taxes on *ushuriya* lands.[110] This idea was not new. In 1876, Cave had suggested placing *ushuriya* taxes on the same level as those of the *kharajiya*, and had estimated that this would result in an annual increase of £700,000. After the formation of the Commission of Inquiry, Ismail himself had agreed in principle to increase the taxes on *ushuriya* holders, whose tax bill in 1877 amounted to a trifling £E 333,000 as against £E 3,143,000 paid by holders of *kharajiya* property.[111] By ironing out this inequity, Wilson hoped to add a considerable amount to the revenue collected by his ministry.

This proposed increase was part of a wider scheme to readjust land taxes in Egypt.[112] Wilson planned to launch a cadastral survey which would classify all land, confirm the titles of landowners, and lead to the establishment of a new system of revenue control. Inaugurated in February when Colvin was appointed to direct the survey, this proposed reform aroused considerable anxiety among the landowners, who feared for the security of their holdings—fears apparently confirmed when Wilson began to force the sale of lands that were in tax arrears.

Egypt's Turks and other large landowners also feared that Wilson intended to abolish the *Muqabala* Law. This law had in fact been abolished in the decree of May 7, 1876, and though it was reestablished the following November, the annual land tax reductions which the government had been giving to those who were paying the *Muqabala* had been suspended.[113] The participants in the scheme were therefore deprived of any immediate benefits while being obliged to continue their *Muqabala* payments. Rumors that Wilson intended to abolish the tax aroused fears among Egypt's landowners that the money which they had already paid would be lost completely.

The new "responsible" ministry also threatened Turkish control of Egypt's administration.[114] It was bad enough that Turks should lose command of the major state departments, but when the "foreigners" began to fill the positions below them with friends and allies, it became clear to many that the days of Turkish domination were numbered. Nubar relied upon his relatives for support. Artin Bey became director of the viceregal cabinet; Tigrane was appointed secretary general of the Council of Ministers; and Boghos Bey, Nubar's son, received a high position in the railway administration. Ali Mubarak appointed Egyptian technicians to offices in the Public Works Department. Wilson and de Blignières packed the positions below them with highly paid Coptic, Syrian, and European officials. The office of accounting, for example, employed twenty-four Europeans during Wilson's tenure as finance director. The rapid increase in the number of European officials became one of the chief complaints of Muhammad Sharif and his party.

While this was happening, other officials were placed on half pay or dismissed altogether. The salaries of some non-European officials were reduced arbitrarily, yet European employees suffered no losses of pay.[115] Within months after Nubar took office, over 500 government employees reportedly had been dismissed. Some were removed for reasons of economy, but political motives also lay behind these dismissals. After a British subject residing in Aswan had protested to the consul general about the rude treatment he had received at the hands of local officials, Nubar, responding to consular pressure, had one official removed from his post—clear proof that Egypt was being governed by the agents of Europe.[116]

Once in control of the administrative machine, Egypt's new rulers sought to consolidate their power and eliminate opposition.[117] In January 1879, the Governorate of Cairo was abolished, its administrations being divided among the Departments of Finance, Public Works, and Interior. In the same month, de Blignières reorganized the Department of Public Works, creating separate executive and administrative branches, and forming six engineering districts, each headed by a chief engineer directly responsible to the ministry. After discovering that services in the provinces were supervised by two inspectors general who came under the orders of the Inspectorate rather than Public Works, de Blignières reduced the influence of these two officials and stipulated that they be given only temporary powers. On September 8, the Inspectorate of lower Egypt was abolished—a convenient way of ridding the administration of Shahin Pasha, one of Ismail's most devoted Turkish officials. This was followed in January by the abolition of the Inspectorate of upper Egypt, an office directed by Umar Lutfi, another prominent Turkish official and supporter of Ismail.

Such measures, however, did not amount to an actual purge of Turkish officeholders. Amin Sami's lists of appointments show that most Turks kept their positions in the governorates and provinces after the establishment of Nubar's government. A wholesale change may not have been deemed wise, but in any case there were simply not enough officials of other types with sufficient authority to replace the Turks. Thus Umar Lutfi was sought out and used by Wilson to help recover tax arrears in upper Egypt.[118] This was important, for the continuing Turkish presence, especially in the provinces, made it possible for Ismail to mount an underground resistance to the new order.

Despite the loss of his property and prerogatives, Ismail's authority remained undiminished. For three-quarters of a century, his family had been feared and obeyed, and nothing so sudden as the events of August 1878 could overcome the deep-seated awe in which Ismail was held by most of his subjects. Nubar's intense personal dislike, even hatred, of Ismail blinded him to the reality that the viceroy was still a power in the land, a man to be reckoned with.[119] Humiliated and angered by the establishment of a government led by a former "servant" who had denied him a role in the administration and openly aimed at crushing him, Ismail quietly began working to upset the new order.

From the beginning, Ismail endeavored to stir up popular resentment against the ministry in Cairo and to intercept government revenue collected in the provinces and divert it to his own coffers. He relied heavily on Turkish loyalists. In mid-September, Shahin Pasha was reported to have entered into discussions with prominent Cairo merchants in hopes of getting up a public protest against the dismantling of khedivial power. The idea of a protest demonstration also had the support of some *ulama*, so we may conjecture that Shahin's activities were part of a wider effort to create discontent at a time when Nubar was preoccupied with the claims of France and Italy for influence in the ministry.[120]

Ismail's Turkish officials raised revenue "illegally" (that is, without authorization from the Department of Finance), and large sums of money were sent to him.[121] An amount equal to £18,000 was collected by the governor of al-Jiza for transmission to the viceroy, and the governor of al-Buhayra collected £50,000 for the same purpose. *Daira* officials caught smuggling money into Cairo at the railway station were "rescued" by Ismail's bodyguard. The amount of money diverted in this way cannot be known, but Ismail's ability to raise revenue contributed mightily to the ministerial government's financial difficulties.

Ismail also availed himself of another group of influential administrators: the provincial notables, whose interests were represented in the Consultative Chamber of Delegates. The alienation and opposition to Nubar of this important group constituted the third major source of weakness of Nubar's ministry. Since 1875, Egypt's provincial notables had watched with deepening concern the deterioration of the country's fiscal position, because in it they saw real threat to their own economic interests. They were particularly concerned about the fate of the *Muqabala* Law, from which they had hoped to derive great benefit. The abolition of the *Muqabala* Law in the decree of May 7, 1876, had aroused grave doubts as to whether contributors would recover the large sums which they had paid into the treasury. As we have seen, this concern created an immediate identity of interest between the notables, the Turkish *dhawat*, and Khedive Ismail, who had reasons of his own for opposing the fiscal policy of Europe.

On August 7, Ismail convened in Tanta a special session of the Consultative Chamber of Delegates, which had not met since 1873. This session was to discuss the *Muqabala*, which the viceroy wanted to see reestablished. Most of the delegates who met on August 7 were new to the Chamber, but many had previously held high administrative positions or were from families of *dhawat* notables. Mustafa Allam (al-Qalyubiya) was related to a family of *shaykh*s who had held high offices in the provinces since the days of Sa'id, while Uthman al-Harmil (al-Gharbiya) could boast of a relative who had been a district chief (*nazir al-qism*) under Muhammad Ali and who later became member of the court (*majlis*) of Tanta.[122] Budayni al-Shari'i (al-Minya) hailed from one of the wealthiest families in upper Egypt. In 1876, one of his brothers was president of the court of appeals in upper Egypt while another brother was agricultural inspector in al-Minya.[123] Muhammad Sultan, the "king" of upper Egypt, left his position as inspector of viceregal properties to take a seat in this Chamber. These delegates not only formed the upper stratum of Egypt's provincial notability, but many were also members of the political/administrative elite.

After the delegates had been convened, a committee of three was appointed to obtain clarification of the government's financial position and to learn whether the money collected for the *Muqabala* could be returned. Upon realizing the impossibility of the government's returning any of the money, the Chamber resolved on August 10 that the *Muqabala* be continued.[124] This, of course, was in keeping with Ismail's wishes.

After the Europeans had restored the *Muqabala* Law on November 18 without its contributors receiving any immediate benefits, Ismail consoled the delegates by telling them that its restoration was due to the Chamber's resolution when in truth it was Goschen and Joubert who had decided to reestablish this measure as a means of obtaining revenue with which to pay Egypt's creditors. No protest was made by the delegates, who in the following session (April 1877) consented to a general increase of ten percent on all taxes in order to set up a contribution to support the Ottomans in their war against the Russians.[125]

While the Chamber voiced no opposition to Ismail and followed his every lead, there can be little doubt that some members had begun to perceive in an alliance with a weakened ruler an opportunity to defend provincial interests and to assert themselves in a limited way. The possibilities created by the new circumstances may be seen in the actions of Sultan Pasha. As a member of the Chamber, Sultan faithfully supported the policies of Ismail; yet, after Nubar's ministry had been formed, he did not hesitate to enter into contact with Nubar and submit to him his own plans for tax relief and reform.[126]

The 1870s were hard for Egypt's peasants and their village leaders, who bore the brunt of a fiscal oppression which may have rivaled even that of the late eighteenth century. The people of Egypt were at the mercy of the viceroy and his administration. Yet if there was, at best, only a quiet protest by the members of the Chamber, the delegates who convened in Cairo in 1876 showed themselves the true defenders of the people of their home districts. Muhammad Hisab (Jirja) won the Chamber's approval for a three-month postponement in the collection of taxes in upper Egypt to permit a brief period of recovery.¹²⁷ At another session, the delegates requested information about the taxes paid by townspeople, with a view to equalizing the tax burden between town and country. In March 1878 the delegates of the Chamber, worried about the dilapidation of the irrigation works and anxious to guard against floods, approved resolutions calling for doubling the number of protective works and forming a committee in every province to obtain information that would be used to provide financial aid to those hard hit by the Nile flood. In 1878, when taxes were being collected in advance to pay the coupon, nine delegates from five provinces in upper Egypt took out a loan from two indigenous banks to pay the provinces' taxes so that the peasants would not have to sell their unripe crops at low prices or go into debt to moneylenders. But such actions were not new; at other times delegates had demonstrated a concern for the welfare of their provinces.

A truly radical departure in the Chamber's attitude occurred during the meeting of January 2, 1879.¹²⁸ Hitherto, the Chamber had not openly protested against European intervention, not even against the formation of the Commission of Inquiry. Paradoxically, this meeting had been initiated by the Council of Ministers because it was planning to raise the taxes on *ushuriya* lands, and also because some of its projects could not be implemented successfully without the cooperation of the notables. Inasmuch as the Chamber had always shown itself amenable, Nubar expected no difficulty. The session opened with the customary speech from the throne by the khedive, who informed the Chamber that the government wished to discuss measures of finance and public works. Few, however, could have predicted the tenor of the reply: "We, the delegates and representatives of the Egyptian nation [*al-umma al-Misriya*]," it began, "the defenders of its rights and seekers of its welfare, which is at the same time the welfare of the government, kindly thank the khedive for the convocation of the Consultative Chamber of Delegates, which is the basis of civilization and order." This speech, read by Abd al-Salam al-Muwaylihi, went on to identify the Chamber as the source of progress and the means of attaining freedom. Ismail was thanked for establishing a ministry responsible to the nation, embodied the Chamber. References were made to the benefit of the fatherland (*manfaʿat al-watan*), the welfare of the nation (maslahat al-umma), and the rights of the subjects (huquq al-raʿiya). The novelty of this reply lay in its glorification of the Chamber rather than the ruler. For the first time, it was claiming a role in politics. This session not only revealed a new self-perception of the Chamber, but also was the opening shot in a round of attacks directed against the "European" government.

Why this sudden and unpredictable development? Certainly the delegates were influenced by the rhetoric and criticism of European intervention found in the Egyptian press. More important, however, they knew that Ismail would not oppose actions directed against his enemies. In fact, as we shall see, Ismail had given them positive encouragement. This identity of interest between the delegates and the viceroy was acknowledged by the Chamber.[129] In the very speech in which the Chamber asserted its "rights," Ismail was praised as the founder of a new era, the leader of civilization and progress, a man whose wishes were in tune with those of the delegates. The self-assertion of the Chamber was directed against Nubar's government rather than against Ismail.

The most important cause of the Chamber's opposition lay in the actions of the new ministry. The chief grievance was the heavy load of taxes being laid upon the country, and, in particular, their collection in advance of the harvest when the country was suffering a severe famine. The primary responsibility for this policy rested with Sir Rivers Wilson. Nubar had objected to the advance collection of taxes on the grounds that it would ruin the peasantry, but his protest was disregarded by Wilson who authorized tax-collecting forays into the countryside without regard to the means used.[130] Not surprisingly, this policy led to a rising chorus of complaints that were expressed in petitions submitted by local shaykhs to the government and in direct representations to the ministers. By early January, large numbers of shaykhs were arriving in Cairo to urge tax relief, but this led only to Vivian's issuing yet another warning to Ismail that he would be held responsible for any action taken against the ministry.[131]

The Chamber also became annoyed by its cavalier treatment by the ministry. Egypt's new rulers realized that without at least the tacit cooperation of the Chamber's delegates their measures stood little chance of success, but they could not bring themselves to work with the Chamber or to offer the delegates anything in return for their support. As Borg noted, the reluctance of Wilson and Nubar even to appear before the Chamber gave umbrage to the delegates who became convinced that the government intended to rule in a heavy-handed manner without regard for their interests.[132]

As we know, the Chamber had been convened in order to receive and discuss measures relating to finances and public works. After several days had passed without an agenda, Mahmud al-Attar (Cairo) proposed that it formally request to see the details of the government's plans.[133] Wilson offered the lame excuse that his financial proposals were not yet complete; de Blignières, however, expressed his willingness to discuss with the Chamber his plan for the reorganization of public works, a comprehensive scheme involving the formation of six committees (one in each delta province) on which *shaykhs* would sit. De Blignières appeared in person before the Chamber, but almost immediately came into conflict with the delegates over a provision that extended the corvée to all peasants, while providing exemptions upon payment of fee.[134] Peasants living on *aba'diya* and other estates had previously been exempted from the corvée, their labor being at the free disposal of the landlords. This provision, delegates complained, placed a new burden upon the landowners who would now have to pay for their labor. But these protests fell upon deaf ears.

Wilson continued to defy the Chamber by refusing to appear. His most conciliatory gesture was to ask the Chamber to send to him a small delegation (of five men) to discuss the details of his proposals. The Chamber agreed on condition that these delegates not be allowed to speak for the Chamber and that Wilson still be obliged to submit his proposals to it. After three weeks, during which time this meeting still had not occurred (despite the Chamber's insistent efforts), the delegates decided to open themselves a general discussion of Egypt's financial problems. The result, as Schölch observes, was an impressive overview of Egypt's taxes, and renewed calls for tax relief.[135]

On February 3, the Chamber launched an attack against the ministry over a decree giving the Commission of Inquiry the power to prepare fiscal and administrative laws. Delegates protested that the Europeans had no right to legislate for Egyptians and to ignore the Chamber as the defender of the laws and representative of the public interest. They argued that the viceroy had respected their rights, had always considered their views in important matters.[136] Through their spokesmen Mahmud al-Attar and Abd al-Salam al-Muwaylihi, they demanded that all important matters be submitted to the Chamber for examination. Had Nubar forgotten that a legislative body already existed to represent the people of Egypt? (Although Nubar had also opposed this scheme, by February his position was so weak that he deferred to Wilson and de Blignières on this matter.)[137] To respond to these charges, Nubar appeared briefly before the Chamber, but would not answer questions directly. Since this was a constitutional matter, he said, it should be discussed by the Council of Ministers; al-Muwaylihi responded that the basis of any progressive government was the people's involvement in constitutional matters. But Nubar would not take a firm stand.

By early February, the problems faced by the new government had become so grave that little imagination was needed to foresee its collapse. In the provinces, there was a further breakdown of security, manifested in the disaffection of the night watchmen (*ghafirs*) assigned to guard the roads and villages. Ismail ascribed this breakdown to the removal of the strong arm of authority, but it can also be attributed to the dissatisfaction of many local *shaykhs al-balad*, the real supervisors of the *ghafirs*.[138]

The situation was more serious in the capital, where the ministry faced rising discontent from the most important segments of society. Handicapped by a nearly empty treasury, Nubar had grown weary and discouraged. His troubles were further compounded when Vivian, who had earlier pledged full support, broke with Nubar and Wilson over their policy of excluding Ismail from council sessions. To restore order and revive confidence, Vivian argued that Ismail should be given some role in the work of the ministry.[139] While this disagreement was raging, an incident occurred that dramatically revealed the true extent of Ismail's authority.

This was the officers' demonstration of February 18.[140] Earlier in the month, the ministry had decided to place on half pay a large number of army officers, whose salaries were already deeply in arrears. Unrest within the army was growing, and most officers held Europe responsible for their plight. On February 17, a petition was drawn up by 400 to 500 officers who demanded, among other things, a settlement of pay arrears. On the morning of the eighteenth, they took their demands to the Chamber, but were told that it could not deal with them. Ten delegates accompanied them to a rallying point, from which they were going to march to the Department of War. On their way, they saw Nubar and Wilson, and attacked them. Nubar and Wilson were finally confined to a room in the Finance Department where they were joined by Riyad and Ali Mubarak. By this time, Ismail had arrived on the scene and confronted the rioters, ordering them to return to their homes and promising them the payment of their arrears. The viceroy's wishes were obeyed after a brief show of force by his loyal troops.

As Schölch shows, the officers' demonstration was instigated by Ismail in an attempt to bring about his return to power. It was organized and led by Latif Salim, who had established contacts with his brother-in-law, Shahin Pasha, and who acted with the full knowledge, support, and encouragement, of the khedive. Ismail was quick to exploit his opportunity. After the riot, he told the consuls that only he could reestablish and maintain law and order. Ismail demanded that Nubar be removed from office and that either he or a man chosen by him be allowed to preside over the Council of Ministers.[141] Having lost the support of the British and French consuls, Nubar acknowledged that he could no longer guarantee public security, and on February 19 resigned from office.

▲▲▲ THE DÉNOUEMENT

Thus began the last phase in the fight between Europe and Ismail for control of the government and its resources. Nubar's resignation gave rise to a cunning and resourceful effort by Ismail to remove European political control and gather into his hands the reins of power, but ironically it was Ismail's very strength, so badly underestimated by Nubar and Wilson, that brought about the big power intervention which led to his deposition on June 26, 1879. In this way, the months following Nubar's resignation form the final chapter in the story of the disintegration of viceregal power in Egypt.

Nubar's departure raised three questions: Who should succeed him as president of the Council? What was to be the relationship between the khedive and the ministry? Who should have seats in a reconstituted ministry? Ismail proposed that measures requiring his approval be submitted to him by the appropriate minister before being discussed by the Council of Ministers as a whole, and that he be allowed to convoke it and preside over its sessions—subject, of course, to a majority vote.[142] Ismail also wanted his son and heir apparent, Tawfiq, to be named president. Britain and France, jealous of each other's influence but not yet prepared to occupy Egypt, offered no proposals for reconstituting the ministry and merely insisted that there be no modifications of existing arrangements.[143]

The Europeans principally concerned with Egypt's administration disagreed about what to do. Fearful that his position could not be long maintained without Nubar, Wilson strongly opposed the appointment of Tawfiq and pressed for Nubar's reinstatement.[144] Wilson was also determined to exclude Ismail from the council's deliberations. He and de Blignières were willing to allow individual ministers to bring their measures to Ismail's attention prior to discussion by the council and even to permit Ismail to examine measures in concert with it, but they refused to allow Ismail to be present at its deliberations. Vivian, on the other hand, vigorously opposed Nubar's return on the grounds that it would lead to a second breakdown which would embroil the European powers even further. He preferred that Tawfiq be appointed council president. Vivian also believed that Ismail's personal power should be taken into account in any future administrative arrangement. Accordingly, he and the French consul proposed that Ismail be allowed to participate in the council's deliberations, but that the two European ministers be given veto powers over its decisions and that the two controllers general be reestablished. The gulf separating Vivian and Wilson was unbridgeable, and their dispute only grew more acrimonious. Wilson attacked Vivian for failing to support Nubar earlier, and Vivian accused Wilson and Nubar of trying to bring about a crisis that would force big power intervention and lead to Ismail's deposition.

The British government, however, supported Wilson. On March 1, the British and French representatives officially demanded that Nubar be appointed to the Council of Ministers and that Ismail not be allowed to preside over its meetings.[145] In return, the two powers were willing to accept Tawfiq's appointment as president of the council. Ismail, however, stood firm against the readmission of Nubar, whose return, he said, would humiliate him before his subjects and stir up even more discontent. Ismail naturally could not reject a demand made by such powerful states as Britain and France, but he told the British representative that he would refuse to accept any responsibility for public security should Nubar be returned to office.

Owing to these events and perhaps to a change of mind by the French government, which had only been lukewarm toward Nubar's return, Britain's demand was modified slightly.[146] On March 9, Ismail was presented with a second declaration which demanded that the two European ministers be given veto power over all council decisions, that Ismail not participate in its deliberations, and that he accept full responsibility for public security, but there was no insistence upon Nubar's reinstatement. The next day, Ismail accepted these provisions, and Tawfiq was appointed council president. Ismail, however, was merely playing for time. Having rid himself of Nubar, he had no intention of accepting a settlement which by Cromer's own admission was designed to reduce him to a political cipher.

Shortly afterward, Ismail precipitated a dispute over appointments to the ministry which further delayed its formation. Claiming a right to name its non-European members, Ismail wanted to transfer Riyad to Foreign Affairs and Justice, and fill the Department of the Interior with a man of his own choice. He pretended to have lost confidence in Riyad whose humble origins disqualified him; the director of the interior, he said, should be a man of greater influence and ability.[147] Wilson's reaction was typically venomous. Ismail, he charged, was making a grab for power in the provinces. Since the director of the interior could obstruct the activities of Finance and Public Works, a cooperative official should be placed in charge. Riyad's removal, said

Wilson, would be a blow to his own authority since he had originally encouraged his cooperation with promises of protection. Ismail was intriguing against him in the capital, and his latest move was only part of a wider strategy aimed at removing the European ministers and overturning the entire settlement. Predictably, Ismail's candidates for appointment to Interior were rejected by Wilson and de Blignières: Ismail Raghib was too old and knew no European languages except Greek; Ahmad Rashid was a well-known client of Ismail; Prince Tawfiq (offered by Ismail as a compromise candidate) was the puppet of his father. The battle was also joined by Vivian, who fervently supported Ismail's arguments and even went so far as to declare Ismail Raghib and Ahmad Rashid—two long-time supporters of the viceroy—to be independent and honest men!

On or about March 17, the governments of France and Great Britain demanded that Riyad remain director of the interior. Two days later, faced with the threatened resignation of Wilson and de Blignières if Riyad were not allowed to stay, Ismail yielded under protest. The British government also took the occasion to recall Vivian, who was replaced as consul general by Frank Lascelles.[148] The deadlock thus broken, Tawfiq's ministry was quickly formed: Riyad received Justice and Interior; Mubarak, Wilson, and de Blignières were reconfirmed in their previous positions; Ali Dhu al-Fiqar was given Foreign Affairs (perhaps to placate Ismail); and Aflatun Pasha was named director of war.[149]

During the month-long ministerial crisis, Egypt's financial situation had gone from bad to worse. Credit dried up; business came to a standstill; and the revenue was woefully inadequate to meet the interest payments on the loans. By March, those Europeans concerned with the management of Egyptian finances knew that the Goschen-Joubert settlement would have to be revised, and discussion on this had already begun.[150] The Commission of Inquiry and Rivers Wilson were each quietly at work on a new financial plan, one of whose features was the repeal of the *Muqabala* Law. Most attention was directed to the work of Wilson, who had begun drafting a project for submission to the Commission on Inquiry and to Ismail. Wilson had concluded that the only way out of Egypt's financial difficulties was a declaration of bankruptcy. He proposed that the interest rate and sinking fund of the Unified Debt be decreased from 7 to 5 percent and that steps be taken to reduce the fiscal advantages enjoyed by Egypt's privileged elements. Among these were a decrease in the civil list from £600,000 to £300,000 a year, an increase in the *ushuriya* tax, and the repeal of the *Muqabala* Law. A confidential draft of this plan was submitted to Ismail.

When on March 28 the Debt Commission had in hand only £44,000 with which to pay a coupon of £240,000 due April 1, the European ministers suggested that payment be postponed for one month. A decree to this effect was submitted to Ismail, but to Wilson's surprise the viceroy announced that he would not sign it, declaring that Egypt was not bankrupt and that it could meet its financial obligations.[151] Since Ismail had long been maintaining that Egypt could not pay, this about-face suggested an ulterior motive. A tip-off to what lay ahead came when the viceroy revealed to Lascelles in an interview that he had recently received a petition from the Consultative Chamber of Delegates protesting Wilson's plan.[152] Wilson's suspicions of viceregal intrigue were about to bear fruit.

On April 7, two weeks after the formation of Tawfiq's ministry, Ismail announced to the European consuls that the grave discontent in the country had obliged him to take radical steps. He said that he had received a project (known as al-La'iha al-Wataniya), representing the views of the entire country, which proposed a modification of Wilson's financial plan and demanded the formation of a purely Egyptian ministry that would be responsible to the Consultative Chamber of Delegates by new constitutional provisions.[153] Yielding to the "will of the nation," Ismail announced the dismissal of the Council of Ministers and appointed Sharif Pasha president of a new ministry; at this, Sharif told the startled Europeans that the country was greatly agitated by the ministry's insulting treatment of the Chamber, and by Wilson's suggestion of declaring bankruptcy and the repeal of the Muqabala Law. The viceroy, Sharif glibly assured the consuls, could not oppose the will of the nation and had little choice but to submit.

The Egyptian historian al-Rafi'i has seen in this development the emergence of a new constitutional order.[154] According to him, in the weeks preceding April 7 a national movement spontaneously arose that found expression in a national party (al-Jam'iya al-Wataniya) composed of the leading elements of Egyptian society. He represents the financial plan submitted to Ismail as having originated in the Consultative Chamber of Delegates, and regards Sharif as a man whose opposition to Ismail's arbitrary rule ran as deep as his resentment of European interference. By accepting the principle of ministerial responsibility to the Chamber and promising to give it a new constitution, says al-Rafi'i, the viceroy recognized his "duty" to follow the opinion of the nation.

Alexander Schölch, however, views this event quite differently: he shows that the coup of April 7 was instigated by Ismail with the aid of Turkish officials and notables in the Chamber, who rallied popular discontent to the viceroy's side. The so-called national party that took shape in late March or early April was in fact created and directed by Ismail's Turkish confidantes to gain support for a financial plan inspired by Ismail himself. Sharif's "truly Egyptian government" was composed entirely of Turkish officials long associated with the Muhammad Ali family. Praised by al-Rafi'i as the founder of constitutionalism in Egypt, Sharif Pasha was in reality one of the Ismail's most loyal agents. The events of April 7 signified not the triumph of constitutionalism but the temporary restoration of the old order.

To appreciate how Ismail and his allies used strategic, personal connections to achieve this stunning but short-lived triumph, we need to examine closely the events preceding the coup of April 7, and particularly Ismail's relations with the Turks and the Consultative Chamber of Delegates.

During Nubar's ministry, Ismail and the Chamber had formed a front against the European ministry, arguing that the Chamber's old rights had been lost and that the ruler had promised their restoration.[155] In the sessions of the Chamber, the "autocrat" Nubar was seen in opposition to the "constitutionalist" Ismail. Realizing that he needed the Chamber's support to defeat the political arrangements foisted upon him, Ismail flattered and cajoled the delegates. In early January, he told a secret meeting of leading delegates that he would not object if they opposed the government. Such efforts were intensified after Nubar's fall; Ismail apparently even gave the delegates a copy (or at least told them the details) of Wilson's financial plan, since they later admitted to having discussed it.[156]

Knowing that Ismail would favor any expression of opposition to the ministry, the delegates precipitated a major clash with the government by challenging the ministry's right to terminate its sessions.[157] On March 27, Riyad announced to the Chamber the expiration of the three-year term fixed by law for its sessions. He thanked the Chamber for its work and said that a new session would be convened at some future date. But they resisted. Muhammad al-Radi demanded a two-month extension of the Chamber's sessions to examine financial matters which the government had withheld from it. Abd al-Salam al-Muwaylihi spoke of the need to make the ministry responsible to the Chamber, and Budayni al-Shari'i insisted that no laws could be issued by the ministry without the Chamber's participation. Riyad denied these claims as inconsistent with the Chamber's constitution, but al-Muwaylihi declared that the Chamber had the right to examine government measures, decide on them, and submit its resolutions to the viceroy. After telling Riyad that they refused to go home until they had received their rights, the delegates passed a resolution to continue in session. The minutes of this meeting were sent to the Council of Ministers and to the khedive.

After Nubar's fall, some Turks became convinced that Wilson's triumph over Vivian would lead to an attempt by Wilson and Nubar to bring down the khedive—a fear not without foundation. After Vivian's recall, Nubar had openly boasted of his "victory"; he still met almost daily with the ministers, journeyed to Alexandria to greet Frank Lascelles upon his arrival, and on the day of Vivian's departure was holding conversations with Wilson, de Blignières, and Riyad at the British agency. These activities especially aroused the fears of Sharif, who suspected Nubar of conspiring with the ministers, perhaps with the connivance of the British government, to remove Ismail from power and change the dynasty. In a March 24 memorandum, Sharif wrote that if the current state of affairs continued, Egypt would fall into anarchy, and that this could only be welcomed by England. He spoke of the occupation of the Suez Canal, and of war.[158]

These two groups—the Turks and the notables in the Chamber—became the principal backers of the financial plan initiated by Ismail as a counterweight to Wilson's project.[159] Schölch believes that this plan may have been drawn up by Ismail's private secretary Barrot. According to Ninet, Ismail summoned the notables and offered them constitutional concessions in exchange for their willingness to sign and support his financial plan. Following this, the Chamber issued a petition stating that after examining Wilson's financial plan and finding it detrimental to Egypt's interests, a counterproject had been drawn up, and that its success would depend upon the Chamber's receiving the same rights and powers in financial and internal affairs as were granted to parliaments in Europe. These included a new electoral law and a provision making the Council of Ministers responsible to the Chamber for all internal and financial matters. This petition, along with a second petition (of March 29), a viceregal decree of April 5 rejecting Egypt's insolvency, and the financial project itself, formed the elements of the La'iha Wataniya that was submitted to the consuls on April 7.

Whoever its formulators, this plan clearly reflected the interests of the privileged groups, and especially of the khedive.[160] Among other things, it condemned the proposed abolition of the Muqabala Law, characterized the proposals for compensation as insufficient, and called for a reduction of the interest rate on the Unified Debt to 5 percent. Unlike Wilson's project, this plan called for no increase in the ushuriya tax, nor for tax reform even though such had often been the request of individual members of the Chamber. Neither did it set up a civil list for the khedive and his family. When asked if its backers were prepared to offer their own estates to guarantee the success of this plan, Ismail replied that this was unnecessary since no greater guarantee existed than the entire population's resolve to make any sacrifice to prevent the loss of dignity implied in national bankruptcy!

Ismail, the Turkish pashas, and members of the Chamber endeavored to find backing for the plan.[161] Meeting at the palace of Ismail Raghib, a group of Turkish *dhawat* issued an appeal for its support, declaring that if Wilson's project were approved, taxes on *ushuriya* lands would rise and the benefits from the *Muqabala* Law would be lost. Ismail also sought help from Shaykh al-Bakri, a prominent member of the *ulama*, who held meetings in his home where provincial notables, *ulama*, and others gathered to hear speakers denounce the government and to sign petitions in support of the *Laʾiha*. Leadership also came from men in the Chamber, who had important connections with the Cairo press. From the outset, the Chamber's sessions had been enthusiastically reported in the newspapers, particularly in *al-Tijara*, a mouthpiece for the revolutionary ideas of al-Afghani. Abd al-Salam al-Muwaylihi, a Freemason and friend of al-Afghani, arose to direct the campaign for the *Laʾiha* in the Chamber while his brother Ibrahim worked to gain the signatures of the *ulama* and grandees in Alexandria.

As a result of these efforts, 331 names representing a cross section of the leading elements in society were collected in support of Ismail's counterproject.[162] These included sixty *ulama*, ninety-three high-ranking military officers, forty-one merchants and notables from Cairo and Damietta, seventy-three higher civil officials, sixty members of the Consultative Chamber of Delegates, the Coptic patriarch, and the chief Jewish rabbi. After these signatures were collected, the *Laʾiha* was put into its final form, and on April 2 it was "passed" in the palace of Ismail Raghib in the presence of Sharif Pasha, Shahin Pasha, Hasan Rasim, Jaʿfar Sadiq, Shaykh al-Bakri, Shaykh al-Adawi and Shaykh al-Khalfawi. In spite of the popular agitation, there was no reason, Borg told the British representative, to fear a riot. Those who supported this project were no revolutionaries but rather the most influential and wealthy men in the country.

Sharif's role in these events is curious. His professed independence was based upon his assertion that he and his fellow ministers would resign if Ismail broke his promises, and that he had agreed to head the new ministry only after becoming convinced that it represented the wishes of the Egyptian people.[163] Yet could anyone really believe that he would oppose his long-time patron and master, to whom he had remained steadfastly loyal throughout the entire crisis, beginning in 1875? On this, Sharif's March 24 memorandum to Vivian, presenting a simple formula to remedy the political situation, is revealing: Ismail was to rule Egypt in concert with a council of ministers consisting of respected Egyptian officials responsible to the khedive both individually and collectively. By "respected" Egyptian officials, Sharif naturally meant himself and a handful of Turkish loyalists. Egypt's Chamber of Delegates did not even warrant mention in Sharif's memorandum, which spoke the khedive's language.[164]

Further proof of Sharif's intentions and sympathies can be found in the officials selected on April 8 to serve in his ministry. Ismail Raghib was reappointed to Finance; Shahin Pasha and Umar Lutfi, whose loyalty to Ismail has already been noted, received the posts of director of war and inspector general of the provinces, respectively; Ali Dhu al-Fiqar, who had been practically raised in the laps of Egypt's viceroys, was made director of justice; Muhammad Thabit, a Circassian, became director of Education and Charitable Endowments; and Muhammad Zaki Pasha, who had served in the households of three viceroys, was given Public Works (Interior and Foreign Affairs were taken by Sharif). This "truly Egyptian ministry" contained not one native Egyptian. Composed entirely of Ismail's Turkish loyalists, it did not represent that cross section of interests temporarily reflected by the signers of the La'iha.[165] Sharif's rhetoric about controlling the khedive and ruling through a ministry responsible to the Chamber was designed to appeal to those elements whose cooperation was vital for Ismail's return to power. Sharif's posture illustrated a style of politics in which certain men came forward claiming to represent an idea or a group, but Sharif himself was certainly not an independent maker of politics.

Ismail's "coup" of April 7, his most dramatic act of self-assertion, was also to be his last. While it completed his actions against the "European" ministry begun soon after the formation of Nubar's government—Wilson and de Blignières were at last chased from the administration, along with their collaborators, Ali Mubarak and Mustafa Riyad—and while the old Turkish ruling elite was returned to power, and Ismail was again a head of government in fact as well as in name, paradoxically Ismail had set in motion the machinery for his removal as viceroy.

Ismail's deposition had been discussed by Europeans before the coup of April 7.[166] Dethronement had been occasionally threatened by the consuls, and even before their dismissal, the European ministers had recommended it as the only way of avoiding a new crisis. Following the coup, however, Britain and France played for time; they refused to admit that Ismail's action was final, and urged him to request the assistance of British and French ministers. Ismail tried hard to convince the powers that he had no intention of ending European control over Egypt's finances. Referring innocuously to his coup as merely a change of cabinet, Ismail declared that he favored the most extensive control over his finances. To prove his intention of abiding by the decree of November 18, 1876, he ordered Sharif to ask Britain and France each to nominate a new controller general.

Ismail soon dispelled any doubts about his true desires. On April 22, he ordered the implementation of the financial plan embodied in the *La'iha Wataniya*, completely disregarding Wilson's project. To appease Europe, Ismail signed a decree which established a new administrative body called the Council of State, modeled after the French Conseil d'Etat.[167] This was to consist of the president of the Council of Ministers as president, two European vice-presidents, eight advisers (four to be Europeans), four investigating officers (two to be Europeans), and a general secretary. Its task was to prepare laws, provide legal counsel, adjudicate administrative disputes, among other functions. But this did not mollify European outrage. Loud cries were raised against Egypt's presumption in claiming the right to regulate its own debts.[168] Arguing feebly that this decree would not override existing rights and contracts, Sharif was forced to admit that it could not withstand European pressure. As he was soon to discover, neither could Ismail's position.

Germany took the initiative. In mid-May, the German consul general, supported by Austria's diplomatic representative, lodged a formal protest against Ismail's unilateral modification of his financial agreements.[169] Declaring the decree of April 22 to be a violation of Egypt's international engagements, the German government refused to recognize its legality, and Austria's representative suggested that Ismail be "persuaded" to abdicate in favor of Tawfiq. By mid-June formal protests against the April 22 decree had been lodged by Britain, France, Russia, and Italy. On June 14, Vivian advised Ismail to abdicate in favor of Tawfiq. Otherwise, Vivian said, Ismail would be deposed by the sultan, who intended to appoint Abd al-Halim Pasha as viceroy, thereby depriving Ismail's sons of their rights of succession. This was followed by a meeting on June 19 between Ismail and the representatives of France and Britain, in which the viceroy was "officially" advised to abdicate. If not, France and Britain would appeal to the sultan, in which case Ismail could count upon neither a civil list nor the right of succession passing to his sons.[170]

Meanwhile, Ismail had been mounting a campaign to strengthen his internal position and to convince Europe and the sultan that he had the unshaken support of the Egyptian people. On May 17, the Consultative Chamber of Delegates received a draft of a new constitution drawn up by Sharif and his Austrian adviser, a Dr. Keller, and on June 2, the Chamber was given a new electoral law.[171] The new constitution stipulated freedom of speech for the delegates and gave the Chamber a veto over laws issued by the Council of Ministers. Early in May, Shaykh al-Bakri visited Vivian and represented himself as the leading figure behind the national movement. Thousands of Egyptians had risen against the European intervention, he said, and had made Ismail swear by the Quran to rule in accordance with a constitution. They had even threatened to depose him if he broke his word. In late June, Shaykh al-Bakri was organizing petitions demanding Ismail's continuation in office, and Abd al-Salam al-Muwaylihi received an order to mobilize support in the Chamber for Ismail, who publicly declared his willingness to make any compromise save the reentry of European ministers into the government.

But the viceroy began losing control over the movement which he had created.[172] The signers of the *La'iha* became divided between a majority supporting Ismail and a minority supporting Tawfiq, who on June 11 had recommended himself to the powers by a timely complaint about his father's unreliability. Tawfiq's supporters came mostly from the clique formed around Jamal al-Din al-Afghani, a fellow Freemason. This charismatic and ambitious personality saw in Tawfiq's accession distinct advantages for himself and his followers. In May or June, Jamal al-Din visited the French consul general and argued for Ismail's removal.

Far more interesting was the defection of the once loyal Sharif. On June 6, 1879, Sharif indicated to the British consul general that he would not oppose Ismail's abdication.[173] About two weeks later, he openly declared that neither the Council of Ministers nor the country had any confidence in him. It has been suggested that Sharif's defection was linked to encouragement from Jamal al-Din's party.[174] Yet Sharif's motive more likely stemmed from fear of Ottoman intervention which would nullify Tawfiq's right to succeed and result in the enthronement of Prince Abd al-Halim, who had no support within Egypt. Such a development, Sharif said, would destroy Egypt's hard-won autonomy and reduce the country to the status of an Ottoman dependency.[175] In addition to not opposing Ismail's removal, he would even work to persuade Ismail to abdicate if Britain and France would assure him that all of the rights won by Muhammad Ali and his successors would be preserved. Under no circumstances would he accept as ruler Abd al-Halim Pasha.

Ismail still hoped that by bribes, professions of loyalty, and displays of popularity in Egypt he could win the support of the sultan and prevent action by the Ottomans against him. To official requests from the

European powers to resign, he replied that the whole matter had been turned over to the sultan and that his fate rested in his hands.[176] But from reports sent by Abraham Bey, Ismail's agent in Istanbul, he knew that Abd al-Halim was meeting daily with the sultan. Only a desperate kind of hope could have prevented him from seeing the inevitable. On June 24, the French representative in Egypt received news from Istanbul that Ismail was to be deposed on the following day and Abd al-Halim proclaimed the new viceroy. Ismail received a hasty visit from the representatives of Germany, Britain, and France, accompanied by Sharif, who again urged him to abdicate. Though Ismail remained firm, the Europeans could not afford to wait. They pressured the sultan to nominate Tawfiq. On June 26, Sharif read to Ismail a telegram from Istanbul addressed to the "ex-khedive" which ordered his removal as viceroy and announced the succession of Tawfiq.

Sharif and Ismail Raghib arranged the transfer of power. Tawfiq was summoned to the Abdin palace where he was ceremoniously greeted by his father, led to Ismail's *diwan*, and saluted as the new viceroy of Egypt. Ismail then retired to Alexandria to make preparations for his departure. On June 30, 1879, amid salvos of farewell from warships and shore batteries, Ismail and his retinue sailed out of Alexandria harbor on his yacht, al-Mahrusa, bound for Naples. Ismail Pasha was never to see Egypt again. Nor was Egypt again to know a despotism as harsh as that which he and his predecessors had laid upon it.

▲8▲
EPILOGUE

As had so often happened in Egyptian history, the breakup of central authority ushered in a period of turmoil and political disorder. The interval between 1879 and 1882, however, differed from the late eighteenth century in two important respects. First, the groups that emerged to provide leadership for society came not from the *ulama* or a coalition of religious brotherhoods and craft guilds, but rather from elements within the new state system. Second, there was no comparable breakdown of Egypt's economic and administrative structures. In fact, there were periods of relatively stable government under Riyad (September 1879–September 1881), who was supported by the Europeans and the Egyptian technicians (including Ali Mubarak), and for about seven months following the appointment of Muhammad Sharif as president of the Council of Ministers in September 1881.

The chief characteristic of the 1879–1882 period was the continued separation of power from authority, and the inability of contending groups to reestablish centralized control. Khedive Tawfiq, the head of state, possessed no influence of his own and was a pawn in the hands of the European consuls. Other forces struggled for control without any group or coalition being able to hold together for long or gather into its hands all the reins of power. Egypt was governed in succession by collaborating officials, *dhawat* notables, and in the months preceding the arrival of British troops, by a group of administrators from the middle levels of the bureaucracy.

Of these efforts to assert control, none was more significant than the stunning but short-lived triumph of *dhawat* notables in the Chamber who carried out an interesting constitutional experiment which had the support of the majority of the Egyptian people. Egypt's Consultative Chamber of Delegates had been dismissed shortly after the deposition of Ismail, and little was heard from its members during Riyad's ministry until January 1881, when a group of Egyptian army officers led by Ahmad Urabi began denouncing the Turco-Circassian officer class and demanding an improvement of material conditions in the army. At this point, leading *dhawat* notables, including Muhammad Sultan, entered into contacts with the *fallah* officers and persuaded them to join the notables in demanding a new constitution. Muhammad Sultan also sounded out Muhammad Sharif on the idea of serving as president of the Council of Ministers in a reconstituted government. This conspiracy bore fruit in September 1881 when a demonstration by Egyptian army officers brought about the downfall of Riyad's government and resulted in Muhammad Sharif's appointment as president of a new Council of Ministers. Sharif Pasha, however, was hardly more than a cipher. It was Egypt's notables who, using the officers as an instrument, had achieved real power.

The men who took their seats in the newly elected Chamber in December 1881 were the wealthiest and most influential members of Egypt's provincial elite—those very persons who had long been associated with high administration in the countryside. Muhammad Shawaribi, Hasan al-Shari'i, Sulayman Abaza, and Muhammad Sultan were well-known figures, but many others, even those delegates new to the Chamber, came from families of provincial *dhawat*. These men were concerned primarily with protecting their social and economic interests, but they also had broad popular support, and in their deliberations showed a real concern for the interests of their constituents.

On the basis of a petition presented to the khedive by a group of *dhawat* notables in September 1881, which stated that there could be no justice or freedom for a society unless its government was willing to listen to the peoples' representatives, the Chamber began its work. On January 2, 1882, Muhammad Sharif resubmitted to the delegates a new draft of the Chamber law of May 1879 in which the Chamber received the right to express its views on the budget but could not control it. As the delegates were discussing this law, the governments of Britain and France, fearing a possible move by the delegates against the khedive, issued the infamous Joint Note of January 8, which contained the threat of intervention. The Joint Note marked the beginning of a process which led to the unraveling of the national coalition. The first casualty was Sharif Pasha who in January defected to the side of the khedive after having become convinced of the inevitability of European intervention.

At first, the Joint Note hardened the attitude of the Chamber. After the formation in February of a new ministry led by Mahmud Sami al-Barudi, a friend and supporter of Urabi, the delegates issued a Basic Law which requested that the Chamber receive control over that half of the budget not allocated to the payment of the debt, and which insisted that no tax be raised without the Chamber's approval. The delegates also proposed a reform of the electoral system. Legislation was passed stipulating that village mayors (*shaykhs al-balad*) be considered government officials and receive fixed salaries; that the position of these officials vis-à-vis the village population and the central administration be defined and regulated by law; that lists of voters be introduced in the provinces; and that the delegates to the Chamber be made independent of the *mudirs*. In effect, the delegates were insisting upon a limited control of the government.

As time passed, however, many of the delegates began to have doubts about the desirability of opposing Europe, especially in light of the vigorous attack against the new order being waged by the khedive. At a critical juncture, Muhammad Sultan, the president of the Chamber, joined the khedive's side. The precise reasons for Sultan's defection are not known, but it must be recalled that Muhammad Sultan had long-standing connections with the viceregal family and with Egypt's collaborating officials, and that he must certainly have recognized the grave threat to his privileges and wealth that could result from continued cooperation with a movement on a collision course with Europe. By July 1882, nearly all of the wealthiest and most influential members of the Chamber had joined the khedive and the European consuls in Alexandria where they were protected by British gunboats. The vast majority of the Egyptian population, including a large number of village *shaykhs*, supported Urabi and his men who were busy organizing Egypt's defenses. The Egyptian bureaucracy, however, remained intact, producing men from the middle levels of government who took over the functions of high administration in a council called *Majlis al-Urfi*. The defeat of Urabi at the battle of Tel al-Kabir in September 1882 sealed the fate of the embryonic nationalist movement.

After 1882, many members of the former elite resumed their administrative positions, but not for long. Muhammad Sultan died of cancer in 1884. Muhammad Sharif, who headed the first ministry formed by the British, died in 1887. Ali Mubarak was pensioned in 1891, and Nubar left office for the last time in 1894. Long before then, however, the British had begun promoting more malleable Syrian and Coptic officials, and had come to rely upon increasing numbers of English advisers imported from British universities. A new order was taking shape, and the age of viceregal absolutism was becoming only a dim memory.

If the 1805–1879 period saw the end of autocracy, it also witnessed the emergence of a new pattern of government. As we have seen, beginning with Muhammad Ali, the functions, structure, and bases of administration in Egypt became radically altered. Government acquired a new role in promoting economic and social development. A hierarchical structure, based upon Western models, was set up, accompanied by a spate of new rules and regulations. Western technology was introduced, bringing new skills and scientific knowledge. Egyptian Muslims were brought into the administration in increasing numbers. By the 1870s, the consequences of these developments were readily apparent. A centralized bureaucracy had emerged to replace the old concessionary system in which administration had been carried out by autonomous social groups. A new administrative elite had appeared, comprised of technocrats who were European in training but not necessarily in outlook, and a strong indigenous element. This "mixed" elite signified the beginning of the end of the monopoly of Egypt's administration by Turks. These and other changes were justified by references to "progress" and "civilization," and by the use of the symbol of an Egyptian nation, which suggested that all Egyptians had a right to be involved in and share the benefits of their country's development.

Practically speaking, however, these changes led to an ever greater centralization of power and government control over society. As the central administration acquired more and more functions, and extended its influence by issuing new regulations, social groups became subordinated to the demands of the state. The Egyptian *ulama*, for example, lost control of education, then later, of justice, as Egyptian society came to be governed by new civil codes rather than the *sharia*. Yet this does not imply that society was totally helpless before the juggernaut. As we have seen, there is a tendency for centralization to go too far until it produces a counterreaction. And society had many ingenious ways of resisting the demands of the central administration. This study has shown how the bureaucracy could be penetrated by groups representing interests outside the government, who endeavored to turn the administration to their own advantage. From the standpoint of the entire society, however, the bureaucracy offered opportunities only to the ruling group and brought hardships and suffering to the vast majority of the subject population.

For good or ill, the new centralized bureaucracy that emerged between 1805 and 1879 had a profound impact upon life in Egypt. It provided a bridge between government and society, altered the character of politics, facilitated the rise of a new administrative elite, made possible the separation of the ruler's household from the administration, and formed a core around which subsequent rulers built up their governing systems. The new bureaucracy thus became a vehicle by which Egypt was brought into the modern age.

Abbreviations Used in Notes

Notes

Glossary

Bibliography

Index

ABBREVIATIONS USED IN NOTES

SOURCES*

AI	*Arshif Ifranji*, European archival section of Egyptian National Archives
al-Abhath	*Mahafiz al-abhath*, copies of orders and documents from various archival sources
Dhawat land register	*Daftar zimam atyan ushuriya: Dhawat. Raqm al-sijill*, 1343
FO	Foreign Office Papers, Public Record Office, London
HP	Hekekyan Papers
Mas	*Masadir wa tarikh Misr*, copies and translations from Arabic and Turkish registers
MDDMS	*Mulakhkhasat dafatir Diwan al-Maʿiya al-Saniya*, Egyptian National Archives
MM	*Milaffat al-mustakhdamin*, pension dossiers for retired officials and their families
Mubarak, *al-Khitat*	Ali Mubarak, *al-Khitat al-Tawfiqiya*
OL (1837)	Organic Law of 1837
OL (1855)	Organic Law of 1855, in F. Jallad, *Qamus al-idara*, vol. 2, pp. 90–111
Sami	Amin Sami, *Taqwim al-Nil*, multivolume collection of archival documents covering the period from Muhammad Ali through Ismail
WM	*al-Waqaʾiʿ al-Misriya*, the *Egyptian Gazette*
WMC	*al-Waqaʾiʿ al-Misriya* collection

MONTHS OF THE HIJRA YEAR (A.H.)

M	*Muharram*, first month	B	*Rajab*, seventh month
S	*Safar*, second month	SH	*Shaʿban*, eighth month
R	*Rabiʿ al-awwal*, third month	N	*Ramadan*, ninth month
RT	*Rabiʿ al-thani*, fourth month	L	*Shawwal*, tenth month
J	*Jumada al-ula*, fifth month	D	*Dhu al-Qaʿda*, eleventh month
JA	*Jumada al-akhira*, sixth month	DH	*Dhu al-Hijja*, twelfth month

*See selected bibliography for publication data.

NOTES

▲2▲ THE THEMES OF EGYPT'S GOVERNMENTAL TRADITION

1. I have found the following works most useful: El Sayed, "The Role of the Ulama"; al-Sayyid Marsot, "The Wealth of the Ulama"; Shaw, *Organization and Development of Ottoman Egypt*; Shaw, "Landholding and Land-Tax Revenues"; Abd al-Rahim, *al-Rif al-misri*; Lapidus, *Muslim Cities*; Hourani, "Some Aspects of Modern Egyptian History"; Hourani, "Ottoman Reform and the Politics of Notables"; Rabie, *Financial System of Egypt*; Ayalon, "Studies in al-Jabarti I"; Holt, "The Pattern of Egyptian Political History"; Raymond, "Quartiers et mouvements populaires"; Raymond, "Quartiers de résidence aristocratique"; Raymond, "Les sources de la richesse urbaine"; Raymond, *Artisans et commerçants au Caire*; Gran, *Islamic Roots of Capitalism*.

2. The "pendulum swing" idea resembles Ibn Khaldun's theory of dynastic cycles and Pareto's concept of the circulation of elites; see Ibn Khaldun, *The Muqaddimah*; Pareto, *Sociological Writings*.

3. See Schölch, "Constitutional Development."

4. Wittfogel, *Oriental Despotism*, sees Egypt as the prototype of a "hydraulic" society where dependence upon a single water supply throws all power into the hands of the government, which alone can maintain the irrigation system. During our period, however, village communities bore the chief responsibility for maintaining local irrigation works, and it was not until the establishment of perennial irrigation in the twentieth century that the central government controlled the water supply.

5. Since Max Weber had little knowledge of Islam or Middle Eastern society, his approach should be used cautiously. For an adaptation of the Weber model, see Findley, *Bureaucratic Reform in the Ottoman Empire*.

6. Hourani, "Ottoman Reform," pp. 36–66.

7. Hourani, "Some Aspects of Modern Egyptian History," p. 13.

8. Ibid., pp. 16–17. Ulama support for the mamluks was, of course, limited; in the late eighteenth century, members of this class vigorously opposed mamluk fiscal policies (El Sayed, "The Role of the *Ulama*," pp. 269–70).

9. See Crecelius, *The Roots of Modern Egypt*.

10. Abd al-Rahim, *al-Rif al-misri*, p. 88.

11. Owen, *Middle East in the World Economy*, pp. 83–84.

▲3▲ THE RECONSTITUTION OF GOVERNMENT BY MUHAMMAD ALI

1. In *Egypt in the Reign of Muhammad Ali*, Afaf Lutfi al-Sayyid Marsot portrays Muhammad Ali as a mamluk whose policies were not fundamentally different from those

of his late eighteenth-century precedessors. This study was not in print at the time I composed this chapter, and I have not seen the manuscript.

2. Owen, *Cotton and the Egyptian Economy*, p. 40.

3. On the viceroy's educational policy, see Heyworth-Dunne, *History of Education*; on his government's intervention in irrigation, transport, industry, and public health, see Rivlin, *Agricultural Policy*, pp. 191-200, 213-49, *passim*; al-Hitta, "The Development of Transport," pp. 406-15; Kuhnke, "Ophthalmological Clinics in Egypt."

4. Rivlin, *Agricultural Policy*, p. 197.

5. Deny, *Sommaire des archives*, p. 138. See also the manuscript by G. B. Brocchi, "Divisions administratives de l'Egypte," 9 July 1824, fols. 94-97, in box 152, *al-Mutafarriqat, AI*; Rivlin, *Agricultural Policy*, p. 86.

6. In 1811, for example, Ibrahim Pasha was named treasurer general to collect government revenues and make changes in the landholding system (Rivlin, *Agricultural Policy*, p. 52).

7. See *WM*, no. 85, 20 J 1245/17 Nov. 1829; no. 191, 2 RT 1246/10 Sept. 1831; Baer, *Egyptian Guilds*, p. 93, and *passim*. On the Coptic scribes and the organization of the Egyptian state archive (*al-Daftarkhana*), see Sami, pt. 2, p. 348; *WM*, no. 350, 8 N 1247/10 Feb. 1832.

8. Rivlin, *Agricultural Policy*, pp. 87-88.

9. Ibid., pp. 78-79.

10. Ibid., pp. 89-101; Campbell, "Report on Egypt," appended to Campbell/Palmerston, unnumbered, 6 July 1840, in FO 78/408b.

11. This paragraph is based on: Deny, *Sommaire des archives*, pp. 108-15; Lane, *Manners and Customs*, pp. 110-11; *WM*, no. 357, 28 N 1247/2 Mar. 1832; no. 388, 5 M 1248/4 May 1832; *WMC*, box no. 1, dossier "al-Idara fi ahd Muhammad Ali," order from *al-Diwan al-Khidiwi* to *al-Muʿawin al-Awwal* of 6 DH 1244/9 June 1829.

12. See Yates, *Modern History*, vol. 1, pp. 458-59; vol. 2, p. 215; Mengin, *Histoire de l'Egypte*, vol. 2, pp. 258-59.

13. See Deny, *Sommaire des archives*, pp. 90-104; 111n1; Hamont, *L'Egypte sous Méhémet-Ali*, vol. 1, pp. 98-99; introduction to volume 1 of *Wizarat al-irshad*. Note that the viceregal cabinet had several designations, including that of council (*majlis*) and that it was basically an entourage composed of the viceroy's aides (*muʿawinun*), some of whom met in council while the others merely served in the cortège (*mawkib*).

14. Rivlin, *Agricultural Policy*, p. 243; Deny, *Sommaire des archives*, p. 105; OL (1837), especially the preface which discusses the problems of overcentralization.

15. Douin, *La mission du Baron de Boislecomte*, p. 127; al-Ayyubi, *Tarikh Misr*, vol. 1, p. 157; OL(1837), pt. 2, art. 6; Rivlin, *Agricultural Policy*, pp. 133, 185.

16. John Bowring, "Report on Egypt and Candia," fol. 405, in FO 78/381; Guémard, *Les réformes*, p. 256; Mengin, *Histoire sommaire*, p. 236.

17. Abd al-Karim, *Tarikh al-taʿlim*, pp. 39-41; Farhi, "Nizam-i Cedid," p. 152; Planat, *Régéneration de l'Egypte*, pp. 179, 202ff.

18. See Clot, *Aperçu*, vol. 1, p. 262.

19. Douin, *La mission du Baron de Boislecomte*, p. 111; Hamont, *L'Egypte*, vol. 1, p. 102; Guémard, *Les réformes*, pp. 277-78.

20. Clot, *Aperçu*, p. lxxxiv.

21. Sami, pt. 3, vol. 1, p. 11.

22. This paragraph is based on: ibid., pt. 2, pp. 372, 492, 591; Cattaui, *Le règne de Mohamed Aly*, vol. 1, pp. 354-56; Rivlin, *Agricultural Policy*, p. 82; HP, MS 37450, fol. 151.

23. See Hamont, *L'Egypte*, vol. 2, pp. 68-69, 343; *WM*, no. 59, 19 RT 1263/6 Apr. 1847; no. 54, 14 R 1264/19 Feb. 1848; Sami, pt. 2, pp. 408, 508; Mubarak, *al-Khitat*, vol. 14, pp. 76-77.

24. On Muhammad Bey, see Douin, *L'Egypte de 1828 à 1830*, p. 250; Yates, *Modern History*, vol. 1, pp. 123–24; Senior, *Conversations*, vol. 1, p. 235. For Muharram Bey and Kamil, see Tugay, *Three Centuries*, pp. 118–22; Deny, *Sommaire des archives*, p. 95n2; Zaki, *A'lam al-jaysh*, pp. 59–61.

25. See Douin, *La mission du Baron de Boislecomte*, p. 101; Douin, *L'Egypte de 1828 à 1830*, p. 189; Douin, *Une mission militaire*, p. 78; Clot, *Aperçu*, vol. 1, pp. lxviii, 272; Hamont, *L'Egypte*, vol. 1, p. 384; vol. 2, p. 33; Heyworth-Dunne, *History of Education*, pp. 117n7, 140; Abd al-Karim, *Tarikh al-ta'lim*, p. 82; HP, MS 37450, fols. 184–85, 211; *MM*, no. 9631, *Mudad istikhdam Khalid Basha*; no. 17199, *Mudad istikhdam Ali Dhu al-Fiqar*.

26. Sami, pt. 2, p. 528n1.

27. The leading Armenian official in Egypt after the death of Boghos in 1844 was Artin Bey, director of foreign affairs from 1844 until 1850.

28. HP, MS 37449, fol. 122; *WM*, no. 93, 13 DH 1263/22 November 1847; Sami, pt. 2, pp. 253–54.

29. This paragraph is based on the following sources: on the *katkhuda*, see Deny, *Sommaire des archives*, pp. 116, 127; on Baqqi Bey, see *MDDMS*, *al-Ma'iya al-Turki*, reg. 62/407, Viceroy/Baqqi Bey, 19 L 1250/18 Feb. 1835; on Muhammad Sharif, see *WM*, no. 28, 11 N 1262/2 Sept. 1846; on Boghos Bey, see Yates, *Modern History*, vol. 1, p. 99; *MDDMS*, *al-Ma'iya al-Turki*, reg. 6/77, Viceroy/Boghos, 26 S 1236/3 Dec. 1820; on Ibrahim, See HP, MS 37450, fol. 162; Dodwell, *Founder of Modern Egypt*, pp. 200–01.

30. Hamont, *L'Egypte*, vol. 2, p. 52; Cadalvene and Breuvery, *L'Egypte et la Turquie*, vol. 1, pp. 109–11.

31. See Deny, *Sommaire des archives*, pp. 63–65; Mubarak, *al-Khitat*, vol. 9, p. 47.

32. OL(1837), pt. 3, art. 19; Sami, pt. 3, vol. 2, p. 816.

33. Heyworth-Dunne, *History of Education*, p. 114; *WMC*, box 31, issue no. 23, 27 L 1244/2 May 1829; box 1, dossier "al-Idara fi ahd Muhammad Ali," copy of Turkish document no. 298, registered in *daftar* 58 of *al-Ma'iya al-Saniya*, 11 JA 1249/26 Oct. 1833; OL (1837), sec. 3, arts. 3, 13. When monthly pensions were assigned to former provincial employees in 1830, the order specified that a pension was *ihsan* (a gift) from the viceroy; in 1848, pensions were still so called. In 1844, a pension was legally designated a *mukafa* (reward, compensation) from the government (*WMC*, box 21, issue 129, 27 J 1246/13 Nov. 1830; *WM*, no. 123, 16 SH 1264/18 July 1848; *al-Abhath*, box 137, *La'ihat al-Ma'ashat*, 12 SH 1260/27 Aug. 1844, preface).

34. Clot, *Aperçu*, p. lxxix; Yates, *Modern History*, vol. 1, p. 458; St. John, *Egypt and Mohammed Ali*, vol. 1, pp. 59–60; Cadalvene and Breuvery, *L'Egypte*, vol. 1, p. 13; Campbell, "Report on Egypt"; Hamont, *L'Egypte*, vol. 1, p. 130; Cattaui, *Le règne de Mohamed Aly*, vol. 1, pp. 220–21; vol. 2, pt. 2, pp. 2–3; Campbell/Wellington, no. 5, 24 Mar. 1835, in FO 78/257.

35. See Owen, *Middle East in the World Economy*, pp. 73–76; Rivlin, *Agricultural Policy*, pp. 203–10.

36. Baer, *Landownership*, p. 13.

37. Owen, *Cotton and the Egyptian Economy*, pp. 65–67.

38. Ibid., pp. 82–83; Heyworth-Dunne, *History of Education*, pp. 223–43.

▲4▲ ADMINISTRATIVE DEVELOPMENT UNDER VICEREGAL ABSOLUTISM

1. Deny, *Sommaire des archives*, pp. 69–74.

2. See Owen, *Middle East in the World Economy*, pp. 64–76, 122–52; Owen, *Cotton and the Egyptian Economy*.

3. See Sabry, *L'empire égyptien*, pp. 224–37.

4. Ibid., p. 46.

5. For this practice in the eighteenth century, see Gibb and Bowen, *Islamic Society*, vol. 1, pt. 1, pp. 310–11.

6. See Landes, *Bankers*; Issa, *Capitalisme*.

7. This paragraph is based on: Landes, *Bankers*, pp. 116–18, 173–77.

8. This paragraph is based on: ibid., pp. 224, 259–60; Hamza, *Public Debt*, pp. 79–82, 186, 189–90, 208.

9. Heyworth-Dunne, *History of Education*, pp. 303–04, 324–25, 342–62, 394.

10. Owen, *Cotton and the Egyptian Economy*, pp. 153–55; Owen, *Middle East in the World Economy*, pp. 148, 150–51.

11. Owen, *Middle East in the World Economy*, pp. 123, 28–129. Rauf Abbas Hamid, *al-Nizam*, p. 49.

12. Owen, *Middle East in the World Economy*, p. 144.

13. Sami, pt. 3, vol. 1, p. 12.

14. Deny, *Sommaire des archives*, pp. 126–29; OL (1837), pt. 2, art. 25.

15. Sami, pt. 3, vol. 1, p. 103; Deny, *Sommaire des archives*, p. 116; see also Sami, pt. 3, vol. 1, pp. 216–17.

16. On the development of these governorates, see Sami, pt. 3, vol. 2, pp. 640, 710; dates are from Sami's annual lists. The post of *muhtasib* was abolished after Muhammad Ali's reign (Baer, *Egyptian Guilds*, p. 44).

17. Sami, pt. 3, vol. 1, p. 15.

18. *Mas, Awamir, Maʿiya Saniya-Arabi*, reg. 1883/66/21, Viceroy/*al-Daqahliya*, 26 S 1272/7 Nov. 1855.

19. The Egyptian government did not keep budgets in the accepted sense of the word. Available information represents only rough estimates (Stanton/Stanley, no. 68, 12 June 1868, in FO 78/2038; Stanton/Derby, no. 154, 4 Dec. 1875, in FO 78/2405).

20. *Mas, al-Majlis al-Khususi*, reg. 66/76/27, *Qarar al-Majlis al-Khususi*, 20 M1280/7 July 1863; reg. 68/135/68, *Qarar al-Majlis al-Khususi*, 2 R 1281/5 Aug. 1864; Sami, pt. 3, vol. 2, p. 669.

21. Zaghlul, *al-Muhama*, pp. 194–95, states that five courts were established in 1852. Other evidence from the Abbas and Saʿid period indicates no more than four of these courts existed at a single time, and that they were subject to viceregal intervention and caprice (Sami, pt. 3, vol. 1, pp. 69, 97, 322, 341, 410–17).

22. Sami, pt. 3, vol. 2, pp. 455–57, 593, 864, 883, and *passim*; al-Rafiʿi, *Asr Ismail*, vol. 2, p. 113; cf. p. 238.

23. The most complete documentation is in *WM*, no. 22, 23 JA 1288/5 Sept. 1871, which reprints not only their statute, but also several discussions held in the Privy Council and the Consultative Chamber of Delegates about them; see also Sami, pt. 3, vol. 2, pp. 943–51; al-Rafiʿi, *Asr Ismail*, vol. 2, pp. 116–17.

24. This paragraph is based on: *WM*, no. 22, 23 JA 1288/5 Sept. 1871, *al-Laʾiha*: [sec. 1] pt. 3, arts. 34–35; [sec. 2] pt. 1, arts. 12–13, 24; Sami, pt. 3, vol. 2, pp. 864, 883, 925, 930.

25. *WM*, no. 22, 23 JA 1288/5 Sept. 1871.

26. Ibid.; al-Rafiʿi, *Asr Ismail*, vol. 2, p. 108; Sami, pt. 3, vol. 2, pp. 972–78, *Tarib*, esp. arts. 1–2, 4, 5; McCoan, *Egypt As It Is*, p. 116.

27. *WM*, no. 22, 23 JA 1288/5 Sept. 1871, *al-Laʿiha*: [sec. 1] pt. 2, arts. 20–33.

28. Sami, pt. 3, vol. 3, pp. 1116–18, *Qarar al-Majlis al-Khususi*, esp. arts. 1, 6–7.

29. Sami, pt. 3, vol. 2, pp. 970–72, *Qarar al-Majlis al-Khususi*, arts. 4, 6, 14.

30. See Sami, pt. 3, vol. 1, pp. 36, 53, 409; pt. 3, vol. 2, pp. 581–82; pt. 3, vol. 3, p. 1232; Deny, *Sommaire des archives*, p. 120; Stanton/Granville, no. 69, 6 Sept. 1872, in FO 78/2229. Muhammad Ali had created a Department of *al-Awqaf*, but it was short-lived (Sami, pt. 3, vol. 1, p. 46).

31. See, for example, Sami, pt. 3, vol. 2, pp. 462, 500, 502.

32. Information about Charitable Endowments, Public Works, Education, and Interior is based on *Mas, al-Majlis al-Khususi*, reg. 68/129/85, *Qarar al-Majlis al-Khususi*, 25 M 1281/30 June 1864; Sami, pt. 3, vol. 2, pp. 520–21, 540, 647–48; *Mas, Awamir, Ma'iya Saniya-Arabi*, reg. 1943/45/94, Viceroy/*al-Majlis al-Khususi*, 28 SH 1289/31 Oct. 1872. In 1859, Interior had 149 employees with a monthly salary of 183,495 piastres; in 1872, there were 24 members at 53,978 piastres a month (Sami, pt. 3, vol. 1, pp. 324–26; *Mas, al-Majlis al-Khususi*, reg. 1956/33/2, *al-Majlis al-Khususi/al-Maliya*, 4 SH 1289/7 Oct. 1872).

33. OL (1837), preface.

34. Deny, *Sommaire des archives*, pp. 34, 115, 138.

35. Information on the Department of Public Works comes from ibid., pp. 115, 125; Sami, pt. 3, vol. 2, pp. 581.–82, 647–48; pt. 3, vol. 3, appendix on the railway administration.

36. See Sami, pt. 3, vol. 1, pp. 215–16, 241–42, 324–26; Minister of Interior/Green, 10 Oct. 1857, in FO 141/33.

37. *Mas, al-Majlis al-Khususi*, reg. 1956/33/2, *al-Majlis al-Khususi/al-Maliya*, 4 SH 1289/7 Oct. 1872; Sami, pt. 3, vol. 3, p. 1191.

38. This paragraph is based on HP, MS 37453, fol. 187; About, *Le Fellah*, pp. 131–33; cf. HP, MS 37449, fols. 30–31.

39. See Deny, *Sommaire des archives*, pp. 120–21; Sami, pt. 3, vol. 1, pp. 17–18; *WM*, no. 49, 9 S 1263/27 Jan. 1847.

40. Sami, pt. 2: p. 541; pt. 3, vol. 1, pp. 17, 86; *al-Abhath*, box 52, dossier "Mawdu' al-Ta'lim," Viceroy/*al-Madaris*, 24 JA 1266/7 May 1850. In 1847, the Privy Council was composed of Ahmad Yagan, Ibrahim Pasha, Abbas Pasha, Hasan Bey, and Burhan Bey.

41. See Sami, pt. 3, vol. 2, pp. 458, 468, 804, 967; pt. 3, vol. 3, pp. 1063, 1065, 1078; see also Sami, pt. 3, vol. 2, years 1287/1288 (1870–1872), *passim*.

42. In 1876, the Privy Council consisted of eight departmental directors, two governors (of Alexandria and Cairo), the presidents of the Council of Justice and the Chamber of Delegates, the supreme commander of the army, the director of the Council for the Affairs of Orphans, the adviser of Public Works, and four unofficial members (Zaki, *Un mot sur Riaz Pacha*, pp. 19–20). In 1877, J. C. McCoan (*Egypt As It Is*, p. 94) placed its number at between seventeen and eighteen men, including one member of the *ulama*.

43. See, for example, al-Rafi'i, *Asr Ismail*, vol. 2, p. 212.

44. When Linant Bey was removed from the Department of Public Works due to old age, he was made a member of the Privy Council; Ahmad Rashid was appointed as a reward for good services (*al-Abhath*, box 111, dossier "Wizarat al-Ashghal," viceregal order of 19 RT 1286/29 July 1869; *WM*, no. 5, 3 SH 1282/21 Dec. 1865).

45. Deny, *Sommaire des archives*, p. 121; see also Sami, pt. 3, vol. 1, p. 18; pt. 3, vol. 2, pp. 516–17, 582, 594, 640, 795, 889–95, 953–54; *Mas, al-Majlis al-Khususi*, reg. 73/74/26, *Qarar al-Majlis al-Khususi*, 17 S 1284/20 June 1867; *WMC*, box 19, dossier "Ma'ashat;" *WM*, no. 219, 7 RT 1285/27 July 1868; *al-Abhath*, box 132, dossier "Majalis," Viceroy/*al-Dakhiliya*, 10 SH 1281/8 Jan. 1865.

46. This paragraph is based on: Sami, pt. 3, vol. 1, p. 18, art. 3; Deny, *Sommaire des archives*, pp. 123–24; Zaghlul, *al-Muhama*, p. 64 and arts. 2, 10; p. 197; *al-Abhath*, box 132, dossier "Majlis Ahkam," Viceroy/*Majlis al-Ahkam*, 23 M 1271/16 Oct. 1854.

47. Judicial matters were handled by the Department of Civil Affairs, the viceregal cabinet, and other official bodies. This paragraph is based on: Deny, *Sommaire des archives*, pp. 94, 109, 114, 121–22, 123; Sami, pt. 3, vol. 1, p. 38; Abbas asked the Council of Justice to specify the penalty for high officials who failed to construct palaces on the land he had given them (Sami, pt. 3, vol. 1, pp. 21–22).

48. OL (1855) p. 104, art. 4; p. 105, arts. 14, 20; p. 106, art. 12; Sami, pt. 3, vol. 2, p. 576.

49. Ismail wrote of the Privy Council's great importance, and Sa'id spoke of it as the only administrative body capable of reconciling the interests of his subjects. Its members, he said, were to be men of experience and long service in the government (Sami, pt. 3, vol. 2, p. 498; *Mas, Awamir, Ma'iya Saniya-Turki*, reg. 558/38/41, Viceroy/Hadhiq Pasha, 23 B 1282/12 Dec. 1865; *al-Abhath*, box 132, dossier "Majlis Ahkam," Viceroy/ *Majlis al-Ahkam*, 18 M 1271/11 Oct. 1854).

50. Abu-Lughod, "Transformation of the Egyptian Elite," pp. 342–43.

51. The organization and operation of this body were defined in an electoral law and in an organic law, both of which are reprinted in Sami (see esp. pt. 3, vol. 2, p. 667, art. 5; pp. 674–75, 676, art. 2.

52. Ibid., p. 925.

53. Ibid., pp. 1056–57.

54. Wallace, *Egypt and the Egyptian Question*, p. 214; Landau, *Parliaments and Parties*, p. 8; Hamza, *Public Debt*, p. 101.

55. Mubarak, *al-Khitat*, vol. 10, p. 32; for peasant revolts, see Colquhoun/Russell, no. 27, 5 Mar. 1865; no. 32, 11 Mar. 1865, in FO 78/1871.

56. al-Rafi'i, *Asr Ismail*, vol. 2, pp. 94–95.

57. Reade/Stanley, no. 17, 17 June 1868, in FO 78/2042.

58. Sami, pt. 3, vol. 2, pp. 785, 788.

59. This paragraph is based on al-Rafi'i, *Asr Ismail*, vol. 2, pp. 93, 95–96, 100–01, 108, 113; Sami, pt. 3, vol. 2, pp. 789, 843; *WM*, no. 22, 23 JA 1288/5 Sept. 1871.

60. Sami, pt. 3, vol. 3, p. 1213.

61. Sami, pt. 2, p. 352.

62. The dossier of Ismail Raghib notes that in 1250/1834–1835 or 1251/1835–1836 a decree was issued which prescribed the awarding of civil ranks to government employees. In 1252/1836–1837, Abd al-Rahman Rushdi received his first civil rank (*MM*, no. 16234, *Mudad istikhdam Ismail Raghib Basha*; no. 17726, *Mudad istikhdam Abd al-Rahman Rushdi Basha*). On the distinction between civil and military spheres in 1829, see Douin, *L'Egypte de 1828 à 1830*, p. 187.

63. *Mas, Awamir, Ma'iya Saniya-Turki*, reg. 61/23, Viceroy/Khurshid Bey, SH 1250/3–31 Dec. 1834; Sami, pt. 3, vol. 1, pp. 121, 126; pt. 3, vol. 2, p. 483.

64. This paragraph is based on: *WM*, no. 380, 5 DH 1247/6 May 1832; *Mas, Awamir, Ma'iya Saniya-Arabi*, reg. 79/405/82, *al-Ma'iya/al-Sharqiya*, 7 JA 1268/29 Mar. 1852; Sami, pt. 3, vol. 1, p. 355; pt. 3, vol. 2, pp. 483, 504.

65. *MM*, no. 815, *Mudad istikhdam Salim Basha*; Sami, pt. 3, vol. 1, p. 355.

66. In 1830, the Department of Civil Affairs (*al-Diwan al-Khidiwi*) fixed pensions for a number of retired district officials on the basis of the quality of their work; lazy officials received less than the others (*WMC*, box 21, *WM*, no. 209, 27 J 1246/13 Nov. 1830). This attitude was held by the viceroy's first lieutenant (*katkhuda*) and perhaps by Muhammad Ali himself (*WM*, no. 380, 5 DH 1247/6 May 1832). For the pension law of 1844, see *al-Abhath*, box 137, *La'ihat al-Ma'ashat*, 12 SH 1260/27 Aug. 1844, art. 1.

67. See art. 1 of *La'ihat al-Ma'ashat*, 5 RT 1271/26 Dec. 1854, in Gelat, *Répertoire général*, vol. 3, pt. 1, p. 681.

68. Art. 1 of *La'ihat al-Ma'ashat*, 18 L 1287/11 Jan. 1871, in Gelat, *Répertoire général*, vol. 3, pt. 1, pp. 693–94.

69. *La'ihat al-Ma'ashat* (1844), art. 3; Sailer/Stanton, 15 Jan. 1866, in FO 141/60.

70. A French translation of the code is enclosed in Murray/Palmerston, no. 7, 24 Mar. 1851, in FO 78/875.

71. See Baer, "Tanzimat in Egypt," in *Social History*, pp. 120–26.

72. This paragraph is based on: Baer, "Tanzimat in Egypt," pp. 127–28; Sami, pt. 3,

vol. 2, pp. 452, 499, 513, 624; Kenny, "Khedive Ismail's Dream," p. 214. Ismail's 1865 order issued during the interim may have referred to the French code on which Egypt's new criminal law was to be based.

73. Colquhoun/Russell, no. 112, 11 Nov. 1861, in FO 78/1591. In 1863, Ismail Raghib received no salary while he was inspector of accounts for the provinces (*MM*, no. 16234, *Mudad istikhdam Ismail Raghib Basha*).

74. Sami, pt. 3, vol. 1, pp. 182, 303; see also p. 285; pt. 3, vol. 3, p. 1220.

75. For Qasim Pasha, Ahmad Khayri, and Hasan al-Shariʿi, see Sami, pt. 3, vol. 3, p. 1400; *MM*, no. 14104, *Mudad istikhdam Ahmad Khayri Basha*; *MM*, no. 11927, *Mudad istikhdam Hasan Basha al-Shariʿi*.

76. Sami, pt. 2, p. 537; pt. 3, vol. 1, pp. 66–67, 218.

77. The remainder of this paragraph is based on: Sami, pt. 3, vol. 2, p. 964; pt. 3, vol. 3, pp. 1052–53; *WM*, no. 833, 10 D 1296/26 Oct. 1879; *Mas*, *Awamir*, *Maʿiya Saniya-Arabi*, reg. 1939/187/213, Viceroy/al-Maliya, 20 R 1289/28 May 1872; *MM*, no. 18037, *Mudad istikhdam Ahmad Nashat Basha*; *MM*, no. 18189, *Mudad istikhdam Muhammad Ratib Basha*.

78. Sami, pt. 3, vol. 2, p. 479; *al-Abhath*, box 132, dossier "al-Maʿashat," Viceroy/al-Daqahliya, 5 DH 1279/24 May 1863.

79. Sami, pt. 3, vol. 1, p. 337; Mubarak, *al-Khitat*, vol. 14, p. 98, records that Thaqib Pasha received his full salary as pension; in 1871 pensions were both higher and lower than the legal amounts (*Mas*, *al-Majlis al-Khususi*, reg. 1954/2/16, *al-Dakhiliya/al-Majlis al-Khususi*, 9 L 1288/22 Dec. 1871).

80. Sami, pt. 3, vol. 1, p. 345; Artin, "Essai sur les causes du renchérissement," p. 75; Sami, pt. 3, vol. 2, p. 461; see also ibid., pt. 3, vol. 1, pp. 233, 347; *Mas*, *al-Majlis al-Khususi*, reg. 74/39/20, *Qarar al-Majlis al-Khususi*, 19 SH 1284/15 Dec. 1867.

81. Baer, "Tanzimat in Egypt," pp. 126–27.

82. Borg/Vivian, no. 29, 19 Sept. 1877, in FO 141/112; see also Rogers/Stanton, unnumbered dispatch, 28 July 1870, in FO 141/72; Carr/Vivian, no. 14, 13 June 1878, in FO 141/120; Wallace, *Egypt and the Egyptian Question*, p. 166.

83. This paragraph is based on Sami's records: on departmental control of accounts, see pt. 3, vol. 1, pp. 89, 156–57; pt. 3, vol. 2, p. 582; on expenditures from departmental treasuries, see pt. 3, vol. 1, p. 280; pt. 3, vol. 2, pp. 466, 884–85; pt. 3, vol. 3, p. 1142; for the practice of not giving receipts, see pt. 3, vol. 2, pp. 882, 923, 931 (irregular accounts are discussed on p. 67); on the authority of the Finance Department, see pt. 3, vol. 1, p. 106; pt. 3, vol. 2, pp. 462, 582–83; on provinces falling behind in submitting records, see pt. 3, vol. 1, p. 113.

84. Ministère des finances, *Rapport*, p. 56, also in FO 78/2998.

85. Commission superieure d'enquête, *Rapport preliminaire*, p. 15, also in dispatch no. 348, 11 Oct. 1878, in FO 78/2857.

86. Cave report, in McCoan, *Egypt As It Is*, p. 388.

87. Sami, pt. 3, vol. 1, p. 130; *Mas*, *Awamir*, *Maʿiya Saniya-Turki*, reg. 526/33, pt. 2, Viceroy/Haqqi Pasha, end of B 1279/21 Jan. 1863; Sami, pt. 3, vol. 1, p. 409; pt. 3, vol. 2, pp. 444, 644, 696, 753.

88. Deny, *Sommaire des archives*, pp. 120, 124.

89. Colquhoun/Russell, no. 22, 21 Feb. 1860, in FO 78/1522.

90. Sami, pt. 3, vol. 3; appendix on the history of the railway and communications administration.

91. This paragraph is based on: Sami, pt. 3, vol. 2, pp. 608, 619, 635, 1015, and annual lists; pt. 3, vol. 3, pp. 1085, 1096, 1264; *WMC*, box no. 1, dossier "al-Idara"; *WM*, no. 432, 2 N 1288/14 Nov. 1871.

92. Deny, *Sommaire des archives*, pp. 96, 34, 98.

93. McCoan, *Egypt As It Is*, p. 92; Lascelles/Salisbury, no. 397, 22 Nov. 1878, in FO 78/2858.

94. Deny, *Sommaire des archives*, pp. 96-97; Sami, pt. 3, vol. 3, pp. 1389-91.

95. This paragraph is based on Sami: on Sa'id's decree on cabinet authority, see pt. 3, vol. 1, p. 158; on delegating viceregal authority to cabinet officials, see pt. 3, vol. 2, p. 632; pt. 3, vol. 3, p. 1230; on giving cabinet officers high positions, see pt. 3, vol. 1, p. 291; pt. 3, vol. 2, pp. 465, 475, 512, 681; on Ismail Raghib's appointments, see ibid., pp. 574, 643, 695; Colquhoun/Russell, no. 24, 24 Feb. 1865, in FO 78/1871.

96. These examples are taken from Sami, pt. 3, vol. 2, years 1863-65: on the confiscation of villages, see esp. 469, 514, 516, 520; on reappropriation of lands given as pensions, see p. 479; on Ismail's order to his director of finance, see p. 500.

97. Gordon, *Letters*, p. 196; see also Senior, *Conversations*, vol. 2, p. 112.

98. Leon, *Khedive's Egypt*, pp. 235-36; see also Vivian/Salisbury, no. 226, 29 June 1878, in FO 78/2855.

99. Sami, pt. 3, vol. 2, pp. 605, 770, 994-95; *al-Abhath*, box 103, dossier "al-Khassa," MS "Nuzzar al-Khassa wa muwazzafuha." For the *dairas* after European intervention, see McCoan, *Egypt As It Is*, pp. 150-60.

100. Muhammad Ali, *Majmu'at Khitabat*, pp. 146-61.

101. Sami, pt. 3, vol. 1, p. 361, art. 4; *MM*, no. 13959, *Mudad istikhdam Muhammad Hafiz Basha*; no. 13727, *Mudad istikhdam Ali Rida Basha*.

102. This paragraph is based on: Sami, pt. 3, vol. 2, pp. 499, 598-99; *al-Abhath*, box 106, dossier "Khassa," Viceroy/*al-Khassa*, 20 S 1280/6 Aug. 1863; for lands brought under *daira* administration, see Sami, pt. 3, vol. 2, years 1863-65; for *daira* inspection offices in 1870 compared with the Inspectorate, see ibid., pp. 880, 648.

103. Sami, pt. 3, vol. 2, pp. 1032, 872.

104. The rest of this paragraph is based on: Sami, pt. 3, vol. 1, pp. 263, 285, 277-78, 279.

105. See HP, MS 37452, *passim*. When the War Department was abolished in 1858, the administrations in its charge, including some military units, were distributed among other bureaucratic departments (Sami, pt. 3, vol. 1, pp. 277-79). At the same time, Egypt's new civil elite showed traces of military influence, often the result of training and education. Complete separation of civil-military spheres did not come until the end of the nineteenth century.

106. This paragraph is based on: Sami, pt. 3, vol. 2, p. 582; Commission supérieure d'enquête, *Rapport préliminaire*, p. 16; Sami, pt. 3, vol. 3, p. 1100, art. 2.

107. This paragraph is based on: OL(1855), pp. 94-95, arts. 2-3, 8-9, and *passim*; Dufferin/Granville, no. 47, 6 Feb. 1883, in FO 78/3566; Sami, pt. 3, vol. 2, p. 619; *Mas, Awamir, Ma'iya Saniya-Turki*, reg. 529/83/3, Viceroy/Raghib Pasha, 14 M 1282/9 June 1865; and reg. 557/8/4, Viceroy/*al-Ashghal*, 21 J 1282/12 Oct. 1865; *Mas, al-Majlis al-Khususi*, reg. 78/140/112, *Qarar al-Majlis al-Khususi,* 29 R 1289/20 May 1872.

108. OL(1855), p. 103, art. 8; *al-Abhath*, box 137, dossier "Qawanin wa Lawa'ih," *Qarar Majlis Mulki Misr*, 23 J 1251/16 Sept. 1835; McCoan, *Egypt As It Is*, p. 119; *MDDMS*, reg. 65, doc. 283, Viceroy/Abbas, 6 N 1251/26 Dec. 1835.

109. Commission supérieure d'enquête, *Rapport préliminaire*, pp. 21-22; see also McCoan, *Egypt As It Is*, p. 385; Amédée and Outrebon, *L'Egypte et Ismail Pacha*, p. 155.

110. Baer, "Tanzimat in Egypt," p. 112.

111. *MDDMS*, reg. 62, doc. 431, Viceroy/Baqqi Bey, 23 L 1250/20 Feb. 1835.

112. See *WM*, no. 12, 10 J 1262/6 May 1846; Mubarak, *al-Khitat*, vol. 10, p. 99; *al-*

Abhath, box 106, dossier 134, "Ahmad Tal'at Basha," Viceroy/Tal'at Pasha, 29 J 1289/4 Aug. 1872; Sami, pt. 3, vol. 1, p. 292. An exception was Habib efendi (Sami, pt. 2, p. 492). In Ottoman Egypt before the nineteenth century, it was apparently the custom for a dismissed or recalled pasha to remain in his house until his accounts were audited (Gibb and Bowen, *Islamic Society*, vol. 1, pp. 2, 47).

113. Sami, pt. 3, vol. 2, p. 633. In 1856, Sa'id had all of the *mudirs* and *ma'murs* in lower Egypt transferred to upper Egypt and vice versa (*Mas, Awamir, Ma'iya Saniya-Arabi*, reg. 1888/9/1, Viceroy/Governor of al-Daqahliya, 7 S 1273/7 Oct. 1856).

114. *WMC*, box 1, dossier "al-Idara fi ahd Muhammad Ali," *Ma'iya Saniya-Turki*, reg. 58, doc. 28, viceroy to all provinces, 21 M 1249/10 June 1833; *WM*, no. 969, 2 DH 1297/5 Nov. 1880; Sami, pt. 3, vol. 2, pp. 576, 629; on rewards for locating unregistered land, see Jallad, *Qamus al-idara*, vol. 3, p. 58; on reclassifying land for tax purposes, see Ministère des finances, *Rapport*, p. 49; Commission supérieure d'enquête, *Rapport préliminaire*, pp. 23–24.

115. Baer, *Landownership*, pp. 8–10; see also Owen, *Middle East in the World Economy*, pp. 141–42.

116. Owen, "The Development of Agricultural Production," p. 533.

117. This paragraph is based on: Baer, *Landownership*, pp. 19, 31; Rauf Abbas Hamid, *al-Nizam*, p. 27.

118. Senior, *Conversations*, vol. 1, p. 56; Leon, *Khedive's Egypt*, p. 263; Gordon, *Letters*, p. 76; Sami, pt. 3, vol. 2, p. 634; pt. 3, vol. 3, p. 1452.

119. Sammarco, *Histoire de l'Egypte moderne*, vol. 3, pp. 32–35.

120. The rest of this paragraph is taken from the following sources: on Ismail's relations with his brother and uncle, see Colquhoun/Russell, no. 39, 13 Mar. 1863, in FO 78/1754; on Abd al-Halim as acting viceroy and president of the council, see Sami, pt. 3, vol. 2, pp. 463, 468, 574.

121. This paragraph is based on the following sources: on salary raises made in 1864, see *Mas, Awamir, Ma'iya Saniya-Turki*, reg. 539/150/69, Viceroy/Ahmad Rashid, 25 N 1280/5 Mar. 1864 (Ismail also gave pensions and promotions as gifts [Sami, pt. 3, vol. 2, p. 621; pt. 3, vol. 3, p. 1098]); on repealing the *ushuriya* taxes, see Artin, *Landed Property*, pp. 104–05; on the payment of officials' debts, see *Mas, Awamir, Ma'iya Saniya-Turki*, reg. 573/43/20, Viceroy/al-Maliya, 21 L 1284/15 Feb. 1868; *Awamir, Ma'iya Saniya-Arabi*, reg. 1942/28/70, Viceroy/Sultan Pasha, 22 B 1288/7 Oct. 1871; Sami, pt. 3, vol. 2, p. 881; for gifts of houses, see *Mas, Awamir, Ma'iya Saniya-Turki*, reg. 539/78/187, Viceroy/Ahmad Rashid, 7 D 1280/14 Apr. 1864, reg. 537/9/19, Viceroy/Rishwan Bey, 4 J 1281/5 Oct. 1864; Sami, pt. 3, vol. 2, pp. 680, 802, 866; on money given to Ismail Siddiq for a house and property, see *Mas, Awamir, Ma'iya Saniya-Turki*, reg. 573/53/13, Viceroy/al-Daira al-Saniya, 7 M 1285/30 Apr. 1868; on the sale of offices, see Borg/Lascelles, 11 July 1879, in FO 78/3002; Sami, pt. 3, vol. 3, p. 1452; on gifts of slaves and officials marrying into the viceroy's family, see Ministry of al-Awqaf, *Qalam al-Sijillat*, *Sijill* 40 *Ahli, hujja* 2686, *Muhammad Ratib Basha*; see also *MM*, no. 20289, *Warathat Ahmad Basha Nashat*; no. 5231, *Sitt Sizawar Hanum*; no. 20289, *Haram Marhum Yusuf Basha Shuhdi*; Sami, pt. 3, vol. 3, pp. 1124n1, 1125; on cash gifts to officials, see Sami, pt. 3, vol. 2, p. 607, and entries for 1863–65, *passim*.

122. These examples are taken from Sami, pt. 3, vol. 2: on Husayn Pasha, p. 443; on Rushdi and Munis Bey, pp. 547, 621; on Daramalli, p. 790; on Nubar Pasha, pp. 615, 582–83; see also *AI, al-Mutafarriqat*, box 152, dossier "Idara," Cazcans-Minister (France), 15 June 1874; on Ismail Siddiq, see Sami, pt. 3, vol. 2, pp. 632, 652.

123. See Colquhoun/Russell, no. 75, 19 June 1865, in FO 78/1871; Stanton/Clarendon, no. 46, 1 May 1866, in FO 78/1925; Stanton/Stanley, no. 3, 12 June 1867, in FO 78/1976; ibid., no. 55, 27 May 1868, in FO 78/2038.

124. Lascelles/Salisbury, no. 236, 19 Apr. 1879, in FO 78/3000; Colquhoun/Russell, no. 32, 11 Mar. 1865, in FO 78/1871.

125. Colquhoun/Russell, no. 74, 25 May 1864, in FO 78/1818.

126. Sami, pt. 3, vol. 2, pp. 483, 585-92; Colquhoun/Russell, no. 76, 11 May 1863, in FO 78/1754; see also Landes, *Bankers*, pp. 149-54.

127. Colquhoun/Russell, no. 115, 4 Aug. 1863, and "Memorandum," in ibid., no. 109, 1 July 1863, in FO 78/1755.

128. Francis/Stanton, 4 Mar. 1868, in FO 141/68; Rogers/Stanton, no. 26, 18 July 1870, in FO 141/72; Arpa/Moore, 18 Sept. 1871, in FO 141/75, pt. 3. Officials were also exploited by their own government in this way.

129. These examples are taken from the following sources: on raises in the *kharajiya* tax, see Artin, *Landed Property*, pp. 90-97; on legal fees and foodstuffs, manufactured items, and prostitution, see Sami, pt. 3, vol. 2, pp. 795, 966-67; pt. 3, vol. 3, p. 1088; Gordon, *Letters*, pp. 292-93, 301-02; on increased revenue since Muhammad Ali's reign, see McCoan, *Egypt Under Ismail*, p. 151.

130. This paragraph is based on: Gordon, *Letters*, pp. 178-79, 140-41, 286, 281.

131. McCoan, *Egypt As It Is*, p. 87; cf. Colquhoun/Russell, no. 24, 24 Feb. 1865, in FO 78/1871.

132. Colquhoun/Russell, no. 111, 18 July 1863, in FO 78/1755; Stanton/Stanley, no. 37, 17 Apr. 1868, in FO 78/2038.

133. These examples are taken from Sami, pt. 3, vol. 2: on Ismail's vigilance in general, pp. 447, 504, 625-26; on his control over work done by officials, p. 542; on his control over officials and their salaries, pp. 466, 514, 519, 548, 619, 827; on his control over expenditures, see, for example, p. 876.

134. These examples are taken from the following: on the location of the Privy Council, see Sami, pt. 3, vol. 2, p. 458 (cf. pt. 3, vol. 3, p. 1393); pt. 3, vol. 2, pp. 683-84; on the War Department and the viceregal cabinet, see pt. 3, vol. 2, p. 609; on the location of Mubarak's administrations, see Mubarak, *al-Khitat*, vol. 9, p. 50; Sami, pt. 3, vol. 2, p. 873; on the relocation of major administrations in the 1870s, see About, *Le Fellah*, p. 131; McCoan, *Egypt As It Is*, p. 91.

135. Sami, pt. 3, vol. 1, pp. 409-10; pt. 3, vol. 2, p. 446.

136. *Mas, Majlis Khususi*, reg. 90/35/36, *Qarar al-Majlis al-Khususi*, 29 L 1290/20 Dec. 1873; *Mas, Awamir, Ma'iya Saniya-Turki*, reg. 529/3/2, Viceroy/*Sikkat Hadid*, 19 SH 1279/9 Feb. 1863; see also Mubarak, *al-Khitat*, vol. 9, p. 43.

137. *Mas, Awamir, Ma'iya Saniya-Turki*, reg. 539/114/257, Viceroy/Ahmad Rashid, 3 R 1281/7 Aug. 1864.

138. This paragraph uses examples from Sami, pt. 3, vol. 2: on Ismail's control over the Alexandria chief of police, see pp. 557-58; over Rushdi and Munis Bey, see pp. 547, 621; over provincial governors' limited powers of appointment, see pp. 632-33; over limited powers to dismiss and appoint clerks in lower Egypt, see p. 624; over Ismail Siddiq's powers, see p. 632; on the viceroy's admonishment of Ismail Siddiq, see pp. 940, 1011 (but shortly after Ismail Siddiq's removal from Finance, he was named director of the viceroy's *daira*).

139. Colquhoun/Russell, no. 84, 17 July 1865, in FO 78/1871.

140. Sami, pt. 3, vol. 2, p. 867; in Muhammad Ali's time, the *wirku* tax was a general professional tax levied upon craftsmen and persons providing services in the cities (Baer, *Egyptian Guilds*, p. 86); Sami, pt. 3, vol. 2, p. 830; *Mas, al-Majlis al-Khususi*, reg. 9/31/21, *al-Majlis al-Khususi*/Governorate of Suez, 18 M 1289/28 Mar. 1872.

141. al-Rafi'i, *Asr Ismail*, vol. 2, pp. 92, 94, 108; Moore/Granville, no. 3, 20 June 1871, in FO 78/2186.

142. See the article from the *Egyptian Gazette* (3 June 1868) in Reade/Stanley, no. 17, 17 June 1868, in FO 78/2042, and the account of al-Rafi'i, *Asr Ismail*, vol. 2, pp. 101-02.

143. al-Rafiʿi, *Asr Ismail*, vol. 2, p. 119; Stanton/Granville, no. 35, 9 May 1873, in FO 78/2283.

144. Abu-Lughod states ("Transformation of the Egyptian Elite," p. 342) that in 1874 the Chamber rose up in arms against Ismail when he asked them to repeal the Law of *Muqabala*; however, the Chamber was not even in session during 1874.

145. Sami, pt. 3, vol. 2, p. 933.

▲5▲ THE FORMATION OF THE BUREAUCRATIC ELITE

1. For the use of this term, see *WM*, no. 619, 12 J 1256/12 July 1840; no. 62, 11 J 1263/27 Apr. 1847; *Mas, Awamir, Maʿiya Saniya-Arabi*, reg. 1881/331/122, Viceroy/*al-Maliya*, 11 SH 1271/29 Apr. 1855; *al-Abhath*, box 55, dossier "Rifaʿa Bey," letter from Department of Education, 2 M 1262/31 Dec. 1845; *al-Abhath*, box 137, *Laʾihat al-Maʿashat*, 12 SH 1260/27 Aug. 1844, art. 1. Wallace, *Egypt and the Egyptian Question*, p. 214, describes *al-dhawat* as official personages, mostly Turks, who owned landed estates and lived in the cities and towns. See Barakat, *Tatawwur*, pp. 183–90.

2. In 1849, when Abbas Pasha granted money to the mothers of Ibrahim Pasha's sons, their courts were referred to as *al-dhawat* households (*dur al-dhawat*) (*MDDMS, Turki*, reg. 1557, doc. 12, note from Abbas Pasha, 22 L 1265/10 Sept. 1849). Elsewhere, however, the viceregal family is distinguished from *al-dhawat* (Sami, pt. 3, vol. 1, pp. 21–22; OL [1855], p. 102, art. 11).

3. Egyptian National Archives, *Daftar zimam atyan ushuriya: Dhawat. Raqm al-sijill*, 1343 (*min* 15 D 1264/13 Oct. 1848 *ila* 6 R 1287/6 June 1870).

4. In November 1871, position rather than rank became the legal basis of salary (*WM*, no. 833, 10 D 1296/26 Oct. 1879).

5. The distinction between higher and lower officials is unclear. The *Egyptian Gazette* of 16 SH 1264/18 July 1848 suggests that the dividing line is the rank of colonel. Whereas pensions had been given to orphaned sons of deceased officials up to and including the rank of lieutenant colonel, but not to sons of *al-dhawat*, henceforth, pensions were also to go to orphaned sons of all officials at the rank of colonel and above. Further, almost all officials mentioned in the *Dhawat* Land Register held first or second ranks, or their military equivalents. Thus I infer that the line of division was second rank (see also Sami, pt. 3, vol. 1, p. 24; *WM*, no. 62, 11 J 1263/27 Apr. 1847).

6. The titles of bey and pasha did not always correspond with rank because the ruler could grant these titles to anyone (see, for example, Sami, pt. 3, vol. 2, p. 467).

7. This paragraph is based on the following sources: on exemption from interrogation by inferiors, see *WM*, no. 62, 11 J 1263/27 Apr. 1847; on favored treatment under the law, see OL (1855), p. 94, art. 2; on equality of all subjects, see ibid., p. 92, art. 1, p. 102, art. 11; on exemption from corporeal punishment, see ibid., p. 94, art. 2; Code of Abbas, art. 21, in Murray/Palmerston, no. 7, 24 Mar. 1851, in FO 78/875; *Qanun al-Muntakhabat*, in Jallad, *Qamus al-idara*, vol. 3, p. 360, art. 85, p. 364, art. 101, p. 365, art. 110.

8. Adham Pasha, a Turk, came to Egypt from Istanbul during the reign of Muhammad Ali. He was sent to study in England, and in 1839 became director of education; his last position was director of education and charitable endowments in 1863 (see Abd al-Karim, *Tarikh al-taʿlim*, pp. 114–15; Mubarak, *al-Khitat*, vol. 12, pp. 5–6).

9. Ali Dhu al-Fiqar was a slave brought from Greece and given by Muhammad Ali to his son Saʿid as a companion in study. According to al-Ayyubi, Ismail Raghib was also a Greek slave (*MM*, no. 17199, *Mudad istikhdam Ali Dhu al-Fiqar*; al-Ayyubi, *Tarikh Misr*, vol. 2, p. 259. See also Politis, *L'Hellénisme*, pp. 205, 219).

10. The phrase "pure element" was used by Abbas (Sami, pt. 3, vol. 1, p. 30). See also Gordon, *Letters*, pp. 182, 226, 301; Gordon wrote in 1867 that in Egypt the division was Arab versus Turk. One of the most humiliating punishments for a member of the *dhawat*

aristocracy was to be dressed as a *fallah* and sent out among the native population, a threat used by the viceroys to keep their men in line (Senior, *Conversations*, vol. 2, p. 85).

11. Mubarak, *al-Khitat*, vol. 9, p. 48.

12. See Leon, *Khedive's Egypt*, pp. 181–82; Bell, *Khedives*, pp. 164, 168, 180 and *passim*; Wallace, *Egypt and the Egyptian Question*, pp. 158–59.

13. See Barakat, *Tatawwur*, pp. 231–60.

14. This paragraph is based on the following sources: on Coptic notables, see *WM*, no. 1447, 15 N 1299/31 July 1882; on the provincial notability, see Baer, "Village Shaykh," in *Social History*, pp. 30–61.

15. Mengin, *Histoire Sommaire*.

16. Baer, "Village Shaykh," in *Social History*, p. 221.

17. These are Hammad Bey, Ali Mubarak, Muhammad Thaqib, Muhammad Mazhar, Ismail Siddiq, Mustafa Bahjat, Ali Ibrahim, and Rifaʿa Tahtawi; Bahjat Pasha was of mixed Turkish-Egyptian parentage.

18. *L'Egypte et l'Europe*, vol. 1, p. 40.

19. The rest of this paragraph is based on the following sources: on Turks refusing to enter new schools, see HP, MS 37449, fol. 89; Douin, *La mission du Baron de Boislecomte*, p. 138; on neglecting their work, see Rivlin, *Agricultural Policy*, p. 108; Muhammad Ali's order appears in an order from the viceregal cabinet, 26 Oct. 1833, in *WMC*, box 1, dossier "al-Idara fi ahd Muhammad Ali."

20. For information on Hekekyan, see Mustafa, "The Hekekyan Papers," pp. 68–75.

21. The following examples are taken from: al-Ayyubi, *Tarikh*, vol. 2, p. 152; Senior, *Conversations*, vol. 2, p. 168; Artin, "Artin Bey," p. 4.

22. The diary (which is being edited for publication) and correspondence of Nubar Pasha are in the custody of Count d'Arschot of Brussels; Hekeyan's papers are in the British Museum.

23. This and the following examples are taken from: Mustafa, "The Hekekyan Papers," p. 73; HP, MS 37450, fol. 34; MS 37449, fol. 212; MS 37450, fols. 133, 99, 211.

24. See Cadalvene and Breuvery, *L'Egypte et la Turquie*, vol. 1, p. 126; Senior, *Conversations*, vol. 1, p. 281, Merruau, *L'Egypte contemporaine*, p. 8.

25. Sami, pt. 3, vol. 1, p. 367.

26. This and the following examples are taken from: Senior, *Conversations*, vol. 2, pp. 93, 58; Marton/Murray, 22 Feb. 1853, in pt. 1, FO 141/21.

27. Sami, pt. 3, vol. 1, p. 260; Marton/Murray, 22 Feb. 1853, in FO 141/21, pt. 1; Bruce/Clarendon, no. 18, 2 Apr. 1857, in FO 141/20.

28. Because of Muhammad Ali's efforts, after 1849 Copts were almost entirely limited to the middle and lower levels of the bureaucracy; however Barakat (*Tatawwur*, p. 183) names one Copt in high office after 1849, and Rauf Abbas Hamid (*al-Nizam*, p. 97) cites two Copts with the title of bey in the central administration.

29. Douin, *Une mission militaire*, p. 77; Planat, *Régéneration de l'Egypte*, p. 166.

30. This paragraph is based on: Abu-Lughod, *Cairo*; HP, MS 37453, fol. 187; Senior, *Conversations*, vol. 2, p. 33.

31. The following examples are taken from: *al-Abhath*, box 106, dossier 134, "Ahmad Basha Talʿat," 25 B 1283/3 Dec. 1866; Sami, pt. 3, vol. 2, p. 546; HP, MS 37450, fol. 11; Abu-Lughod, *Cairo*, pp. 115–16; Mubarak, *al-Khitat*, vol. 9, p. 48; Ministry of *al-Awqaf*, *al-Daftarkhana, waqfiyat al-mahfuza*, vol. 1, no. 955, Khalil Bey Khulusi; vol. 2, no. 3218, Hasan Basha Munastarli.

32. This paragraph is based on: Leon, *Khedive's Egypt*, pp. 56–58; Edmond About, *Le Fellah*, pp. 105–06.

33. *MM*, no. 10511, *Mudad istikhdam Hasan Basha Rasim*.

34. Mubarak, *al-Khitat*, vol. 14, p. 98; Ministry of *al-Awqaf, Qalam al-Sijillat, Sijill* 12, *Ahli, Alif, hujja* 36, Muhammad Sultan Basha.

35. Ministry of *al-Awqaf, Qalam al-Sijillat, Sijill* 330 *Qadim, hujja* 2296, Rifaʿa Tahtawi; *MM*, no. 18001, *Warathat marhum Hasan al-Shariʿi Basha*.

36. Muhammad Hafiz, Abdallah Fikri, and Mustafa Bahjat were officials of mixed Turkish-Egyptian background (Zakhura, *Mirʾat al-asr*, vol. 2, p. 322; Mubarak, *al-Khitat*, vol. 2, p. 46; vol. 16, p. 56).

37. Douin, *La mission du Baron de Boislecomte*, p. 111.

38. *WMC*, box 1, dossier, "al-Idara fi ahd Muhammad Ali," *Maʿiya Saniya-Turki*, reg. 56, Viceroy/Governor of *al-Daqahliya*, 10 S 1250/18 June 1834.

39. This paragraph is based on: Senior, *Conversations*, vol. 2, p. 110; HP, MS 37449, fol. 112; MS 37450, fol. 63; on Muhammad Ali's control, see Rivlin, *Agricultural Policy*, p. 64; on the expense of bringing land under cultivation, see Hamont, *L'Egypte*, vol. 1, pp. 119–21.

40. Barakat, *Tatawwur*, pp. 169–72; Baer, *Landownership*, pp. 14–15.

41. Owen, *Cotton and the Egyptian Economy*, pp. 74–75.

42. Ibid., pp. 70–71.

43. The *uhda* system did not end completely; Abbas revoked most but not all of Muhammad Ali's *uhdas*; Saʿid and even Ismail continued to grant *uhdas*, which continued in existence until the late 1860s (Baer, *Landownership*, pp. 14–15).

44. This and the following examples are taken from: Barakat, *Tatawwur*, pp. 77–78, 111, 79; *al-Abhath*, box 132, dossier "al-Maʿashat," Viceroy/*al-Maliya*, 19 RT 1280/1 Oct. 1863.

45. Sami, pt. 3, vol. 2: years 1863–65.

46. Baer, *Landownership*, pp. 16–17.

47. Barakat, *Tatawwur*, p. 84.

48. Mubarak, *al-Khitat*, vol. 12, p. 50; figures for the other officials come from the *Dhawat* Land Register.

49. Examples are taken from: *MM*, no. 633, *Mudad istikhdam Muhammad Bayk Khulusi*; no. 3579, *Mudad istikhdam Muhammad Thaqib Basha*; Mubarak, *al-Khitat*, vol. 16, pp. 56–58.

50. Owen, *Middle East in the World Economy*, p. 130.

51. Shortly after his accession, Ismail allegedly forced officials to surrender productive agricultural land and to take tracts of uncultivated land in return (Gordon, *Letters*, p. 86; *MM*, no. 7791, *Mudad istikhdam Yusuf Basha Fahmi*).

52. Unless otherwise stated, this paragraph is based on: Barakat, *Tatawwur*, pp. 112, 134, 136–39, and *passim*, and Rauf Abbas Hamid, *al-Nizam*, pp. 83–85, 88, 182, and *passim*.

53. Owen, *Middle East in the World Economy*, p. 130.

54. Barakat, *Tatawwur*, p. 139.

55. OL (1855), p. 100, art. 1; in his biography of Salih Majdi Bey, Mubarak (*al-Khitat*, vol. 8, p. 24) commented that Salih was promoted to the rank of major by the direct order of Saʿid without the mediation (*tawassut*) of anyone.

56. Colquhoun/Russell, no. 5, 16 Jan. 1861, in FO 78/1590.

57. The following examples are taken from: McCoan, *Egypt As It Is*, p. 377; *MM*, no. 8613, *Warathat Ahmad Basha al-Daramalli*; Ministry of *al-Awqaf, al-Daftarkhana, waqfiyat al-mahfuzah*, vol. 2, no. 2644, Muhammad Asim; *al-Abhath*, box 105, MS "Kashf asma kibar muwazzafi al-hukuma al-misriya fi awwal al-maghfur lahu Jannatmakan Ismail Basha Khidiwi Misr," D 1279/20 Apr.–19 May 1863.

58. This paragraph is based on: Artin, "Artin Bey," p. 1; Senior, *Conversations*, vol. 2, p. 168; on Arakil, see Sami, vol. 3, pt. 1, pp. 58, 194, and list of appointments for 1857; on

Iram, see About, *Le Fellah*, p. 130; on Abraham and Kevork, see al-Ayyubi, *Tarikh*, vol. 2, p. 152; Sami, pt. 3, vol. 2, p. 516; Holynski, *Nubar*, p. 12.

59. Artin, "Artin Bey," pp. 2, 4; Gilbert/Palmerston, no. 24, 7 Aug. 1850, in FO 78/840.

60. See Artin, "Artin Bey," *passim*; *MM*, no. 1625, *Mudad istikhdam Istafan Bayk*, and no. 1757, *Warathat Istafan Bayk*; Heyworth-Dunne, *History of Education*, p. 160; and Sami, annual lists of appointments.

61. Nubar and his family directed Foreign Affairs during the following periods: Boghos Bey: 1824–1844; Nubar: 1866–1874, 1875–1876, 1878–1879, 1884–1888; Tigrane Pasha: 1891–1894; Artin was director between 1844 and 1850, and Stephen Bey from 1854 to 1857.

62. Hekekyan did suspect, however, that Muhammad Ali tried to have him poisoned (Senior, *Conversations*, vol. 2, pp. 142–45).

63. The following examples are taken from: Murray/Palmerston, no. 12, 5 Mar. 1849, in FO 78/804; Murray/Canning, no. 1, 14 July 1851, in FO 195/348; HP, MS 37452, fol. 55.

64. Abd al-Karim, *Tarikh al-ta῾lim*, p. 566; Heyworth-Dunne, *History of Education*, p. 253.

65. Douin, *La mission du Baron de Boislecomte*, p. 138.

66. This and the following are based on: HP, MS 37449, fol. 109; Hamont, *L'Egypte*, vol. 1, pp. 440–41; Heyworth-Dunne, *History of Education*, pp. 169, 241; HP, MS 37452, fol. 53, 55; Abdel-Rahim Mustafa, "The Hekekyan Papers," p. 69.

67. On *al-watan*, see Dozy, *Supplément aux dictionnaires arabes*, vol. 2, pp. 819–20. *Patrie* was not a new meaning, only one to which these officials gave greater emphasis.

68. Hamont, *L'Egypte*, vol. 1, p. 287; Urabi, *Mudhakkirat Urabi*, vol. 1, p. 16. Egypt's rulers used *al-watan* and appealed to their subjects' patriotic spirit. See *WM*, no. 93, 13 DH 1263/22 Nov. 1847; Farhi, "Nizam-i Cedid," p. 173; Sami, pt. 3, vol. 1, pp. 185–86.

69. The following examples are taken from: Senior, *Conversations*, vol. 2, pp. 205–06, 11, 8–17, *passim*, 209–10; vol. 1, p. 271.

70. Mustafa, "The Breakdown of the Monopoly System," p. 303; Senior, *Conversations*, vol. 2, p. 209; Sabry, *L'empire égyptien*, p. 231; Sami, pt. 3, vol. 1, pp. 67, 68–69.

71. Bruce/Clarendon, no. 35, 17 July 1854, in FO 78/1036; HP, MS 37454, fol. 359.

72. Landau, "Secret Societies in Modern Egypt."

73. Dr. Pruner, Abbas's private physician, was the trustworthy channel of communication between the British consul general and the viceroy (Murray/Canning, 12 Dec. 1848, in FO 352/32; Murray/Pruner, 15 Apr. 1849, in FO 141/16, pt. 3). I wish to thank Frederick J. Cox for these references.

74. This and the following are based on: Francis/Governor of Alexandria, and Jones/Stanton, 27 July and 22 Sept. 1866, in FO 141/60; Reade/Raghib, no. 94, 7 June 1867, in FO 78/1976; Stanley/Omar Pasha, 3 Jan. 1871, in FO 141/76; on Sa῾id's exemption of Europeans from his salary withholding, see *al-Abhath*, box 135, dossier "Murattabat al-muwazzafin," viceregal order of 26 J 1275/1 Jan. 1859; on the flogging incident, see Moore/Granville, no. 22, 7 Sept. 1871, in FO 78/2186; on the British engine drivers' strike, see Stanton/Stanley, no. 7, 23 Jan. 1868, in FO 78/2038; on Lee Green's license, see Bruce/Clarendon, no. 18, 2 Apr. 1857, in FO 140/20; Sami, pt. 3, vol. 1, pp. 191–92; for Hekekyan's comment, see HP, MS 37449, fol. 125.

75. Barnett/Aberdeen, no. 29, 14 Dec. 1844, in FO 78/582; Bertrand, *Nubar*, pp. 26–27.

76. Stratford Canning Papers, Stratford de Redcliffe/Bruce, 27 July 1854, in FO 352/40; Murray/Canning, 12 Dec. 1848, in FO 352/32, in *AI*. Both were made available to me by Frederick J. Cox.

77. Green/Clarendon, no. 39, 7 Sept. 1857, in FO 78/1314; Murray/Stratford de Redcliffe, no. 16, 25 Nov. 1853 in FO 195/412.

78. This and the following examples are taken from: HP, MS 37450, fol. 2; Green/ Clarendon, no. 92, 22 Dec. 1857, in FO 78/1314; Colquhoun/Russell, no. 52, 26 Apr. 1864, in FO 142/27; HP, MS 37450, fol. 211; Green/Malmesbury, no. 35, 1 Apr. 1859, in FO 78/1467.

79. Murray/Canning, no. 1, 14 July 1851, in FO 195/348; HP, MS 37452, fols. 48–50.

80. Rauf Abbas Hamid, al-Nizam, pp. 174–75.

81. WM, no. 1483, 25 L 1299/9 Sept. 1882.

82. Examples are taken from the following sources: on Muhammad Sultan, see G. Fahmi, Souvenirs, p. 82; on the Shawaribi family, see Mubarak, al-Khitat, vol. 14, p. 116; on the Abaza family, see MM, no. 12707, Mudad istikhdam Sulayman Basha Abaza; Mubarak, al-Khitat, vol. 14, p. 3; on the Shari'i family, see Zakhura, Mir'at al-asr, vol. 2, p. 257.

83. See Baer, "Village Shaykh," pp. 38–45; for their supervision of the ghafirs, see Jallad, Qamus al-idara, vol. 3, p. 369, art. 121.

84. In addition, Ibrahim al-Shari'i was appointed inspector of Samallut by Ismail (Zakhura, Mir'at al-asr, vol. 2, p. 260).

85. This was true of Muhammad al-Shawaribi, al-Sayyid Pasha Abaza, and Bahjat Pasha; Ali Badrawi received Fuwwa and Shayasat as uhdas (Mubarak, al-Khitat, vol. 14, p. 116; ibid., vol. 16, p. 57; Jallad, Qamus al-idara, vol. 3, p. 504; Baer, Landowner-ship, p. 58).

86. Sami, pt. 3, vol. 1, p. 214; Zakhura, Mir'at al-asr, vol. 2, p. 260.

87. Mubarak, al-Khitat, vol. 9, pp. 14, 99; vol. 15, p. 73; Rogers/Stanton, no. 36, 7 Nov. 1871, in FO 141/75, pt. 3.

88. This letter, written in Luxor on 19 Dec. 1856, is discussed in Bruce/Clarendon, no. 61, 30 Dec. 1856, in FO 78/1222.

89. Ministry of al-Awqaf, Qalam al-Sijillat, Sijill 12, Ahli, Alif, hujja 36, Muhammad Sultan Basha.

90. Mubarak, al-Khitat, vol. 12, p. 50.

91. Ministère de l'intérieur, Recensement général, vol. 2, pt. 1.

92. For example, in the village of al-Jaradat in al-Buhrayra, where he owned 1,206 faddans, Ismail Siddiq built a mosque, a storehouse, a house for his estate-manager, an office for his employees, and a farmhouse (Mubarak, al-Khitat, vol. 10, p. 55). In Saman-nud, Ali Badrawi built a mosque and donated revenues in his waqfiya to support the poor and the orphans, and to instruct the young in the Quran (Ministry of al-Awqaf, Qalam al-Sijillat, sijill 28, Qadim, hujja 1413, Ali Bayk Badrawi). Cf. the waqfiya of Muham-mad Sultan, cited in note 89.

93. Rogers/Stanton, no. 36, 7 Nov. 1871, in FO 141/75, pt. 3.

94. Zakhura, Mir'at alasr, vol. 1, p. 444.

95. Senior, Conversations, vol. 1, p. 293.

96. Alexander Schölch, Egypt for the Egyptians!, pp. 35–36.

▲6▲ EGYPT'S OFFICIALS AND THEIR INTERESTS

1. See Bell, Khedives, pp. 192–93.

2. Mubarak, al-Khitat, vol. 9, p. 39.

3. See Delanoue, Moralistes, pp. 452–520. Professor Darrell Dykstra wrote his doc-toral dissertation on Mubarak, but has not yet published it. Arabic biographies (see bibliography) are based on Mubarak, al-Khitat, vol. 9, pp. 37–61; pp. 38–42 focus on his youth.

4. Mubarak, al-Khitat, vol. 9, p. 41.

5. Tussun, al-Ba'athat al-Ilmiya, pp. 226–367.

6. *AI*, *Ahd Muhammad Ali*, *daftar* 5, docs. 6858 (notes by Poinçoit) and 6864; *daftar* 9, dossier "Education," doc. 7571; *daftar* 11.

7. *AI*, *Ahd Muhammad Ali*, *daftar* 9, dossier "Education," doc. 7719.

8. This paragraph is based on Mubarak, *al-Khitat*, vol. 9, pp. 43–44.

9. The rest of this paragraph is based on: ibid., p. 44; the Privy Council debate is in *al-Abhath*, box 52, dossier "Mawduʿ al-Taʿlim," Viceroy/*al-Madaris*, 24 JA 1266/7 May 1850.

10. Mubarak, *al-Khitat*, vol. 9, pp. 45–46. Mubarak maintains that he was maligned by jealous men, but he was probably dismissed because of his close association with Abbas, Saʿid's enemy. Ali Ibrahim and Hammad Bey were also dismissed by the new viceroy.

11. Ibid., p. 47. The viceroy's order of dismissal cites the need to transfer all civil officials to the War Department (Sami, pt. 3, vol. 1, p. 220).

12. Mubarak, *al-Khitat*, vol. 9, p. 48; *Mas*, *Awamir*, *Maʿiya Saniya-Arabi*, reg. 1898/94/60, Viceroy/*al-Maliya*, 28 RT 1278/2 Nov. 1861.

13. Mubarak, *al-Khitat*, vol. 9, pp. 48–49.

14. *Mas*, *Awamir*, *Maʿiya Saniya-Turki*, reg. 582/7/65, Viceroy/Linan Bey, 19 RT 1286/29 July 1869.

15. Mubarak, *al-Khitat*, vol. 9, p. 49; see Abu-Lughod, *Cairo*, pp. 105–12; Heyworth-Dunne, *History of Education*, pp. 342–424.

16. *Mas*, *Awamir*, *Maʿiya Saniya-Turki*, reg. 582/7/65, Viceroy/Linan Bey, 19 RT 1286/29 July 1869; Sami, pt. 3, vol. 2, pp. 695, 808, 824, 826; cf. Mubarak, *al-Khitat*, vol. 9, pp. 53–54.

17. Mubarak, *al-Khitat*, vol. 9, p. 54.

18. Ibid.

19. This paragraph is based on ibid., pp. 40, 43, 61.

20. See ibid., pp. 46–47.

21. Ibid., p. 48.

22. Ibid., p. 46.

23. See Tussun, *al-Baʿathat*, pp. 416–86.

24. Sami, pt. 3, vol. 2, p. 925; see *Mas*, *Awamir*, *Maʿiya Saniya-Arabi*, reg. 1919/6/1 and 118/17, Viceroy/*al-Jihadiya*, 7 J 1283/17 Sept. 1866; 3 DH 1283/8 Apr. 1867.

25. See Mubarak, *al-Khitat*, vol. 8, pp. 22–25; and Zakhura, *Mir'at al-asr*, vol. 1, pp. 410–12.

26. Bell, *Khedives*, p. 193; Ninet, *Arabi Pacha*, p. 38.

27. McCoan, *Egypt As It Is*, p. 389.

28. Ibid., p. 385.

29. Sami, pt. 3, vol. 2, p. 860.

30. Mubarak, *al-Khitat*, vol. 9, p. 46.

31. Sami, pt. 3, vol. 2, p. 542.

32. Sami, pt. 3, vol. 3, p. 1452.

33. Ali Mubarak, *Nukhbat al-Fikr*, pp. 115–16.

34. Mubarak, *al-Khitat*, vol. 9, p. 45; the following examples are taken from: ibid., pp. 45, 48.

35. *WM*, no. 93, 13 DH 1263/22 Nov. 1847.

36. Ali Mubarak, *Alam al-Din*, vol. 1, p. 6.

37. Ibid., p. 7.

38. Ali Mubarak, *Tariq al-hija*, pt. 2, pp. 105–06.

39. Mubarak, *Nukhbat al-Fikr*, pp. 173–74.

40. Delanoue, *Moralistes*, p. 489.

41. Mubarak, *Nukhbat al-Fikr*, p. 189.

42. See G. Fahmi, *Souvenirs*, pp. 23–25, 82–91; a manuscript of the memoirs of Huda Sha'rawi, Sultan's daughter, owned by Mrs. Margot Farranto Badran, formerly of St. Antony's College, Oxford; *MM*, no. 11369, *Warathat Muhammad Sultan Basha*; Amin Sami's records; al-Rafi'i, *al-Thawra*, pp. 590–94; Taymur, *Tarajim*, pp. 31–39; Mujahid, *al-A'lam al-Sharqiya*, vol. 1, pp. 157–59.

43. G. Fahmi, *Souvenirs*, pp. 82, 88.

44. Zakhura, *Mir'at al-asr*, vol. 1, p. 343.

45. This paragraph is based on G. Fahmi, *Souvenirs*, p. 82; Barakat, *Tatawwur*, p. 249; Ministry of *al-Awqaf, Qalam al-Sijillat, Sijill* 22, *Misr, hujja* 2176, Umar Bayk Sultan. Fahmi writes that Muhammad Sultan's family may have had ties with Bedouin tribes who had settled in al-Minya.

46. See G. Fahmi, *Souvenirs*, pp. 82–83; and Sultan Pasha's pension dossier (*MM*, no. 11369).

47. Sulayman Abaza served as district leader in his home province of al-Sharqiya and was later its governor; Ali Badrawi was *hakim al-khutt* and *nazir al-qism* of Sammanud, his home village (*MM*, no. 12707, *Mudad istikhdam Sulayman Basha Abaza*; Mubarak, *al-Khitat*, vol. 12, p. 49).

48. Blunt, *Secret History*, p. 313.

49. G. Fahmi, *Souvenirs*, pp. 83–85.

50. This paragraph is based on Sami, pt. 3, vol. 1, p. 345; pt. 3, vol. 2, pp. 492, 503, 498; *MM*, no. 11369, *Warathat Muhammad Sultan Basha*.

51. G. Fahmi, *Souvenirs*, p. 21.

52. See Sami, pt. 3, vol. 2, pp. 648, 649–50, 970–72; Vivian/Derby, no. 320, 30 Nov. 1877, in FO 78/2634.

53. al-Rafi'i, *al-Thawra*, p. 591; Stuart, *Egypt After the War*, p. 445; Ministry of *al-Awqaf, Qalam al-Sijillat, Sijill* 12, *Ahli, Alif, hujja* 36, *Muhammad Sultan Basha*; Ministère de l'intérieur, *Recensement général*, vol. 2, pt. 1.

54. G. Fahmi, *Souvenirs*, p. 87.

55. See note 53.

56. This paragraph and the following one are based on the Sha'rawi memoirs, pp. 6–7, and *n1*.

57. G. Fahmi, *Souvenirs*, p. 85.

58. Sami, pt. 3, vol. 3, p. 1450.

59. *Mas, Awamir, Ma'iya Saniya-Arabi*, reg. 1940/59/61, Viceroy/al-Dakhiliya, 13 JA 1289/18 Aug. 1872.

60. G. Fahmi, *Souvenirs*, p. 85.

61. See Wilson, *Chapters*, pp. 94–97; al-Ayyubi, *Tarikh*, vol. 2, pp. 263–66, 358–408; Sami, pt. 3, vol. 3, pp. 1449–55; Leon, *Khedive's Egypt*, pp. 183–98; McCoan, *Egypt Under Ismail*, pp. 69–70, 135–36, 151.

62. Wilson, *Chapters*, p. 95; see also Leon, *Khedive's Egypt*, pp. 183–84.

63. al-Ayyubi, *Tarikh*, vol. 2, p. 263; McCoan, *Egypt Under Ismail*, p. 70.

64. Leon, *Khedive's Egypt*, p. 183; McCoan, *Egypt Under Ismail*, p. 70.

65. Although Sami (pt. 3, vol. 3, p. 1449) asserts that the *mufattish* was never dismissed he was briefly demoted in 1872 from his position as director of finances to membership on the Privy Council, but quickly returned to favor; the reference to "little khedive" is from al-Ayyubi, *Tarikh*, vol. 2, p. 360.

66. This paragraph is based on: Sami, pt. 3, vol. 3, pp. 1450–51.

67. This paragraph is based on ibid., and on the following sources: for the promotion of 1863, see *Mas, Awamir, Ma'iya Saniya-Turki*, reg. 526/50/56 and 95/741, Viceroy/al-Maliya, 13 SH 1279/3 Feb. 1863, and 14 DH 1279/2 June 1863; on not being appointed to the regency council, see Sami, pt. 3, vol. 2, p. 641; for the land grants, see ibid., entries

for 1863 and 1864; for the appointments of 1865, see ibid., p. 613; for the appointment of 1867, see ibid., p. 711.

68. Sami, pt. 3, vol. 3, p. 1125; *Dhawat* Land Register, entry for Ismail Siddiq.

69. Leon, *Khedive's Egypt*, p. 184; McCoan, *Egypt Under Ismail*, p. 70; Wilson, *Chapters*, p. 94.

70. This and the following paragraphs on the loan of 1868 and Ismail Siddiq's role are based on: Hamza, *Public Debt*, pp. 138–51; Sabry, *L'empire égyptien*, pp. 138–47; al-Ayyubi, *Tarikh*, vol. 2, pp. 264–65.

71. Sabry, *L'empire égyptien*, p. 142; Hamza, *Public Debt*, p. 141.

72. *AI*, *Ahd Ismail*, Collection 139/8/42–, Viceroy/Abraham Bey, 15 Feb. 1874.

73. Sami, pt. 3, vol. 2, p. 632.

74. Ibid., p. 652. Ismail Siddiq was also authorized to appoint officials to fill the administrative offices created in 1866. (ibid., pp. 669–700).

75. See ibid., pp. 663–64, 669, 700.

76. Ibid., pt. 3, vol. 3, pp. 1451–52; Ninet, "Origins of the National Party in Egypt," p. 122.

77. Sami, pt. 3, vol. 2, p. 940.

78. McCoan, *Egypt As It Is*, p. 95; al-Ayyubi, *Tarikh*, vol. 2, pp. 90–91; Stanton/ Derby, no. 39, 28 May 1874, in FO 78/2342.

79. Sami, pt. 3, vol. 2, p. 650. The wife of Muhammad Shakir Pasha was a freed slave of Ismail Siddiq, and Ahmad Nashat was his nephew (Butler, *Court Life in Egypt*, p. 178; *MM*, no. 20873, *Warathat Muhammad Shakir Basha*).

80. Sami, pt. 3, vol. 3, p. 1452.

81. McCoan, *Egypt As It Is*, p. 95*n1*.

82. This paragraph is based on Leon, *Khedive's Egypt*, pp. 191–97; McCoan, *Egypt Under Ismail*, pp. 200–01; al-Ayyubi, *Tarikh*, vol. 2, pp. 361–62, 401–08; Sami, pt. 3, vol. 3, pp. 1453–55; Vivian/Derby, no. 27, 11 Nov. 1876, in FO 78/2504.

83. In 1865, for example, the *mufattish* received a gift of £5,000 from the viceroy (Sami, pt. 3, vol. 2, p. 632). The following information is taken from: McCoan, *Egypt Under Ismail*, p. 151; Wallace, *Egypt and the Egyptian Question*, p. 152; Sami, pt. 3, vol. 3, p. 1452.

84. al-Ayyubi, *Tarikh*, vol. 2, p. 401.

85. Sami, pt. 3, vol. 2, pp. 802, 940, 964; Mubarak, *al-Khitat*, vol. 10, p. 55; *al-Abhath*, box 106, dossier "Ismail Basha Siddiq," reference to *WM*, no. 729, 23 N 1294/1 Oct. 1877; *Mas, Awamir, Maʿiya Saniya-Arabi*, reg. 1927/145/48, Viceroy/*al-Daira al-Saniya*, 26 J 1286/3 Sept. 1869; *Maʿiya Saniya-Turki*, reg. 573/65/57, Viceroy/*al-Daira al-Saniya*, 20 M 1285/13 May 1868; al-Ayyubi, *Tarikh*, vol. 2, p. 401.

86. The following examples are taken from: *Mas, Awamir, Maʿiya Saniya-Turki*, reg. 573/86/23, Viceroy/*al-Daira al-Saniya*, 16 R 1285/7 July 1868; *Maʿiya Saniya-Arabi*, reg. 1935/78/104, Viceroy/*al-Maliya*, 21 N 1287/15 Dec. 1870; McCoan, *Egypt Under Ismail*, p. 200.

87. Sami, pt. 3, vol. 2, p. 624.

88. *Dhawat* Land Register; Mubarak, *al-Khitat*, vol. 19, p. 88; see also ibid., pp. 12, 17, 55.

89. Mubarak, *al-Khitat*, vol. 10, p. 55.

90. *MM*, no. 9598, *Mudad istikhdam Muhammad Sharif Basha*; on the life and career of Muhammad Sharif, see also al-Rafiʿi, *Asr Ismail*, vol. 2, pp. 206–23; Zakhura, *Mirʾat al-asr*, vol. 1, pp. 125–29; al-Ayyubi, *Tarikh*, vol. 2, pp. 166–72; Blunt, *Secret History*, pp. 146, 149, 190, and *passim*; Bell, *Khedives*, pp. 163–81; Zaki, *Aʿlam al-Jaysh*, pp. 110–12; Cromer, *Modern Egypt*, vol. 2, pp. 334–35.

91. *al-Abhath*, box 135, dossier 33, contains reports on the genealogy of Muhammad Sharif, whose grandfather, according to one account, was chief treasurer (*daftardar*) of

Egypt. The remainder of this paragraph is based on al-Ayyubi, *Tarikh*, vol. 2, pp. 166–68.

92. This paragraph is based on: al-Ayyubi, *Tarikh*, vol. 2, p. 168; and *MM*, no. 9598; *Mudad istikhdam Muhammad Sharif Basha*.

93. al-Ayyubi, *Tarikh*, vol. 2, pp. 168–69; *MM*, no. 9598, *Mudad istikhdam Muhammad Sharif Basha*.

94. For this and the following, see Leon, *Khedive's Egypt*, pp. 181–82; Dicey, *Khedivate*, p. 182; Bell, *Khedives*, p. 168; al-Ayyubi, *Tarikh*, vol. 2, pp. 170–72.

95. *AI*, *al-Mutafarriqat*, box 108, "al-Siyasa, 1828–1879," United States Consular reports, Farman/Evarts, no. 237, 17 June 1878; Bell, *Khedives*, pp. 166–68; Green/Clarendon, no. 16, 8 Feb. 1858, in FO 78/1401.

96. This paragraph is based on: Wallace, *Egypt and the Egyptian Question*, pp. 158–59; Dicey, *Khedivate*, pp. 182–83; Cromer, *Modern Egypt*, vol. 2, p. 334; on Sharif's indolence, see *AI*, *al-Mutafarriqat*, box 152, "Administration," United States Consular Reports, Beardsley/Fish, no. 363, 28 Sept. 1878; on his dismissal from Sa'id's army and general apathy, see *MM*, no. 9598, *Mudad istikhdam Muhammad Sharif Basha*; Bell, *Khedives*, p. 166; on his attitude toward Armenians and native Egyptians, see Vivian/Salisbury, no. 422, 14 Dec. 1878, in FO 78/2858; *L'Egypte et l'Europe*, vol. 1, p. 95n1; Blunt, *Secret History*, p. 149; Cromer, *Modern Egypt*, vol. 2, p. 334.

97. Bell, *Khedives*, pp. 164, 180; Colquhoun/Russell, no. 119, 6 Aug. 1863, in FO 78/1755.

98. Bell, *Khedives*, pp. 165–66.

99. Sami, pt. 3, vol. 2, p. 482; Colquhoun/Russell, no. 76, 11 May 1863, in FO 78/1754.

100. Sami, pt. 3, vol. 2, pp. 452, 474, 499.

101. Stanton/Stanley, no. 26, 20 Mar. 1868; no. 32, 4 Apr. 1868; no. 42, 25 Apr. 1868, in FO 78/2038; no. 21, 27 Feb. 1867, in FO 78/1976.

102. Sami, pt. 3, vol. 2, pp. 490, 606, 693; *al-Abhath*, box 106, dossier 38, "Sharif Basha," Viceroy/al-Maliya, 18 JA 1280/30 Nov. 1863; *Mas*, *Awamir*, *Ma'iya Saniya-Arabi*, reg. 1943/88/105, Viceroy/al-Maliya, 6 DH 1289/4 Feb. 1873.

103. On Ismail's favors to Sharif, see *al-Abhath*, box 106, dossier 38, "Sharif Basha," Viceroy/al-Qalyubiya, 25 DH 1280/1 June 1864; Viceroy/al-Maliya, 18 JA 1280/30 Nov. 1863; on his holdings in 1879 and 1885, see Barakat, *Tatawwur*, p. 177; Ministère de l'intérieur, *recensement général*, vol. 2, pt. 1.

104. Bell, *Khedives*, pp. 178–79.

105. In June 1865, Robert Colquhoun, the British consul general, wrote that Sharif was acting in concert with the Council of State; in July, he observed that the real business of government was being carried out by Nubar, who had a powerful influence over Sharif (Colquhoun/Russell, no. 75, 19 June 1865; no. 84, 17 July 1865, in FO 78/1871).

106. On the life and career of Mustafa Riyad, see *MM*, no. 27656, *Mudad istikhdam Mustafa Riyad Basha*; al-Ayyubi, *Tarikh*, vol. 2, pp. 197–211; Zaki, *Un mot sur Riaz Pacha*; Abbate Pacha, *Séance solennelle*; Zakhura, *Mir'at al-asr*, vol. 1, pp. 74–76; Wallace, *Egypt and the Egyptian Question*, pp. 112–13, 115; Milner, *England in Egypt*, pp. 126–28; al-Rafi'i, *al-Thawra*, pp. 45–48; Bell, *Khedives*, pp. 121–41; Cromer, *Modern Egypt*, vol. 2, pp. 342–45; Abd al-Karim, *Tarikh al-ta'lim*, vol. 2, pp. 67–74.

107. See, for example, Bell, *Khedives*, p. 131; Wallace, *Egypt and the Egyptian Question*, p. 113; McCoan, *Egypt Under Ismail*, p. 180n1.

108. McCoan, *Egypt Under Ismail*, p. 180n1.

109. al-Ayyubi, *Tarikh*, vol. 2, p. 197. Wallace, *Egypt and the Egyptian Question*, p. 115, and McCoan, *Egypt Under Ismail*, p. 180n1, both state that Riyad was Jewish. al-Ayyubi also states that Riyad's father had been director of the mint under Muhammad Ali.

110. Milner, *England in Egypt*, p. 126.

111. My thanks to Ms. Sana Hassan for this piece of family gossip. Barakat, *Tatawwur*, p. 185.

112. Bell, *Khedives*, pp. 121-22; Wallace, *Egypt and the Egyptian Question*, p. 115.

113. McCoan, *Egypt Under Ismail*, p. 180*n1*; Bell, *Khedives*, p. 127.

114. The information contained in this and the following paragraph is taken from Riyad's pension dossier, *MM*, no. 27656; al-Ayyubi, *Tarikh*, vol. 2, p. 198, Zaki, *Un Mot sur Riaz Pasha*, p. 15; and Sami, pt. 3, vol. 1, p. 55.

115. al-Ayyubi, *Tarikh*, vol. 2, p. 198.

116. Zaki, *Un Mot sur Riaz Pasha*, pp. 16-17.

117. Sami, pt. 3, vol. 2, pp. 448, 482.

118. *al-Abhath*, box 107, dossier no. 4, "al-Khassa," MS "Nuzzar al-Khassa wa muwazzafuha"; Sami, pt. 3, vol. 2, p. 721.

119. Sami, pt. 3, vol. 2, pp. 540, 642, 854.

120. Bell, *Khedives*, pp. 123-24, 131.

121. Zaki, *Un Mot sur Riaz Pasha*, p. 18; for the order of dismissal, see Sami, pt. 3, vol. 2, p. 764.

122. Bell, *Khedives*, pp. 121, 131-32.

123. Sami, pt. 3, vol. 2, p. 791.

124. Zaki, *Un Mot sur Riaz Pasha*, p. 18; al-Ayyubi, *Tarikh*, vol. 2, p. 199; *MM*, no. 27656, *Mudad istikhdam Mustafa Riyad Basha*.

125. This paragraph is based on Sami, pt. 3, vol. 2, p. 1028; pt. 3, vol. 3, p. 1144; *MM*, no. 27656, *Mudad istikhdam Mustafa Riyad Basha*.

126. See Abd al-Karim, *Tarikh*, vol. 2, pp. 67-74.

127. Cromer, *Modern Egypt*, vol. 2, p. 345, and Wallace, *Egypt and the Egyptian Question*, p. 112, recognize Riyad's sense of justice, though Cromer notes that Riyad's notions of right and wrong were higher than any law.

128. Milner, *England in Egypt*, p. 392; Ministry of *al-Awqaf*, *Qalam al-Sijillat*, *Sijill* 17, *Ahli*, *hujja* 147, *Mustafa Riyad Basha*.

129. Blunt, *Secret History*, pp. 97-98; Cromer, *Modern Egypt*, vol. 2, p. 343.

130. Bell, *Khedives*, p. 137.

131. Ibid., p. 128; Milner, *England in Egypt*, pp. 126-27.

132. Cromer, *Modern Egypt*, vol. 2, p. 343.

133. Malortie, *Egypt*, p. 94.

134. The following views are taken from: Holynski, *Nubar*, pp. vii, 76-77, *passim*; Emile Bertrand, *Nubar*; Dicey, *Khedivate*, pp. 117, 125, 130; Wallace, *Egypt and the Egyptian Question*, p. 160; McCoan, *Egypt Under Ismail*, p. 262. See also Archarouni, *Nubar Pacha*; Zakhura, *Mir'at al-asr*, vol. 1, pp. 77-79; Makhluf, *Nubar Basha*.

135. This paragraph is based on the following sources: on Nubar's education, see Holynski, *Nubar*, p. 5; on his arrival in Egypt, see al-Ayyubi, *Tarikh*, vol. 2, p. 149; on Boghos, see Sami, pt. 2, p. 528*n1*; Holynski, *Nubar*, p. 9; on Nubar's entering government service, see Campbell/Palmerston, "separate," 30 Nov. 1833, in FO 78/228; Bertrand, *Nubar*, p. 14; *MM*, no. 8321, *Mudad istikhdam Nubar Basha*; on work in translation office, see *MM*, no. 8321, *Mudad istikhdam Nubar Basha*; Barnett/Aberdeen, no. 4, 17 Jan. 1844, in FO 78/582.

136. This paragraph is based on: Bertrand, *Nubar*, p. 15; al-Ayyubi, *Tarikh*, vol. 2, pp. 151-52; Holynski, *Nubar*, pp. 12-13; About, *Le Fellah*, p. 130; Sami, pt. 3, vol. 2, pp. 492, 516, 519.

137. Bertrand, *Nubar*, p. 21.

138. See Rivlin, "The Railway Question" pp. 365-88.

139. Murray/Palmerston, no. 9, Apr. 17, 1851, in FO 78/875.

140. Except for the quotation from Cromer, this paragraph is based on: Bell, *Khe-*

dives, pp. 146, 151, 160; al-Ayyubi, *Tarikh*, vol. 2, pp. 149, 162, 164; Holynski, *Nubar*, pp. 7–10; Bertrand, *Nubar*, pp. 16–17; Cromer, *Modern Egypt*, vol. 2, p. 339; Malet, *Egypt, 1879–1883*, p. 45.

141. Cromer, *Modern Egypt*, vol. 2, p. 342.

142. Bertrand, *Nubar*, pp. 22–24; Tagher, "Portrait Psychologique," pp. 357–58.

143. See McCoan, *Egypt Under Ismail*, p. 26*n1*; Green/Clarendon, no. 23, 18 July 1857, in FO 78/1314; Sami, pt. 3, vol. 1, p. 234, 318.

144. Green/Malmesbury, no. 35, 1 Apr. 1859, in FO 78/1467.

145. Landes, *Bankers*, p. 162*n1*.

146. Sabry, *L'empire égyptien*, p. 24; Bertrand, *Nubar*, pp. 26–27; Green/Clarendon, no. 23, 28 July 1857, in FO 78/1314.

147. Holynski, *Nubar*, p. 21; for Murray's special relationship with Abbas, see Rivlin, "The Railway Question," pp. 366, 369.

148. *AI*, *al-Mutafarriqat*, box 152, dossier "Administration," Outrey/French Minister of Foreign Affairs, no. 35, 2 June 1865.

149. Stanton/Derby, no. 45, 6 June 1874, in FO 78/2342.

150. Colquhoun/Russell, no. 90, 1 June 1863, in FO 78/1755; Tagher, "Portrait Psychologique," pp. 364–66.

151. Colquhoun/Russell, no. 24, 24 Feb. 1865; no. 84, 27 July 1865, in FO 78/1871.

152. About, *Le Fellah*, p. 130; Elgood, *The Transit of Egypt*, p. 125.

153. The following examples are taken from: Sami, pt. 3, vol. 2, pp. 582–83, 584; *MM*, no. 18266, *Mudad istikhdam Dikran Basha*; Colquhoun/Russell, no. 84, 17 July 1865, in FO 78/1871.

154. Colquhoun/Russell, no. 59, 17 Apr. 1863, in FO 78/1754.

155. Bell, *Khedives*, p. 132.

156. Vivian/Salisbury, no. 228, 29 June 1878, in FO 78/2855; Kusel, *An Englishman's Recollections*, p. 120.

157. Bell, *Khedives*, pp. 159–60; Sami, pt. 3, vol. 2, pp. 802, 839, 853; *al-Abhath*, box 106, dossier "Nubar Basha," Viceroy/Mustafa Pasha, 29 SH 1279/19 Feb. 1863; *Mas, Awamir, Ma'iya Saniya-Arabi*, reg. 1935/103/136, Viceroy/*al-Maliya*, 3 DH 1287/24 Feb. 1871.

158. This and the following paragraph is taken from Bell, *Khedives*, pp. 145–60, *passim*; Bertrand, *Nubar*, p. 34; Cromer, *Modern Egypt*, vol. 2, pp. 336, 343; Holynski, *Nubar*, p. 130; Dicey, *Khedivate*, pp. 134–35, 166–68, 195.

159. See al-Ayyubi, *Tarikh*, vol. 2, p. 156; Landes, *Bankers*, pp. 116–17.

160. Landes, *Bankers*, p. 162.

161. This and what follows is drawn from ibid., pp. 248–75, *passim*.

162. See Hamza, *Public Debt*, pp. 88–92.

163. Landes, *Bankers*, p. 275.

164. Douin, *Règne du Khédive Ismail*, vol. 1, p. 205.

165. A. Sammarco, *Histoire de l'Egypte moderne*, vol. 3, p. 130.

166. See ibid., vol. 3, ch. 7.

167. McCoan, *Egypt As It Is*, pp. 284–86.

168. Brinton, *Mixed Courts*, pp. 8–12.

169. Ibid., pp. 13–24, *passim*.

▲7▲ THE DISMANTLING OF KHEDIVIAL ABSOLUTISM

1. Schölch, *Egypt*, pp. 44–47.

2. Stanton/Derby, no. 182, 24 Dec. 1875, in FO 78/2405. On the Cave mission, see McCoan, *Egypt Under Ismail*, pp. 176–78.

3. Rothstein, *Egypt's Ruin*, pp. 16–18; Stanton/Derby, no. 24, 23 Jan. 1876, in FO 78/2500.

4. Stanton/Derby, no. 52, 19 Feb. 1876, in FO 78/2500.

5. McCoan, *Egypt Under Ismail*, pp. 184–85; Stanton/Derby, no. 86, 17 Mar. 1876; no. 110, 30 Mar. 1876, in FO 78/2501.

6. Rothstein, *Egypt's Ruin*, p. 20; Stanton/Derby, no. 86, 17 Mar. 1876, in FO 78/2501

7. Stanton/Derby, no. 80, 14 Mar. 1876, in FO 78/2501.

8. Pierre Crabites, *Ismail*, pp. 231–32.

9. Ibid., p. 232; Rothstein, *Egypt's Ruin*, p. 22; McCoan, *Egypt Under Ismail*, p. 185.

10. Hamza, *Public Debt*, pp. 119–20.

11. Ibid., p. 237; McCoan, *Egypt Under Ismail*, pp. 174–75.

12. Cromer, *Modern Egypt*, vol. 1, p. 12; Dicey, *Khedivate*, pp. 146–51.

13. Rothstein, *Egypt's Ruin*, pp. 24–26; Cromer, *Modern Egypt*, vol. 1, p. 12.

14. This paragraph is based on: McCoan, *Egypt Under Ismail*, pp. 187–89; Hamza, *Public Debt*, pp. 78, 157, and 157$n1$; Sabry, *L'empire égyptien*, p. 180; Landes, *Bankers*, pp. 64$n2$, 117, 117$n2$, 162, 169.

15. This paragraph is based on: Sabry, *L'empire égyptien*, pp. 180–81; McCoan, *Egypt Under Ismail*, pp. 188–89; Michels, *Souvenirs de carrière*, pp. 115, 119, 124–26.

16. Rothstein, *Egypt's Ruin*, p. 30.

17. See Commission de la caisse spéciale de la dette publique d'Egypte, *Compte rendu*, pp. 6–11.

18. McCoan, *Egypt Under Ismail*, p. 191; Sabry, *L'empire égyptien*, pp. 182–84; Dicey, *Khedivate*, pp. 104–05, 158–59; Vivian/Derby, no. 27, 11 Nov. 1876, in FO 78/2504.

19. Vivian/Derby, no. 12, 27 Oct. 1876, in FO 78/2503; ibid., no. 21, 4 Nov. 1876, in FO 78/2504; Commission de la caisse spéciale de la dette publique d'Egypte, *Compte rendu*, p. 11.

20. This paragraph is based on: McCoan, *Egypt Under Ismail*, pp. 180–83, 190; Dicey, *Khedivate*, pp. 126–29; on the use of these courts by European subjects against Egyptian debtors, see Cookson/Derby, no. 214, 3 June 1876, in FO 78/2503.

21. Vivian/Derby, no. 24, 10 Nov. 1876; no. 27, 11 Nov. 1876, in FO 78/2504.

22. See al-Ayyubi, *Tarikh Misr*, vol. 2, pp. 361–401; Vivian/Derby, no. 27, 11 Nov. 1876, in FO 78/2504.

23. Rothstein, *Egypt's Ruin*, p. 27; Cromer, *Modern Egypt*, vol. 1, p. 13; McCoan, *Egypt Under Ismail*, p. 205.

24. McCoan, *Egypt Under Ismail*, pp. 205–07; Rothstein, *Egypt's Ruin*, p. 28.

25. Vivian/Derby, no. 221, 19 July 1877, in FO 78/2633.

26. McCoan, *Egypt Under Ismail*, p. 222; Rothstein, *Egypt's Ruin*, p. 50.

27. This paragraph is based on: Rothstein, *Egypt's Ruin*, p. 50; Cromer, *Modern Egypt*, vol. 1, pp. 26–27, 31$n1$; McCoan, *Egypt Under Ismail*, pp. 215–17; Borg/Vivian, unnumbered, 27 Dec. 1877, in FO 141/112.

28. Leon, *Khedive's Egypt*, p. 423; McCoan, *Egypt Under Ismail*, p. 211.

29. Vivian/Derby, no. 84, 3 Apr. 1877, in FO 78/1632; ibid., no. 297, 28 Sept. 1877, in FO 78/2634.

30. Ibid., no. 297, 28 Sept. 1877, in FO 78/2634.

31. Ibid., no. 20, 27 Jan. 1877, in FO 78/2631; ibid., no. 38, 15 Feb. 1877, in FO 78/2631; Cromer, *Modern Egypt*, vol. 1, pp. 32–33.

32. Cromer, *Modern Egypt*, vol. 1, p. 26.

33. Sabry, *L'empire égyptien*, p. 191; McCoan, *Egypt Under Ismail*, pp. 225–26.

34. The rest of this paragraph is based on the following sources: on Vivian's pressure, see McCoan, *Egypt Under Ismail*, p. 223; on Ismail's resistance, see Cromer, *Modern Egypt*, vol. 1, pp. 42–44; on the mixed courts suit, see Keay, *Spoiling the Egyptians*, pp.

NOTES TO PAGES 189-96 ▲ 255 ▲

38-39; on Ismail's capitulation, see McCoan, *Egypt Under Ismail*, p. 227; on establishing the commission, see Cromer, *Modern Egypt*, vol. 1, p. 45.

35. McCoan, *Egypt Under Ismail*, pp. 230-31.

36. Sami, pt. 3, vol. 3, pp. 1125, 1465; McCoan, *Egypt Under Ismail*, pp. 193n1, 200; *Egypt for the Egyptians*, pp. 70-71; al-Ayyubi, *Tarikh*, vol. 2, p. 407.

37. Cromer, *Modern Egypt*, vol. 1, p. 45; Vivian/Derby, no. 81, 22 Mar. 1878, in FO 78/2854.

38. Vivian/Derby, no. 81, 22 Mar. 1878, in FO 78/2854; Bell, *Khedives*, pp. 132-33.

39. Vivian/Derby, no. 88, 28 Mar. 1878, in FO 78/2854.

40. Vivian/Salisbury, no. 176, 17 May 1878, in FO 78/2854; ibid., no. 124, 15 Mar. 1879, in FO 78/2999.

41. This paragraph is based on the following sources: on Riyad's belief in clean government, see Bell, *Khedives*, pp. 131-32; on his dislike of oppressive and heavy-handed methods, see Cromer, *Modern Egypt*, vol. 2, p. 344; on his faith in Islam, see ibid., p. 343; Butler, *Court Life in Egypt*, pp. 267-68; on his attitude toward outsiders, see Milner, *England in Egypt*, pp. 129, 341.

42. Blunt, *Secret History*, pp. 97-98.

43. Keddie, *Jamal ad-Din*, p. 81; Kedourie, *Afghani*, p. 7; Shafiq, *Mudhakkirati*, vol. 1, pp. 108-09; Amin, *Zu'ama al-islah*, pp. 62-63; Ahmed, *Intellectual Origins*, pp. 15-16.

44. Kedourie, *Afghani*, pp. 7-8; Keddie, *Jamal ad-Din*, p. 83.

45. Keddie, *Jamal ad-Din*, p. 93.

46. Kedourie, *Afghani*, p. 28; Keddie, *Jamal ad-Din*, pp. 100-01; see also Sabry, *La gènese*, pp. 142-43.

47. This paragraph is based on: Sabry, *La gènese*, p. 126; Vivian/Derby, no. 77, 30 Mar. 1877, in FO 78/2631; ibid., no. 100, 19 Apr. 1877, in FO 78/2632; ibid., no. 130, 14 June 1877, in FO 78/2633; ibid., no. 350, 26 Dec. 1877, in FO 78/2634.

48. Sabry, *La gènese*, p. 2, and *passim*.

49. The rest of this paragraph is based on the following sources: on Ismail's press sponsorship, see Gendzier, *Practical Visions*, p. 49; *Egypt for the Egyptians*, p. 87; on Abd al-Halim's activities, see Vivian/Derby, no. 187, 21 June 1877, in FO 78/2633; Keddie, *Jamal ad-Din*, pp. 96, 120-21; Jerrold, *Egypt Under Ismail Pacha*, pp. 253-54; Gendzier, *Practical Visions*, p. 7.

50. This paragraph is based on: Keddie, *Jamal ad-Din*, pp. 83-87, 96, 101-02, 104-07, 109; Kedourie, *Afghani*, p. 23.

51. Keddie, *Jamal ad-Din*, pp. 107-08.

52. Bell, *Khedives*, p. 193.

53. Abbate Pacha, *Séance solennelle*, p. 9; *WMC*, box 21, issue 528, 15 SH 1290/8 Oct. 1873.

54. *WMC*, box 5, issue 529, 22 SH 1290/15 Oct. 1873.

55. Ahmed, *Intellectual Origins*, p. 17.

56. Mubarak, *Nukhbat al-Fikr fi tadbir Nil Misr*, pp. 110-11, 176, 184, 197.

57. See ibid., pp. 153-54, 158-65, 186, 198, *passim*.

58. McCoan, *Egypt As It Is*, p. 104; *Mas, Ma'iya Saniya-Arabi*, reg. 8/77/157, Viceroy/al-Maliya, 6 S 1293/3 Mar. 1876.

59. Schölch, *Egypt*, p. 52; Wallace, *Egypt and the Egyptian Question*, p. 160; Kusel, *An Englishman's Recollections*, p. 122.

60. Dicey, *Khedivate*, pp. 166-67, 194-95; see also Wilson, *Chapters*, pp. 158-59, 216.

61. Dicey, *Khedivate*, pp. 128-29.

62. Malet, *Egypt, 1879-1883*, p. 45; Bell, *Khedives*, pp. 146, 155; McCoan, *Egypt Under Ismail*, p. 262.

63. Ninet, "Origins of the National Party in Egypt," p. 123.

64. Sabry, *La gènese*, p. 103; McCoan, *Egypt Under Ismail*, p. 262.

65. Dicey, *Khedivate*, pp. 166–69.

66. Cave/Derby, no. 4, 25 Dec. 1875, in FO 78/2538.

67. Stanton/Derby, no. 13, 9 Jan. 1876; ibid., no. 1, 1 Jan. 1876; ibid., no. 13, 9 Jan. 1876, in FO 78/2500.

68. Cave/Derby, no. 103, 5 Feb. 1876, in FO 78/2539b.

69. Stanton/Derby, no. 6, 5 Jan. 1876; ibid., no. 13, 9 Jan. 1876, in FO 78/2500.

70. The following two paragraphs are based on: Dicey, *Khedivate*, pp. 166–74.

71. Ibid., pp. 179–80, 198; Wilson, *Chapters*, pp. 125–26, 133.

72. This paragraph is based on: Wilson, *Chapters*, pp. 99–101, 111–12, 124, 133, 147, 157.

73. Vivian/Salisbury, no. 207, 8 June 1878, in FO 78/2855; Dicey, *Khedivate*, pp. 182–83.

74. The rest of this paragraph is based on: Wilson, *Chapters*, pp. 130–31, 133; Dicey, *Khedivate*, pp. 182–83; Vivian/Salisbury, no. 207, 8 June 1878, in FO 78/2855.

75. Wilson, *Chapters*, pp. 132–33; Vivian/Salisbury, no. 228, 29 June 1878, in FO 78/2855; Schölch, *Egypt*, p. 52.

76. Schölch, *Egypt*, p. 52; Wilson, *Chapters*, p. 145.

77. Dicey, *Khedivate*, pp. 193–94; Foreign Office/Vivian, unnumbered, 29 July 1878, in FO 78/2851; Vivian/Salisbury, no. 259, 23 July 1878, in FO 78/2856; Wilson, *Chapters*, p. 147.

78. This paragraph is based on: Vivian/Salisbury, no. 279, 18 Aug. 1878, in FO 78/2856; Schölch, *Egypt*, pp. 52–55.

79. Wilson, *Chapters*, pp. 151–52.

80. Vivian/Salisbury, no. 286, 22 Aug. 1878, in FO 78/2856.

81. This paragraph is based on: Wilson, *Chapters*, pp. 153–55, 161; Dicey, *Khedivate*, p. 179.

82. Vivian/Salisbury, no. 375, 1 Nov. 1878, in FO 78/2858; ibid., no. 265, 7 May 1879, in FO 78/3001; ibid., no. 20, 11 Jan. 1879, in FO 78/2998. Lascelles/Salisbury, no. 374, 29 Oct. 1878; ibid., no. 371, 28 Oct. 1878, in FO 78/2857; the viceregal family's holdings were 425,729 *faddans*.

83. Dicey, *Khedivate*, pp. 189–90.

84. Ibid., p. 188; Schölch, *Egypt*, pp. 54–56.

85. See the enclosures from *Moniteur égyptien* in Vivian/Salisbury, no. 293, 30 Aug. 1878, in FO 78/2856; ibid., no. 423, 14 Dec. 1878, in FO 78/2858; cf. also Wilson, *Chapters*, p. 179; *WM*, no. 796, 11 S 1296/4 Feb. 1879.

86. Vivian/Salisbury, no. 85, 28 Feb. 1879, in FO 78/2998.

87. Wilson, *Chapters*, p. 155; Lascelles/Salisbury, no. 310, 10 Sept. 1878, in FO 78/2857.

88. Vivian/Salisbury, no. 422, 14 Dec. 1878, in FO 78/2858. This paragraph is also based on: Cromer, *Modern Egypt*, vol. 1, pp. 66–68; Wilson, *Chapters*, p. 176; Vivian/Salisbury, no. 286, 22 Aug. 1878, in FO 78/2856; ibid., no. 424, 14 Dec. 1878; ibid., no. 433, 21 Dec. 1878, in FO 78/2858; Lascelles/Salisbury, no. 310, 10 Sept. 1878, in FO 78/2857.

89. For two months prior to Nubar's appointment as Minister of Foreign Affairs and Justice, these departments were directed by Riyad; see Sami, pt. 3, vol. 3, pp. 1530, 1534–35.

90. This paragraph is based on: Wilson, *Chapters*, pp. 145–46; Lascelles/Salisbury, nos. 296, 298, 3 Sept. 1878; ibid., nos. 304, 306, 7 Sept. 1878; ibid., no. 326, 19 Sept. 1878; ibid., no. 332, 23 Sept. 1878, in FO 78/2857.

91. Lascelles/Salisbury, no. 317, 16 Sept. 1878; ibid., no. 321, 17 Sept. 1878, in FO 78/ 2857.

92. Ibid., no. 310, 10 Sept. 1878; ibid., no. 322, 18 Sept. 1878, in FO 78/2857.

93. See ibid., no. 324, 18 Sept. 1878; ibid., no. 332, 23 Sept. 1878; ibid., no. 334, 25 Sept. 1878, in FO 78/2857.

94. Nubar/Vivian, 30 Aug. 1878, in FO 78/2856; Lascelles/Vivian, no. 332, 23 Sept. 1878, in FO 78/2857.

95. Lascelles/Salisbury, no. 298, 3 Sept. 1878; ibid., no. 308, 9 Sept. 1878; ibid., no. 310, 10 Sept. 1878, in FO 78/2857.

96. This paragraph is based on: Lascelles/Salisbury, nos. 323 and 324, 18 Sept. 1878; ibid., no. 331, 21 Sept. 1878; and Vivian/Salisbury, no. 319, 17 Sept. 1878, in FO 78/2857. By Sept. 21, the British government had formally sanctioned Wilson's appointment.

97. Lascelles/Salisbury, no. 339, 27 Sept. 1878, in FO 78/2857; see also Dicey, *Khedivate*, pp. 191–92.

98. Lascelles/Salisbury, no. 336, 26 Sept. 1878, in FO 78/2857; Dicey, *Khedivate*, p. 191.

99. Vivian/Salisbury, no. 341, 27 Sept. 1878, in FO 78/2857; Schölch, *Egypt*, p. 59; Lascelles/Salisbury, no. 352, 12 Oct. 1878; ibid., no. 355, 16 Oct. 1878, in FO 78/2857.

100. See Lascelles/Salisbury, no. 353, 14 Oct. 1878; ibid., no. 365, 25 Oct. 1878, in FO 78/2857; Vivian/Salisbury, no. 422, 14 Dec. 1878, in FO 78/2858.

101. Lascelles/Salisbury, no. 404, 29 Nov. 1878, in FO 78/2858.

102. Lascelles/Vivian, no. 342, 27 Sept. 1878, in FO 78/2857.

103. See enclosure from *Moniteur égyptien* in Vivian/Salisbury, no. 423, 14 Dec. 1878, in FO 78/2858.

104. Sami, pt. 3, vol. 3, pp. 1549–50.

105. See Lascelles/Salisbury, no. 351, 12 Oct. 1878, in FO 78/2857; ibid., no. 379, 2 Nov. 1878; ibid., no. 382, 5 Nov. 1878; and Vivian/Salisbury, no. 432, 20 Dec. 1878, in FO 78/2858.

106. Vivian/Salisbury, no. 65, 21 Feb. 1879, in FO 78/2998.

107. Ibid., no. 245, 15 July 1878, in FO 78/2855. In March, Vivian wrote that Wilson two months previously had desired Sharif's entry into the ministry and had made overtures to him (ibid., no. 89, 1 Mar. 1879, in FO 78/2999); see also ibid., no. 82, 27 Feb. 1879, in FO 78/2998.

108. al-Rafiʿi, *Asr Ismail*, vol. 2, p. 76; Bell, *Khedives*, p. 173; Schölch, *Egypt*, p. 59; Vivian/Salisbury, no. 422, 14 Dec. 1878, in FO 78/2858.

109. This paragraph is based on: *MM*, no. 18189, *Mudad istikhdam Muhammad Ratib Basha*; Sami, pt. 3, vol. 3, p. 1504; al-Ayyubi, *Tarikh*, vol. 2, pp. 89–92; Ministry of al-Awqaf, Qalam al-Sijillat, *Sijill* 40, *Ahli, hujja* 2686, Muhammad Ratib Basha.

110. Vivian/Salisbury, no. 422, 14 Dec. 1878, in FO 78/2858; Schölch, *Egypt*, p. 85; see Cromer, *Modern Egypt*, vol. 1, pp. 68–69.

111. Stanton/Derby, telegram, 28 Apr. 1876, in FO 78/2502; Cromer, *Modern Egypt*, vol. 1, pp. 114–15.

112. This paragraph is based on: Wilson, *Chapters*, pp. 180–81; Cromer, *Modern Egypt*, vol. 1, p. 115; Dicey, *Khedivate*, p. 204; Keay, *Spoiling the Egyptians*, p. 55.

113. This paragraph is based on: Blunt, *Secret History*, p. 34; Artin, *Landed Property*, p. 113; Vivian/Derby, no. 33, 18 Nov. 1876 in FO 78/2504.

114. This paragraph is based on the following sources: on Nubar's appointments, see Schölch, *Egypt*, p. 59; on Mubarak's appointments, see *WM*, no. 793, 19 M 1296/13 Jan. 1879; on Wilson's and de Blignières's appointments, see ibid., no. 792, 14 M 1296/7 Jan. 1879; ibid., no. 795, 4 S 1296/26 Jan. 1879; Malet/Granville, no. 94, 27 Feb. 1882, in FO 78/3435; Schölch, *Egypt*, p. 85.

115. Mubarak, *al-Khitat*, vol. 9, p. 55; Blunt, *Egypt*, p. 34.

116. Keay, *Spoiling the Egyptians*, p. 48; on the removal of the *ma'mur* of Aswan, See Borg/Lascelles, no. 32, 19 Oct. 1878; Nubar/Lascelles, no. 642, 23 Nov. 1878, in FO 141/121.

117. This paragraph is based on the following sources: on the abolition of the Cairo governorate, see *WM*, no. 794, 26 M 1296/19 Jan. 1879; on the reorganization of the Ministry of Public Works, see extract from *Moniteur égyptien* in Vivian/Salisbury, no. 13, 8 Jan. 1879, in FO 78/2998; on the abolition of the Inspectorate of lower Egypt, see *WMC*, box 1, dossier "al-Idara"; *WM*, no. 777, 10 N 1295/8 Sept. 1878; Sami, pt. 3, vol. 3, p. 1292; on the abolition of the Inspectorate of upper Egypt, see *WM*, no. 794, 26 M 1296/19 Jan. 1879; Sami, pt. 3, vol. 3, p. 1457.

118. Wilson, *Chapters*, p. 182.

119. Vivian/Salisbury, no. 422, 14 Dec. 1878, in FO 78/2858; ibid., no. 65, 21 Feb. 1879, in FO 78/2998.

120. Lascelles/Salisbury, no. 314, 14 Sept. 1878; ibid., no. 325, 18 Sept. 1878, in FO 78/2857.

121. Ibid., no. 303, 6 Sept. 1878, in FO 78/2857. The following is based on McCoan, *Egypt Under Ismail*, pp. 238–39.

122. Mubarak, *al-Khitat*, vol. 9, p. 14; ibid., vol. 15, p. 34.

123. *MM*, no. 11927, *Mudad istikhdam Hasan al-Shari'i Basha*; Zakhura, *Mir'at al-asr*, vol. 2, p. 260.

124. Schölch, *Egypt*, p. 75.

125. Ibid., pp. 75–76.

126. G. Fahmi, *Souvenirs*, pp. 86–87.

127. This paragraph is based on: Schölch, *Egypt*, pp. 76–77; al-Rafi'i, *Asr Ismail*, vol. 2, p. 158; Sami, pt. 3, vol. 3, p. 1432, extract from *WM*, no. 688, 1 DH 1293/18 Dec. 1876; Vivian/Derby, no. 115, 4 May 1877, in FO 78/2632.

128. This paragraph is based on: Schölch, *Egypt*, pp. 78–80; al-Rafi'i, *Asr Ismail*, vol. 2, pp. 159–62.

129. Schölch, *Egypt*, p. 80.

130. Vivian/Salisbury, no. 422, 14 Dec. 1878, in FO 78/2858; Wilson, *Chapters*, p. 182.

131. Vivian/Salisbury, no. 24, 18 Jan. 1879, in FO 78/2998.

132. Borg/Vivian, no. 1, 18 Feb. 1879, in FO 141/128.

133. al-Rafi'i, *Asr Ismail*, vol. 2, p. 162.

134. De Blignières's report is found in *WMC*, no. 18, dossier "al-Majalis"; *WM*, no. 794, 26 M 1296/20 Jan. 1879; for the clash between de Blignières and the Chamber, see Schölch, *Egypt*, p. 81.

135. Schölch, *Egypt*, pp. 82–83; see also al-Rafi'i, *Asr Ismail*, vol. 2, pp. 162–64.

136. Schölch, *Egypt*, pp. 83–84.

137. See Vivian/Salisbury, no. 437, 21 Dec. 1878, in FO 78/2858; ibid., no. 15, 10 Jan. 1879; ibid., no. 21, 11 Jan. 1879, in FO 78/2998.

138. Ibid., no. 57, 15 Feb. 1879, in FO 78/2998; *WM*, no. 794, 26 M 1296/20 Jan. 1879.

139. Vivian/Salisbury, no. 57, 15 Feb. 1879, in FO 78/2998; see also Cromer, *Modern Egypt*, vol. 1, pp. 70–71.

140. The following two paragraphs are based on Schölch, *Egypt*, pp. 65–69.

141. Vivian/Salisbury, no. 61, 19 Feb. 1879, in FO 78/2998.

142. Ibid., no. 79, 26 Feb. 1879, in FO 78/2998.

143. Cromer, *Modern Egypt*, vol. 1, pp. 87–88.

144. This paragraph is based on: Wilson, *Chapters*, pp. 187, 190; Vivian/Salisbury, nos. 63, 65, 79, 82, 83; 20, 21, 26, 27 Feb. 1879, in FO 78/2998; Cromer, *Modern Egypt*, vol. 1, pp. 94–96; Vivian/Salisbury, no. 128, 15 Mar. 1879, in FO 78/2999.

145. This paragraph is based on: Vivian/Salisbury, no. 94, 2 Mar. 1879; ibid., no. 96, 3 Mar. 1879, in FO 78/2999.

146. This paragraph is based on: Cromer, *Modern Egypt*, vol. 1, p. 89; Schölch, *Egypt*, p. 71; Vivian/Salisbury, no. 110, 10 Mar. 1879, in FO 78/2999; Cromer, *Modern Egypt*, vol. 1, p. 97.

147. This paragraph is based on: Schölch, *Egypt*, pp. 71–72; Vivian/Salisbury, no. 117, 13 Mar. 1879; ibid., no. 119, 14 Mar. 1879; ibid., nos. 124 and 127, 15 Mar. 1879, in FO 78/2999.

148. Vivian/Salisbury, no. 117, 13 Mar. 1879; ibid., no. 141, 20 Mar. 1879; ibid., no. 130, 17 Mar. 1879, in FO 78/2999; Schölch, *Egypt*, p. 72.

149. Lascelles/Salisbury, no. 151, 22 Mar. 1879, in FO 78/2999.

150. This paragraph is based on: Cromer, *Modern Egypt*, vol. 1, pp. 88, 117–21; Mc-Coan, *Egypt Under Ismail*, pp. 256–57; Wilson, *Chapters*, p. 191.

151. Cromer, *Modern Egypt*, vol. 1, p. 98.

152. Lascelles/Salisbury, no. 163, 30 Mar. 1879, in FO 78/2999; see also Cromer, *Modern Egypt*, vol. 1, pp. 98–99.

153. See Lascelles/Salisbury, no. 187, 7 Apr. 1879; ibid., no. 201, 9 Apr. 1879, in FO 78/3000.

154. al-Rafiʿi, *Asr Ismail*, vol. 2, pp. 181–91.

155. Schölch, *Egypt*, pp. 80–81.

156. Vivian/Salisbury, no. 21, 11 Jan. 1879, in FO 78/2998; Schölch, *Egypt*, p. 90; see also al-Rafiʿi, *Asr Ismail,* vol. 2, p. 180.

157. This paragraph is based on: Schölch, *Egypt*, pp. 86–87; and al-Rafiʿi, *Asr Ismail*, vol. 2, pp. 178–80.

158. Letter from Vivian, in Lascelles/Salisbury, no. 228, 15 Apr. 1879, in FO 78/3000; Schölch, *Egypt*, p. 86.

159. This paragraph is based on Schölch, *Egypt*, pp. 88–90.

160. This paragraph is based on: ibid., pp. 90–91.

161. This paragraph is based on the following sources: on the support by Turkish *dhawat*, see Lascelles/Salisbury, no. 180, 4 Apr. 1879, in FO 78/3000; Vivian/Salisbury, no. 273, 10 May 1879, in FO 78/3001; on the support of *ulama*, see Lascelles/Salisbury, no. 175, 1 Apr. 1879; ibid., no. 191, 8 Apr. 1879, in FO 78/3000; on press support, see al-Rafiʿi, *Asr Ismail*, vol. 2, p. 159; Keddie, *Jamal ad-Din*, p. 98; on the work of the al-Muwaylihi brothers, see ibid., pp. 101, 116; Schölch, *Egypt*, p. 88; Sabry, *La genèse*, p. 146.

162. This paragraph is based on: Lascelles/Salisbury, no. 189, 7 Apr. 1879; ibid., no. 180, 4 Apr. 1879, in FO 78/3000; Schölch, *Egypt*, pp. 88–89.

163. Vivian/Salisbury, no. 526, 4 May 1879; ibid., no. 290, 16 May 1879, in FO 78/3001; Keay, *Spoiling the Egyptians*, p. 66.

164. Schölch, *Egypt*, pp. 85–86.

165. Ibid., p. 92.

166. This paragraph is based on ibid., pp. 93–94; Cromer, *Modern Egypt*, vol. 1, pp. 132–33; Lascelles/Salisbury, no. 204, 10 Apr. 1879, in FO 78/3000.

167. Schölch, *Egypt*, p. 94; Lascelles/Salisbury, no. 251, 27 Apr. 1879, in FO 78/3000.

168. Vivian/Salisbury, no. 341, 8 June 1879, in FO 78/3002.

169. Schölch, *Egypt*, p. 96.

170. Vivian/Salisbury, unnumbered, 14 June 1879; ibid., no. 368, 19 June 1879, in FO 78/3002.

171. This paragraph is based on: Schölch, *Egypt*, pp. 94–97; al-Rafiʿi, *Asr Ismail*, vol. 2, pp. 194–200.

172. This paragraph is based on: Schölch, *Egypt*, pp. 96–97; Kedourie, *Afghani*, pp. 25–26, 28.

173. Vivian/Salisbury, no. 338, 7 June 1879, in FO 78/3002.
174. Schölch, *Egypt*, p. 96.
175. Vivian/Salisbury, unnumbered 14 June 1879; ibid., no. 365, 18 June 1879, in FO 78/3002; Schölch, *Egypt*, p. 96.
176. This and what follows is based on: Schölch, *Egypt*, pp. 97-99; Cromer, *Modern Egypt*, vol. 1, pp. 139-42; Bell, *Khedives*, pp. 31-35; Dicey, *Khedivate*, pp. 218-20.

▲▲▲
GLOSSARY

ab'adiya	Uncultivated lands granted to notables, high officials, and others.
afandis, afandi	Honorific title of respect taken by Egyptian government employees; a Turkish word, written *efendi* in Turkish.
al-awqaf (sing. *waqf)*	Charitable endowments for pious or public purposes.
alim (pl. *ulama*)	Muslim scholar trained in religious law & science; some served as local judges
aliq	Fodder for horses.
amin	Salaried tax agent under the Ottomans.
amir	Title held by leading mamluk officers.
ayn (pl. *ayan*)	"Notable," local or communal leader.
'ayn al-sawab	"Source of all truth" (honorific title for ruler).
Azhar	Famous Muslim theological seminary and university in Cairo, founded in 973 A.D.
badal ta'yin	Food allowances given to officials.
al-bahri	Lower Egypt (see also *al-qibli*).
bandar	Provincial capital where governor lived.
bashmu'awin	Chief assistant; director-in-chief, viceregal cabinet.
bashmutarjim	Chief translator or interpreter.
bayt	Mamluk household.
bey	Title held by leading mamluk officials; later a title of honor in state service.
bikbashi	Major (in military hierarchy); in Turkish, written *binbashi* (head of thousand); also given to civil official of fourth rank.
daira	Office or agency set up to administer estates of individual members of viceregal family.
Daira Saniya; the *Daira*	Central office for management of estates and properties belonging to members of the viceregal family

	(the *dairas* of individual family members were sometimes appended to this office, sometimes were independent of it).
al-dhawat	Upper class or aristocracy; in nineteenth-century Egypt, persons of high state rank.
diwan	State department or administrative office.
Diwan al-Abniya	Office of Construction and Repair (under Muhammad Ali).
Diwan al-Ashghal	Department of Public Works, estab. 1864.
Diwan al-Dakhiliya	Department of Interior, estab. 1857
Diwan al-Katkhuda	Office of Viceroy's First Lieutenant.
Diwan al-Khidiwi	Another name for *al-Diwan al-Mulki*, or Department of Civil Affairs.
Diwan al-Mulki	Department of Civil Affairs.
Diwan Umum al-Taftish	Department of Inspection.
faddan	Unit of land measurement, equivalent to 1.038 acres.
fallahin	Peasant cultivators.
firman	Imperial Ottoman decree.
ghafir	Village watchman.
hakim al-khutt	Head of subdistrict.
hijaz	Mountainous region in western Arabia.
hijra	Muslim era, beginning with Muhammad's emigration from Mecca to Madina in 622 A.D.—year one of the Muslim calendar.
hisabat	"Accounts"; also refers to an office of accounting.
hissa	A section or part of a village.
hubb al-watan	Love of country.
al-Hukuma al-Saniya	Viceregal government.
ihsan	A gift from the ruler.
iltizam, iltizamat	A tax farm of revenue-producing land; the source of mamluk wealth and power; confiscated in 1811–14 by Muhammad Ali.
imam	Muslim prayer leader.
izba	Hamlet where field hands who worked the great estates lived.
al-intisab	Personal connections.
al-Jamʿiya al-Wataniya	Designation for political party formed in 1879.
jurnal	Daily report presented by an administration to a household official in order to facilitate viceregal control (under Muhammad Ali).
kashif	Subordinate to Turkish *nazir*, or governor general.
katib	Scribe.
Katib Arabi	Clerk of Arabic documents.
katkhuda	First lieutenant of the viceroy under Muhammad Ali and Abbas.

kharaj	Land tax established by Muhammad Ali.
kharajiya property	Land paying the *kharaj* tax; according to 1858 law, the state could requisition these lands for public use without compensating their owners, who were mostly small peasant proprietors.
al-khassa	The viceroy's private office for the administration of his estates and other properties.
khatib	Muslim preacher.
khawli	Supervisor of agricultural lands.
khaznadar	Chief treasurer.
khedive	Although used informally earlier, a title officially granted to Ismail in 1867 to assure him a higher status than that of previous Ottoman governors; from Persian word meaning lord, master, god.
khutt	Subdistrict of a province.
kiswa	Official uniform.
lawaʾih (sing. *laʾiha*)	Laws, statutes.
madani	Civil, as opposed to military.
madrasa (pl. *madaris*)	Secondary school.
mahafiz al-abhath	Collections of copies of orders and documents from various archival sources.
al-maʿiya al-saniya	Viceregal entourage or cabinet.
majlis	Council or court.
Majlis al-Ahkam, or *Majlis al-Ahkam al-Misriya*	Council of Justice (or Supreme Court)—along with the Privy Council *(Majlis Khususi)* one of the two main, conciliar bodies of the period 1849–1879.
majlis baladi	Administrative council in a provincial capital.
majlis daʿawi al-balad	Village-level court.
Majlis daʿawi al-bandar	Court located in a provincial capital.
Majlis ibtidaʾi	Court of first instance (estab. during Abbas's reign).
Majlis idarat mash-yakhat al-balad	Village administrative council.
majlis istiʾnaf	Appeals court.
Majlis Khususi	Privy Council.
Majlis al-Nuzzar	Council of Ministers (estab. 1878).
Majlis Shura al-Nuwwab	Consultative Chamber of Delegates (or the Chamber), estab. 1866.
Majlis taftish al-ziraʿa	One of a number of agricultural councils founded in 1869.
Majlis al-Urfi	Council established in 1882.

maktab (pl. *makatib*)	Primary school.
Maktab al-Khanka	Primary school for male children of the Muhammad Ali family.
al-Mamlaka al-Misriya	Ismail's "Egyptian kingdom."
mamluk, Mamluk	Originally a white male slave of non-Arab extraction (from southern Russia) recruited to fight in a *corps d'élite* of Turkish slave-soldiers who served under the Ayyubids (1169–1250). By the thirteenth century, the Mamluks had reached positions of power and ruled Egypt until the Ottoman conquest of 1517; after 1517 this ruling caste disappeared, but Ottoman military commanders continued to recruit white male slaves for their armies. By the seventeenth century these mamluks organized themselves into powerful groups that eventually took over the state. The mamluks were crushed as a political force by Muhammad Ali by 1811.
ma'mur	Head of a unit of provincial administration.
ma'mur al-idara	Administrative chief.
ma'muriya	Unit of provincial administration.
markaz	Synonymous with *ma'muriya;* a unit of provincial administration.
mashrabiya	Wooden latticework on Egyptian buildings.
maslaha	Administration.
mawkib	Cortège (as: the viceroy's cortège).
mir alay	Designation given to civil officials of second rank, second grade; also means colonel; in Arabic, written *amir alay.*
mir al-liwa	Designation given to civil officials of second rank, first grade; also means brigadier general; in Arabic, written *amir al-liwa.*
mirmiran	Designation given to officials of the first civil rank (*al-rutba al-ula*).
mu'awin (pl. *mu'awinun*)	Assistant(s) to provincial officials; aides.
mudir	Governor of a province or director of a state department; title emerged under Muhammad Ali.
mudiriya	Province.
mufattish	Inspector.
Mufattish Umum	Inspector General; head of Office of Inspectorate.
muhafaza	Reward.
muhafiz	Governor of governorate.
muhafiza	Governorate (not under jurisdiction of a province).
muhtasib	Market inspector in Cairo and Alexandria.
muhurdar	Keeper of the seal.

multazim	Tax-farmer (one holding an *iltizam*).
mulki	Civil affairs.
muqabala	Land tax measure issued in 1871 to reduce Egypt's debt.
muwazzafun	Junior state employees.
nazir al-qism	District chief.
Nizam Jadid	"New Order," an army organized in 1820 by Muhammad Ali, consisting first of black Sudanese slaves, then of Egyptian conscripts; despite its deficiencies, an improved military force enabling Muhammad Ali to make significant military advances.
nizara	Department of state.
octroi (Fr.)	Tax levied on commodities entering a town.
qadi	Judge in Muslim courts
qaʾim maqam	Administrator of a number of villages; also lieutenant colonel; designation given to civil officials of the third rank.
qalam	Office.
qanun (pl. *qawanin*)	Administrative law(s).
al-qibli	Upper Egypt.
qism	District of a province.
rutba ula	First civil rank.
Ruznama	Executive department of Ottoman treasury.
saghqul aghasi	Adjutant major; designation given to civil official of fifth rank.
Sahib al-Izza	Honorific title for bey.
Sahib al-Saʿada	Honorific title for pasha.
Saʿid	The southernmost part of Egypt.
salamlik	Parlor; sitting room.
sarraf	Tax collector; treasurer.
sarraf pasha	Chief treasurer or banker.
shaflik	Land owned by the viceroy and his family; a Turkish word, spelled *çiftlik* in Turkish.
sharia	The revealed or canonical law of Islam.
sharia court	Court applying Islamic law, presided over by *qadi*.
shaykh	Chief or leader.
shaykh al-balad	Village leader or mayor.
shaykh al-hissa	Notable with administrative responsibility for a section of a village.
shilla	Gang; brotherhood; fraternity; group; used in this work to mean a temporary alliance among equals.
Taftish	Inspectorate.
Tanzimat	Reform measures issued in Istanbul and applied in various parts of the Ottoman empire, 1839–1876.
taqarir	Resolutions passed by the Privy Council.
taqsit	Title deed to land.

tasarruf	Right of free disposal of landed property.
tashrifati	Grand master of ceremonies.
uhda	Land (containing villages) conceded by ruler to an individual who guaranteed the payment of its taxes.
ulama (sing. *alim*)	Muslim scholars and theologians trained in religious law and science; some served as local judges.
ushr	A tithe levied in 1854 by Sa'id.
ushuriya	Land paying the *ushr* tax and held in full private ownership.
wakil	Deputy.
wali	Ottoman viceroy.
Wali al-Ni'am	"Great Benefactor," title given to Muhammad Ali.
waqf (pl. *al-awqaf*)	Endowment given for religious or charitable purpose.
waqfiya	Endowment deed of a *waqf*.
warsha	Workshop.
watan	Fatherland.
wirku tax	General professional tax; a Turkish word, spelled *vergu* in Turkish.
ziyadat al-masaha	Unregistered and unsurveyed lands.

▲▲▲
BIBLIOGRAPHY

I have used my style of transliteration for Arabic words and have modified the titles of published works accordingly, except in cases where this would have significantly altered the spelling.

▲▲▲ PRIMARY SOURCES

EGYPTIAN ARCHIVAL SOURCES (CAIRO)

Dar al-Kutub (Egyptian National Library):
al-Waqa'i' al-Misriya, 1245–1300/1829–1883. Issues of the *Egyptian Gazette*. During the time of my research (1968–1970), the Egyptian National Archives also contained typescript copies of this newspaper.

Dar al-Mahfuzat al-Umumiya archives:
Milaffat al-mustakhdamin wa udhun rabt al-ma' ashat al-mulkiya, 1830–1948. Pension dossiers for retired officials and the heirs *(waratha)* of deceased officials, containing employment records and information on the families of state functionaries.

Dar al-Watha'iq al-Qawmiya (Egyptian National Archives):
Arshif Ifranji (Archives européenes). *al-Mutafarriqat. Ahd Muhammad Ali, Ibrahim, Abbas, wa Sa'id* (30 boxes). *Ahd Ismail* (45 boxes). Government correspondence and other Egyptian state documents written in French. This collection also contains copies of dispatches from the archives of major Western countries.
Mahafiz al-Abhath al-mawjuda bi-Dar al-Watha'iq. A large collection comprising 155 boxes of dossiers containing copies of reports, decrees, statutes, organic laws, and information on members of the viceregal family and other prominent personalities. The subject index *(kashf)* lists these boxes by number and the dossiers by title. Box 137 of this collection contains the Organic Law of 1837.
Masadir wa tarikh Misr. Collection of materials copied or translated from the Turkish and Arabic registers of the *Ma'iya Saniya, Daira Saniya, Majlis Khususi* and other important holdings; arranged by subject.
Mulakhkhasat dafatir Diwan al-Ma'iya al-Saniya. Arabic summaries and translations from the registers of the viceregal cabinet; most are viceregal orders.
Taqasit al-Ruznama. Title deeds and registration certificates for lands held by officials and others. This collection is formed principally of three smaller collections listed under the generic title *al-Hujaj al-Shar'iya*. This collection also contains the

Dhawat Land Register, whose full title is *Daftar zimam atyan ushuriya: Dhawat.* *Raqm al-sijill:* 1343, *min* 15 D 1264/13 Oct. 1848 *ila* 6 R 1287/6 June 1870.

al-Waqa'i' al-Misriya Collection. Boxes of dossiers arranged by subject and containing copies of articles from the *Egyptian Gazette* between 1828 and 1880.

Wizarat al-awqaf (Ministry of Charitable Endowments):
Collections of deeds of endowment *(waqfiyas)* housed in the basement *(al-Daftarkhana)* and roof archives of this ministry. Endowments are indexed in registers by donor. References to these documents contain the number of the register *(sijill)*, and all other pertinent data, including the number of the title deed (also called *al-hujja)* and name of donor.

BRITISH ARCHIVAL SOURCES (LONDON)

Public Record Office:
Foreign Office dispatches and other correspondence from series 78 and 141. A document entitled "Etat nominatif des fonctionnaires européens au service du gouvernement égyptien" (in FO 78/3436) provided the data for table 14.

PAPERS, REPORTS, MEMORANDA, AND MEMOIRS

Abbate Pacha. *Seance solennelle pour Riaz Pacha, dans la Salle du conseil legislatif.* Cairo: n.p., 1911. Mimeographed.

Bowring, John. "Report on Egypt and Candia." In FO 78/381.

Brocchi, G. B. "Divisions administratives de l'Egypte." 9 July 1824, in box 152, *al-Mutafarriqat, AI.*

Campbell, Mr. "Report on Egypt." Appended to Campbell/Palmerston, unnumbered, 6 July 1840, in FO 78/408B.

Cave, Stephen. "Memorandum on the Financial Position of Egypt and on Measures for Restoring Its Credit." In FO 78/2539A.

Code of Abbas (Code d'Abbass). Enclosure in Ch. Murray/Palmerston, no. 7, 24 Mar. 1851, in FO 78/875.

Hekekyan Papers, MSS 37448-71. Papers, including the diary, of Joseph Hekekyan. British Museum, London.

Murray, Ch. "Note sur les pachas d'Egypte." In Murray/Palmerston, no. 1, 1 Jan. 1847, in FO 78/707.

Sha'rawi, Huda. Memoirs of the daughter of Muhammad Sultan Pasha and leader of the movement for female emancipation in Egypt. Manuscript currently in the possession of Mrs. Margot Farranto Badran, formerly of St. Antony's College, Oxford.

Zaki, Ahmad. *Un mot sur Riaz Pacha.* Speech followed by a biography of Riyad, presented in Cairo, 1911. Mimeographed.

OFFICIAL EGYPTIAN PUBLICATIONS AND EDITED DOCUMENTS

Commission de la caisse spéciale de la dette publique d'Egypte. *Compte rendu du 10 juin 1876 au 10 janvier 1877.* 2nd ed. Alexandria: Imprimerie du commerce, 1879.

Commission supérieure d'enquête. *Rapport préliminaire addressé à S. A. le khedive.* Cairo: n.p., 1878.

Gelat, Phillippe. *Répertoire général annoté de la legislation et de l'administration égyptiennes, 1840-1908.* Vol. 3, pt. 1. Alexandria: Lagoudakis, 1909.

Jallad, Filib. *Qamus al-idara wa al-qada* [Dictionary of Administration and Justice]. 7 vols. Alexandria: al-Matba'a al-Bukhariya, 1890-1896.

Ministère des Finances. *Dictionnaire geographique de l'Egypte.* Cairo: Imprimerie Nationale, 1890.

————. *Rapport sur l'organization de la compatabilité dans les provinces par G. Fitzgerald.* Cairo: Delbos -Demouret, Jablin, 1878.

Ministère de l'intérieur. *Recensement général de l'Egypte.* 2 vols. Cairo: Imprimerie Nationale, 1884–1885.

Muhammad Ali, Prince. *Majmuʿat Khitabat wa Awamir Khassa al-Maghfur lahu Abbas Basha al-Awwal* [A Collection of Speeches and Orders of the Late Abbas Pasha the First]. Cairo, n.p., n.d.

Régny, E. de. *Statistique de l'Egypte d'après des documents officiels.* Alexandria: Imprimerie Française Moures, 1871.

Sami, Amin. *Taqwim al-Nil* [Calendar of the Nile]. 3 pts. Cairo: al-Matbaʿa al-Amiriya and Dar al-Kutub al-Misriya, 1916–1936.

Wizarat al-thaqafa wa al-irshad al-qawmi [Ministry of Culture and National Guidance]. *Diwan al-Maʿiya al-Saniya. al-Sijill al-Awwal* (8 July 1829–23 Dec. 1830). Cairo: al-Matbaʿa al-ʿAlamiya, 1960.

▲▲▲ SECONDARY SOURCES

Abbas Hamid, Rauf. *al-Nizam al-ijtimaʿi fi Misr fi zill al-milkiyat ziraʿiya al-kabira 1837–1914* [The Social Order in Egypt Under Large Agricultural Estates]. Cairo: Dar al-Fikr al-Hadith, 1973.

Abd al-Karim, Ahmad Izzat. *Tarikh al-taʿlim fi asr Muhammad Ali* [History of Education in the Age of Muhammad Ali]. Cairo: al-Nahda al-Misriya, 1938.

————. *Tarikh al-taʿlim fi Misr min nihayat hukm Muhammad Ali ila awaʾil hukm Tawfiq, 1848–1882* [History of Education in Egypt from the End of the Reign of Muhammad Ali to the Beginning of the Reign of Tawfiq]. 2 vols. Cairo: Matbaʿ at al-Nasr, 1945.

Abd al-Karim, Muhammad. *Ali Mubarak: Hayatuhu wa Maʾathiruhu* [Ali Mubarak: His Life and Accomplishments]. Cairo: Mutbaʿat al-Risala, n.d.

Abd al-Rahim, Abd al-Rahim Abd al-Rahman. *al-Rif al-misri fi al-qarn al-thamin ashar* [The Egyptian Countryside in the Eighteenth Century]. Cairo: Ayn Shams University Press, 1974.

Abdel-Malek, Anouar. *Idéologie et renaissance nationale: L'Egypte moderne.* Paris: Editions Anthropos, 1969.

About, Edmond. *Le Fellah: Souvenirs d'Egypte.* 3rd ed. Paris: Hachette, 1873.

Abu-Lughod, Ibrahim. "The Transformation of the Egyptian Elite: Prelude to the Urabi Revolt." *Middle East Journal* 21 (1967): 325–44.

Abu-Lughod, Janet. *Cairo: 1001 Years of the City Victorious.* Princeton, N.J.: Princeton University Press, 1971.

Ahmed, Jamal Mohammed. *The Intellectual Origins of Egyptian Nationalism.* London: Oxford University Press, 1960.

Amédée, Sacré, and Louis Outrebon. *L'Egypte et Ismail Pacha.* Paris: J. Hetzel, 1865.

Amici Bey, F. *L'Egypte ancienne et moderne et son dernier recensement.* Alexandria: V. Penasson, 1884.

Amin, Ahmad. *Zuama al-islah fi al-asr al-hadith* [Leaders of Reform in the Modern Period]. Cairo: al-Nahda al-Misriya, 1948.

Amin, Samir. *Accumulation on a World Scale: A Critique of the Theory of Underdevelopment.* New York: Monthly Review, 1974.

Anderson, Perry. *The Lineages of the Absolutist State.* London: New Left Books, 1974.

Archarouni, Victoria. *Nubar Pacha: Un grand serviteur de l'Egypte, 1825–1899.* N.p., n.d. [1948?].

Artin, Yacoub. "Artin Bey." *Revue d'Egypte* [Cairo], Nov. 1895, pp. 1–9.

————. "Essai sur les causes du renchérissement de la vie matérielle au Caire dans le courant du XIX^{e}siècle, 1800 à 1907." *Mémories de l'Institut égyptien* 5 (1908): 57–140.

————. *The Right of Landed Property in Egypt.* Trans. Edward Abbott Van Dyck. London: Wyman, 1883.

Ayalon, D. "Studies in al-Jabarti I. Notes on the Transformation of Mamluk Society in Egypt Under the Ottomans." *Journal of the Economic and Social History of the Orient* 3 (1960): 275–325.

Ayubi, Nazih N. M. *Bureaucracy and Politics in Contemporary Egypt.* London: Ithaca Press, 1980.

al-Ayyubi, Ilyas. *Tarikh Misr fi ahd al-Khidiwi Ismail Basha min sanat 1863 ila sanat 1879* [History of Egypt in the Time of Khedive Ismail from 1863 to 1879]. 2 vols. Cairo: Dar al-Kutub al-Misriya, 1923.

Baer, Gabriel. *A History of Landownership in Modern Egypt, 1800–1950.* London: Oxford University Press, 1962.

————. *Egyptian Guilds in Modern Times.* Jerusalem: Israel Oriental Society, 1964.

————. *Studies in the Social History of Modern Egypt.* Chicago: University of Chicago Press, 1969.

Barakat, Ali. *Tatawwur al-milkiya al-zira'iya fi Misr wa atharuhu ala al-haraka al-siyasiya, 1813–1914* [The Development of Agricultural Property in Egypt and Its Influence on the Political Movement]. Cairo: Dar al-Thaqafa al-Jadida, 1977.

Bell, Charles Frederic Moberly. *Khedives and Pashas: Sketches of Contemporary Egyptian Rulers and Statesmen.* London: Sampson Low, Marston, Searle, and Rivington, 1884.

Bendix, Reinhard. *Max Weber: An Intellectual Portrait.* London: Methuen, 1966.

Benis, Adam Georges. *Une mission militaire polonaise en Egypte.* Cairo: Société royale de géographie d'Egypte, 1938.

Berger, Morroe. *Bureaucracy and Society in Modern Egypt.* Princeton, N.J.: Princeton University Press, 1957.

————. *Military Elite and Social Change: Egypt since Napoleon.* Princeton, N.J.: Wilson School of Public and International Affairs, 1960.

Berque, Jacques. *L'Egypte: Impérialisme et révolution.* Paris: Gallimard, 1967.

Bertrand, Emile. *Nubar Pacha, 1825–1899.* Cairo: le Journal *L'Egypte*, 1904.

Binder, Leonard. *In a Moment of Enthusiasm: Political Power and the Second Stratum in Egypt.* Chicago: University of Chicago Press, 1978.

Blignières, M. de. *Le contrôle anglo-français en Egypte.* Paris: Quantin, 1882.

Blunt, Wilfred Scawen. *Secret History of the English Occupation of Egypt.* 1922; rpt. New York: Howard Fertig, 1967.

Bouvier, J. "Les interêts financiers et la question d'Egypte." *Revue Historique* 224 (1960): 75–104.

Brinton, Jasper Yeates. *The Mixed Courts of Egypt.* 2nd ed. New Haven, Conn.: Yale University Press, 1968.

Brown, L. Carl. *The Tunisia of Ahmad Bey, 1837–1855.* Princeton, N.J.: Princeton University Press, 1974.

Butler, Alfred J. *Court Life in Egypt.* London: Chapman and Hall, 1887.

Cadalvene, Ed. de, and J. de Breuvery. *L'Egypte et la Turquie de 1829 à 1836.* 2 vols. Paris: Bertrand, 1836.

Cattaui, Rene. *Le règne de Mohamed Aly d'après les archives russes en Egypte.* 3 vols. Cairo and Rome: Société royale de géographie d'Egypte, 1931–1936.

Centre national de la recherche scientifique. *L'Egypte au XIXe siècle.* Paris: Imprimerie Louis Jean, 1982.

Clot, Antoine B. *Aperçu général sur l'Egypte.* 2 vols. Paris: Fortin, Masson, 1840.

Collins, Jeffrey Garden. "The Egyptian Elite Under Cromer." Ph.D. diss., University of California, Los Angeles, 1981.
Colvin, Aukland. *The Making of Modern Egypt*. London: T. Nelson, 1906.
Combe, Etienne, Jacques Bainville, and Edouard Driault. *L'Egypte ottomane, l'expedition française en Egypte et le règne de Mohamed-Aly (1517–1849)*. Volume 3 of *Précis de l'histoire d'Egypte par divers historiens et archéologues*. Cairo: L'Institut français d'archéologie orientale du Caire, 1933.
Crabites, Pierre. *Ismail the Maligned Khedive*. London: George Routledge, 1933.
Crecelius, Daniel. "The Ulama and the State in Modern Egypt." Ph.D. diss., Princeton University, 1967.
————. *The Roots of Modern Egypt: A Study of the Regimes of Ali Bey al-Kabir and Muhammad Bey Abu al-Dhahab, 1760–1775*. Chicago: Bibliotheca Islamica, 1982.
Cromer, Earl of. *Modern Egypt*. 2 vols. London: Macmillan, 1908.
Darwish, Hasan Muhammad. *al-Wizarat al-Misriya fi zill hukm al-usra al-ulwiya* [Egyptian Ministries Under the Rule of the Muhammad Ali Dynasty]. Cairo: Matbaʿat al-Ibtihaj, 1924.
Davis, Eric. *Challenging Colonialism: Bank Misr and Egyptian Industrialization, 1920–1941*. Princeton, N.J.: Princeton University Press, 1983.
Delanoue, Gilbert. *Moralistes et politiques musulmans dans l'Egypte du XIXème siècle, 1798–1882*. Lille: University of Lille, 1980.
Deny, J. *Sommaire des archives turques du Caire*. Cairo: Société royale de géographie d'Egypte, 1930.
Dicey, Edward. "Our Route to India." *Nineteenth Century* 1 (1877): 665–85.
————. *The Story of the Khedivate*. London: Rivington, 1902.
Dodwell, Henry. *The Founder of Modern Egypt: A Study of Muhammad Ali*. 1931; rpt. Cambridge: Cambridge University Press, 1967.
Domínguez, Jorge I. *Insurrection or Loyalty: The Breakdown of the Spanish-American Empire*. Cambridge, Mass.: Harvard University Press, 1980.
Douin, Georges. *L'Egypte de 1828 à 1830: Correspondance des consuls de France en Egypte*. Rome: Société royale de géographie d'Egypte, 1935.
————. *Histoire du règne du Khédive Ismail*. 3 vols. Rome and Cairo: Société royale de géographie d'Egypte, 1933–1941.
————. *La mission du Baron de Boislecomte: L'Egypte et la Syrie en 1833*. Cairo: Société royale de géographie d'Egypte, 1927.
————. *Une mission militaire française auprès de Mohamed Aly: Correspondance des Generaux Belliard et Boyer*. Cairo: Société royale de géographie d'Egypte, 1923.
Dozy, Reinhart. *Supplément aux dictionnaires Arabes*. Leiden: E. J. Brill, 1881.
Dykstra, Darrell Ivan. "A Biographical Study in Egyptian Modernization: Ali Mubarak (1823/4–1893). Ph.D. diss., University of Michigan, 1977.
Egypt for the Egyptians: A Retrospect and a Prospect. London: Cecil Brooks, 1880.
L'Egypte et l'Europe [par un ancien juge mixte]. 2 vols. Leiden: E. J. Brill, 1884.
Elgood, P. G. *The Transit of Egypt*. London: Edward Arnold, 1928.
Elton, Geoffrey Rudolph. *The Tudor Revolution in Government: Administrative Changes in the Reign of Henry VIII*. Cambridge: Cambridge University Press, 1953.
Fahmi, Gallini. *Souvenirs du Khédive Ismail au Khédive Abbas II*. Cairo: n.p., n.d. [1943?].
Fahmi, Zaki. *Safwat al-asr fi tarikh wa rusum mashahir rijal Misr* [The Best of the Age in the History and Records of Famous Egyptian Men]. Cairo: Matbaʿat al-Iʿtimad, 1926.
Farhi, David. "Nizam-i Cedid—Military Reform in Egypt under Mehmed Ali." *Asian and African Studies* 8 (1972): 151–83.

Farman, Elbert E. *Egypt and Its Betrayal.* New York: Grafton, 1908.

Fikri, Muhammad Amin. *Jughrafiyat Misr* [Geography of Egypt]. Cairo: Wadi al-Nil, 1296/1878–1879.

Findley, Carter V. *Bureaucratic Reform in the Ottoman Empire: The Sublime Porte, 1789–1922.* Princeton, N.J.: Princeton University Press, 1980.

Fu'ad, Faraj Sulayman. *al-Kanz al-thamin li ʿuzamaʾ al-Misriyin* [Valuable Treasure of the Great Egyptians]. Cairo: al-Iʿtimad, 1917.

Gendzier, Irene L. *The Practical Visions of Yaʿqub Sanuʿ.* Cambridge, Mass.: Harvard University Press, 1966.

Gibb, H. A. R., and Harold Bowen. *Islamic Society and the West.* Vol. 1. 1950–57, rpt. London: Oxford University Press, 1962–63.

Gordon, Lady Duff. *Letters from Egypt, 1862–1869.* Reedited by Gordon Waterfield. London: Routledge and Kegan Paul, 1969.

Gran, Peter. *Islamic Roots of Capitalism: Egypt, 1760–1840.* Austin: University of Texas Press, 1979.

Grigorian, Mesrop G. *Armenians in the Service of the Ottoman Empire, 1860–1908.* London: Routledge and Kegan Paul, 1977.

Guémard, Gabriel. *Les réformes en Egypte d'Ali-Bey El Kébir à Mehemet-Ali, 1760–1848.* Cairo: Paul Barbey, 1936.

Hamont, P. N. *L'Egypte sous Méhémet-Ali.* 2 vols. Paris: Léauty et Lecointe, 1843.

Hamza, Abdel-Maksud. *The Public Debt of Egypt, 1854–1876.* Cairo: Government Press, 1944.

Heaphey, J. "The Organization of Egypt: Inadequacies of a Non-political Model for Nation-Building." *World Politics* 18 (1966): 177–93.

Hermassi, Elbaki. *Leadership and National Development in North Africa: A Comparative Study.* Berkeley and Los Angeles: University of California Press, 1972.

Heyworth-Dunne, James. *An Introduction to the History of Education in Modern Egypt.* London: Luzac, 1938.

al-Hitta, Ahmad Ahmad. "The Development of Transport, 1800–1870." In *The Economic History of the Middle East, 1800*–1914, ed. Charles Issawi. Chicago: University of Chicago Press, 1966, pp. 406–15.

Holt, Peter Malcolm. "The Pattern of Egyptian Political History from 1517 to 1798." In *Political and Social Change in Modern Egypt,* ed. P. M. Holt. London: Oxford University Press, 1968, pp. 79–90.

Holt, Peter Malcolm, ed. *Political and Social Change in Modern Egypt.* London: Oxford University Press, 1968.

Holynski, Alexandre. *Nubar-Pacha devant l'histoire.* Paris: E. Dentu, 1886.

Hourani, Albert H. *Arabic Thought in the Liberal Age, 1798–1939.* London: Oxford University Press, 1962.

————. "History." In *The Study of the Middle East: Research and Scholarship in the Humanities and the Social Sciences,* ed. Leonard Binder. New York: John Wiley, 1976, pp. 97–135.

————. "The Middleman in a Changing Society: Syrians in Egypt in the Eighteenth and Nineteenth Centuries." In *The Emergence of the Modern Middle East.* Berkeley and Los Angeles: University of California Press, 1981, pp. 103–23.

————. "Ottoman Reform and the Politics of Notables." In ibid., pp. 36–66.

————. "Some Aspects of Modern Egyptian History." Presented at the Colloquium on Tradition and Change in the Middle East held at Harvard University in Oct. 1969. Mimeographed, St. Antony's College, Oxford University.

Hunter, F. Robert. "The Cairo Archives for the Study of Elites in Modern Egypt." *International Journal of Middle East Studies* 4 (1973): 476–88.

Huseyn Efendi. *Ottoman Egypt in the Age of the French Revolution.* Trans. with introduction and notes by Stanford J. Shaw. Cambridge, Mass.: Harvard University Press, 1964.

Ibn Khaldun, Abd al-Rahman. *The Muqaddimah: An Introduction to History.* Trans. Franz Rosenthal. 3 vols. New York: Pantheon, 1958.

Issa, Hossam M. *Capitalisme et sociétés anonymes en Egypte: Essai sur le rapport entre structure sociale et droit.* Paris: R. Pichon et R. Durand-Auzias, 1970.

Jerrold, Blanchard. *Egypt Under Ismail Pacha.* London: Samuel Tinsley, 1879.

Keay, J. Seymour. *Spoiling the Egyptians: A Tale of Shame.* New York: Putnam, 1882.

Keddie, Nikki R. *Sayyid Jamal an-Din "al-Afghani": A Political Biography.* Berkeley and Los Angeles: University of California Press, 1972.

Kedourie, Elie. *Afghani and Abduh. An Essay on Religious Unbelief and Political Activism in Modern Islam.* London: Frank Cass, 1966.

Kenny, Lorne M. "Ali Mubarak: Nineteenth Century Egyptian Educator and Administrator." *Middle East Journal* 21 (1967): pp. 35–51.

———. "The Khedive Ismail's Dream of Civilization and Progress." *Muslim World* 55 (1965): 142–55, 211–21.

Kremer, Alfred von. *Agypten.* 2 vols. Leipzig: Brockhaus, 1863.

Kuhnke, Laverne. "Early Nineteenth Century Ophthalmological Clinics in Egypt." *Clio Medica* (Vienna) 5 (1972): 209–14.

Kusel, Baron de. *An Englishman's Recollections of Egypt, 1863–1887.* London: John Lane, 1915.

Lacour, Raoul. *L'Egypte d'Alexandrie à la seconde cataracte.* Paris. Hachette, 1871.

Landau, Jacob M. *Jews in Nineteenth Century Egypt.* New York: New York University Press, 1969.

———. "Notes on the Introduction of Ministerial Responsibility into Egypt." *Journal of Modern History* 28 (1956): 21–34.

———. *Parliaments and Parties in Egypt.* Tel Aviv: Israel Oriental Society, 1953.

———. "Prolegomena to a Study of Secret Societies in Modern Egypt." *Middle Eastern Studies* 1 (1965): 135–86.

Landes, David S. *Bankers and Pashas: International Finance and Economic Imperialism in Egypt.* Cambridge, Mass.: Harvard University Press, 1958.

Lane, Edward William. *An Account of the Manners and Customs of the Modern Egyptians.* 1860; rpt. New York: Dover, 1973.

LaPalombara, Joseph, ed. *Bureaucracy and Political Development.* 2nd ed. Princeton, N.J.: Princeton University Press, 1967.

Lapidus, Ira Marvin. *Muslim Cities in the Later Middle Ages.* Cambridge, Mass.: Harvard University Press, 1967.

Leon, Edwin de. *The Khedive's Egypt.* New York: Harper, 1877.

Makhluf, Najib. *Nubar Basha wa ma tamma ala yadihi* [Nubar Pasha and His Achievements]. Cairo: n.p., n.d. [1903?].

Malet, Edward. *Egypt, 1879–1883.* London: John Murray, 1909.

Malortie, Baron de. *Egypt: Native Rulers and Foreign Interference.* 2nd ed. London: William Ridgeway, 1883.

McCoan, J. C. *Egypt As It Is.* London: Cassell Petter and Galprin, 1877.

———. *Egypt Under Ismail: A Romance of History.* London: Chapman and Hall, 1889.

Mengin, Félix. *Histoire de l'Egypte sous le gouvernement de Mohammed-Aly.* 2 vols. Paris: A. Bertrand, 1823.

———. *Histoire sommaire de l'Egypte sous le gouvernement de Mohammed-Aly, 1823–1838.* Paris: Firmin Didot, 1839.

Merruau, M. Paul. *L'Egypte contemporaine de Mehemet-Ali à Said Pacha, 1840–1857.* Paris: Didier, 1858.

Michels, Baron des. *Souvenirs de carrière, 1855–1886.* Paris: Plon-Nourrit, 1901.

Milner, Viscount. *England in Egypt.* 1920; rpt. New York: Howard Fertig, 1970.

Moore, Clement Henry. "Authoritarian Politics in Unincorporated Society—The Case of Nasser's Egypt." *Comparative Politics* 6 (1974): 193–218.

———. *Images of Development: Egyptian Engineers in Search of Industry.* Cambridge, Mass.: MIT Press, 1980.

el-Mouelhy, Ibrahim. "Les Mouelhy en Egypte: Ibrahim el Mouelhy Pacha." *Cahiers d'histoire égyptienne* 2 (1950): 313–28.

———. "Les Mouelhy en Egypte: Mohammed el Mouelhy Bey." *Cahiers d'histoire égyptienne* 6 (1954): 168–79.

Mubarak, Ali. *Alam al-Din.* 4 vols. Alexandria: Matbaʿat Jaridat al-Mahrusa, 1882.

———. *al-Khitat al-Tawfiqiya al-Jadida li-Misr al-Qahira wa muduniha wa biladiha al-qadima wa al-shahira* [New Plans under Tawfiq for Egypt—Cairo, Its (Other) Cities and Towns, Old and New]. 20 vols. Bulaq: al-Matbaʿah al-Kubra al-Amiriya, 1304–1306/1886–1889.

———. *Nukhbat al-Fikr fi tadbir Nil Misr* [The Best Thinking on the Management of the Egyptian Nile]. Cairo: Wadi al-Nil, 1297/1879–1880.

———. *Tariq al-hija wa al-tamrin ala al-qiraʾa fi al-luga al-Arabiya* [The Spelling Method and Exercise in the Reading of the Arabic Language]. Pt. 2. Bulaq: al-Matbaʿah al-Kubra al-Amiriya, 1303/1885–1886.

Mujahid, Zaki Muhammad. *al-Aʿlam al-Sharqiya fi al-miʾa al-rabiʿa ashara al-hijriya* [Prominent Eastern Personalities in the fourteenth Muslim century]. 4 vols. Cairo: Dar al-Tibaʿa al-Misriya al-haditha, 1949–1963.

Mustafa, Ahmed Abdel-Rahim. "The Breakdown of the Monopoly System in Egypt After 1840." In *Political and Social Change in Modern Egypt,* ed. P. M. Holt. London: Oxford University Press, 1968. pp. 291–307.

———. "The Hekekyan Papers." In ibid., pp. 68–75.

Naff, Thomas, and Roger Owen, eds. *Studies in Eighteenth Century Islamic History.* Carbondale: Southern Illinois University Press, 1977.

al-Najjar, Husayn Fawzi. *Ali Mubarak: Abu al-Taʿlim* [Ali Mubarak: The Father of Education]. Cairo: Dar al-Kutub, 1967.

Ninet, John. *Arabi Pacha.* Berne: Chez l'auteur, 1884.

———. "Origins of the National Party in Egypt." *Nineteenth Century* 13 (1883): 117–34.

Owen, E. R. J. *Cotton and the Egyptian Economy, 1820–1914: A Study in Trade and Development.* Oxford: Clarendon Press, 1969.

———. "The Development of Agricultural Production in Nineteenth-Century Egypt: Capitalism of What Type?" In *The Islamic Middle East, 700–1900: Studies in Economic and Social History,* ed. A. Udovitch. Princeton, N.J.: Darwin, 1981, pp. 521–46.

———. *The Middle East in the World Economy, 1800–1914.* London: Methuen, 1981.

Owen, Roger, and Bob Sutcliffe, eds. *Studies in the Theory of Imperialism.* London: Longman, 1972.

Pareto, Vilfredo. *Sociological Writings,* ed. S. E. Finer; trans. D. Mirfin. London: Pall Mall, 1966.

Pintner, Walter McKenzie, and Don Karl Rowney, eds. *Russian Officialdom: The Bureaucratization of Russian Society from the Seventeenth to the Twentieth Century.* Chapel Hill: University of North Carolina Press, 1980.

Planat, Jules. *Histoire de la régéneration de l'Egypte.* Paris: J. Barbezat, 1830.

Platt, Desmond Christopher St. Martin. *Finance, Trade, and Politics in British Foreign Policy, 1815–1914*. Oxford: Clarendon Press, 1968.

Politis, Athanase G. *L'Hellenisme et l'Egypte moderne*. Paris: Félix Alcan, 1929.

Polk, William R., and Richard L. Chambers. eds. *Beginnings of Modernization in the Middle East: The Nineteenth Century*. Chicago: University of Chicago Press, 1968.

Pye, Lucian W., and Sidney Verba. *Political Culture and Political Development*. 1969; rpt. Princeton, N.J.: Princeton University Press, 1972.

Rabie, Hassanein. *The Financial System of Egypt, A.H. 564–741, A.D. 1169–1341*. London: Oxford University Press, 1972.

al-Rafiʿi, Abd al-Rahman. *Asr Ismail* [The Age of Ismail]. 2 vols. 2nd ed. Cairo: al-Nahda al-Misriya, 1948.

———. *al-Thawra al-Urabiya wa al-ihtilal al-Injlizi* [The Urabi Rebellion and the English Occupation]. 3rd ed. Cairo: Dar al-Qawmiya, 1966.

Raymond, André. *Artisans et commerçants au Caire au XVIIIᵉ siècle*. 2 vols. Damascus: Institut français, 1973–1974.

———. "Essai de géographie des quartiers de résidence aristocratique au Caire au XVIIIᵉ siècle." *Journal of the Economic and Social History of the Orient* 6 (1963): 58–103.

———. "Quartiers et mouvements populaires au Caire au XVIIIᵉ siècle." In *Political and Social Change in Modern Egypt*, ed. P. M. Holt. London: Oxford University Press, 1968, pp. 104–16.

———. "Les sources de la richesse urbaine au Caire au dix-huitième siècle." In *Studies in Eighteenth Century Islamic History*, ed. Thomas Neff and Roger Owen. Carbondale: Southern Illinois University Press, 1977, pp. 187–204.

Reid, Donald M. *The Odyssey of Farah Antun: A Syrian Christian's Quest for Secularism*. Chicago: Bibliotheca Islamica, 1975.

Richards, Alan. *Egypt's Agricultural Development, 1800–1980: Technical and Social Change*. Boulder, Colo.: Westview Press, 1982.

Rivlin, Helen Anne B. *The Agricultural Policy of Muhammad Ali in Egypt*. Cambridge, Mass.: Harvard University Press, 1961.

———. "The Railway Question in the Ottoman-Egyptian Crisis of 1850–1852." *Middle East Journal* 15 (1961): 365–88.

Robinson, Ronald. "Non-European Foundations of European Imperialism: Sketch for a Theory of Collaboration." In *Studies in the Theory of Imperialism*, ed. Roger Owen and Bob Sutcliffe. London: Longman, 1972, pp. 117–42.

Robinson, Ronald, and John Gallagher. *Africa and the Victorians: The Climax of Imperialism and the Dark Continent*. New York: St. Martin's Press, 1961.

Rosenberg, Hans. *Bureaucracy, Aristocracy, and Autocracy: The Prussian Experience, 1660–1815*. Cambridge, Mass.: Harvard University Press, 1958.

Rothstein, Theodore. *Egypt's Ruin: A Financial and Administrative Record*. London: Fifield, 1910.

Sabry, Muhammad. *L'empire égyptien sous Ismail et l'ingérence anglo-française, 1863–1879*. Paris: Paul Geuthner, 1933.

———. *La genèse de l'esprit national égyptien, 1863–1882*. Paris: Association Linotypist, 1924.

Safran, Nadav. *Egypt in Search of Political Community: An Analysis of the Intellectual and Political Evolution of Egypt, 1804–1952*. Cambridge, Mass.: Harvard University Press, 1961.

Saint-Hilaire, J. Barthélemy. *Lettres sur l'Egypte*. Paris: M. Lévy, 1856.

Sammarco, Angelo. *Le règne du Khedive Ismail de 1863 à 1875*. Volume 3 of *Histoire de l'Egypte moderne depuis Mohammed Ali jusqu'à l'occupation britannique, 1801–1882.* Cairo: Société royale de géographie d'Egypte, 1937.

———. *Les règnes de Abbas, de Said et d'Ismail, 1848–1879.* Volume 4 of *Précis de l'histoire d'Egypte par divers historiens et archéologues.* Rome: Société royale de géographie d'Egypte, 1935.

Santerre des Boves, J. *Son excellence Chérif Pacha: Notice biographique.* Cairo: n.p., 1887.

al-Sayyid Marsot, Afaf Lutfi. *Egypt in the Reign of Muhammad Ali.* Cambridge: Cambridge University Press, forthcoming.

———. [El Sayed, Afaf Loutfi]. "The Role of the Ulama in Egypt During the Early Nineteenth Century." In *Political and Social Change in Modern Egypt,* ed. P. M. Holt. London: Oxford University Press, 1968, pp. 264–80.

———. "The Wealth of the Ulama in Late Eighteenth Century Cairo." In *Studies in Eighteenth Century Islamic History,* ed. Thomas Naff and Roger Owen. Carbondale: Southern Illinois University Press, 1977, pp. 205–16.

Schölch, Alexander. "Constitutional Development in Nineteenth Century Egypt—A Reconsideration." *Middle Eastern Studies* 10 (1974): 3–14.

———. *Egypt for the Egyptians! The Sociopolitical Crisis in Egypt, 1878–1882.* Translated from the German. London: Ithaca Press, 1981.

———. "Wirtschaftliche Durchdringung und politische Kontrolle durch die europäischen Mächte im Osmanischen Reich (Konstantinopel, Kairo, Tunis)." *Geschichte und Gesellschaft* 4 (1975): 404–46.

Senior, Nassau William. *Conversations and Journals in Egypt and Malta.* 2 vols. London: Sampson Low, Marston, Searle, and Rivington, 1882.

Shafiq, Ahmad. *Mudhakkirati fi nisf qarn* [My Memoirs During Half a Century]. 3 vols. Cairo: Matbaʿat Misr, 1934–1936?

al-Sharqawi, Mahmud, and Abdallah al-Mishadd. *Ali Mubarak: Hayatuhu wa daʿ-watuhu wa atharuhu* [Ali Mubarak: His Life, His Mission, His Work]. Cairo: al-Injlu al-Misriya, 1962.

Sharubim, Mikhaʾil. *Al-Kafi fi tarikh Misr al-qadim wa al-hadith* [The Complete History of Ancient and Modern Egypt]. 4 vols. Bulaq: al-Matbaʿa al-Kubra al-Amiriya, 1898–1900.

Shaw, Stanford J. "The Central Legislative Councils in the Nineteenth Century Ottoman Reform Movement before 1876." *International Journal of Middle East Studies* 1 (1970): 51–84.

———. *The Financial and Administrative Organization and Development of Ottoman Egypt.* Princeton, N.J.: Princeton University Press, 1962.

———. "Landholding and Land-Tax Revenues in Ottoman Egypt." In *Political and Social Change in Modern Egypt,* ed. P. M. Holt. London: Oxford University Press, 1968, pp. 91–103.

Sirhank, Ismail. *Haqaʾiq al-akhbar an duwal al-bihar* [The True Information About Maritime States]. 2 vols. Bulaq: al-Matbaʿa al-Amiriya, 1312–1314/1894–1897.

Springborg, Robert. "Patterns of Association in the Egyptian Political Elite." In *Political Elites of the Middle East,* ed. George Lenczowski. Washington, D.C.: American Enterprise Institute, 1975, pp. 83–107.

St. John, James Augustus. *Egypt and Mohammed Ali; or, Travels in the Valley of the Nile.* 2 vols. London: Longman, Rees, Orme, Brown, and Green, 1834.

Stein, Stanley J., and Barbara H. Stein. *The Colonial Heritage of Latin America: Essays on Economic Dependence in Perspective.* London: Oxford University Press, 1970.

Stuart, Villiers. *Egypt After the War.* London: John Murray, 1883.

Tagher, Jacques. "Portrait psychologique de Nubar Pacha." *Cahiers d'histoire Egyptienne* 1 (1948): 353–72.

Taymur, Ahmad. *Tarajim ayan al-qarn al-thalith ashar wa awaʾil al-rabiʿ ashar* [Biographies of Prominent Men of the Thirteenth Century and Early Fourteenth Century]. Cairo: n.p., 1940.

Tignor, Robert L. *Modernization and British Colonial Rule in Egypt, 1882–1914*. Princeton, N.J.: Princeton University Press, 1966.

Tugay, Emine Foat. *Three Centuries. Family Chronicles of Turkey and Egypt*. London: Oxford University Press, 1963.

Tussun, Umar. *al-Baʿathat al-Ilmiya* [Educational Missions]. Alexandria: Matbaʿat Salah al-Din, 1934.

Urabi, Ahmad. *Mudhakkirat Urabi* [The Memoirs of Urabi]. 2 vols. Cairo: Dar al-Hilal?, 1954?

Vatikiotis, P. J. *The Modern History of Egypt*. London: Weidenfeld and Nicolson, 1969.

Wallace, D. MacKenzie. *Egypt and the Egyptian Question*. London: Macmillan, 1883.

Walz, Terence. *Trade between Egypt and bilad as-Sudan, 1700–1820*. Cairo: Institut français d'archéologie orientale du Caire, 1978.

Ward, Robert E., and Dankwart A. Rustow, eds. *Political Modernization in Japan and Turkey*. Princeton, N.J.: Princeton University Press, 1964.

Wehr, Hans. *A Dictionary of Modern Written Arabic*. Ed. J. Milton Cowan. Ithaca, N.Y.: Cornell University Press, 1961.

Wendell, Charles. *The Evolution of the Egyptian National Image: From Its Origins to Ahmad Lutfi al-Sayyid*. Berkeley and Los Angeles: University of California Press, 1972.

Weygand, Le General. *Histoire militaire de Mohammed Aly et de ses fils*. 2 vols. Paris: Imprimerie nationale, 1936.

Wickwar, W. Hardy. *The Modernization of Administration in the Near East*. Beirut: Khayats, 1963.

Wilkinson, J. G. *Modern Egypt and Thebes*. 2 vols. London: John Murray, 1843.

Wilson, C. Rivers. *Chapters from My Official Life*. London: Edward Arnold, 1916.

Wittfogel, Karl A. *Oriental Despotism: A Comparative Study of Total Power*. New Haven, Conn.: Yale University Press, 1957.

Yates, William Holt. *The Modern History and Condition of Egypt*. 2 vols. London: Smith, Elder, 1843.

Zaghlul, Ahmad Fathi. *al-Muhama* [The Lawyer's Profession]. Cairo: n.p., 1900.

Zakhura, Ilyas. *Kitab mirʾ at al-asr fi tarikh wa rusum akabir al-rijal li-Misr* [The Mirror of the Age in the History and Records of Influential Men of Egypt]. 3 vols. Cairo: al-Matbaʿa al-Umumiya, 1897–1916.

Zaki, Abd al-Rahman. *Aʿlam al-jaysh wa al-bahriya fi Misr athnaʾa al-qarn al-tasiʿ ashar* [Prominent Personalities of the Egyptian Army and Navy During the Nineteenth Century]. Cairo: Matbaʿat al-Risala, 1947.

Zaydan, Jurji. *Mashahir al-Sharq fi al-qarn al-tasiʿ ashar* [Famous Men of the East in the Nineteenth Century]. 2 vols. Cairo: Matbaʿat al-Hilal, 1902, 1911.

al-Zirikli, Khayr al-Din. *al-Aʿlam: Qamus tarajim li ashar al-rijal wa al-nisaʾ min al-Arab wa al-mustaʿribin fi al-Jahiliya wa al-Islam wa al-asr al-hadir* [Prominent Personalities: A Biographical Dictionary of the Most Famous Men and Women from Among Arabs and Arabicized Persons in the Pre-Islamic and Islamic Era and in the Modern Age]. 2nd ed. 10 vols. Cairo: al-Matbaʿah al-Arabiya, 1927–?

INDEX

Elite, bureaucratic: common interests among, 99, 110–13; corruption of, 67–69; dependence of on viceroy, 36, 67–70, 179; development of, 35, 36, 41, 55, 66–67, 229; ethnic rivalries among, 99; growing independence of, 117, 189; intermarriage among, 102; landholdings of, 103–10; life style of, 5, 82, 99–103; native Egyptians among, 41; under Ismail, 80–83; under Muhammad Ali, 23, 29, 31, 32; under the Ottomans, 10; wealth of, 99–100; westernization of, 100–03, 112–13. *See also* Bureaucracy

Europe: consular intervention of, 36, 37–38, 115–17, 196, 229; influence of, on the elite, 100–03, 112, 117, 171–72; intervention of, 4, 31, 35, 156, 168–70, 174–76, 179–90, 203; and mamluk rulers, 12; and Muhammad Ali, 15, 22; study missions to, 32, 85, 88, 90, 113; technology and science of, 164, 165; and trade, 10, 13, 36, 74

European Affairs, Office of, 48

Europeans: among the viceroy's elite, 38, 84, 93, 98–99; and the Capitulations, 37–38; and the power struggle of the 1870s, 211, 216–26; hostility toward, 35, 192; investment houses of, 38, 147, 205, 206; landholdings of, 107–08; scorn of, for Egyptians, 137

Factory system, 32
Fahmi, Zaki, 142–43, 144
Finance, Department of, 21, 46, 47, 66
Foreign Affairs, Department of, 21, 46
France, 3, 13, 22, 70, 181–85, 203, 204–06, 217
Freemasonry, 115, 192–93

Galice Bey, 128
Gordon, Lady Duff, 65, 75
Goschen, G. J., 184, 185, 187, 188
Goschen-Joubert settlement (1876), 183–88, 204, 206, 211, 218
Governorates, 42, 43
Governors, provincial, 45, 46
Green Bey (Lee Green), 98–99, 116

Hammad Abd al-Ati, 88, 127, 128
Hasan al-Munastarli, 133, 159

Hasan al-Shari'i (Ismail's son), 58, 188, 228
Hekekyan, Joseph. *See* Yusuf Hikakyan
High Court of Justice (1842–49), 51
Holynski, Alexandre, 165
Hourani, Albert, 11
Huda Sha'rawi, 143, 144
Husayn Kamil, Prince (Ismail's son), 65, 73, 111, 132

Ibraham, Prince (Muhammad Ali's son), 23, 25, 27, 167–68
Ibraham Yagan, 25, 72, 111
Ilhami Pasha (Abbas's son), 65
Iltizam system (tax farming), 12–13, 14
Ilyas al-Ayyubi, 152
Industry, Department of, 21, 46
Industry and trade, 32, 40, 138
Inspectorate, Department of, 18, 42, 46, 141–42, 148
Interior, Department of, 46, 47–48
Iram Bey, 111, 170
Irrigation system, 40, 45, 53
Ismail: achievements of, 35, 44, 57, 70; bankruptcy of, 219–20; and Consultative Chamber of Delegates, 49, 53, 212–14, 219, 227–29; *daira* of, 65–66; deposition of, 179, 180, 189, 210, 223–24; elite of, 55, 58, 59, 63–64, 81, 143–44, 147–48, 156, 162–63; land policy of, 65, 69, 74, 105–08; loans made by, 39, 181, 182, 205; power of, 29, 65, 72, 75–79, 209–10; and public debt, 173, 181, 184, 187–89, 201; tax policy of, 39, 54, 75
Ismail Pasha, 61
Ismail Raghib, 64, 147–48, 170
Ismail Siddiq: background of, 145; career of, 141, 144, 145–49, 174, 184; corrupt practices of, 150; loyalty of, to khedive, 72, 123, 132; murder of, 185–86, 189; power of, 73, 77–78, 146–49; wealth and landholding of, 149–50
Italy, 203–04

Jamal al-Din al-Afghani, 192–93
Jasmund, Consul General (Germany), 170
Joint Note of 1882, 228
Joubert, M., 184, 185
Journalism, 70, 192–93
Judicial system, 19–20, 171, 174–76. *See also* Courts